GW00643742

Trademark Valuation

Founded in 1807, John Wiley & Sons is the oldest independent publishing company in the United States. With offices in North America, Europe, Australia, and Asia, Wiley is globally committed to developing and marketing print and electronic products and services for our customers' professional and personal knowledge and understanding.

The Wiley Finance series contains books written specifically for finance and investment professionals as well as sophisticated individual investors and their financial advisors. Book topics range from portfolio management to e-commerce, risk management, financial engineering, valuation, and financial instrument analysis, as well as much more.

For a list of available titles, visit our Web site at www.WileyFinance.com.

Trademark Valuation

A Tool for Brand Management

Second Edition

GORDON V. SMITH AND
SUSAN M. RICHEY

WILEY

Cover image: © iStockphoto.com/Warchi
Cover design: Wiley

Copyright © 2013 by Gordon V. Smith and Susan M. Richey. All rights reserved.

Published by John Wiley & Sons, Inc., Hoboken, New Jersey.

Published simultaneously in Canada.

No part of this publication may be reproduced, stored in a retrieval system, or transmitted in any form or by any means, electronic, mechanical, photocopying, recording, scanning, or otherwise, except as permitted under Section 107 or 108 of the 1976 United States Copyright Act, without either the prior written permission of the Publisher, or authorization through payment of the appropriate per-copy fee to the Copyright Clearance Center, Inc., 222 Rosewood Drive, Danvers, MA 01923, (978) 750-8400, fax (978) 646-8600, or on the Web at www.copyright.com. Requests to the Publisher for permission should be addressed to the Permissions Department, John Wiley & Sons, Inc., 111 River Street, Hoboken, NJ 07030, (201) 748-6011, fax (201) 748-6008, or online at http://www.wiley.com/go/permissions.

Limit of Liability/Disclaimer of Warranty: While the publisher and author have used their best efforts in preparing this book, they make no representations or warranties with respect to the accuracy or completeness of the contents of this book and specifically disclaim any implied warranties of merchantability or fitness for a particular purpose. No warranty may be created or extended by sales representatives or written sales materials. The advice and strategies contained herein may not be suitable for your situation. You should consult with a professional where appropriate. Neither the publisher nor author shall be liable for any loss of profit or any other commercial damages, including but not limited to special, incidental, consequential, or other damages.

For general information on our other products and services or for technical support, please contact our Customer Care Department within the United States at (800) 762-2974, outside the United States at (317) 572-3993 or fax (317) 572-4002.

Wiley publishes in a variety of print and electronic formats and by print-on-demand. Some material included with standard print versions of this book may not be included in e-books or in print-on-demand. If this book refers to media such as a CD or DVD that is not included in the version you purchased, you may download this material at http://booksupport.wiley.com. For more information about Wiley products, visit www.wiley.com.

Library of Congress Cataloging-in-Publication Data:

ISBN 978-1-118-24526-2 (cloth)
ISBN 978-1-118-28627-2 (ePDF)
ISBN 978-1-118-28318-9 (ePub)

Printed in the United States of America

10 9 8 7 6 5 4 3 2 1

In my 50 years as an appraiser, I have been blessed by the acquaintanceship of many colleagues and professionals around the globe. There are too many to mention by name, but I treasure their friendship and the opportunity to serve a myriad of clients together. What is written here is an attempt to distill my experiences enhanced by the contributions of this body of world class professionals.

—Gordon V Smith, Sanibel, Florida

I am indebted to my co-author for the opportunity to work on the second edition of his foundational book on the valuation of trademarks. Beyond Gordon Smith's impressive professional accomplishments in the field of intellectual property valuation, he is a true gentleman and a good friend. I would also like to acknowledge the able editorial and research assistance of Ryan O'Rourke, who gave us every spare moment a third-year law student could spare.

—Susan M. Richey, Concord, New Hampshire

Contents

Preface   xi

Acknowledgments   xiii

CHAPTER 1
The Nature of a Trademark   1
    Trademark Defined   2
    The Legal Underpinnings of Trademarks   17
    Trademarks, Brands, and the Products and
        Services They Represent   20
    Summary   29

CHAPTER 2
Valuation Basics   31
    The Business Enterprise   31
    Valuation Principles   46
    Property and Rights to Property   50
    Premise of Value   51
    Valuation Methods   57
    Summary   59

CHAPTER 3
Using Financial Information   61
    Financial Reporting   62
    Financial Statements and Value: Disaggregating
        S&R's Assets   65
    Tax Issues   77
    Summary   81

CHAPTER 4
Trademark Valuation   83
    Cost Method   84
    Estimating Reproduction and Replacement Cost 87
    Using the Cost Method for Trademarks   90
    Market Method   94
    Using the Market Method for Trademarks   98

Income Method   101
Using the Income Method for Trademarks   106
Summary   106

CHAPTER 5
Trademark Economic Benefit   **107**
Future Economic Benefit   107
Quantifying Economic Benefit   116
Direct Techniques   118
Indirect Techniques   133
Summary   137

CHAPTER 6
Income Method: Economic Life and Risk   **139**
Defining Economic Life   140
Trademark Economic Life and Pattern   144
Survivor Curves and Studies of Historical Life   154
Forecasting Growth   157
S-Curves in General   161
Elements of Risk   164
Summary   171

CHAPTER 7
The Income Method: Putting It All Together   **173**
Trademark Valuation by Residual   173
Multiple Exploitation Scenarios   184
Valuation Based on Income Allocation   186
Summary   187

CHAPTER 8
Trademark Licensing Economics   **189**
Licensing Economics   189
Some General Thoughts   193
Royalty Quantification   195
Quantification Techniques   197
Scoring and Rating Techniques   201
Discounted Cash Flow Model   205
Dividing the Economic Benefit   208
Another Analytical Technique   210
Rules of Thumb   211
Summary   212

CHAPTER 9
Quantification of Harm in Trademark Enforcement Cases   **213**
Civil Trademark Enforcement Actions   214
Monetary Recovery in Civil Actions   217
Enhancement of Monetary Recovery   227

Valuing Counterfeits for Purposes of Criminal Sentencing   232
Summary   234

CHAPTER 10
Special Trademark Valuation Situations   **235**
Trademarks in Finance   235
Trademarks in Bankruptcy   238
Valuation Directions   244
Trademarks and Ad Valorem Taxes   248
Summary   249

CHAPTER 11
Global Trademark Issues   **251**
Trademark Holding Companies   252
The Scourge of Trademark Trolls   253
International Valuation Standards   255
Counterfeiting: A Worldwide Contagion   257
Political/Investment Risk   259
Summary   261

APPENDIX A
Basic Investment Principles   **263**
A Certificate of Deposit Example   263
The Arithmetical Foundation   266

APPENDIX B
**Theoretical Foundations for the Determination of a Fair
Rate of Return on Intellectual Property**   **269**

APPENDIX C
Investment Rate of Return Requirements   **271**
Investment Risk   272
Required Rate of Return Components   273
Rate of Return Models   274
Arbitrage Pricing Theory   278
Venture Capital   279
Weighted Average Cost of Capital   281
References   284

APPENDIX D
Predicting Sales and Revenues for New Ventures with Diffusion Models   **285**
New Product Sales Forecasting Models: Product Diffusion   286
Types of Product Diffusion Models   288
The Bass Model   290
Caveats of the Bass Model   293
Summary   294
References   295

APPENDIX E

Dealing with Uncertainty and Immeasurables in Trademark Asset Valuation   **297**

Elements of Valuation Analysis   298

Decision Analysis and Decision Trees   301

Monte Carlo Techniques   309

Obtaining Information from Indirect Observation   317

Option Pricing Models   323

Good Enough Decision Making   325

Summary   332

About the Authors   **333**

Index   **335**

Preface

This book is about brands and the trademarks that carry their flag. Brands have been with us for as long as private enterprise. The first time a skillful baker of bread realized that he or she could bake more bread than the family needed, a business was born. It is not difficult to imagine a time, shortly after that, when a child was given some money and instructions—"go buy bread for today . . . make sure to buy it from the store on the corner." Unbeknown to the proprietor of the corner shop, a brand was born.

Now we have come to understand the tremendous business power that brands have. When someone mentions "intellectual property," most of us think of patents. We are a technology savvy society. However, it may well be that brands are more influential in the success of a business enterprise than technology.

Managers cannot manage effectively unless they have some grasp of the value of the assets entrusted to them. So this book is written for the business community whose members are responsible for creating, recognizing, and exploiting their trademarks and brands; for the members of the legal community who wish to understand the principles of valuation; and for governments and regulators who must maintain an intellectual property environment for the good of everyone.

A valuation of intellectual property is, of necessity, a multidisciplinary task. It is necessary to have some understanding of the legal underpinnings that give intellectual property its meaning. We must also have some understanding of technology as well as the creative arts in order to appreciate how intellectual property comes into existence. We need to understand basic business concepts because it is through commercial exploitation that intellectual property achieves value. Lastly, we need to understand basic financial and investment principles in order to quantify the results of these efforts.

Superimposed over all of these essentials is the need for diligent, unbiased analysis, and just plain common sense.

So this book journeys through several landscapes that may seem at first to be unconnected. But we wanted to include them all so that those who may be familiar with one can move on to the next and benefit from a new experience.

Gordon V. Smith, Sanibel, Florida
Susan M. Richey, Concord, New Hampshire
October 2013

Acknowledgments

We wish to extend our special thanks to Mr. William J. Murphy who authored Appendix E, Dealing with Uncertainty and Immeasurables in Trademark Asset Valuation He also contributed to our discussion in Chapters 10 and 11. Mr. Murphy is a Professor of Law and Chair of the Commerce and Technology Law Graduate program at the University of New Hampshire School of Law.

We also express our appreciation to Dr. Richard A. Michelfelder of Rutgers University School of Business and Dr. Maureen Morrin of Temple University Fox School of Business for their study "Predicting Sales and Revenues for New Ventures with Diffusion Models" that is Appendix D.

We thank Dylan D'Ascendis for his contribution to Appendix C. He is a Principal of AUS Consultants and a Certified Rate of Return Analyst (CRRA).

We have excerpted and paraphrased material from Gordon V. Smith and Russell L. Parr, *Intellectual Property: Valuation, Exploitation and Infringement Damages*, 4th ed. (Hoboken, NJ: John Wiley & Sons, Inc., 2005) and these are not footnoted in every case.

CHAPTER 1

The Nature of a Trademark

It is September 21, 2012, and thousands of people are lined up outside Apple stores in San Francisco, New York, Hong Kong, Singapore, and many other places, waiting to purchase an "iPhone 5" smartphone. Three days later 5 million had been sold worldwide.

The iPhone 5 had been announced just two weeks prior to when the lines were forming. Philip Schiller, Apple's senior vice president commented, "iPhone 5 is the most beautiful consumer device that we've ever created."[1]

The iPhone 5 was the latest in a series of upgrades to the original iPhone, a revolutionary smartphone product that was introduced in 2007. Seventy-four days after its introduction, the late Steve Jobs, and Apple's former CEO, commented, "1 million iPhones in 74 days—it took almost 2 years to achieve this milestone with the iPod®.

"Three days," "two years," "74 days"—what has driven this phenomenal success story?

Yes, the mobile telephone market has expanded dramatically in the past 10 years to the point where there are over 6 billion subscribers worldwide. Apple, however, does not have a dominant market share in the mobile phone marketplace by any means. And the iPhone is one of the more expensive units on the market. In spite of this, we observed the intense market interest in the iPhone 5, which is essentially an upgrade of an existing product.

So what drove buyers to queue up outside stores in September? Was it the iPhone 5's new display, its new high-performance chip, extended battery life, or faster wireless technology? Or was it the redesign of the unit with a new, thinner, lighter, aluminum body? Or was it the jewelry-like fit and finish? Possibly it was because Apple stores are conveniently located or because store personnel are helpful and knowledgeable. Or was it the confident expectation of high quality performance that prospective buyers felt, based on the past performance of the products and services delivered by Apple under its family of i-prefaced trademarks and service marks?

Or was it all of the above?

We suggest to you that the answer to this question is "yes." Those folks were standing in line because they were influenced in varying degrees by all the factors that we just noted and likely other influences that we did not list.

This is a book about trademark valuation. Certainly the sale of 5 million iPhone 5 smartphones in three days (together with the sales of millions more previously) had a

---

[1] This quote as well as Steve Jobs's and iPhone sales data is from various press releases provided by Apple Corporation, http://www.apple.com.

significant positive economic impact on Apple Corporation. If our task was to opine on the value of the iPhone trademark, one of our tasks would be to estimate the portion of that economic impact that could be ascribed to the trademark. Clearly, iPhone 5 sales are also driven by the product's design features and the many elements of its built-in technology that deliver the performance smartphone buyers are seeking.

This is not a simple task. But there are tools and methods of analysis available to us and that is what this book is about. Our first step is to examine what a trademark is, not just in the legal sense, but also in the economic/business context.

Trademarks are images with many levels of meaning. They can be nostalgic reminders of times and products past, examples of outstanding graphic design, or the symbols of powerful institutions that influence our lives. As pleasant as it might be to contemplate their nostalgic or artistic aspects, however, we must focus on the role of trademarks in commerce. Trademarks are business assets and must be viewed primarily in the context of a commercial enterprise. Their task is to contribute to the profitability of the parent enterprise. Commerce is driven by *return on investment* (ROI) principles, and trademarks are not exempted from that requirement. Even trademarks that are associated with nonprofit, governmental, or institutional organizations are used for a purpose and promoted with an objective in mind. They must be judged by how well they meet those objectives.

TRADEMARK DEFINED

A trademark generally identifies the source of a product or service and distinguishes that product or service from those coming from other sources.[2] As defined in the U.S. Trademark Act of 1946 (the Lanham Act), a trademark is "any word, name, symbol or device or any combination thereof [used by someone to] identify and distinguish his goods, including a unique product, from those manufactured or sold by others and to indicate the source of the goods[.]"[3] A trademark also serves as an assurance of quality—the consumer comes to associate a level of quality with the goods or services bearing a given trademark. Trademarks have also been described as the embodiment of goodwill.

In the United States, the federal law and the courts have addressed these aspects of trademarks in various ways:

> *Trademarks help consumers to select goods. By identifying the source of the goods, they convey valuable information to consumers at lower costs. Easily identified trademarks reduce the costs consumers incur in searching for what they desire, and the lower costs of search the more competitive the market. [...]*[4]

---

[2] A few specialized trademarks—collective marks and certification marks—are used in conjunction with goods and services but the former indicate commercial origin in a member of a group or the latter certify that certain standards or a level of quality have been met. Trade names refer to a business or enterprise as a whole and do not single out a specific product or service of that entity.

[3] 15 U.S.C. § 1127.

[4] *Scandia Down Corp. v. Euroquilt, Inc.*, 772 F2d 1423, 1429 (7th Cir. 1985), cert. denied, 475 U.S. 1147 (1986).

A trademark also may induce the supplier of goods to make higher quality products and to adhere to a consistent level of quality. The trademark is a valuable asset, part of the "goodwill" of the business. If the seller provides an inconsistent level of quality, or reduces quality below what consumers expect from earlier experience, that reduces the value of the trademark. The value of a trademark is in a sense a "hostage" of consumers; if the seller disappoints the consumers, they respond by devaluing the trademark.
—Scandia Down Corp. v. Euroquilt, Inc.[5]

The protection of trade-marks is the law's recognition of the psychological function of symbols. If it is true that we live by symbols, it is no less true that we purchase goods by them. A trade-mark is a merchandising short-cut which induces a purchaser to select what he wants, of what he has been led to believe he wants. The owner of a mark exploits this human propensity by making every effort to impregnate the atmosphere of the market with the drawing power of a congenial symbol . . . to convey, through the mark, in the minds of potential customers, the desirability of the commodity upon which it appears. Once this is attained, the trade-mark owner has something of value.
—Mishawaka Mfg. Co. v. Kresge Co.[6]

The European Court of Justice offered the following summary:

In addition to its function of indicating origin and, as the case may be, its advertising function, a trade mark may also be used by its proprietor to acquire or preserve a reputation capable of attracting consumers and retaining their loyalty.

Although that function of a trade mark—called the investment function *may overlap with the advertising function, it is none the less distinct from the latter. Indeed, when the trade mark is used to acquire or preserve a reputation, not only advertising is employed, but also various commercial techniques.*

When the use by a third party, such as a competitor of the trade mark proprietor, of a sign identical with the trade mark in relation to goods or services identical with those for which the mark is registered substantially interferes with the proprietor's use of its trade mark to acquire or preserve a reputation capable of attracting consumers and retaining their loyalty, the third party's use must be regarded as adversely affecting the trade mark's investment function.[7]

Trademark Types

The word *trademark* is used in an umbrella sense to refer to the array of specific types of marks in the upcoming discussion. "Trademark" also may be used in a discrete sense to indicate marks that are physically affixed or attached to goods, in contrast, for example, to service marks that are used in advertising to promote specific

---

[5] Ibid.
[6] *Mishawaka Mfg. Co. v. Kresge Co.*, 316 U.S. 203,205 (1942).
[7] *Interflora, Inc. and Interflora British Unit v. Marks & Spencer plc and Flowers Direct Online Ltd.*, C-323/09, ECJ 2011 (Sept. 22, 2011).

services. Trademark holders give notice of their ownership of marks by denoting federally registered marks with the symbol ® or, if unregistered, by the symbols ™ or ℠ to indicate trademark or service mark use, respectively.

While they may or may not be protected as trademarks, some "spokespersons" or "spokescharacters" can take on a form of secondary meaning with respect to a product or service. Even Charlie Brown's dog "Snoopy," with a strong identity of his own, has become associated with MetLife's financial services.[8] In fact, some trademark holders prefer to create their own spokescharacters to enhance the brand and, in the process, these creations take on trademark significance of their own. Mars, Inc., has used this marketing strategy to maximum effect in the creation of "spokescandies" (referred to by the company as "M&M's Characters")[9] made to look like animated M&M's chocolate candies but exhibiting personality characteristics unique to the color of their candy shell and filling, such as the seductive Ms. Green (dark chocolate), the know-it-all Red (milk chocolate), the gullible but likeable Yellow (peanut), the confident and hip Blue (almond), the slightly paranoid Orange (crispy), and so on.

Trademark   Many common trademarks are a form of the name of the entity that holds the mark, oftentimes shown in distinctive type style, or in conjunction with a logo. Examples include:

Source:[10]

Source:[11]

13.

12.

Source:[14]

---

[8] Charlie Brown and Snoopy are characters in the famous comic strip *Peanuts* by Charles M. Schulz.
[9] See http://www.mmsworld.com/charactercategorygroupdisplay.aspx?id=1326.
[10] USPTO Registration No. 238,146 (Owned by The Coca-Cola Co.).
[11] USPTO Registration No. 3,002,164 (Owned by International Business Machines Corp.).
[12] USPTO Registration No. 912,210 (Owned by Goodyear Tire & Rubber Co.).
[13] USPTO Registration No. 878,049 (Owned by General Electric Co. Corp.).
[14] USPTO Registration No. 3,858,395 (Owned by AT&T Intellectual Property II, L.P.).

Trademarks most familiar to consumers are those associated with the merchandise they purchase for private consumption, such as "L'eggs" hosiery, "Birds Eye" frozen foods, and "Tide" detergent.

Service Mark   For all practical purposes, service marks function the same way that trademarks do except that they identify services rather than products. Examples would be "MetLife" and "American Express", financial service providers, and "United", which provides commercial aviation services.

Trade Name   A trade name is the name of a business, association, or other organization, used to identify it. There is no symbolic identifier associated with trade names and trade names may not be federally registered. Ownership would be governed by common or state law. A trade name is typically not an asset of material value, unless it also functions as a trademark because the buying public recognizes goods and services by their trademark and, in many cases, may be unaware of the actual name of the producing company. As an example, many are unaware that such famous brand names as "Grey Poupon" mustard, "A.1." steak sauce, "Baker's" chocolate, and "Planters" peanuts are products of Kraft Foods. The Coca-Cola Company markets beverages and juices that are branded "Sprite," "Fanta," "Lift," and "Nestea" (under a sublicense agreement with the mark's owner, Nestlé S.A.). Yet other companies, such as Samsung Electronics, choose to include their trade name on nearly every product they have.

Trade names are often incorrectly identified as a trademark or service mark. It is not uncommon for the United States Patent and Trademark Office (USPTO) to reject applications for registration of such marks when the specimen showing actual use of the mark includes the terms, "Corp." or "Inc." For example, letterhead on which the only use of the phrase "Weight Watchers" is at the bottom, followed immediately by the words "International, Inc." and, possibly, a corporate address would be considered evidence of trade name use but not evidence of service mark use, such as "Weight Watchers" weight loss planning, or trademark use, such as "Weight Watchers" frozen meals.

Certification Mark   Certification marks identify products that have specific characteristics, such as those marked with the "Cotton" mark of the National Cotton Council or the "Woolmark" registered by The Wool Bureau. Some certification marks signify that specific goods or services comply with certain known standards, such as the Underwriter's Laboratories' "UL" stamp. Standard & Poor's Corporation has registered some of its ratings used to denote the quality of certain types of securities, and the Motion Picture Association of America has registered the phrase, "Restricted under 17 Requires Accompanying Parent or Guardian."

Certification marks are used on goods or services that are not provided by the owner of the mark. The owner of the mark must exert some control over the use of the mark by third parties, however, so that the public is not deceived by its certifying function.

Collective Mark   Collective marks are owned by an organization, association, or collective entity but generally are used to indicate that the product or service bearing the designation was manufactured or is being provided by someone who is a member of that specific group. Professional organizations or trade associations permit their members to use the organization's mark in provision of specific goods or services: illustrations include the Society of Certified Public Accountants "CPA", the Institute of Electrical and Electronics Engineers "IEEE", the American Society of Appraisers "ASA", Screen Actors Guild-American Federation of Television and Radio Artists "SAG-AFTRA", and the Financial Analysts Society "CFA". Again, the presumption is that the group supervises the use of its mark to prevent unqualified or nonmember individuals from using it. To the extent that the collective entity itself offers services or goods, it may do so under the same mark.

One variant of collective marks—collective membership marks—is the only type of trademark not designed for use in conjunction with the sale or marketing of goods or services or the running of a business as a whole. Members of the collective use the mark solely to denote membership in the group. As a result, ownership of collective membership marks is not confined to professional organizations and trade associations but also extends to social clubs and beneficial fraternal societies. Examples include the Royal Order of Jesters and the numerous Greek fraternities and sororities inhabiting college campuses nationwide. Once again, the collective must monitor use of the mark by its members.

Trade Dress   Trade dress has been defined as "the total image of a product and may include features such as size, shape, color or color combinations, texture [...] or graphics."[15]

W. Mack Webner offers the following comprehensive description:

> [W]hat catches the consumer's eye, and he or she may come to identify a 'product' with the focal point of its 'package' [...] The elements of a consumer product package: the trademark, the color scheme, the use of opaque or clear containers, geometric design features, the arrangement of the elements—and, in retail establishments, the arrangement of service areas and other public spaces—can all come together to provide a distinctive image, the trade dress, that the public recognizes.[16]

Some aspects of product appearance that are recognized as protectable trade dress in the United States, such as a distinctive product configuration or distinctive product color, are not protected under trademark law in other countries of the world. In particular, there is no international consensus that three-dimensional marks, such as a product's shape, constitute legitimate trademarks. For example, many countries enact industrial design laws to protect product shape or they limit protection for that aspect of a product's appearance to design patents or copyright law. Additionally, like other nontraditional trademarks, a single color alone may be subject to objections that it lacks distinctiveness or does not meet the requirement found in some countries that a trademark must be capable of graphical representation.[17] As a result, product appearance may be handled differently from country to country.

---

[15] *John H. Harland Co. v. Clarke Checks, Inc.*, 711 F.2d 966, 980 (11th Cir. 1983).
[16] W. Mack Webner, "Protecting Trade Dress or, Not All Packaging Is Political," *Remarks: Trademark News for Business* (International Trademark Association) 5, no. 3 (1992): 2.
[17] Other matters that appeal to human perception and may be considered to be nontraditional trademarks are sound, scent, motion, taste, and texture.

Virtual Marks　Virtual marks, whether used to test virtual products or services before their introduction in the physical world or to designate virtual products and services that are exchanged for real-world currency, represent value in the real world although they do not constitute traditional trademarks. Because such marks are not affixed to physical goods or used to advertise services available in the physical world, their use may not constitute the type of use necessary to attain legal trademark significance.

Sometimes dubbed "reverse product placement," the practice of launching new brands in a virtual world to gauge their popularity before introducing them in the real world is gaining acceptance among a wide variety of consumer product and service companies. David Edery, video game insider and former MIT academic, explains the reasoning behind the phenomenon: "Why spend tens or hundreds of millions of dollars fighting mature competitors for mindshare and shelf space in the physical world when you can launch a new offering in an uncluttered fictional one?"[18] One commonly cited example is Starwood Hotels' introduction of the "Aloft" hotel brand in *Second Life*, an online virtual world operated by Linden Labs (http://secondlife.com/). Starwood, owner of such renowned brands as "Westin" and "Sheraton," utilized the virtual world launch as a kind of test marketing by allowing visitors in *Second Life* to tour its planned space and offer feedback before Aloft Hotels were opened to the public in the real world.[19] In like fashion, Calvin Klein, a leading designer and marketer of fashion apparel, accessories, and fragrances, premiered a new perfume brand in *Second Life* by giving away virtual fragrance bubbles followed by offers of actual samples of the fragrance.[20]

Sometimes the popularity of the virtual brand suggests creation of a real world product or service. Consider the iconic Harry Potter series of books and movies and its references to "Bertie Botts' Every Flavor Beans," a brand of virtual candy converted into a real world confection by Cap Candy, a division of Hasbro.[21] Similarly, Square Enix, publisher of the *Final Fantasy* video game recognized the commercial possibilities of the game's virtual healing item "Potion" and partnered with beverage manufacturer Suntory to market the "Potion" energy drink in Japan.[22]

Other virtual marks, while not translated to real world products or services, become the subject of commercial transactions in the virtual or real world. Eros LLC, a virtual supplier of erotic products in *Second Life*, is thought to have earned in excess of $1 million in real world currency over a five-year span by selling its products, in which it has asserted trade dress rights, for Linden dollars.[23] Linden dollars can be earned through play in *Second Life* or may be purchased with real world currency.

---

[18] David Edery, "Reverse Product Placement in Virtual Worlds," *Harvard Business Review* 84, no. 12 (December 2006).

[19] Reena Jana, "Starwood Hotels Explore *Second Life* First," *Bloomberg Businessweek*, August 22, 2006.

[20] Douglas Macmillan, "Big Spenders of *Second Life*," *Bloomberg Businessweek*, April 16, 2007; and Clement James, "Calvin Klein Launches *Second Life* Virtual Perfume," *ITNEWS*, March 22, 2007.

[21] Edery.

[22] Ibid.

[23] Barry Werbin, "Trademarks in Virtual Worlds," *INTA Bulletin*, December 1, 2009.

Brand-Based gTLDs   The widespread incorporation of trademarks into domain names has facilitated transformation of the Internet into a global marketplace. The importance of leveraging a brand through its use in a domain name has been noted by the Internet Marketing Association:

> *The brand is usually part of a company's web site address. It is often entered into search engines to find a company, its products and services. . . . [T]he brand is vital to how a company's consumer traffic is generated on the Internet[.]*[24]

Recent developments suggest that brand incorporation in domain names will assume even greater importance for commercial interests wishing to grow their Web-based presences.

On June 11, 2011, the governing board of ICANN (Internet Corporation for Assigned Names and Numbers) voted that almost any word in almost any language can become a *generic top level domain* (gTLD). This vote paves the way for businesses to apply to become a domain name registrar for what has been termed a "brand" or "vanity" gTLD. According to branding consultancy, Interbrand, "What this means is that companies or associations can now secure a URL address that embeds the brand name even more deeply into its composition."[25] Among the first companies to announce the intention to seek a brand gTLD was Japanese-based Canon. The option of using ".canon" instead of—or more likely in addition to—"canon.com" affords the company enhanced flexibility as it formulates its Internet marketing strategy.

Just how companies will leverage their trademarks by controlling brand space remains to be seen but internet marketers have begun to speculate as to the potential benefits of brand-based gTLDs. Some suggested benefits include:

- Fostering a greater sense of security for clients and customers by reassuring them of the authenticity of the website[26]
- Creating an online community of interests that allows targeted marketing[27]
- Enabling online auction sites to assign a personalized URL to each seller under the auction site's umbrella[28]
- Allowing merging or reorganizing companies to project a single, cohesive brand[29]

The value of brand-based gTLDs, while difficult to estimate at present, promises to be substantial.

---

[24] Internet Marketing Association, "Protecting Your Valuable Brand: The Importance of Trademarks," *IMA*, February 22, 2013, http://www.imanetwork.org/protecting-your-valuable-brand-the-importance-of-trademarks/.

[25] Paola Norambuena, Jeff Mancini, and Jerome McDonnell, "What's in a Domain? Generic Top-Level Domains and the New Dotbrand Frontier," *Interbrand,* http://www.interbrand.com/en/Interbrand-offices/Interbrand-New-York/dotbrand-whitepaper.aspx.

[26] Alexa Raad, "Why ICANN's New Domain-Name System Could Benefit Brands," *Advertising Age*, August 16, 2011.

[27] Ibid.

[28] Norambuena, Mancini, and McDonnell.

[29] Ibid.

Trademark Significance

Not every word, symbol, or other indicator is acceptable as a trademark. As the several definitions of trademark illustrate, in its most basic sense, a trademark must perform a distinguishing function. Words that describe a quality or characteristic of the good or service with which it is used, and geographic names or surnames that do not signify a distinctive commercial source, generally cannot be registered in any jurisdiction, and the same is true of commonly used words for an object or good, such as "knife," "cotton," or "cup," otherwise known as generic terms. Marks that would be misleading (vis-à-vis the intended goods or services), or those in poor taste are not registrable. Word marks are categorized by U.S. courts as follows:

- *Fanciful or coined marks.* These are words that are invented and have no built-in meaning, such as "Kodak," "Exxon," "Lexus," and "Cheerios."
- *Arbitrary marks.* These are existing words with no relation to the goods or services with which they are associated, such as "Apple" (computers) or "Shell" (petroleum products).
- *Suggestive marks.* These are words that suggest some attribute of or benefit from the goods or services, but do not describe the goods themselves, such as "Coppertone" (tanning lotion), "Caterpillar" (tractors), or "Whirlpool" (clothes washers).

The foregoing categories are considered to be "technical trademarks" capable of protection from the date of their first use in commerce.

Descriptive Marks   These describe some aspect of the goods or services or a characteristic of them. They cannot be protected until they have achieved distinctiveness through use and advertising in commerce, which is called *acquiring secondary meaning.* Examples are "Car-Freshener" for an auto deodorizer, "Rich 'n' Chips" for chocolate-chip cookies, or the descriptor "Gold Medal" for flour or "Blue Ribbon" for beer.

Generic Terms   These words represent the name of a product or service category or subcategory and, so, constitute "the name of the thing" and cannot be rendered proprietary for public policy reasons. The National Biscuit Company (Nabisco) learned this lesson almost a century ago in its unsuccessful attempt to claim the words "shredded wheat" as the trademark for its cereal made from strands of whole wheat. Declaring the term to be generic, the U.S. Supreme Court reasoned that competitors would be harmed unfairly if they were unable to advise the consuming public of the name of the thing they wished to sell.[30]

Terms may be generic from the outset, as "shredded wheat" or they may begin their existence as legitimate trademarks but become generic through improper use. The following list details actions on the part of the trademark holder or the public at large that can threaten the trademark significance of a term:

- Use of the trademark as a noun (e.g., "hand me my Nikon")
- Use of the trademark as a verb (e.g., "please Xerox that letter")

---

[30] *Kellogg Co. v. National Biscuit Co.*, 305 U.S. 111, 116 (1938).

- Use of the trademark without its descriptor (e.g., "this recipe calls for Tabasco")
- Pluralizing a trademark ("move all the Buicks to the showroom")
- Using the trademark as a noun-descriptor (e.g., "it's the Rolls-Royce of electric drills")
- Using a trademark in the possessive (e.g., "the IBM's tape drive is turned off")
- Failing to capitalize, put in quotation marks, or otherwise set apart a trademark in writing

Improper usage will, in time, lead to an inevitable slide toward genericism. Savvy trademark holders are aware of this and police the usage of their marks and conduct campaigns to promote proper use. Xerox Corporation, which has a particularly difficult battle, has placed very imaginative advertising campaigns in the media, encouraging proper use of their marks—"Xerox has two Rs" (one in the word and one in a circle denoting registration). They remind us that a trademark is an adjective and never a verb or a noun. Trademark owners continually monitor the media and remind transgressors of their misuse. This is an exceedingly difficult task because, on the one hand trademark owners *want* their marks to be on everyone's lips yet, on the other, they need to encourage proper usage.

U.S. courts acknowledge that the categories discussed in the preceding are useful in determining the distinctiveness of word marks and logos but are not helpful in making that same determination with regard to trade dress. Courts divide trade dress into the following categories: (1) packaging, generally the label, wrapping, or container for the product; (2) product design, generally the shape or configuration of the product itself; and (3) whatever is not included in the foregoing two categories. Distinctiveness of packaging is generally assessed by how unusual it is in the field in which it is used—consider the distinctive container for baby pants made to look like an ice cream cone, marketed by Playtex International Corp. Product design is treated like descriptive word marks and requires the acquisition of secondary meaning in order to be protected—for example, consumers eventually came to associate the pinched glass decanter with "Pinch" whiskey. A single color alone—think of the color brown used in advertising "UPS" package delivery services—also requires acquisition of secondary meaning. Courts approach other types of "dress" not included in the preceding categories, such as the look and feel of a retail establishment or restaurant, on a case-by-case basis with a presumption toward requiring secondary meaning in the face of uncertainty.

In addition to being distinctive, trade dress must be non-functional to merit protection. The functionality concept in trade dress law represents an area of the law that many find confusing because it is not a reference to utilitarian functionality. In an effort to clear up the confusion, early decisions in this area drew a distinction between de facto or utilitarian functionality, which does not necessarily block trade dress protection, and de jure functionality, which does block trade dress protection for public policy reasons. Consider the iconic shape of the "Coca-Cola" beverage bottle—it performs the utilitarian function of holding liquid and allowing it to be poured for consumption. That function, however, is not dependent upon the bottle's curved and ribbed sides; numerous bottle shapes exist capable of performing the same functions. If, however, the bottle's shape represented the most effective way to contain or pour the liquid, or it facilitated the least expensive manufacturing process, the shape would be considered de jure functional and, therefore, unprotectable. To confer trade dress protection on such an essential design feature would prohibit fair competition. Later court cases omit any reference to "de jure" and simply use the word "functional."

When a purely aesthetic design feature is in issue, courts will attempt to determine whether protecting that feature through trade dress law would impose a significant non-reputation-related disadvantage on competitors. The color black has been held to be functional for outboard motors because it provided an aesthetic advantage to boat owners who wanted a color that was compatible with different boat colors and one that would render a relatively unattractive piece of equipment less conspicuous.[31]

Trademarks and Brands

"You like to-may-toes and I like to-mah-toes."[32] Here, however, we say, "You call it a trademark and I call it a brand."

If asked the meaning of the word "Budweiser," someone in the marketing world would immediately identify it as a famous brand of beer. Someone in the legal or accounting or valuation professions might well identify it as a trademark of the Anheuser-Busch InBev Company. So we need to define how we are going to use those terms in this book.

A trademark, in any one of its various forms, is a bundle of property rights that are defined by law and protected within a legal system. There will be more about that in this chapter, but we keep it simple for this purpose.

It is more difficult to define what is referred to as a *brand*. There does not seem to be any universal agreement as to what a brand is or is not. For our purposes here, we will define a brand as an aggregation of attributes that buyers have come to associate with a particular product or service or organization. The brand terminology is used by those in the marketing field, perhaps because brand attributes attempt to describe the characteristics of the intersection of a product or service with the marketplace.

There is another concept that we believe also contributes to this confusion. It is common in the marketing disciplines, to speak of "brand equity." The equity word, to those in the legal, accounting, and valuation disciplines, as well as individuals on the financial side of the business world, is a monetary term rather than a subjective description. The term "brand equity" as it is commonly used seems to us to primarily refer to the strength of the brand. That is, a strong brand (i.e., well known and with enduring customer loyalty), has high brand equity. We will be revisiting this concept in the next chapter when we discuss the financial aspects of brand valuation.

One of the reasons why there may be little agreement about the definition of a brand is that there are different perceptions of a brand depending upon whether you are its owner or whether you are a buyer of it.

---

[31] *Brunswick Corp. v. British Seagull Ltd.*, 35 F.3d 1527, 1531 (Fed. Cir. 1994).

[32] This is a famous line from the song "Let's Call the Whole Thing Off" by George and Ira Gershwin, which is featured in the film *Shall We Dance* (1937), starring Fred Astair and Ginger Rogers. The song lyrics highlighted different pronunciations of "tomato" and the like.

GOING GLOBAL

The Chinese computer firm Lenovo Group Limited was founded in the 1980s by some engineers at the Chinese Academy of Sciences. Years were spent developing the business in China and in 2005 the firm purchased the personal computer business of IBM Corporation and the "ThinkPad" laptop trademark that IBM had built. With the acquisition of this well-established brand, Lenovo's leap from a national brand to an international one was facilitated. The cost? $1.75 billion, including debt assumed. Today Lenovo directs its operations in 60 countries from a headquarters in North Carolina.

Lenovo accomplished the leap from being a national brand to a global brand using ThinkPad as its vaulting pole. Many other enterprises are starting from humbler beginnings and are trying to negotiate the chasm from contract manufacturing to being branded, innovative enterprises. And branding is an important key.

This progression is especially evident in the developing world. In that milieu, a nation or geographic area is often in the position of being able to offer abundant labor and perhaps natural resources in order to gain access to more speedy economic development. Many enterprises in that situation become contract manufacturers for multinational enterprises headquartered elsewhere. We have observed a natural progression that, as a contract manufacturer becomes more skilled, it begins to develop improvements in manufacturing technology and even the design of the product being manufactured for others. Typically, a contract manufacturer is operating under license from its client, who is the primary beneficiary of these advances. At some point, a contract manufacturer or some of its managers or key personnel may decide to break away and use their newfound knowledge to build a branded, innovative enterprise. The next step, of course, is to transcend the national boundaries of the business's origin and go global. This is happening often today and we believe that this business evolution will continue strongly as the world economy improves.

Owner's Perspective   To its owner, a brand that is pervasive in the marketplace is valuable because it enhances profitability. The proof of this is everywhere. Brands now fly across national boundaries with ease. But one does not attempt such a flight in a single-engine light plane. It takes a jetliner, with all of the costs that go with the trip.

Buyer's Perspective   The buyer of a brand may see and appreciate a different set of attributes such as function, style, color, or current popularity as being the most important.

While it is possible to list all sorts of brand attributes, not all brand attributes are present or associated with every product or service. As an example, a strong brand is dependable—it can be counted upon to deliver what it is supposed to deliver. But things change. Since its beginnings, we have come to expect that any ballpoint pen will write dependably without skipping. So the attribute of dependability is no longer a consideration for a buyer choosing between brands of ballpoint pens. Nor does a high degree of dependability enable the maker of ballpoint pens to charge a higher price. It is a brand attribute that has become irrelevant. Today, a comfortable gripping surface, or simply price, may be more of a defining attribute. So, defining attributes are continually changing as product development takes place and as consumer tastes evolve. The brand landscape is continually changing and the view is different depending on your vantage point. This makes it more difficult to firmly establish the parameters of brand.

In his discussion of the role of brands, David Aaker relates:

> *A brand is a distinguishing name and/or symbol (such as a logo, trademark, or package design) intended to identify the goods or services of either one seller or a group of sellers, and to differentiate those goods or services from those of competitors. A brand thus signals to the customer the source of the product, and protects both the customer and the producer from competitors who would attempt to provide products that appear to be identical.*[33]

This description bears much similarity to the legal definitions of a trademark, and illustrates how the concepts of trademark and brand are intertwined. An example of how brands are built might help clarify the distinction.

Let us assume for a moment that we have developed some technology that would enable us to produce a lawnmower that would be quieter and easier to start than lawnmowers presently in the marketplace. We believe in our ideas and so we decide to form a business to manufacture our lawnmowers. As we form the enterprise, we design a trademark and logo, research other existing marks, and successfully register our new mark and logo.

At this point, our brand is comprised of a registered trademark and logo that are known only to us and some folks at the USPTO. We begin to manufacture lawnmowers that are placed in home improvement and garden centers for sale. We decide to paint all of our models of lawnmower yellow. Our business is launched.

After a year or so, our quieter- and easier-to-start lawnmower is being enthusiastically purchased by homeowners. Happily, these buyers recognize the unique features of our mowers and our market research additionally informs us that our customers appreciate the dependability and long life of our machines. Our customers are also are starting to identify the distinctive yellow color with our machines.

At this point we have begun to build a brand in the fuller sense. We have begun to build the aggregation of attributes that are at the intersection between our marketing efforts and the perception of our customers. If the attributes that are perceived by our customers are positive in nature, then our brand will continue to be enhanced. It may well be that we could extend the use of our brand to other types of lawn care equipment and further grow our business.

Some liken a brand to a "promise." That is, if a customer purchases a lawnmower bearing our trademark, we promise to deliver the brand attributes that the marketplace has come to expect and value. If we deliver, the brand will grow in value.

---

[33] David A. Aaker, *Managing Brand Equity: Capitalizing on the Value of a Brand Name* (New York: Free Press, 1991), 7.

At this point the bundle of legal rights associated with our trademarks is unchanged. However, the economic impact on our business of those rights is greatly enhanced. The potential economic benefit available from exploiting our trademarks enhances its value. And the source of that value is the positive brand attributes that we have built.

Stated another way, our trademarks insure that the economic benefit of the brand attributes that we have carefully built stays in our possession. The legal protection of our marks has been firmly linked to the economic benefit of our brand attributes. And that leads us to conclude that trademarks are inextricably combined with the aggregation of brand attributes. As a practical matter, it becomes impossible to separate the trademarks' intellectual property rights from the attributes of the brand. They become, for business and economic purposes, a single business asset. Their future is linked together. If, as an example, we neglected to pay the proper renewal fees to maintain our trademark registrations and thereby lost the rights conferred by registration, our lawnmower business would certainly suffer seriously. We might have to dispose of the business in a distressed sale, or incur the cost of rebranding our mowers and hope to survive the market disruption and consumer confusion. Alternatively, if one of the brand attributes of our lawnmowers turned out to be false or undependable, the economic usefulness of our intellectual property trademark rights would erode.

This concept of a symbiotic relationship of legal rights and economic benefit is not unlike the case of a patent in which the intellectual property rights granted by the patent include, as a practical matter, the right to receive the economic benefits of exploiting the patent. So the value of the patent is dependent on the economic benefit of its exploitation. And so it is with trademarks. The positive or negative essence of the brand attributes resulting from the successful exploitation of a trademarked product or service is the foundation of the mark's value.

AN UNHAPPY TRADEMARK STORY

We are reminded of the example of the "Edsel" automobile that was introduced to the marketplace by the Ford Motor Company in 1958. After years of market research and development of this new automobile line by Ford Motor Company and the expenditure of millions of dollars, the Edsel auto turned out to be a flop. Its end was announced late in 1959 after a total of 84,000 sales have been made. Reportedly Ford lost $350 million (in 1950s dollars) on this venture. Many have opined about the reasons for the model's demise, but it is not important to us to struggle with that. The point here for us is that Ford's intellectual property rights in the Edsel trademark lost whatever value they may have had because the brand attributes were negative. In fact, Edsel became a word of informal usage in America to denote "failure" (e.g., "That idea is a real Edsel."). Obviously, Ford Motor Company could never again use that trademark because it had been so spectacularly damaged.

SEPARATING THE WHEAT FROM THE WHEAT

Early in 2013, Hostess Brands, Inc., a major U.S. baking company, began winding down its operations with the intention of liquidating all of its assets. This large company owned quite a number of well-known brands. The company carefully considered how best to liquidate its assets in order to meet its liabilities. While not likely, it was conceivable that some of the company's large portfolio of trademarks could end up being separated from the recipes, bakeries, distribution centers, and delivery routes that supported these well-known brands. In essence, that would be separating the trademarks from the brand attributes. If that were to happen, the buyers of these separate assets would likely discover that the sum of the parts did not equal the former whole. By mid-year, the first tranche of assets was sold to a newly formed entity, Hostess Brands, LLC. Included were production facilities and the snack cake brands including "Twinkies". By July, 2013 these brands began to appear on store shelves. So far so good, it would seem. We discuss this case in more detail in Chapter 10.

Conclusion   In our discussions of trademark valuation, we will assume that a trademark carries with it the other elements ascribed to a brand, that is, the trademark carries with it a "full complement" of all the ingredients necessary to also be recognized as a brand. We will therefore use these terms interchangeably. We will assume that when we refer to a trademark in *economic terms*, we include with the legal rights the drivers of economic benefit.

The reader should not assume, however, that this is always the case. Brand and trademark are, under unusual circumstances, separable. In any trademark valuation, (or a valuation of any other type of property) the task begins with a careful definition of the property rights to be valued.

The distinction between a brand and a trademark is especially important when one considers the economic life of each. Economic life will be discussed in detail in Chapter 5, but the reader can visualize how the economic life of a brand (comprised as it is of many elements) could be quite different from that of a trademark. Within the brand, there may be a constant turnover of its constituent parts, as advertising programs and marketing strategies come and go in order to respond to the *Sturm und Drang* of business and competition, like an actor may appear on the stage now as a cowboy and then as a butler. The economic life of a trademark can even be independent of a particular product if it is sufficiently strong, versatile, and if the transition is carefully managed.

Trademarks and Goodwill

A trademark, or brand, identifies a product or service as coming from a particular source (usually a commercial enterprise). Siegrun Kane describes trademarks as "symbols of goodwill. The value of this goodwill increases with length of use, advertising, and sales. Trademarks used for a long time on successful, highly advertised products have developed tremendous goodwill"[34].

In a 1942 decision, the Supreme Court described this trademark/goodwill relationship as follows:

> *The protection of trademarks is the law's recognition of the psychological function of symbols. If it is true that we live by symbols, it is no less true that we purchase goods by them. A trademark is a merchandising shortcut which induces a purchaser to select what he wants, or what he has been led to believe he wants. The owner of a mark exploits this human propensity by making every effort to impregnate the atmosphere of the market with the drawing power of a congenial symbol. Whatever the means employed, the aim is the same—to convey through the mark, in the minds of potential customers, the desirability of the commodity upon which it appears. Once this is attained, the trademark owner has something of value. If another poaches upon the commercial magnetism of the symbol he has created, the owner can obtain legal redress.[35]*

This linkage of a trademark and "goodwill" is both understandable and the source of confusion. At one time, a business enterprise was thought to consist of only tangible assets and goodwill, but references to "blue sky" persist when valuing the fixtures and inventory of a retail business. Careful analysis reveals, however, several components encompassed within the goodwill "catchall" That analysis enables the valuation expert to understand the difference between computer software, an assembled workforce, or a favorable contract. It is much less clear that there is a difference between goodwill and a trademark, especially when goodwill is described as patronage, or the proclivity of customers to return to a business and recommend it to others, or as above—"commercial magnetism."

The courts have addressed this linkage in considering the assignment (transfer of ownership) of trademarks. Kane explains that, "A trademark does not exist in a vacuum. A trademark is attached to a business—it symbolizes the goodwill of the business. When the trademark is assigned without the goodwill of the business, the assignment is invalid. Some courts characterize the effect of such an invalid assignment (also known as an assignment in gross) as abandonment. It is not precisely clear exactly what must be transferred, along with a trademark assignment, to avoid this potentially disastrous result. In some cases, it has been judged sufficient that tangible assets necessary to carry on the assignor's business were transferred along with the trademark. The overriding principle seems to be that enough other assets are transferred so that the assignee is able to produce the product or service at a quality level indistinguishable from that of the assignor, so that the public is not deceived by the presence of the trademark on the goods or services of the new trademark owner.

No benefit arises from struggling with the unclear concept of goodwill or attempting to draw a bright line between goodwill and trademarks, if indeed that were possible. The remainder of this book will not use the term "goodwill" because

---

[34] Siegrun D. Kane, *Trademark Law: A Practitioner's Guide*, 2nd ed. (New York: Practising Law Institute, 1991), 10.

[35] *Mishawaka Mfg. Co. v. Kresge Co.*

skillful identification of all the elements of a business enterprise, including the constituent intangible assets, will account for the existence of goodwill.

THE LEGAL UNDERPINNINGS OF TRADEMARKS

A trademark possesses all the attributes of property, a fact apparent from the definitions recited earlier in this chapter. A trademark achieves this status from civil or common law, under which protection is obtained by registration or use in commerce.

The Lanham Act as amended is the primary federal law in the United States governing trademark rights and its protections exist alongside those afforded by state and common law. In order to be protected or registered at the federal level, a mark must be used in a manner that has an effect on interstate commerce, that is, commerce between the states or commerce between the United States and a foreign nation. Each of the various states extends protection or registration to marks that are used intrastate, that is, within the state, whether or not use of the mark or the effect of that use crosses state boundaries. Since the Internet has become a virtual marketplace in which commerce crosses geographic boundaries seamlessly, it is hard to imagine any trademark use that is not interstate in nature. As a consequence, state registration of trademarks offers very few advantages to trademark holders and registration in the USPTO reigns supreme over state registration for those trademark holders who opt to protect their mark in this manner.

Although not required to protect a mark in the United States, federal trademark registration offers numerous advantages to the registrant, advantages that are important for valuation purposes. First, the registration acts as constructive notice of a claim to trademark rights in specific goods or services and may also be cited by the USPTO against applications to register confusingly similar marks. Additionally, a registration confers nationwide priority in the mark as of the date of filing of the application, even though actual use of the mark may have been confined to a small geographic region. Additionally, the registration may form a basis for obtaining trademark protection in other countries or regions of the world. In an enforcement proceeding in the United States, the registration constitutes prima facie evidence of ownership, validity, and the exclusive right to use the registered mark. If the registration has been granted incontestable status by the USPTO, it may be conclusive evidence as to matters of ownership, validity, and use. Finally, a federal registration must exist to pursue counterfeiting remedies, an enforcement mechanism that can lead to harsh sanctions on the civil and criminal fronts and detention and seizure of counterfeit items at the border.

A hallmark of the civil law system is that trademark rights are secured by registration, unaccompanied by any required showing of use of the mark in commerce. Specifically, the system allows non-users to register a mark with an eye toward selling the registration to the foreign holder of the mark when the foreign holder exhibits plans to enter the registrant's national market. Countries such as China that are struggling to gain a handle on the counterfeiting issue must now confront actions within their borders that other nations often consider to be trademark trolling. Harmonization attempts, through multinational treaties providing for equal treatment of foreign trademark holders with domestic trademark holders, widespread enactment of model trademark statutes, or creation of international registration systems, has eased the problem somewhat but much work remains to be done.

Trademark Application

An application for federal trademark registration in the United States is made to the Trademark Office of the USPTO. Most trademark registrations in the United States are filed on the basis of (1) actual use of the mark on specified goods and services in commerce[36] or (2) a bona fide intent to use the mark on specified goods or services in commerce.[37] Although the Trademark Office will examine the latter type of application prior to actual use, no registration will issue until the applicant notifies the Trademark Office that actual use has taken place.[38]

Under the Lanham Act, the Trademark Office bears the burden of proving that a requested registration falls within one of the statutory bars to registration and should not issue.[39] In conformance with that obligation, the Trademark Office conducts a search of its own records for potentially conflicting registrations and the Trademark Office examines the application to determine whether any of the bars to registration exist, including: nondistinctive terms that reflect some aspect or characteristic of the goods or services, including the geographic locale from which they emanate, or terms that falsely describe any of the foregoing; fraudulent or scandalous subject matter; and subject matter that is generic or functional in nature.[40] In addition to the foregoing substantive review, applications are reviewed for compliance with certain formalities. Formalities include generally a signed oath or declaration from an identified individual or entity and address attesting to right of exclusive use of the mark, a description of the mark and the goods or services with which it is in use or is intended for use, a date of first use anywhere and a date of first use in commerce, a drawing of any graphically represented mark, the appropriate fee, and, for marks in use, a specimen of the goods or advertising for the services bearing the subject mark.[41]

There are procedures in place that enable an applicant to respond to a refusal to register and attempt to work out a solution to the condition that gave rise to the

---

[36] Lanham Act § 1(a), 15 U.S.C. § 1051(a) (2009).

[37] Lanham Act § 1(b), 15 U.S.C. § 1051(b) (2009).

[38] Less common bases for federal registration exist to enable U.S. compliance with international agreements and treaty obligations. Specifically, the Trademark Office allows foreign applicants for federal trademark registration to obtain issuance of a registration by declaring a bona fide intent to use the mark in U.S. commerce, without making a showing of actual use in commerce in two instances: (1) where they rely upon a foreign trademark registration issued in their country of origin in accordance with the Paris Convention, under section 44(e) of the Lanham Act, 15 U.S.C. § 1126(e) (2009); or (2) when they hold an international trademark registration issued by a country other than the United States that is a signatory to the Madrid Protocol under section 66 of the Lanham Act, 15 U.S.C. § 1141h(a)(3) (2009).

[39] The prefatory language of section 2 of the Lanham Act allocates the ultimate burden of proof to the Trademark Office: "No trademark by which the goods of the applicant may be distinguished from the goods ofothers shall be refused registration on the principal register on account of its nature unless" one of the listed bars to registration pertains. Lanham Act § 2, 15 U.S.C. § 1052 (2006).

[40] Lanham Act § 2, 15 U.S.C. § 1052 (2006).

[41] Lanham Act § 1, 15 U.S.C. § 1051 (2009); 37 C.F.R. § 2.61(a) (2011).

refusal. If the Trademark Office maintains its refusal, the applicant has access to several forums for appeal.[42]

If the Trademark Office determines that no reason exists to refuse registration, it will publish its decision so that anyone who believes he will be harmed by the registration may file an opposition to registration with an administrative tribunal in the Trademark Office.[43] In like manner, one who believes he is harmed by an issued registration may petition for its cancellation in front of the same tribunal[44] or in a court proceeding under section 37 of the Lanham Act.[45]

Evidence of continued use of the registered mark must be filed with the PTO during the fifth year after registration and in conjunction with requests to renew the registration every 10 years.[46] After the registration has passed its fifth year, an additional filing can be made, attesting that the mark has been in use for five consecutive years, a filing that generally results in a grant of incontestable status.[47] Incontestability is not bulletproof, however, and the registration may still be canceled if it was obtained by fraud, or if the mark is vulnerable to several specific challenges, including abandonment and genericism.[48]

In today's global economy, trademark holders very often seek multi-national protection for their intellectual property. In addition to seeking trademark registrations from individual foreign nations, several mechanisms exist to allow trademark holders to obtain international registrations. The International Trademark Association website provides the following summary and links to detailed procedures for each mechanism:

> *Several international agreements coordinate the procedure of filing applications for trademark registration in more than one country. A registration with the Benelux Office for Intellectual Property (BOIP) covers Belgium, Luxembourg and the Netherlands. A Community Trade Mark (CTM) protects a trademark in all of the member countries of the European Union. The Madrid Agreement and Madrid Protocol provide an opportunity to file an application for an international registration that will cover multiple member countries. Filing with the African Intellectual Property Organization (OAPI) protects trademarks in all of the member countries in Africa. There is also the possibility of filing with the African Regional Industrial Property Organization (ARIPO), under which a trademark owner can protect its trademark in the member states in southern Africa.[49]*

---

[42] The first appeal is taken to the Trademark Trial and Appeal Board, an administrative tribunal in the Trademark Office, and further appeal may be had to the U.S. Court of Appeals for the Federal Circuit or to a federal district court where new evidence may be submitted, with a subsequent appeal available to the appropriate regional court of appeals.

[43] Lanham Act § 13, 15 U.S.C. § 1063 (2009).

[44] Lanham Act § 14, 15 U.S.C. § 1064 (2009).

[45] Lanham Act § 37, 15 U.S.C. § 1119 (2009).

[46] Lanham Act § 9, 15 U.S.C. § 1059 (Supp. 2012).

[47] Lanham Act § 15, 15 U.S.C. § 1065 (Supp. 2012).

[48] Lanham Act § 33(b), 15 U.S.C. § 1115(b) (2006).

[49] See International Trademark Association, "Fact Sheets Introduction to Trademarks," *INTA*, http://www.inta.org/TrademarkBasics/FactSheets/Pages/InternationalTrademarkRights FactSheet.aspx.

TRADEMARKS, BRANDS, AND THE PRODUCTS AND SERVICES THEY REPRESENT

We have presented trademark categories from a legal standpoint, and it is useful to know this in order to better understand the legal "roots" of a given type of mark. There is a system of international classes of goods and services which is used to describe the type of product or service with which a trademark will be associated.

These categories do not, however, provide much help in the valuation process. For that we need to think of trademarks using a different structure that will help us differentiate marks by using some of the criteria that affect potential value. To be useful, our valuation methodologies must apply all along the trademark spectrum. For most of us, the word "trademark" equates to the identity of some good or service that we use in everyday life. There are, however, millions of brands developed by those who provide intermediate goods and services (those used in the manufacturing process or in business-to-business transactions), or by governments, organizations, and institutions. Intermediate buyers are motivated differently than consumers, and their needs are more specific and better defined. The trademarks they use must be included in such a classification scheme, and we suggest the following as a structure:

Governmental/Institutional
> Federal Government
> State Governments
> City Government
> Governmental Agencies
> Armed Forces
> Post Office
> Internal Revenue Service
> Transportation
> Hospitals
> Universities
> Trade Organizations
> Charitable Organizations
> Fraternal Organizations
> Professional Organizations

Extractive/Commodity
> Oil & Gas
> Coal
> Metals
> Electric, Gas, and Water Utilities

Lumber

Grain

Cotton

Chemicals

Semicommodity

Industrial/Commercial/Residential Construction

Paper

Fruits/Nuts

Meats/Poultry

Dairy Products

Plywood/Dimension Lumber

Specialty Chemicals

Transportation/Freight

Intermediate Goods/Services

Services for Industry

Design/Engineering/Construction to Industry

Parts/Component Manufacturers

Machine Tools

Textiles

Leather

Plumbing/Heating/AC/Electrical/Masonry Contractors

Wholesalers/Distributors

Finished Goods

Automobiles

Appliances

Computer Software (business to business)

Electrical/Electronic Goods

Apparel

Retailers

Mass Marketers

Malls

Department/Specialty Stores/Supermarkets

Small/Intermediate Retail Stores

Dealers

Franchisees

Industrial/Commercial Services
  Construction
  Advertising
  Market Research
  Management Consulting
  Accounting
  Legal
  Financial (i.e., investment banking, commercial credit)

Consumer Services
  Banks/Financial
  Telecommunications
  Cable Television
  Insurance
  Hotels
  Publishers
  Newspapers
  Transportation
  Restaurants/Fast food

Consumer Products
  Soap
  Personal Care Products
  Apparel
  Computer Software (shrink-wrap)
  Food Products
  Beverage Products

Entertainment
  Motion Pictures
  Television
  Stage
  Characters/Personalities/Sports Figures
  Sports Teams
  Toys/Games

There is a pattern to the list of classifications just mentioned. Generally speaking, as we read down the list, it can be observed that there is *value being added* along the way. Another observation is that the classes move from industrial to consumer goods. Intuitively, we might feel that the importance (and relative value) of trademarks associated with these categories of business activity might also increase from the beginning to the end of the series.

We can test our intuition by examining the categories further. Obviously some trademarks could be placed in more than one classification or it might be somewhat unclear which classification might best describe a given mark. Anything as ubiquitous in our lives as trademarks will resist strict compartmentalization. But our purpose is to superimpose a rationalization that can assist in our specific analysis.

Governmental/Institutional

We tend to dismiss the trademarks associated with organizations in this category, perhaps because we feel that they do not *need* trademarks and just have them because they have to identify themselves in some way or other. To some extent this is true, but we find that trademarks provide these organizations with some of the same benefits that they provide to others. They have their own brand attributes that are emblematic, identifying a vast organization by means of a symbol. The Great Seal of the United States on an aircraft in the farthest reaches of the world carries an unmistakable message. The symbols of the Red Cross, Salvation Army, and United Nations are instantly recognized everywhere. The light blue of equipment and uniforms used by United Nations personnel in conflict zones might well be judged to have achieved secondary meaning.

These trademarks can be guideposts. Anyone who has visited London has come to appreciate the symbols of the Underground and British Rail as they provide guidance through an effective, but potentially confusing public transport system. The symbols of the "T" in Boston, the "METRO" in Washington, and "BART" in San Francisco accomplish the same purpose. All that is needed on a sign is a symbol and an arrow and we are on our way.

Sometimes these symbols are intended to be motivators. The Postal Service wants us to use its services, as do hospitals (which are moving toward a competitive environment), and public transportation systems. The armed services want to encourage recruitment and colleges and universities seek applicants. These symbols are also used as a means of seeking the acceptance of an idea.

Will we ever see a *New Yorker* magazine cartoon where one subway rider says to another, "I really prefer PECO Energy electricity, it's so smooth and uninterrupted"? Electric power customers have a choice about whose electrons they consume. Many electric and gas utilities are brushing off their images and shaping them in entirely new ways. Brands of electricity are a natural result of this progression. Communications services are strongly into branding.

Extractive/Commodity

Extractive industries, such as oil, natural gas, coal, and mining do not depend on their trademarks in the way consumer products companies do. They and commodity producers sell to other industries for the most part and theirs are price, delivery, or technology-based buying decisions. Even commodity products such as plywood, lumber, coal, and fuel oil that find their way to a consumer market are more likely to be identified, in the mind of the consumer, with the retailer than with their original provider. The retailer's trademark is then more important than that of the cutter of trees, or the miner of coal. There are exceptions to this, however, and these serve to illustrate our classification system. Sodium chloride, as an example, is mined or obtained by evaporation. It is a commodity chemical. Some is bound for chemical processes (e.g., as a feedstock for chlorine), or for our roads in wintertime, and some is destined for our tables.

The former uses are "unbranded," though chemical specifications, price, and location are very important. The latter is granulated, processed, and packaged, wholesaled, distributed, house branded, or company branded, and sold to us from the shelves of our food market. A trademark has little importance at the beginning of the process, but can be very important at the end.

Crude oil is also a commodity. It is not described by the name of the party who drilled for it, but by its characteristics (e.g., "light sweet crude," or "Texas intermediate"). By the time it is refined into motor oil or gasoline, however, its identity is very important and refiners spend considerable amounts of money to make sure that we as consumers are aware of the unique properties of their product and of their trademark.

Semicommodity

As we have noted, there can be "crossovers" along our spectrum, as specific products move along the manufacturing continuum. Trademarks may be present all along, but their relative importance changes. A container of polystyrene granules coming from The Dow Chemical Company is so marked and is clearly identifiable to the buyer. To what extent, however, did the Dow trademark influence the decision to buy this raw material? We suggest that the decision to buy was made on the basis of chemical specifications, price, delivery (time and quantity), and perhaps other contractual terms, and that the Dow name and reputation as embodied in the trademark was of secondary importance. There is no question that suppliers of commodities and/or intermediate goods or services or components work hard to build strong reputations and are justifiably proud of what their trademarks stand for in the business world. We submit, however, that those reputations provide less "inertia" (in terms of retaining a customer) than that of consumer brands. These buying decisions are (should be) based on more "rational" thinking, and less emotion. One's reputation is only as good as the products or services delivered yesterday. Therefore, product performance, technology, service, support, innovation, and price loom much larger than they do in a consumer's decision to purchase bread, a shaver, or a DVD player, where a buyer does not have the skill or information to perform a technical evaluation of the product and tends to depend on the manufacturer's reputation as embodied in the trademark.

This is not to say that trademarks cannot become important quite early in the process. Assume that Dow Chemical developed a process by which to make polystyrene granules magnetic, and that this property greatly facilitated processing of this material by those who manufacture goods from it. Dow would certainly differentiate this breakthrough product in the marketplace by distinctively trademarking it. This trademark would become important to the manufacturers buying it, though it might not be important to the end user of products made from it (especially if it lost the magnetic property in the processing) because the magnetic property would be important only to the manufacturer, not the consumer. The distinctive trademark would serve as a "shorthand" identifier of the product, enabling a buyer to quickly specify the needed material.

This polystyrene example adds yet another example of branding in the intermediate industries. The Dow Chemical Company itself manufactures foam insulation from polystyrene, which is branded with the trademarked name "Styrofoam." This product and Dow's "Saran Wrap" plastic film are both used in industrial packaging and construction applications, but are also well known by consumers. This "early differentiation" of a product from commodity into brand would be expected to affect value.

Intermediate Goods/Services—Finished Goods

Steel, metal castings, plastic, and paint, are commodity components of subassemblies that eventually become finished products such as automobiles and appliances. The trademark we know as a consumer goes on when the finished product is assembled. Automobile antifreeze is a mixture of chemicals and dyes that is sold to us in distinctive packaging. The trademark goes on at the end. Many trademarked products we buy move a long way through the manufacturing chain before the trademark that we recognize is applied.

There are, however, trademarks in use all along the chain. Some of these are associated with the materials used, with subassemblies, or with the manufacturing process itself. There is a myriad of trademarks associated with goods and services that are used to make the products we buy. As a buyer of the final product, we are totally unaware that "Drierite"[50] desiccants or a "Hytrol"[51] conveyor system may have been used in its manufacture. There are those, however, to whom these names represent a product image that is important to them in their work. In the commercial or industrial sales cycle, a new vendor is thoroughly "vetted" and their goods or services are subjected to tests and trials. Once this is done, the successful candidates are put on an approved bidders list. Under the banner of a trademark, such an approved product or service greatly facilitates the approval process for new or related products or services. The trademark paves the way and the selling effort can get right to the essentials, without the "who are we," "how long have we been in business," "who else have we served" preamble. This results is both a cost saving and a better opportunity for the trademark owner. A trademark also helps to bridge the gap as sales persons and buyers change employment.

These marks have a role in their particular commerce, but are not as critical as other product attributes that we have discussed. As proof, companies are acquired and it is not uncommon for the acquirer to begin to market the products of the former owner under its own brand "umbrella." This is done carefully of course, but it is not uncommon. Another way to view this is to imagine that a consumer brand in a competitive market lost its trademark for some reason. This could well mean the demise of the brand. If such an event befell an industrial or commercial brand, a severe result would be much less likely.

The best of all worlds for the manufacturer of industrial or commercial goods or services is to achieve a level of quality or uniqueness that results in being

---

[50] Trademark of W. A. Hammond Drierite Co., Xenia, Ohio.
[51] Trademark of Hytrol Conveyor Company, Inc., Jonesboro, Arkansas

"specified." That is, when construction or design specifications are written, the description of a unit is stated as "Electric motor, 20 h.p . . . GE Model XXXXX or equivalent." This type of brand strength is built by performance and price, not massive advertising.

Trademarks in the industrial or business setting may be important because of their "implied guarantee" attribute. We are sure that there have been at least some "lemons" among the many models of copier sold by Xerox or Ricoh over the years, but overall they have established strong reputations and it would be an uphill battle for a newcomer to compete. A company purchaser would be hesitant to put his or her reputation on the line by recommending the purchase of a "just as good as" copier, no matter what the price or claims for quality. Everyone wants a trademark that can be inserted in the phrase, "no one ever was fired for buying _____."

When the attributes of a trademarked intermediate product are important (or can be made important) to the end consumer, these trademarks can be made to carry through to the marketplace. There are many examples of this such as Dupont's "Teflon" lubricant and "Kevlar" high-strength material, "Gore-Tex" membrane, Intel computer chips, and the like. When this happens, we have "dual billing" in the marketplace, such as outerwear by L.L. Bean, with "Gore-Tex" lining, or a personal computer from Sony with "Intel Inside."

A commercial or industrial trademark can also be extremely useful as an umbrella, under which new products or services can be introduced. Brand extensions can be an important strategy outside of the consumer markets. In Chapter 5, we note how this type of trademark can facilitate an expansion or acquisition strategy.

Retailers

Even after all the hands have carried and added value to a product to bring it to its final, finished state, we may see it and buy it in a retail establishment that has its own trademark. So another brand layer has been added. The retailer's value added is to provide us with a one-stop shop (ample selection), provide display and education, perhaps credit or payment facilities and delivery services, and to act as our "ombudsman" with the maker of the goods.

Retailers can themselves become customer magnets in the marketplace. Manufacturers of goods may vie for display or shelf space in the establishment of a successful retailer. We comment in a later chapter how this can lead to brand extension strategies for some retailers.

Trademarks can be very important in retailing, but there is usually a balancing of importance between the mark of the retailer and the marks of the goods being sold. Some retail locations such as auto dealers, apparel stores, and service stations use the trademark of the manufacturer or service provider. The actual identity of the location owner is immaterial to the consumer. Other retail locations, such as Macy's, Bloomingdales, Eckerd's, or Smith's Toy Shop, have an identity separate from that of the goods sold. That identity, by itself, may be very strong or relatively insignificant, but will always have some relationship to the goods sold or services provided. That is, a retailer's name will become associated with the type, quality, and price of the goods sold. The characteristics of the wares become part of the retailer's "persona."

Industrial/Commercial Services

This is a business classification in which one intuitively realizes a wide range of importance for trademarks. Services are provided by people and so there can be a variety of combinations of personal and trademark power to drive such a business. As a general rule, the character of smaller service firms is formed by their personnel, while that of large firms is more of a "corporate character." Employees of small firms may take customers or clients with them if they move to another firm. This is much less likely to happen with larger service providers. There tends to be a much more personal relationship between the customers and employees of a small advertising, accounting, or legal practice than there is at larger firms.

The relative power of a trademark is still quite evident in professional services. As an example, one could assume that an audit performed in accordance with *generally accepted accounting principles* (GAAP) by a *certified public accountant* (CPA) would be essentially the same service, no matter which firm provided it. We have, however, observed a price difference in the audit services of small versus large accounting firms. In addition, a small- or middle-market company (which would have a free choice between a large or small auditing firm) will most often opt for the large firm if it is contemplating a public offering of stock or seeking other significant financing. The motivation is that investors, and perhaps regulators, take a higher degree of comfort in an audit by a larger, more well-known accounting firm and the process may be smoother as a result. For the same reason, a public company involved in a major transaction will seek the assistance of a major investment banker. It is a bit more difficult, in this case, to ascribe this entirely to the power of the trademark (because of the nature of the services required), but unquestionably the directors of such a company derive some comfort by this action, given the litigious nature of our financial society.

Obviously, a large professional firm, advertising agency, market research, consultant, designer, or constructor can offer "one-stop-shopping" and an ability to handle large tasks. So the advantage is not only from its trademark. But a firm's trademark does become a symbol of its particular prowess and is an attraction in its own right. There are those that feel that receiving a letter from a prestigious law firm will strike more fear and trepidation in the heart of an alleged transgressor than that from an attorney or firm less well known.

Hiring a world renowned management consulting firm can provide an element of insurance against criticism that may not be available from a less well known firm, even though the advice received may be the same. This is the power of a trademark.

Consumer Services

We are becoming a service-driven economy, and so it is not surprising to observe the development of regional, national, and international trademarks for consumer services. This includes banking, insurance, credit card services, brokerage and investment services, and even legal and accounting services. There are also national brands of health care, tax preparation, and funeral services.

We tap into a whole infrastructure when we write a check or buy a mutual fund or make a mortgage payment. The "retailer" with the trademark may have little to do with the whole process. He or she is just the agency through which we obtain access to the system. When we write a check and send it to a mail-order company across the country, we have no knowledge of all the back-office operations involved in accomplishing the flow of funds that enables this transaction. Our contact is with our "value-added reseller"—our local bank branch. That bank is the party that must build brand equity and a trademark in order to create and maintain customer relationships like ours.

Consumer Products

Even though this is one of the largest classifications, in terms of number and importance of trademarks, little needs to be said about this classification of trademarks, because these are what we think of when we use that term. This classification is populated by consumer products bearing marks such as, "Eveready," "Amazon," "Coca-Cola," and a host of other consumer goods. These are the trademarks that are written about, sung about, and are part of our lives on a daily basis. Trademarks in this classification are very important building blocks in the brand equity structure. McCarthy and Perreault provide an interesting analysis of differences within this category.[52] *Staples* are products bought often and routinely and branding is important to assist shoppers in saving time and to locate products of previous satisfaction. *Impulse* products are purchased in an unplanned manner, and their display location becomes very important. *Shopping* products are defined as either homogeneous or heterogeneous. *Homogeneous* products are seen by the consumer as basically the same, and price becomes a dominant force in the purchase decision. *Heterogeneous* products are seen as different and the buyer wants to carefully inspect for quality and performance. Branding may be less important here. *Specialty* products are those for which the consumer is willing to search. This may involve a specific insistence on a particular brand. Finally, there are *unsought* products that are either brand-new in the market or not regularly needed, such as a cemetery plot. It is in this world of consumer products that trademarks loom the largest, in terms of fiscal importance.

Entertainment

At the other end of the range from commodities are the products and services associated with entertainment, games, sports, and toys. This is where trademark is everything. Well, not everything, but certainly extremely important. The fact that licensing of marks and characters is a multibillion dollar industry within this industry underlines the importance of the images that drive profits in this business.

As with all things financial (that are legal) investments with relatively low risk tend to have surer, but relatively low rewards. People *need* automobile tires, so we at least have that need assisting us if we decide to invest money to build a tire brand. People do not need entertainment or toys or t-shirts with a cartoon character on them, so the sale is dependent on the persuasiveness of the image alone. The investment to build a "character" (living or not) is a large and risky one. But the rewards can be huge, if the effort is one of the few successful ones. The owner of such a character can rest assured that "the world will beat a path to his door"[53].

---

[52] E. Jerome McCarthy and William D. Perreault, *Basic Marketing* (Homewood, IL: Richard D. Irwin, Inc., 1987).
[53] This popular misquotation, originally attributed to Ralph Waldo Emerson, is actually based on two different statements.

SUMMARY

We are presenting this classification system in order to facilitate our analysis of trademark value. It is intended to provide a structure for a consideration of the elements that contribute to trademark value. It is also intended, as we describe in a later chapter, to provide a structure for an analysis of empirical evidence as to whether those elements are indeed value-influencing. Further chapter highlights include:

- There is an economic business asset created when legal trademark rights are combined with positive market attributes built by its related product or service. The asset is most commonly called a "brand."
- While trademark legal rights and brand attributes are distinct, they achieve their highest value in combination.
- There are many different types of trademarks and the roster is likely to increase as technology enables new means of mass communication to come into existence.
- Trademark and brand issues are international in scope.
- Within the spectrum of industries, the role and value of the trademark-brand asset can vary greatly.
- A trademark valuation must begin with a carefully defined description of the subject property.

CHAPTER 2

Valuation Basics

Intellectual property is a category of property rights that includes *trademarks, patents, copyrights,* and *trade secrets,* or *know-how.* Intellectual property is an intangible creation, distinguished by the fact that its owner is legally protected from unauthorized exploitation by others.

In today's world, intellectual property may have immense value. Investors value the Facebook enterprise in the neighborhood of $100 billion. No doubt the "Facebook" trademark represents a substantial portion of that value.[1] But what was the value of the Facebook trademark when it was first registered in 2006? Very little. This lack of intrinsic value is characteristic of intellectual property in general.

Valuation Precept

Intellectual property has little or no intrinsic value. It attains value for its owner when it produces economic benefit through exploitation.

A trademark gains value by being associated with a successful product or service that finds favor in the marketplace. This success is measured by its contribution to the profitability of a business enterprise. So it is essential that we understand the context of the business enterprise within which a trademark attains value.

Intellectual property is unlike other types of property because, with the owner's consent, many entities can exploit it simultaneously. That is, the owner's rights can be subdivided among many entities, each of whom may exploit the intellectual property, as an example, in a particular geography, or for a specific time period or for a specific use. Or the owner may elect to retain all of the rights of ownership. In either case, a major challenge of valuing intellectual property lies in identifying the breadth of its exploitation possibilities.

THE BUSINESS ENTERPRISE

A business enterprise is an aggregation of assets assembled in order to provide entrepreneurial profit. Every enterprise, from the smallest to the largest, can identify its assets in one of three categories: monetary assets, tangible assets, and intangible assets.

---

[1] "Facebook," Registration No. 3,041,791, owned by Facebook, Inc.

These groupings comprise the portfolio of assets needed by a business enterprise in order to provide products or services to the marketplace. The relative importance of these three groupings varies widely from business to business, but all three asset groups are present to some degree. It stands to reason, therefore, that the total value of the business enterprise is equal to the aggregate value of these three asset categories within it. This is an important valuation concept that we will return to again and again in this book. Our purpose here is to present a discussion on the valuation of trademarks. However, we must be cognizant throughout that discussion that a trademark attains value by being successfully exploited in the marketplace. That successful exploitation requires the presence of other intangible, tangible, and monetary assets. So, whatever value estimate we might conclude for a trademark must coexist with the values of the many other assets that comprise the enterprise and its value must be commensurate with the value of the whole in a reasonable and supportable way.

That said, it is essential that we have a clear understanding of the other assets, in addition to trademarks, that comprise the enterprise whole. We will discover that, as this discussion expands, it is necessary to winnow out the potential economic benefit produced by a trademark from that resulting from exploitation of the whole asset portfolio. It therefore makes sense to know something about nontrademark assets and how they contribute.

Valuation Precept

The sum of the values of the monetary, tangible, and intangible assets is equal to the value of the enterprise (see Exhibit 2.1).

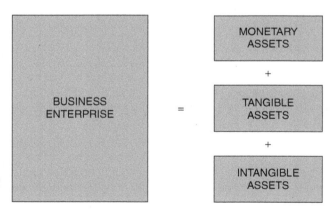

EXHIBIT 2.1   Business Enterprise Value Elements
Source: John Wiley & Sons, Inc. Reprinted with permission.

Asset Types

Monetary Assets   Monetary assets, also called "*net working capital*," are defined as *current assets less current liabilities*, as shown on the subject company's balance sheet.

Current assets include:

- Cash
- Short-term investments, such as marketable securities
- Accounts receivable, less reserves
- Inventories, including raw materials, work in process, and finished goods
- Prepayments

Current liabilities include:

- Accounts Payable
- Current portion of long-term debt
- Income taxes and other accrued items

In most cases, there is an excess of current assets over current liabilities, and so net working capital is a positive amount. In a simple analogy, this could be thought of as the "money in the cash drawer." It is an amount that must be committed in order to keep the enterprise running on a day to day basis.

There are some businesses that are able to operate with an excess of current liabilities, or negative net working capital. Generally, these businesses have customers that pay in advance for services rendered.

Tangible Assets Tangible assets, sometimes referred to as *fixed assets*, are usually shown as "Plant, Property, and Equipment" on an accounting balance sheet. Typically included in this asset category are the following classifications of property:

- Land
- Land improvements, such as paving, fencing, landscaping, yard lighting, sewerage, and fire protection
- Buildings, including building construction and services
- Improvements to leased property, which may comprise structural improvements, building services, power wiring, piping, and the like
- Machinery and equipment, including machinery, power wiring, plant piping, laboratory equipment, tools, and the like
- Special tooling, such as dies, jigs, fixtures, molds
- Drawings
- Office furniture and equipment
- Licensed vehicles
- Construction in progress

Intangible Assets Intangible assets typically do not appear on a company's balance sheet except in response to certain financial reporting conventions that are discussed in a following chapter. Accounting theory defines intangibles as assets that do not have physical substance, or that grant rights and privileges to a business owner, and that are inseparable from the enterprise.

The Financial Accounting Standards Board (FASB), in its Accounting Standards Codification, defines *intangible assets* as: "Assets (not including financial assets) that lack physical substance."[2]

---

[2] Financial Accounting Standards Board, *Accounting Standards Codification Glossary* (2009).

The same source defines *goodwill* as an "asset representing the future economic benefits arising from other assets acquired in a business combination."[3]

The International Valuation Standards Council (IVSC) offers more useful definitions as follows:

> *Intangible Assets: A non-monetary asset that manifests itself by its economic properties. It does not have physical substance but grants rights and privileges to its owner that usually generate income.*
> *Goodwill: Any economic benefit arising from an asset or assets that is not capable of being individually identified and separately recognized.*

International Financial Reporting Standards define intangible assets as: "An intangible asset is an identifiable non-monetary asset without physical substance."[4]

To qualify as an intangible, an asset must be identifiable:

> *An asset is identifiable if it either:*
>
> *(a) is separable, i.e. is capable of being separated or divided from the entity and sold, transferred, licensed, rented or exchanged, either individually or together with a related contract, identifiable asset or liability, regardless of whether the entity intends to do so; or (b) arises from contractual or other legal rights, regardless of whether those rights are transferable or separable from the entity or from other rights and obligations.[5]*

To qualify as an intangible, an asset must also meet *recognition* criteria:

> *An intangible asset shall be recognized if, and only if:*
>
> *(a) it is probable that the expected future economic benefits that are attributable to the asset will flow to the entity; and (b) the cost of the asset can be measured reliably.[6]*

We define intangible assets as all the elements of a business enterprise that exist beyond monetary and tangible assets. They are the elements, after working capital and fixed assets, that make the business work and contribute to the earning power of the enterprise. Their existence is dependent on the presence, or expectation, of earnings. They usually appear last in the development of a business and most often disappear first in its demise. We categorize intangible assets as:

- Rights
- Relationships
- Undefined intangibles
- Intellectual property

---

[3] Ibid.
[4] International Accounting Standards Board (IASB *Technical Summary, IAS 38 Intangible Assets.*
[5] Ibid.
[6] Ibid.

Rights

Every business enterprise acquires rights by establishing contractual agreements with other businesses, individuals, or governmental bodies. A large enterprise may have a bundle of rights comprising thousands of elements. These rights exist according to the terms of a written contract that defines: the parties to the agreement; the nature of the rights, goods, or services transferred; the transfer consideration; and the duration of the agreement. To have real value, the contract's provisions must result in an economically beneficial exchange.

Some contracts are valuable because they enable an enterprise to obtain goods or services *from* others at an advantageous price. The most common types of such a contract include:

- Leases at rates or terms that are better than what is available in the current market. Such an advantageous lease is called a leasehold interest.
- Advantageous distribution agreements for the sale, warehousing, and movement of products
- Employment contracts that help retain key personnel
- Financing arrangements that provide access to capital at more favorable terms or rates
- Insurance coverage at better than market rates
- Contracts for the supply of raw materials or purchased products at advantageous terms
- Contracts for services, such as equipment maintenance, data processing, or utility services
- Licenses or governmental certifications that are in short supply or are costly to obtain
- Rights to receive goods or services in limited supply, such as radio or television network affiliations, or film distribution rights
- Covenants by a former owner or employee not to compete
- Contractual rights of a franchisee to an exclusive territory or product line
- License contracts for the use of intellectual property that will reduce costs or create a profit opportunity

Some contractual rights are valuable because they afford an opportunity to provide goods or services *to* others at a profit. Such a contract represents "presold" business. They can provide a positive earnings stream that exceeds what is required to provide a return on the other assets employed. This type of contract can include:

- Mortgage servicing rights to collect, process, and manage escrow and insurance matters on a portfolio of mortgages for a fee
- Loan agreements purchased as part of a business enterprise on which there will be a future return of principal and interest
- Agreements to provide food service, health care, data processing, advertising, or consulting services
- Agreements to provide goods under contract for future delivery
- Student enrollments or subscriptions that are prepaid

- Licenses granted to another for the use of intellectual property in return for royalties
- Franchises that protect a territory or product line and produce fee income

Trademark valuation is integral to the challenging process of valuing the intangible asset rights of a franchisee and franchisor. The owner of intangible assets creates a franchise relationship by contracting with another entity to distribute products or services supported by those assets, provide marketing assistance to that entity, and exert some controls over that entity's operations. The franchisee typically pays an amount in excess of an arm's length price for the specific products or services, and that excess is a payment for the use of the intangible assets and intellectual property owned by the franchisor and licensed to the franchisee.

Most often, the prominent asset in a franchising transaction is a trademark created and developed by the franchisor and "rented" by the franchisee. As in a license, the rights in intangible assets are divided among franchisor and franchisee(s) according to the terms of their contractual agreement. We must therefore be careful to consider this apportionment properly when valuing the rights of either party or the collective value of the intangible assets or intellectual property involved. Perhaps because of the strong identification of goodwill with trademarks, the conventional wisdom leads us to conclude that the business of the franchisee, viewed alone, has little or no intangible assets. This is, however, not necessarily true, depending on the specific characteristics of the franchise.

In what we might call "strong" franchises, the parties specify and control every element of the business enterprise. An example is a fast food operation, in which the franchisor rigidly specifies and controls the building design, interior furnishings, signage, methods of food preparation, menu, ingredients, employee uniforms, and other procedures. If the business operates according to specifications, whatever good or bad happens is largely due to the employment of the franchisor's assets. In this case, there are probably few valuable intangible assets in the franchisee's enterprise, although there may be some. A skillful and energetic franchisee, even under strictly controlled conditions, ought to enjoy superior earnings and create some amount of goodwill.

By contrast, in "weak" franchises the franchisor provides only an umbrella business concept and trademark. We use "weak" and "strong" not in a pejorative sense, but to depict the degree of control exerted by the franchisor. An example of a weak franchise is one that provides a territory in which a franchisee sells a line of cosmetics or household goods. Even though the franchisor might provide training, accounting systems, and national advertising in support of a brand, the success of the territory will be much more dependent on the skills, personality, and ingenuity of the franchisee. This situation permits the franchisee much more latitude to employ personal marketing or selling skills. The franchisee in this situation might even be able to switch to a competing line of products without a hitch in the earnings of his or her business, demonstrating the existence of the body of intangible assets that he or she has created as part of the enterprise.

We must therefore examine each franchise situation on its own merits without undue dependence on the "conventional wisdom."

Relationships

Every business has established relationships with outside agencies, other companies, and other individuals. These are noncontractual and can, at the same time, be both ephemeral and extremely important to the enterprise. They include:

- Assembled workforce
- Customer relationships
- Distributor relationships

Assembled Workforce   One of the most obvious relationships of an enterprise is between the business and its employees. It can be very costly to locate, hire, and train a workforce, as evidenced by the expenditures made to retain employees and reduce turnover. The more specialized the workforce, the greater the cost of its assemblage and the larger its potential value to the enterprise.

Generally, accounting rules and financial reporting standards do not recognize an assembled workforce as an identifiable asset, preferring instead to lump it together with "goodwill." However, this practice does not obviate the need to recognize an assembled workforce as a potentially valuable asset that is a part of the business enterprise portfolio.

Customer Relationships   Every business has customers, but not every business has customer relationships. For example, a newsstand in a large city probably has a number of customers who habitually purchase a daily newspaper. Perhaps the walk from the bus stop to their place of work takes them past this particular stand. There are probably other convenient locations to make the purchase, but whatever the reason, these customers use this one. The newsstand proprietor does not know the identity of customers or where they work, maintains no customer account records, and could not contact them to research their interest in additional publications or services. If the proprietor moved the newsstand to another location, these customers would probably not seek him or her out, but would instead patronize another stand better located to their route. This is not a customer relationship in the sense that we are using the term.

Two aspects of a business's relationship with its customers are primary value drivers. One is the amount of *inertia* in the relationship, and the other is the amount of *information available* about the customer.

The newsstand example is representative of a low-inertia customer relationship. This term describes the situation in which there is little to hold the customer to the relationship. It is relatively easy for a customer to migrate to another source of the goods or services obtained.

Businesses that can lock in their clientele to some degree sit at the high end of the inertia scale. Typically, these businesses provide goods or services that are sharply differentiated from their competition, are not "location dependent," and are less dependent on branded merchandise for customer attraction.

These businesses have formed strong customer relationships that would persist through a change in ownership, changes in personnel, or even relocation. The value of customer relationships in such a situation is very high. The buyer of such a business would recognize the likelihood of earnings stability brought about by the solid clientele and would therefore pay a premium compared to a similar business with low-inertia customer relationships.

At the highest point of the inertia scale, we find a true monopoly business. The best example of this might be a water utility. Such a business has a territorial monopoly, provides a service (water delivery) essential to life, and owns a distribution system unfeasible for a competitor to duplicate. Especially in urbanized areas, there is no reasonable alternative to being a customer of one's local water utility. Sales and earnings of such an enterprise are steady, and the prospect of business failure is remote. Perhaps curiously, the value of customer relationships in this scenario is *low*. A true monopoly obtains its customers by virtue of its franchise, not by building relationships.

Distributor Relationships   A business that depends on others to distribute or sell its products may have established relationships of considerable value. There are companies whose representatives sell cosmetics, cookware, and cleaning products in the residential market. These companies have no retail stores, and the relationship with their representatives is extremely important.

Other businesses may sell complex products in a highly technical market through manufacturers' representatives. While there may be a contract between the company and its representatives, usually either party can terminate it on short notice. Therefore, the contract does not ensure a continuation of the relationship. Locating, hiring, training, and maintaining such representation can be a very costly process, and, once accomplished, the relationship is an asset of value to the enterprise.

It is important to note that, in this situation, the relationship between distributor and customer may be stronger than the relationship between company and customer. Therefore, the company–distributor relationship may be very crucial to the welfare of the business.

Undefined Intangibles

In spite of the fact that in recent years appraisers have analyzed, identified, and valued many intangible assets, a residual often remains. That residual of undefined intangibles is commonly referred to as "goodwill" or "going concern value." Some combine these two assets, but we believe them to be separate and distinct.

Goodwill   Business people, attorneys, accountants, and judges have all had a try at defining goodwill, the most elusive of intangibles. For many years, the bundle of assets that we now define as intangibles was simply called "goodwill." While there seemed to be little difficulty in naming this mysterious asset, there was much more difficulty in defining it. In 1936, Frank S. Moore wrote:

> *What is commercial goodwill? "Lord Eldon, the great English judge, said that it meant nothing more than the probability that the old customers will return to the old place."*
>
> *Cruttwell v. Lye,* (1810) 17 Ves. Jr., 335, 346.

> *[Quoting Justice Joseph Story]: "Goodwill may be properly enough described to be the advantage or benefit which is acquired by an establishment beyond the mere value of the capital, stock, funds, or property (meaning physical property) employed therein, in consequence of the general public patronage and encouragement which it receives from constant or habitual customers on account of its local position, or common celebrity, or reputation for skill, or affluence, or punctuality, or from other accidental circumstances or necessities, or even from ancient partialities or prejudices."*
>
>

Faust v. Rohr, 166 N.C. 187 (1914).[7]

The accounting profession examined the subject of goodwill at length in *Accounting Research Study No. 10*, published by the American Institute of Certified Public Accountants:

> *The idea of goodwill appears to have existed long before the advent of modern business concepts. P. D. Leake mentions some early references to goodwill, including one in the year 1571 in England, "I gyve to John Stephen . . . my whole interest and good will of my Quarrell . . . . [i.e., quarry]."*
>
> *In the simpler business organizations of [an] earlier period, goodwill was often of a rather personal nature, attaching in large measure to the particular personality, friendliness, and skill of the proprietor or partners of a business . . . . As the industrial system developed and business increased in complexity, the various advantages which a business possessed and which contributed to its profitability became less personal in nature. The individual advantages which a company enjoyed became more varied, were integrated with all facets and activities of a business, and thus became less distinguishable. Manufacturing processes, financial connections, and technological advantages all assumed increasing importance. Goodwill came to be regarded as everything that might contribute to the advantage which an established business possessed over a business to be started anew.* [8]

It is important to carefully consider the concept of goodwill because it is so closely allied to trademarks and brands. While a trademark is more narrowly defined in its role as intellectual property, the concept of brand seems to borrow some aspects of goodwill, as it has been defined from time to time.

Patronage   Many equate goodwill with patronage, or the proclivity of customers to return to a business and recommend it to others. This results from superior service, personal relationships, advertising programs, and business policies that meet with favor in the marketplace.

Excess Earnings   Another common aspect of a goodwill definition is the presence of so-called "excess earnings." That is, a business that possesses significant goodwill is

---

[7] Frank S. Moore, *Legal Protection of Goodwill* (New York: The Ronald Press Company, 1936), 6, 8.

[8] George Catlett and Norman Olson, *Accounting for Goodwill, Accounting Research Study No. 10*, (New York: American Institute of Certified Public Accountants, 1968).

likely to have earnings that are greater than those required to provide a fair rate of return on the other assets of the business. Such earnings are not "excess" in the sense of exorbitant or usurious profits, but indicate the presence of earning assets in addition to monetary, tangible, and identifiable intangibles.

Residual   Goodwill can be represented by the residual between the value of the enterprise as a whole and the value of the other identifiable assets. This is really a permutation of the excess earnings concept because the value of the enterprise will exceed the value of the identifiable assets (and create room for the residual) only if there are excess earnings.

This residual is prominent in mergers and acquisitions of public companies. One well-used strategy is for the acquiring company to offer to the shareholders of the target a price in excess of that at which the target's stock is trading on an exchange. Acquiring companies may do this for a number of reasons. They may need to motivate all (or at least a majority) of shareholders to sell their holdings, to obtain control of the target's assets, to exploit potential synergies, or to thwart competition for the transaction. The end result may be a value indication for the acquired company that exceeds that formerly in evidence in the marketplace. This increased business enterprise value may be ascribable to specific underlying assets or may be an increase in the value of goodwill represented by a residual.

It is unwise to depend entirely on one definition to the exclusion of the others. Can there be goodwill in a business that is losing money? Of course. A temporary escalation of expenses, a casualty loss, the opening of a new plant, or the development of a new product line can temporarily eliminate earnings, but goodwill can remain. Even over a longer period, persistent mismanagement can result in losses, but the earning *capability* can be present, as can goodwill.

Can there be excess earnings and no goodwill? Certainly. Suppose a business has a single customer who is locked in for several years under a lucrative contract. There might well be excess earnings, but they are attributable to the contract, not goodwill. As another example, the local franchisee of a well-known company may have a very successful business with earnings in excess of those required to provide a fair return on other assets. It is entirely possible, however, that those excess earnings are attributable (exercising the caveats noted) to the franchise and that the goodwill may really be trademark value or an advantageous interest in the trademark. Goodwill is an elusive concept, but a value can be determined after identifying and segregating the other assets.

If valuation practitioners were skilled enough in the identification and quantification of the intangible assets in the enterprise portfolio, they would not need to resort to the catch-all term "goodwill." There is, at times, no economic justification for the analysis necessary to do this, and in those cases, the term is useful, as long as valuation practitioners recognize that it represents an aggregation of intangible assets.

Going Concern Value   The so-called "going concern value" has been defined as "the additional element of value which attaches to property by reason of its existence as part of a going concern."[9] The measure of that value is the cost incurred to assemble

---

[9] *VGS Corp. v. Commissioner*, 68 T.C. 563, 569 (1977), appeal dismissed (5th Cir.).

and organize the myriad of small assets and incidental relationships that enable a business to "get going." One must obtain licenses, register with governmental and regulatory authorities, establish bank accounts, establish relationships with suppliers and advisors, buy paper, pencils, signs, and so on. These are the elements of a "going concern."

Intellectual Property

The final element of the intangible asset category is intellectual property. This classification of property includes trademarks, patents, copyrights, and trade secrets or know-how. Chapter 1 provides an extensive discussion of trademarks.

Here we provide a discussion about the other forms of intellectual property. Our purpose is to remind the reader that a business is truly a complex portfolio of assets. The valuation techniques described in the following chapters all depend on recognizing this fact. As much as we might wish to ascribe impressive value to trademarks, we must always bear in mind the existence of the other assets in an enterprise. Therefore, we must have some speaking acquaintance with them and be able to recognize them and appreciate their contribution to the earnings and worth of the enterprise.

A business enterprise that owns intellectual property can internally utilize its benefits or transfer interests in the property to others who will exploit it, or both. Later chapters examine in detail how intellectual property is exploited and valued. As with other types of intangible property, not all intellectual property has value. Its value is usually determined by the marketplace, either directly or indirectly.

Proprietary Technology The term *proprietary technology* refers to trade secrets and know-how. Our discussion of intellectual property begins with this classification because in our experience it is often of primary importance in the success of an enterprise. We also note that all technology-related intellectual property is a trade secret at the time of its creation. Those responsible for the creation can either maintain secrecy or elect to obtain other forms of statutory protection, such as a patent, in return for divulging its content.

Proprietary technology is very often more valuable to an enterprise than its patents. According to Karl F. Jorda:

> *Patents are but the tips of icebergs in a sea of trade secrets. Over 90% of all new technology is covered by trade secrets and over 80% of all license and technology transfer agreements cover proprietary know-how, i.e., trade secrets, or constitute hybrid agreements relating to patents and trade secrets.*[10]

Jorda also opines that the decision as to which type of protection to seek is not simply a "patent or padlock" question, but one in which the inventor must decide "what to patent and what to keep a trade secret and whether it is best to patent as well as padlock, i.e., integrate patents and trade secrets for optimal protection of innovation."[11]

---

[10] Quoted in David Rines [Professor of Intellectual Property Law and Industrial Innovation], *Germeshausen Center Newsletter* (Spring 1999).
[11] Ibid.

Trade secrets have been defined in several ways, for example:

[As] information, including a formula, pattern, compilation, program, device, method, technique or process that: (i) derives independent economic value, actual or potential, from not being generally known to, and not being readily ascertainable by proper means by, other persons who can obtain economic value from its disclosure or use, and (ii) is the subject of efforts that are reasonable under the circumstances to maintain its secrecy.[12]

[As] any formula, pattern, patentable device or compilation of information which is used in one's business and which gives an opportunity to obtain an advantage over competitors who do not know or use it. It may be a formula for a chemical compound, a process of manufacturing, treating or preserving materials, a pattern for a machine or other device, or a list of customers . . . or it may . . . relate to the sale of goods or to other operations in the business such as a code for determining discounts, rebates or other concessions in a price list or catalog, of bookkeeping or other office management."[13]

[As] any information that can be used in the operation of a business or other enterprise and that is sufficiently valuable and secret to afford an actual or potential economic advantage over others.[14]

With the passing of the Uniform Trade Secrets Act, there is U.S. federal law prohibiting the misappropriation of trade secrets. Most states have modified their laws to conform to the provisions of this Act and most litigation on this issue takes place in state venues.

Some trade secrets are patentable inventions that have not been patented in order to avoid making them public and limiting them to the statutory life of a patent. By not seeking a patent, the owner of proprietary technology also is relieved of the necessity of administering registrations (perhaps internationally) and the cost of legal and filing fees. It is not unusual to forego a patent because the subject technology may be changing so rapidly that obsolescence may occur before the governments grants a patent. However, one must consider the risk of having valuable information subject to being inadvertently divulged, independently developed, or "reverse engineered" by another.

Whatever its character, in order for a company's proprietary technology to receive trade secret protection under the law it should:

- Not be known outside of the company
- Be known only by a relatively few employees
- Be subject to stringent procedures to protect its secrecy
- Be of significant economic value to the enterprise
- Have been the result of development expenditures by the company
- Not be information that could be easily obtained by others

---

[12] Uniform Trade Secrets Act § 1(4) (amended 1990).
[13] Restatement of Torts, (1939).
[14] Restatement (Third) of Unfair Competition, Sec. 39 (1995).

STRADIVARIUS

Violins and cellos made by Antonio Stradivari in the late 1600s to early 1700s are famous throughout the world for the reputed unsurpassed quality of their sound. At auction, these instruments have brought millions of dollars. The name "Stradivarius" has even come to be used to describe superlative quality itself (e.g., "the Stradivarius of watchmaking").

Let us assume for a moment that we have been engaged to opine on the market value of the assets that comprised the successful Stradivari family enterprise. Instruments were made in a small shop on the ground floor of the family residence, so tangible assets would not seem to loom large. The family saved the money received for violins sold to live on until the next sale, so there would be a monetary asset. But business was thriving and the price of a Stradivari instrument was higher than for others. So we turn our attention to intangibles.

Many scientists and craftsmen have studied examples of Antonio Stradivari's instruments in an attempt to discern the reasons for their superiority. Some have conjectured that the dimensions of his instruments are the key, while others have theorized about the types of wood he used, or that he treated the wood or finished it in some special way. Some suggest that the climate in which the trees grew was a factor. But none of these theories has stood up for long. No one, it seems, has been successful at reverse engineering Stradivari's proprietary technology. Of course it is conceivable that he had no trade secrets—he simply used materials at hand and that the size of the materials dictated the size of the instrument and he was simply very lucky at his trade. The length of his career and the number of fine instruments he crafted, however, strongly suggests otherwise.

Others have conducted extensive, science-based tests of the sound of a Stradivarius versus other fine instruments, and yet there is not universal agreement about the superiority of its sound.

So what makes a Stradivarius instrument famous, sought-after, and valuable? Is it the hitherto unknown trade secrets of Antonio Stradivari's craftsmanship? Is it the superior sound? Or has Stradivarius come to be a world-class brand? Or is it all of the above?

We cannot satisfy the reader with definitive answers to these questions, but we raise them using this interesting example because these are precisely the sort of questions that a valuer must ask in order to winnow out the economic benefit that can be ascribed to a specific intangible or intellectual property that is embedded within the asset portfolio of an enterprise.

Patents   A patent is the legal process whereby technology or proprietary methods may be turned into property with defined rights associated with its ownership. In the United States, a patent is the grant of a property right by the U.S. government to the inventor (or his or her heirs and assigns), by action of the U.S. Patent and Trademark Office. This structure is pretty universal worldwide, though the governments and agencies differ. The right conferred by the patent grant is the right to exclude others from making, using, or selling the invention.

In defining a Utility Patent, Section 101 of the U.S. Code states: "Whoever invents or discovers any new and useful process, machine, manufacture or composition of matter, or any new and useful improvement thereof, may obtain a patent therefore."[15]

The word "process" typically refers to industrial or technical processes and describes a methodology for treating materials to manufacture a product. The "machine" element would describe a device that provides an innovative performance of some operation. The "composition of matter" element relates to innovative mixtures of ingredients or to new chemical compositions. The "manufacture" element is somewhat of a catch-all to accommodate patentable innovations that do not fall into the process, machine or composition of matter categories.

Copyrights   A copyright protects the expression of an idea, not the idea itself, just as a patent does not protect an idea, but rather its embodiment in a product or process. Copyright protection commences from the time when that expression is fixed in some tangible form, even prior to its publication, not the time at which some application is accepted by the federal government. In fact, full copyright protection is present whether the work is registered with the Copyright Office of the Library of Congress or not. A copyright owner may reprint, sell, or otherwise distribute the copyrighted work, prepare works that are derived from it, and assign, sell, or license it.

For works created after January 1, 1978, copyrights are protected for a period of the life of the author plus 70 years. The terms of copyright protection were extended in a new law passed in October 1998, the Sonny Bono Copyright Term Extension Act, bringing U.S. law into conformity with European standards. Copyright protection on "works for hire" extends for 95 years from date of publication, or 120 years from the date of creation, which ever expires first.

Section 102 of Title 17 of the U.S. Code defines a copyright as follows:

Copyright protection subsists . . . in original works of authorship fixed in any tangible medium of expression, now known or later developed, from which they can be perceived, reproduced or otherwise communicated, either directly or with the aid of a machine or device. [Included are:]

1. *Literary works;*
2. *musical works, including any accompanying words;*
3. *dramatic works, including any accompanying music;*
4. *pantomimes and choreographic works;*
5. *pictorial, graphic, and sculptural works;*
6. *motion pictures and other audiovisual works;*
7. *sound recordings.*

An unpublished work may be registered by:

1. *Reducing the work to tangible form*
2. *Transmitting an application form to the Copyright Office*
3. *Transmitting a copy of the work and the registration fee to the Copyright Office*

---

[15] 35 U.S.C. § 101.

A work to be published is protected by:

1. *Publishing with the appropriate identifying marks*
2. *Following steps 2 and 3 above, but furnishing two copies to the Copyright Office*[16]

In December 1990, Congress amended the Copyright Act to include protection for "architectural works": "the design of a building as embodied in any tangible medium of expression, including a building, architectural plans, or drawings. The work includes the overall form as well as the arrangement and composition of spaces in the design, but does not include individual standard features."[17]

In October 1992, the Copyright Office published final regulations for the registration of architectural works, which includes some definitions and registration instructions. As with other registerable works, the issue of intellectual property ownership here is very important because the design and ownership of a building are often separated.

Computer Software   Computer software is an intangible asset that is included in this discussion of intellectual property because it is subject to patent, copyright, or trade secret protection.

The Copyright Act defines a computer program as "a set of statements or instructions to be used directly or indirectly in a computer in order to bring about a certain result."[18]

Computer software here includes the project description and research, source code, object code, program documentation, user instructions, and operating manuals. This intangible asset can be extremely important to a business enterprise, and we categorize it as being either *product* or *operational* software.

Product Software   Businesses develop this category of software for resale as a product. Product software ranges from individual, stand-alone programs to more complex modular systems that interface with one another, such as a general ledger system. The software may be sold with or without consultant support and related services.

Operational Software   A company uses this category of software in its own internal operations. Operational software may be purchased, licensed, developed by an outside firm under contract, or developed internally. Businesses may require operational software to operate the computer system itself or to manage a specific task or application.

Valuation Precept

IP value depends on successful exploitation. Successful exploitation necessitates gathering a portfolio of appropriate complementary assets around the IP.

---

[16] 17 U.S.C. § 102.
[17] 17 U.S.C. § 102(a)(8).
[18] 17 U.S.C. § 101.

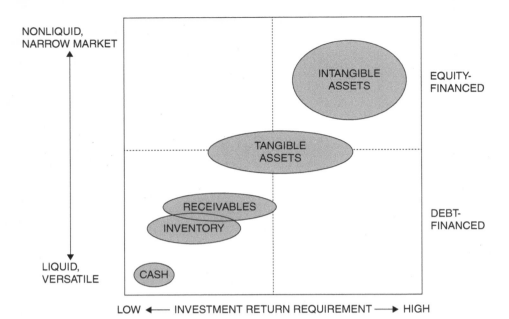

EXHIBIT 2.2 Enterprise Asset Characteristics
Source: John Wiley & Sons, Inc. Reprinted with permission.

Intellectual property cannot be exploited by itself. Even the most clever and innovative patented technology on the planet must be embedded in a product or service that people want to buy. And to make that product or service, complementary assets—tangible, monetary, and intangible—must be gathered around it. In other words, a business enterprise must be built around the technology.

As we leave this discussion about the enterprise context surrounding intellectual property, we point out some essential characteristics of the other assets that comprise this context (see Exhibit 2.2).

Exhibit 2.2 illustrates the relationship between enterprise assets and several financial characteristics. The right ordinate indicates the type of financing that is typically available to create these assets. Traditional loan sources (e.g., a commercial bank) are typically not interested in intangible assets or intellectual property as loan collateral. Therefore, businesses must rely on internal funding or the sale of equity to develop these assets. The left ordinate indicates a range of asset characteristics. Monetary assets tend to be versatile (i.e., useful in a wide range of businesses) and are liquid, or able to be easily converted into cash. Intangible assets, including intellectual property, tend to be unique to their enterprise and therefore illiquid. Along the abscissa the investors' required rate of return ranges from low for monetary assets (little risk) to high for intangibles (significant risk).

VALUATION PRINCIPLES

Up to now we have used the term "value" without defining it so that we can make a more global approach to the discussion of IP and its role within a business enterprise.

We also recognize that most readers will have an intuitive understanding of value, just as they might have an understanding of snow. An expert skier or geologist, however, may use a number of terms to describe different types of snow, such as corn, grits, powder, snirt, or firn. In the same way, a valuation professional has a need to be more specific about permutations of value. Now, it is necessary to more precisely define what this term means.

We start by defining what a valuation is and is not. First, valuation professionals commonly use the term "valuation" and "appraisal" interchangeably. We will do so as well.

Describing the Transaction

The most useful way to conceptualize a valuation is to think of it as a virtual transaction. That is, our objective is to estimate the price at which the subject property would change hands between a buyer and seller at a specific moment in time. We need to think a bit about the words we are using to describe this virtual transaction:

- *Price*. A valuation is usually stated in terms of money, but it could also be equated to "total consideration" in the event that the transaction involved bartering or non-monetary compensation.
- *Estimate*. It is very important to understand that the only way we would ever know the "true" price in a transaction is if the transaction actually took place in the real world. We make valuations because we need that information for one purpose or another, even though an actual transaction has not taken place and may not even be contemplated. Therefore, the price in our virtual transaction is the result of an estimate or an opinion on the part of the valuer.
- *Buyer and seller*. Obviously, in our virtual transaction, the seller wants to get the highest possible price and the buyer wants to pay the lowest possible price. But beyond that simplistic view, we recognize that a myriad of additional factors may motivate both buyer and seller. Do externalities compel either buyer or seller to enter into the transaction? Are there time pressures to make the transaction? Are there other unusual motivations to buy or sell? It is easy to see that we must take these factors into consideration when we estimate the virtual transaction price.
- *Specific time*. We all know that when we buy an automobile, we pay a negotiated price to the dealer. When we drive it away from the dealership, our formerly new automobile becomes a "used car," with a different price. A value estimate is only valid as of a specific moment or, at best, for a rather short period of time.

While this may sound quite imprecise, we should not be deterred because countless business decisions are made every day all over the globe based on evaluations of the possibility and probability of future events.

Misconceptions

Murphy, Orcutt, and Remus have provided an excellent book on the valuation of patents.[19] In it, they discuss some popular misconceptions about the valuation

---

[19] William J. Murphy, John L. Orcutt, and Paul C. Remus, *Patent Valuation: Improving Decision Making through Analysis* (Hoboken, NJ: John Wiley & Sons, Inc., 2012).

process and why related anxieties may be unfounded. We paraphrase that discussion in brief form in the following:

- *Valuation analysis can only be conducted by experts.* The valuation of intellectual property is not easy, to be sure. It is also not "rocket science." It requires diligent research, unbiased judgment, and some pretty simple arithmetic.
- *The value conclusion is more important than the valuation process.* In the real world of business, the research and the inputs to the valuation process may, in the end, be more valuable than the result. Yes, in litigation the value conclusion may be the important keystone.
- *Mathematical complexity produces a precise result.* We hope to convince the reader that it is the research and analysis of inputs to the valuation process that influence the quality of the result, not complex mathematics.
- *A value conclusion that is not precise is useless.* In the real world of business, multiple value conclusions or ranges of value may be quite useful and it may not be necessary to devote the time and resources necessary to come to a single conclusion.

There is no "magic bullet" method. In this book, we will present the three primary valuation methodologies and a number of techniques that are used to develop the required inputs to those methodologies. The facts and circumstances of a particular valuation may suggest the use of multiple methods.

The Inputs Are Difficult, the Arithmetic Is Easy

It is quite understandable that people who are learning about valuation or observing the process from the outside would focus on the calculations necessary to convert a myriad of information into a conclusion of value. There is a natural tendency to look for the secret of valuation in its mathematics. We who teach and consult about intellectual property and valuation commonly get requests for a case study. Case studies are useful in the learning process, but these requests are often founded in a desire for a recipe. The hope is that there is a repeatable, step-by-step series of mathematical calculations that will lead one directly to a valuation conclusion. This is a hope that cannot be fulfilled, in our view.

A valuation may appear to be a haphazard process from the outside, but it is not. In another field, a skilled builder has a good grasp of the tasks and tools necessary to construct a house. However, every house is different and so a craftsman must select those specific tasks and tools necessary for the facts and circumstances of a particular construction project. Stated another way, there is a solid body of knowledge about home building, but the application of that knowledge is different in every case. There can be no "one size fits all" application in the form of a recipe. Similarly, with valuation, there is a body of principles (primarily from the financial/investment world) and their application is dependent on the particular set of facts and circumstances associated with a particular property and valuation needs.

We use the concept of a funnel, as shown in Exhibit 2.3, to illustrate the valuation process.

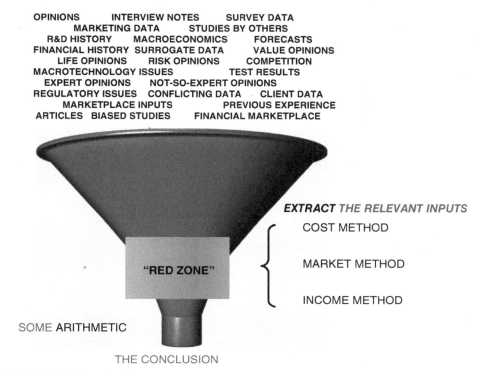

OPINIONS   INTERVIEW NOTES   SURVEY DATA
MARKETING DATA   STUDIES BY OTHERS
R&D HISTORY   MACROECONOMICS   FORECASTS
FINANCIAL HISTORY SURROGATE DATA   VALUE OPINIONS
LIFE OPINIONS   RISK OPINIONS   COMPETITION
MACROTECHNOLOGY ISSUES   TEST RESULTS
EXPERT OPINIONS   NOT-SO-EXPERT OPINIONS
REGULATORY ISSUES   CONFLICTING DATA   CLIENT DATA
MARKETPLACE INPUTS   PREVIOUS EXPERIENCE
ARTICLES   BIASED STUDIES   FINANCIAL MARKETPLACE

EXTRACT THE RELEVANT INPUTS

COST METHOD

"RED ZONE"

MARKET METHOD

INCOME METHOD

SOME ARITHMETIC

THE CONCLUSION

EXHIBIT 2.3   Valuation Elements

As we demonstrate in upcoming chapters, each of the valuation methodologies concludes with some mathematical calculations. And for each methodology, there are critical inputs to the calculations. Those critical inputs are the result of a distillation of information of many kinds and from many sources. The appraiser must make that distillation in an unbiased way after an exhaustive investigation.

This is the mountain of information that we analyze in our illustrative funnel. This information may include factual data, historical information, forecasts of various types, opinions of others, reliable data, unreliable data, and conflicting information. We must gather this data with some plan in mind, rather than simply grabbing whatever information comes to hand. We must also proceed in an unbiased manner. That is, we should not reject data that appears to be contrary to some preconceived notion of ours. Our search should be as exhaustive as possible.

More often than not, there are no direct sources of specific information needed in the process. Assume, for example, that our analysis requires an estimate of the cost of a Toyota Camry automobile three years from now. There is no authoritative source of that data, so we must develop it ourselves. We might consider:

■ The current cost of a Toyota Camry
■ Historical Camry prices

- Generalized automobile price trends
- The onset of electric automobiles and sales forecasts
- Future gasoline prices
- History of automobile model changes
- History and forecasts of inflation
- Forecasts of world automobile markets
- Price trends of steel, aluminum, and labor

Our task is to utilize available data to derive our own opinion of a needed input—in this case the future price of a Toyota Camry. In a sense, this is a "minifunnel" because that future price is but one of the essential inputs to a larger valuation issue.

Extracting the essential inputs is the crucial task and so we have designated part of the funnel as the "red zone." This is the most difficult task in the entire process. Here we must be thoughtful, logical, and unbiased. There must be some logical, explainable connection between the information gathered and the essential inputs that we are going to rely on. It is useful to remember that at some point (in a report or litigation, or before a Board of Directors or a peer group), we have to explain why we accepted or rejected some inputs, why we relied on some data and not others, and the basis for judgments that we made. Smoke, mirrors, and computerized black boxes have no place here.

Once the appraiser has settled on the essential inputs, the mathematics is straightforward; and a more complex mathematics does not guarantee a more precise or correct result. The quality of the value opinion is determined long before the arithmetic is applied.

PROPERTY AND RIGHTS TO PROPERTY

The first step in any valuation is to carefully develop a description of the property. It's important to understand that we are never valuing property per se, but rather rights to the property. As an example, our assignment might be to value an acre of undeveloped land. Our first step is to develop a physical description to include the boundaries and area covered, as well as whether it is flat, hilly, dry or wet, and so forth. However, the assignment is not really to place a value on the earth or the rocks and stream that might be on the land, but rather our task is to value the rights that the seller is offering to a buyer of the land. We can envision a situation in which the seller might want to retain the mineral rights of the land or, in another case, governmental regulations limit land use. There is an almost infinite variety of rights that we would have to consider as available to a buyer in a particular case.

These issues arise with various levels of importance in all types of property, and especially with regard to intellectual property, because, as we noted at the beginning of this chapter, intellectual property is unique in the myriad of ways its rights can be subdivided among various parties. We therefore must have a firm grasp on the particular rights to be appraised.

PREMISE OF VALUE

Henry Babcock describes value as being:

> *expressible in terms of a single lump sum of money considered as payable or expended at a particular point in time in exchange for property, that is, the right to receive future benefits beginning at that particular timepoint.*[20]

Oliver Wendell Holmes recognized that value has many meanings when he said:

> *A word (value) is not a crystal, transparent and unchanged; it is the skin of a living thought, and may vary greatly in color and content according to the circumstances and the time in which it is used.*[21]

Value is not the same as price or cost, although at times they are equivalent. When we speak of "getting a bargain" or "paying dearly" for something, we recognize the difference between price and value.

Value is the representation of all future benefits of ownership, compressed into a single payment. Therefore, value is continually changing as the future benefits increase or decrease with the passage of time. Therefore, we can only express an opinion of value relative to a specific time—an "as of" date. We must also define the future benefits of ownership in terms of whose ownership is assumed and/or the underlying purpose of the appraisal.

Valuation Precept

A valuation is always forward looking. Value is based on the economic benefits that an asset can be expected to produce in the future.

The distinction of ownership and purpose are essential to the appraisal process. A valuation cannot proceed without defining the premise of value under which it is to be made. One cannot, for example, meaningfully answer the question "What is my car worth?" because additional information is necessary. Value does not exist in the abstract and must be addressed within the context of time, place, potential owners, and potential uses. If value, like beauty, is in the eye of the beholder, we need to know who the "beholder" will be. Is it:

- An insurance company?
- A used car dealer?
- A next-door neighbor?

---

[20] Henry A. Babcock, FASA, *Appraisal Principles and Procedures* (Washington, DC: American Society of Appraisers, 1980).
[21] Quoted in American Institute of Real Estate Appraisers of the National Association of Realtors, *The Appraisal of Real Estate* (Chicago: 1978).

- A tax assessor?
- An accountant?
- The executor of my estate?
- A dealer in scrap metal?

Sometimes identifying the recipient of the appraisal will also define the value premise, since, by custom, certain users have defined requirements. In other cases, it is necessary to ascertain how users plan to use the valuation. Some examples include using the valuation to:

- Estimate the cost of replacing property
- Determine how much insurance to carry
- Assist in setting a selling price
- Set the amount of a charitable donation
- Calculate the amount of estate, gift, or income taxes
- Determine the amount of a damage claim
- Estimate the value of property as collateral in a loan transaction
- Estimate the price a property would bring at auction

Each of these combinations of appraisal use and purpose has a specific premise of value that is appropriate.

We can apply these same questions and answers to intellectual property. Because of its versatility, we must form an opinion as to its most promising use. The "highest and best use" (a phrase frequently used by real property appraisers) is that which provides the highest net return. That may vary considerably, depending on how the intellectual property is exploited, when it is exploited, and with whom it is exploited.

The more a property is designed, constructed, or suited for a special purpose, the greater difference there will be in value measured by different premises. An extreme example would be a nuclear power plant constructed at great cost. As a source of electric power it may have great market value and its cost justified. But if the plant shuts down, what alternative use is there for this massive facility? Its market value under that circumstance could be zero (or negative). In less dramatic fashion, this is true for a trademark expected to have its highest value within the business enterprise of which it is a part, and associated with the product or service for which it was created. Removed from that milieu, the trademark's value could drop significantly. In varying degrees, this is true for most intangible assets and intellectual property.

In following sections, we introduce several definitions of value as well as several types of cost and indicate for each its most common usage in the valuation process. We will also present examples of valuation concepts applied to physical property to better illustrate the underlying theories.

Market Value

This measure of value is the most commonly used and is, unfortunately, the most misunderstood. Appraisal literature, financial reporting standards, the law, and court cases also contain the terms fair market value, fair value, true value, and exchange value. The general misunderstanding and fuzziness surrounding this value concept is in no small way related to its indefinite use by attorneys in contracts and by legislators in law. Both situations lead to litigation that, in turn, involves more attorneys and expert witnesses and, in the end, a judge who attempts to interpret all of their misinterpretations. With that aside, we make yet another attempt to clarify this concept.

There are two recognized definitions of market value. One describes it in terms of the conditions under which a property exchange occurs. The second describes it in economic terms.

Conditions of Exchange   Market value embodies the concept of an exchange of property. Further, it defines the conditions of that exchange. There are, therefore, different types of market value, as those conditions change. All, however, proceed from these basic concepts:

1. *The amount at which a property would exchange.* For example, two persons come together for the purpose of exchanging property for money since an appraisal is made in terms of money.
2. *Between a willing buyer and a willing seller.* These two persons want to make the exchange.
3. *Neither being under compulsion.* Neither of the parties is forced, by the other or by circumstances, to make the transaction.
4. *Each having full knowledge of all relevant facts.* Both parties are aware of what is included in the sale, the condition of the property, its history and possible use, and any liabilities against it.
5. *And with equity to both.* The exchange will be fair to both parties, and neither will gain particular advantage in negotiation or in the terms of the sale.

This is the definition of market value in its purest form. Some may introduce minor modifications, such as substituting the words "might exchange" in place of "would exchange" because no one knows the precise amount. To find it is the purpose of having an appraisal. Another common modification is the substitution of "reasonable knowledge" for "full knowledge," presumably since no one ever has absolutely full knowledge of anything. With the possibility of these minor changes, that is the essence of market value.

Alternative Exchange Conditions   There are times when a valuation must reflect that there are unwilling buyers and sellers, there is an element of compulsion present, or that a buyer intends to use the property for a purpose that differs from the current use. These conditions introduce further modifications to the definition outlined. The most common example arises in a bankruptcy wherein the present owner of property must dispose of it to satisfy creditors. The property must be liquidated (turned into cash). The term *liquidation* also connotes some form of compulsion on the part of the owner (seller), perhaps because the financial return on the property has not met expectations or because there are other, better opportunities for investment. The speed with which the seller hopes to achieve liquidity is a key value factor.

Orderly liquidation is the situation in which there is a "reasonable" time in which to accomplish the sale. What is reasonable can vary considerably, depending on the type of property. Very unique property, suited for a narrow purpose, would appeal to a very small market. It might take six months to a year to advertise, engage intermediaries, and close such a transaction. A steel mill or petrochemical plant are more extreme examples and might require several years of worldwide marketing efforts and substantial conversion costs to achieve the same objective. If we place intellectual property on the market, it could easily require a year or more to locate a buyer whose particular business circumstances would result in a reasonable exchange price.

Forced liquidation implies the same transaction carried out more quickly, even at some sacrifice in selling price. Often this means selling to an intermediary, such as a real estate developer or other dealer, who buys with the intent of "repackaging" the property and reselling it at a profit. The exchange price is further reduced by the dealer's holding costs and return on investment.

Auction is likely to result in the lowest exchange price because there is no particular effort to contact the best possible buyer prospects and because there is an objective to dispose of the property "now." Auctions of machinery and equipment, store fixtures, and so on, are usually conducted on an "as-is, where-is" basis. Therefore, the buyer also considers the cost to remove and transport the property. Intangible assets and intellectual property are not often exchanged separately from the business enterprise of which they are a part and not often under conditions of forced sale. This is because, as stand-alone property, they tend to have sharply reduced value outside of the enterprise that created them. Patents can be an exception, as illustrated by the well-publicized auctions of the Nortel and Kodak patent portfolios. We discuss auction sales of trademark rights in a subsequent chapter.

Economic Criteria   The second definition of market value is quite important and provides a most useful guide for the valuation process itself. By this standard, *fair market value* is equal to the present value of the future economic benefits of ownership.

In subsequent chapters, we provide an explanation of the methods by which we can estimate this present value to directly indicate market value.

Fair Value

In order to explain the derivation of this value premise it is necessary to digress a bit into the development of current financial reporting standards.

The accounting profession has long been reticent about showing intangible assets on corporate financial statements (i.e., the balance sheet). This reflects the opinion that intangibles are difficult to identify precisely, are difficult to separate from the business, and have unclear financial benefits and economic life are unclear.[22] If a newspaper company purchases a printing press (a tangible asset), presumably none of these drawbacks are apparent, so there is no question about that investment showing up on the balance sheet.

At the same time, some investors and lenders, as well as some in the academic community, have advocated the inclusion of intangible assets in financial statements because that provides a "complete picture" of an enterprise. This has been a long-standing tension.

---

[22] For a detailed discussion of these issues, see Gordon V. Smith and Russell L. Parr, Chapter 5 in *Intellectual Property: Valuation, Exploitation and Infringement Damages,* 4th ed. (Hoboken, NJ: John Wiley & Sons, Inc., 2005).

In 2001, the FASB issued two statements that substantially altered U.S. accounting for intangible assets and intellectual property acquired in business combinations and thereafter:

- Statement of Financial Accounting Standards No. 141 – Business Combinations (SFAS 141)
- Statement of Financial Accounting Standards No. 142 – Goodwill and Other Intangible Assets (SFAS 142)

These Statements have since (July 1, 2009) been designated as Accounting Standards Codification (ASC) 805 and 350.

We have seen similar developments outside the United States. The International Accounting Standards Board (IASB), reorganized from the International Accounting Standards Committee (IASC) in 2000, has been working since 1973 to develop accounting standards acceptable to nearly 200 participating countries. Its regulations are called International Financial Reporting Standards (IFRS). The marked increase in cross-border acquisitions and mergers provides considerable incentive for the adoption of standardized accounting practices. World equity markets are growing and maturing with the accompanying need to provide world investors with consistent financial information.

Within the IFRS, the section dealing with intangible assets is International Accounting Standard (IAS) 38. It is, in essence, similar to ASC 805 and 350 just referred to.

The essential point, at this stage in our discussion, is that these accounting standards introduce the concept of *fair value*, defined generally as follows: the price that would be received to sell an asset or paid to transfer a liability in an orderly transaction between market participants at the measurement date.

Market participants are buyers and sellers in the principal (or most advantageous) market for the asset or liability that are:

- Independent of the reporting entity; that is, they are not related parties
- Knowledgeable, having a reasonable understanding about the asset or liability and the transaction based on all available information, including information that might be obtained through due diligence efforts that are usual and customary
- Able to transact for the asset or liability
- Willing to transact for the asset or liability; that is, they are motivated but not forced or otherwise compelled to do so

Readers will notice the similarity between this definition of fair value and the previous discussion of market value. The differences are somewhat subtle. We describe the difference as a change of viewpoint. That is, market value considers the positions of both buyer and seller equally. Fair value views the transaction more from the view of the seller, presumably because accountants focus on what could be realized in the distressed sale of assets.

The emphasis on market participants and the principle or most advantageous market reflects the difficulties experienced by companies and their auditors in valuing some of the complex financial instruments that were at the center of the financial meltdown of recent times.

Fair value is the required standard when making valuations following a business combination. Company A acquires Company B for $100 million, the purchase price is reflected on A's balance sheet only *after* it is allocated to all the monetary, tangible, and intangible assets acquired. The fair value of those individual assets is the basis for the purchase price allocation.

Cost of Reproduction   This is value measured by the cost that would be incurred as of the appraisal date to construct a replica of the subject property. It is often the basis for an insurance policy since the purpose of some casualty insurance is to restore property to its original condition. Cost of reproduction can also be useful as a starting point to develop other measures of value.

For an intangible asset, this value could be based, for example, on the work effort that would be necessary to reproduce a software system. For a trademark, the costs of planning, design, research, legal work, advertising, and promotion incurred to originate the mark and develop it to its status as of the appraisal date represent the cost of reproduction.

Cost of Replacement   This is value measured by the cost, as of the appraisal date, to obtain a property with equivalent utility to the subject. For the computer software, it would be a system written in the newest, most efficient language for current hardware configurations that would perform the currently required tasks. It would have the same utility as the old system, but would likely accomplish its required tasks in a quite different manner.

Cost of Reproduction/Replacement Less Depreciation   These terms refer to a type of value calculated by reducing either cost of reproduction or cost of replacement by an amount to reflect the loss in value due to physical deterioration and, in some cases, obsolescence.

Original Cost   This is the cost recorded at some previous time for the purchase, construction, or creation of an asset. It is typically the amount recorded on the books of an enterprise and may be a combination of materials, labor, overheads, taxes, interest, and other costs. It represents the costs incurred by a specific party, at a particular time, and in accordance with particular conditions. It is only related to value by coincidence, since the costs, even at the time they were incurred, may have been unusually high or low. In the valuation of intangible assets and intellectual property, one must be cautious in using any accounting or tax-based value. In a valuation, original cost can be useful as:

- A rough guide as to reproduction cost at an earlier time
- Part of the balance sheet of a business enterprise
- A starting point in the development of reproduction cost by the use of price trends

Book Cost   *Book cost* is also known as *book value* or *net book value*, and it refers to the original cost reduced by accounting depreciation as carried on the books of a business. In order to distinguish between "accounting depreciation" and "appraisal depreciation," we use the term capital recovery to refer to depreciation for accounting purposes.

Capital recovery is an allocation of cost. When a business purchases an asset that it expects to be useful for several years, it would distort the financial statements to reflect that expenditure entirely at the time of purchase. Therefore, the business spreads the cost over the asset's useful life:

$$\frac{\text{Original life}}{\text{Useful life}} = \frac{\$1,000,000}{40 \text{ years}} = \$25,000 \text{ per year}$$

Using this example, the business reduces the original cost of the asset by $25,000 per year until, in the fortieth year, it is zero. During the intervening years, we refer to the declining amount as book cost or net book value. Intangible assets and intellectual property acquired in a business combination are typically subject to a capital recovery (i.e., amortization) on financial statements. We observe this again in Chapter 3.

Though many business people think of book cost as equivalent to some form of value, it is not. Property accounting practices vary widely. In some cases, accounting books continue to show disposed of property, and in others, businesses write off and remove depreciated property from the accounting records. Capital recovery practices also vary widely, and so methods and lives are not consistent from company to company. Therefore, it is unlikely that accounting depreciation (capital recovery) matches the decline in value over time. Therefore, even if the original cost starting point was representative of value at some previous moment, depreciated original cost is not likely to equal current value. Book cost is, except for the regulated (utility) environment, useful only as a rough benchmark suitable for "order of magnitude" comparisons.

Tax Basis   This is the same as book value described except that the calculation of capital recovery is in accordance with tax requirements. Some form of accelerated method is usually used to calculate capital recovery, and the life is the result of some legislation rather than being based on actual service life.

The government changes tax depreciation methods and lives so often and so significantly that tax basis is of no use as a measure of any form of value.

VALUATION METHODS

In this section, we provide a brief description of valuation methods. In following chapters, these methods are described more fully and examined as to their suitability for appraising trademarks.

Many have attempted to invent methods for valuing intangible assets, especially brands and trademarks. Professional firms in the fields of advertising, marketing, and related consulting are eager to coin their own proprietary brand valuation schemes on which they can bestow their own trademark.

Many have also devised systems for "scoring" brands on different attributes, such as versatility, internationality, leadership, protection, and so forth. These can be useful checklists and might be helpful in comparing one brand with another, but there is no supportable connection between a score and a dollar amount of market value.

In reality, there are three accepted valuation methodologies: the market, cost, and income methods.[23] When observing some long list of valuation methods, some analysis will reveal that these are really permutations of the market, cost, and income methods and that some methods are in reality simply techniques for deriving the inputs that are needed for the market, cost, and income methods.

Market Method

The market method is the most direct and the most easily understood appraisal technique. Using it, we construct our virtual transaction based on actual transactions in the marketplace. Information about an "arm's length" transaction of property comparable to our subject is required. Ideally, we have more than one transaction from an active marketplace.

The residential real estate market is a good example of a situation in which these conditions are usually present. There is typically some activity in this market in a given area, and selling, asking, and exchange prices are public. Of course, not all residential properties are similar, but given enough activity, reasonable comparisons are possible. Where these optimal market conditions do not exist, using this approach involves more judgment, and it may become a less reliable measure of value. As we will discuss in subsequent chapters, this technique is rarely used for the valuation of trademarks because their uniqueness and symbiotic relationship to a given product or service precludes it.

Cost Method

The cost method provides input to our virtual transaction by informing us about what buyer and seller would consider as the cost of a realistic alternative to the contemplated transaction. One of the theoretical threads running through appraisal methodology is the principle of substitution, that is, that one would not pay more for property than the cost of an equally desirable substitute. So there is a price-cost-value equivalency if certain conditions are met.

One assumption underlying the cost method is that the price of new property is commensurate with the economic value of the service that the property can provide during its life. The marketplace is the test of this equation. If, for example, the price of a new machine is set at a level far above the present value of the future economic benefits of owning the machine, then no machines would sell. If the opposite were true, then demand would outstrip supply, and presumably the price would rise. The price of a new machine, absent some market aberration, is therefore equal to its market value at the time of purchase.

Property to be appraised is typically not new, however, so the use of the cost approach therefore nearly always brings with it the complexity of quantifying the reduction from ("brand new") value due to the action of some form of depreciation.

---

[23] The International Valuation Standards Council in its Guidance Note No. 4 describes these as "the market comparison approach, the income capitalization approach and the cost approach."

Income Method

The income method provides input to our virtual transaction by informing us about how buyer and seller would consider the future economic benefit of owning the subject property. The underlying theory is that the value of property can be measured by the present worth of the net economic benefit (cash receipts less cash outlays) to be received over its life. This concept is nicely described by Campbell and Taylor:

> It has often been stated, but bears repeating, that assets (whether bricks and mortar, land, equipment, or corporate shares) are only worth in the open market what they can earn, and the true measure of worth is the assets' earnings when related to the risk inherent in the business situation.[24]

The four essential ingredients of the income method are:

1. A forecast of the *amount* of the income stream that the property can generate in the future
2. An assumption as to the *duration* and *pattern* of the income stream
3. An assumption as to the *risk* associated with the realization of the forecasted income

Because business property is owned for the express purpose of earning a return on investment, the income approach is a strong indicator of value for this type of property. In the chapters that follow, we concentrate on the use of the income approach for the valuation of trademarks. We also provide a much more detailed discussion on how to develop the four ingredients needed in these calculations.

SUMMARY

This chapter's highlights include:

- A trademark comes into the business world with very little value. It attains value through an association with a successful product or service.
- A business must combine a trademark with a portfolio of other monetary, tangible, and intangible assets before the trademark attains value.
- That portfolio of assets comprises a business enterprise and it is essential, for trademark valuation, to understand the contributions of the assets in the portfolio.
- A valuation is like a "virtual transaction." It is a forward-looking estimate based on a careful gathering of data and a logical, unbiased analysis of that data.
- The basis of every valuation is one or more of three accepted methods: the cost, market, and income methods.

In the next chapter, we begin to apply those methods on a macrolevel that focuses on the whole enterprise.

---

[24] Ian R. Campbell and John D. Taylor, "Valuation of Elusive Intangibles," *Canadian Chartered Accountant*, May 1972, 41.

CHAPTER 3

Using Financial Information

In the previous chapter, we used the concept of a funnel (Exhibit 2.3) to illustrate the valuation process. A competent valuation begins with the collection of data and proceeds to an analysis of that information in order to extract the necessary valuation inputs. Nearly every valuation includes gathering and analyzing financial information. This can include:

- Information about the economy as a whole
- Information about a specific industry
- Information about a group of companies within a specific industry
- Information about a specific business enterprise

Valuation Precept

A valuation of intangible assets or intellectual property properly begins with an analysis of financial statements

Values are expressed in terms of money. It is inescapable, therefore, that financial information, of various kinds and from various sources, forms an essential part of the factual basis for a value opinion.

In this chapter, we focus on the financial statements of a single company and discuss methods for analyzing and drawing conclusions from them. This exercise is useful for several reasons:

- As the first step to understand the business and operations of a client, adversary, or transaction target
- As part of an aggregation of financial data on an industry segment
- To obtain competitive intelligence

Financial reporting by business enterprises can vary from the voluminous regulatory reports and annual reports to shareholders of major public corporations down to a two-page balance sheet and income statement of a small retail establishment. There is every degree of complexity between these two extremes. We begin this discussion by observing a situation in which financial reporting is at its most complete. We are going to use, as an example, a report of the Coca-Cola Company to the U.S. Securities & Exchange Commission (SEC). This is one of many reports of a publicly traded company to the SEC. We will be referring to the so-called Form 10-K, which is filed annually. As of this writing, the most current report of the Coca-Cola Company is for the fiscal year ended December 31, 2011. Readers can download a copy of this report from the Company's website.[1] This report begins with a substantial narrative by company management covering the following subjects:

- Description of the business and some history
- Acquisitions made by the company during the reporting year
- Description of how the company segments its operations geographically
- An extensive description of products and brands
- The company's distribution organization
- A discussion of competition
- The sourcing of essential raw materials
- A discussion of patents, copyrights, trade secrets, and trademarks
- Governmental regulations affecting the business
- An extensive discussion of risk factors affecting the business
- A description of the physical properties owned by the company
- Legal proceedings that may affect company operations
- Brief biographies of the executive officers of the company
- Information about the markets for the company's common equity
- An extensive discussion by management of financial conditions and results of operations
- Discussion concerning market risk

Taken together, the preceding sections in the Coca-Cola Company 10-K report (which is comprised of nearly 80 pages) provide a wealth of information about that business enterprise. The next section of the Coca-Cola Company 10-K report presents financial statements and supplementary data. This comprises about 60 pages, of which the Notes to Consolidated Financial Statements are the largest part. These notes are a very important part of this report, providing additional detail on line item dollar amounts contained in the financial statements.

Were we to be engaged to appraise the trademarks of the Coca-Cola Company, a careful study of this report would provide a wealth of information to that task prior to interviews and fact finding with company personnel at their locations.

FINANCIAL REPORTING

In the discussion that follows, we will use the less complex financial statements of a fictitious company, Smith & Richey Enterprises (S&R).

Consolidated Statement of Earnings

In Exhibits 3.1 and 3.2, we provide the primary financial statements for this business. Exhibit 3.1 is a consolidated statement of earnings that reports total revenues

---

[1] Coca-Cola Company, "Annual & Other Reports," *Coca-Cola Journey,* http://www.coca-colacompany.com/investors/annual-other-reports.

EXHIBIT 3.1   Consolidated Statement of Earnings

SMITH & RICHEY ENTERPRISES
Consolidated Statement of Earnings
($ millions)

Year ended December 31,	2012	%
Net operating revenues	$ 30,900	100.0
Cost of goods sold	14,500	46.9
Gross profit	16,400	53.1
Selling, general and administrative expenses	9,000	29.1
Other operating charges	275	0.9
	9,275	30.0
Operating income	7,125	23.1
Interest income	340	1.1
Interest expense	450	1.5
Other income — net	80	0.3
Income before income taxes	7,095	23.0
Income taxes	2,838	9.2
Net income	$ 4,257	13.8
Earnings per Common Share	$ 1.70	
Common Shares (Mill)	2,500	

for the company over the course of a year; in this case, the year ended December 31, 2012. From those revenues are subtracted various expenses incurred by the business in order to calculate the net income from the year's operations, the so-called "bottom line."

The bottom of Exhibit 3.1 shows the number of shares of common stock outstanding as well as the earnings (net income) per common share. We have made a calculation of the line items of the income statement expressed as a percentage of revenues. This is data not usually included on a typical income statement, but we have made this calculation as a part of our analysis and will refer to its results subsequently.

Consolidated Balance Sheet

The consolidated balance sheet of the company is shown as Exhibit 3.2. Balance sheets give a financial picture of the company at a particular moment in time, in this case, December 31, 2012. This is different from the income statement which captures the income and expense results during the entire year.

You will observe that the balance sheet is divided into two sections—"Assets" at the top and "Liabilities & Shareowners Equity" at the bottom. A nontechnical

EXHIBIT 3.2 Consolidated Balance Sheet

SMITH & RICHEY ENTERPRISES
Consolidated Balance Sheet
($ millions)

Year ended December 31,	2012	%
ASSETS		
Current Assets		
Cash and cash equivalents	$ 7,000	
Marketable securities	2,300	
	9,300	18.9
Trade accounts receivable	3,800	
Inventories	2,400	
Prepaid expenses and other assets	2,250	
Total current assets	17,750	36.0
Investments and Other Assets		
Investments in other enterprises	6,500	
Other assets	2,000	
	8,500	17.2
Property, Plant and equipment		
Property, plant and equipment at cost	17,100	
Less allowance for depreciation	(7,000)	
Net book value	10,100	20.5
Intangible Assets		
Intangible assets at cost	15,750	
Less allowance for amortization	2,800	
	12,950	31.9
Total Assets	$49,300	100.0%
LIABILITIES and SHARE-OWNERS' EQUITY		
Current Liabilities		
Accounts payable and accrued expenses	$ 6,600	
Loans and notes payable	6,850	
Current maturities of long-term debt	120	
Accrued income taxes	350	
Total Current Liabilities	13,920	28.2
Long-term Debt	5,010	10.2
Other Liabilities	3,000	6.1
Deferred Income Taxes	1,790	3.6
Shareowners' Equity		
Common stock	900	
Capital surplus	9,600	
Reinvested earnings	40,080	
	50,580	
Less treasury stock	25,000	
	25,580	51.9
Total Liabilities and Shareowners' Equity	$49,300	100.0%

explanation of these two sections might be that the assets section of the balance sheet describes what the company owns, while the liabilities section describes what the company owes. You will again note that we have made a calculation of the line items in these two sections expressed as a percentage of total assets and total liabilities, respectively.

FINANCIAL STATEMENTS AND VALUE: DISAGGREGATING S&R'S ASSETS

Let us now assume that we are in the beginning stages of a valuation of the trademark portfolio of S&R. What information can we glean from S&R's financials that can help us?

First, we must recognize a fundamental difference between a business enterprise and its assets as reflected on its financial statements and the picture of those same assets as reflected in a valuation. The reader will recall the business enterprise equation that was Exhibit 2.1 in the previous chapter. It illustrated the concept that the value of a business enterprise is equal to the combined values of its monetary, tangible, and intangible assets, recognizing that the value relationships among these three asset classes may change from time to time and is certainly different from enterprise to enterprise. In total, however, the equation holds.

A quick scan of the balance sheet of S&R will reveal that there are entries for monetary assets (as we defined them in Chapter 2), tangible assets ("Property, Plant & Equipment") and intangible assets. Are these the same as shown in Exhibit 2.1? The answer is no, and we need to understand the difference.

Cost versus Value

The fundamental difference is between cost and value. The simplest example of that might be our experiences connected with the purchase of a new automobile. At the time we are handed the keys to our new automobile, the price that we have agreed to pay is both the cost of the automobile and its market value. That is, we, as a willing buyer, have agreed with the automobile dealer, as a willing seller, on a price that seems fair to both of us. Otherwise, the sale would not have taken place. By definition, this transaction reflects the results of a virtual transaction that we might construct to estimate market value.

We all know, however, that the moment we drive that car away from the automobile dealer's premises, it becomes a "used car" and its value is reduced by some amount instantaneously. During the period that we will own the car, it acquires some wear and tear, new automobile models come out, and the features that made the automobile so attractive to us when we bought it are superseded by improvements. Thus, the market value of the car continues to change due to the action of a host of external factors. But its cost remains the same—the price we paid for it.

The same basic principles apply to the assets of a business enterprise. When we look at the company's balance sheet, we are seeing a record of costs, not values. As in our automobile example, however, we know that those recorded costs were at one time value equivalents. As an example, we can observe on the balance sheet of S&R, an entry to "Property, Plant & Equipment at Cost" in the amount of $17.1 billion dollars. This presumably includes all of the land, buildings and machines, and so forth that S&R is currently utilizing in its business. So, if the land under the headquarters building was originally purchased in 1952 for $100,000, that amount is included in the $17.1 billion. Reason tells us, however, that the value of that land is probably significantly higher today. So the question remains, is there any information on the balance sheet of S&R that might assist us in the valuation of whatever trademarks the company owns?

With an understanding of the cost versus value issue and the discussion about Exhibit 3.1, we can infer the following:

- Whatever the market value of S&R's trademarks, it is subsumed in the value of the whole S&R enterprise.
- We know that the value of the S&R enterprise is equal to the value of its monetary assets plus the value of its tangible assets plus the value of its intangible assets.
- We know that the value of its trademarks is buried somewhere in the intangible asset category along with the values of other intangible assets and intellectual property.

So it becomes clear that if we could come to an opinion about the value of the intangible asset classification of S&R, we would be part of the way down the road toward our objective of valuing its trademark portfolio.

Monetary Assets

In Chapter 2, we noted that our classification of monetary assets can also be called net working capital. Net working capital is defined as the excess of current assets over current liabilities. Returning to S&R's balance sheet, the reader can observe that there are amounts contained thereon for current assets and current liabilities. As we noted previously, however, S&R's balance sheet reflects costs rather than values.

Current Assets   The reader will also note that one item listed under current assets is "Cash and Cash Equivalents." It is quite reasonable to assume that the amount shown is equal to market value. Cash is cash. However, the amounts for other items that comprise current assets, such as marketable securities, trade accounts receivable, inventories, and prepaid expenses may or may not reflect value.

For insight into this situation, we can refer to the Accounting Standards Codification (ASC) of the FASB, the U.S. accounting standards-setting body. The ASC describes, in part, the obligation of a company such as S&R to examine the amounts shown on the balance sheet for these items in light of whether they represent realizable amounts.[2] That is, to examine whether in fact the amount shown for marketable securities is realizable based on current market prices, whether the amount shown for trade accounts receivable can reasonably be expected to be realized and so forth. Company management is directed to make adjustments to these amounts to reflect those factors and those adjustments are subject to audit by the Company's outside accountants.

---

[2] FASB ASC 605-10-25.

In the business world, managements do in fact review their current assets and make adjustments or set up reserves that have the effect of reducing the current asset balance. So there is a bias toward conservatism with respect to these amounts. So we are reasonably safe in assuming that balance sheet amounts for current assets are equivalent to value, especially in the case of audited financial statements.

Current Liabilities   This section of S&R's balance sheet reflects obligations which are expected to be satisfied during a current business cycle, which is currently taken to be one year. Again, company management is expected to analyze these forecasted expenses in the light of whether they are reasonably expected to occur. Again, the amounts shown on the balance sheet are subject to audit by the company's outside accountants. For these reasons, we are reasonably justified in accepting these amounts as indications of value.

Monetary Assets   For these reasons, we can be reasonably confident that we can use the amounts shown for current assets and current liabilities in an audited financial statement as the basis for a calculation of S&R's monetary assets as follows in Exhibit 3.3.

Tangible Assets   S&R's balance sheet shows an entry for property, plant, and equipment. It indicates that the original cost of tangible assets is $17.1 billion and that the company has accumulated an allowance for depreciation of $7 billion. The net of these two is the net book value shown on the balance sheet of $10.1 billion. While this information provides something for us, it is not very informative about what

EXHIBIT 3.3   Calculation of Monetary Asset Value

Current Assets	
Cash and cash equivalents	$ 7,000
Marketable securities	2,300
	9,300
Trade accounts receivable	3,800
Inventories	2,400
Prepaid expenses and other assets	2,250
Total current assets	17,750
LESS	
Current Liabilities	
Accounts payable and accrued expenses	$ 6,600
Loans and notes payable	6,850
Current maturities of long-term debt	120
Accrued income taxes	350
Total current liabilities	13,920
= MONETARY ASSETS	**$ 3,830**

EXHIBIT 3.4 Notes to Financial Statements

NOTES to Financial Statements	
1. Selling, general and administrative expenses	
Distribution and promotion expense	9,750
Advertising expenses	1,260
Other expenses	540
	11,550
2. Plant property & equipment	
Land	800
Buildings and improvements	4,050
Machinery and equipment	10,450
Other equipment	1,800
	17,100
3. Intangible assets	
Trademarks with Indefinite Lives	6,500
Goodwill	5,000
Other intangible assets	4,250
	15,750
Less allowance for amortization	2,800
	12,950

kinds of tangible assets S&R owns. For that information, we can turn to the notes that are a part of S&R's financial statements in Exhibit 3.4.

Item 2 in Exhibit 3.4 tells us that S&R owns land, buildings and improvements, machinery and equipment, and so-called "other equipment." This is a fairly typical mix of tangible assets.

In the previous chapter, we discussed the nature of net book value as it is carried on a balance sheet. That discussion included an explanation of accounting depreciation, or, better termed capital recovery. That is a system for spreading the cost of capitalized assets over the period of time during that they will be useful to the business. Typically, that allocation of costs is done on a straight-line basis, that is, it is spread in equal parts over an estimate of the number of years of usefulness. One might be tempted to utilize net book value as a measure of market value, but in our experience it is rare that a tangible asset loses market value on an even, straight-line pattern. So the balance sheet amount of net book value is not very useful as an indicator of market value.

The proper way to estimate the market value of such a body of tangible assets is to inventory and inspect them and to apply the cost, market, and income methods that we introduced in the previous chapter to appraise them. That can be an extensive undertaking and it is impractical to do so for the purpose of this example. We therefore introduce a rough rule of thumb that we have found to be reasonable for a typical complement of assets that S&R owns. As a starting point, we combine the detail contained in the notes with the net book value as shown on the balance sheet in a single schedule as shown in Exhibit 3.5.

EXHIBIT 3.5   Tangible Assets

Property, Plant and Equipment	
Land	800
Buildings and improvements	4,050
Machinery and equipment	10,450
Other equipment	1,800
	17,100
Less allowance for depreciation	(7,000)
Net Book Value	**10,100**
Rule of Thumb Valuation Formula	
Original cost	17,100
Plus: Net book value	10,100
	27,200
Divided by: 2	**$13,600**

Our rule of thumb valuation formula calculates an average of the original cost and net book value as shown in Exhibit 3.6. This simply comes from having observed many tangible asset appraisals over the years and is a very general relationship. Using this formula, our estimated market value for tangible assets is $13.6 billion.

We would caution against using this rule of thumb for companies that have a large investment in land development, forest preserves, or large holdings of natural resources such as oil, gas, and mineral reserves. The original cost of such assets can be misleading as well as the methods used for depreciation, which is usually closely related to the extent of depletion of the resources, rather than their remaining market value. In this situation, one must make a separate appraisal of these assets using whatever method is appropriate.

Intangible Assets   Addressing the third asset classification, intangible assets, we note that the balance sheet records intangible assets at cost in the amount of $15.75 billion less an allowance for amortization of $2.8 billion (see Exhibit 3.7).

We again turn to the notes to financial statements to learn a bit more about what makes up this entry on S&R's balance sheet. That portion of the financial notes is

EXHIBIT 3.6   Tangible Asset Value

Rule of Thumb Valuation Formula	
Original cost	17,100
Plus: Net book value	10,100
	27,200
Divided by: 2	**$13,600**

EXHIBIT 3.7   Intangible Assets from Balance Sheet

Intangible Assets	
Intangible assets at cost	15,750
Less allowance for amortization	2,800
	12,950

EXHIBIT 3.8   Intangible Assets—Value?

3. Intangible assets	
Trademarks with indefinite lives	6,500
Goodwill	5,000
Other intangible assets	4,250
	15,750
Less allowance for amortization	2,800
	12,950

contained in Exhibit 3.8, which informs us that intangible assets are comprised of trademarks with indefinite lives, goodwill, and so-called other intangible assets.

Now we must address the question of whether either the $15.75 billion of cost or the $12.95 billion of cost after amortization are representative of the market value of S&R's intangible assets.

To address this question, we would direct the reader back to the discussion in a previous chapter under the heading "Fair Value." There, we pointed out that in a merger or acquisition, the acquiring company must allocate the total purchase price to all of the assets acquired. That allocation is based upon the fair value of those assets and in nearly every case, will include some intangible assets. Accounting rules in the United States, and elsewhere under IFRs, do not permit the inclusion of self-created intangible assets to be placed on the balance sheet.[3]

Based on this information, we must conclude that the amounts shown on S&R's balance sheet for intangible assets represent intangibles purchased as part of mergers and acquisitions with other companies and do not reflect in any way the intangible assets that S&R has created during its existence.

To address this difficulty, we can expand the business enterprise equation as illustrated in Exhibit 3.9. We have added a third way by which the value of the total business enterprise can be expressed. That is, the value of the business enterprise is equal to the value of its invested capital, which is divided into two types—the value

---

[3] See IASB, Intangible Assets, International Accounting Standard No. 38 (1999), to wit: "Internally generated goodwill shall not be recognised as an asset. No intangible asset arising from research (or from the research phase of an internal project) shall be recognized . . . . Internally generated brands, mastheads, publishing titles, customer lists and items similar in substance shall not be recognised as intangible assets."

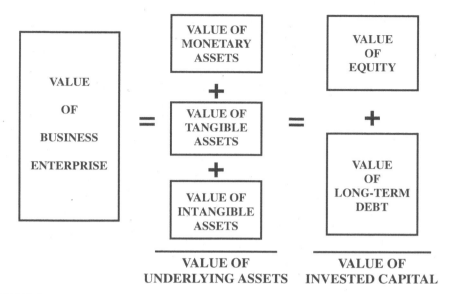

EXHIBIT 3.9 Business Enterprise Equation Expanded

of its long-term debt and the value of its shareholders' equity. This view of the value of a business enterprise is well-accepted in the investment community.

We have estimated the value of Concord's monetary assets and tangible assets. We have been unable to discover any information on Concord's financial statements that would assist in the value of its intangible assets. If, however, we could value the whole S&R business enterprise by adding together the value of its long-term debt and the value of its shareholders' equity, we could make a subtraction to calculate the value of its intangible assets.

So we can turn to the task of valuing the S&R business enterprise by valuing its invested capital. Here, we can find some assistance again on the balance sheet. We find an entry on the liability side of the S&R balance sheet for long-term debt in the amount of $5.01 billion. We focus on long-term debt because that is the amount that S&R has borrowed from lenders to finance its long-term assets, typically its tangible assets. We can assume that this book value of long-term debt is equal to its market value. Long-term debt value can vary from its book value as interest rates change in the marketplace, but it is safe to assume that rates don't change drastically over the short-term. This is a consideration, however.

The valuation of shareholders' equity is a bit more complicated. We can observe that there is an amount shown for shareholders' equity on S&R's balance sheet in the amount of $25.58 billion. This, however, represents the amount that S&R has received from investors from time to time in public offerings of its stock, plus an accumulation of its earnings over time which, while the amount belongs to share-owners, S&R has reinvested in its business. It becomes obvious that this is not necessarily the amount that a buyer would pay to shareholders for their capital stock (see Exhibit 3.10).

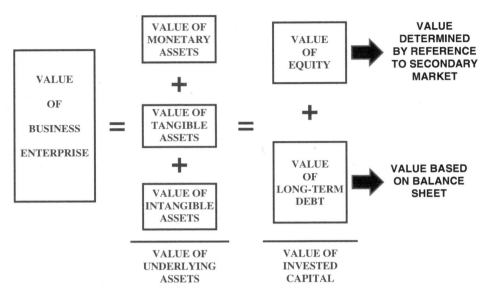

EXHIBIT 3.10   Business Enterprise Equation—Enterprise Value

Because S&R is a public company, that is, its shares are traded on a public marketplace, we can look to this secondary market as to what buyers and sellers think S&R's shares are worth.

S&R's income statement informs us that the company had $2.1 billion common shares outstanding as of the end of 2012. Some research will discover the price of S&R's common shares as of 12/29/2012, and we discover that to be $20.40 per share. Multiplying, we discover that the market value of Concord's common equity is $42.84 billion. We add to that the value of long-term debt and we have an estimate of the Concord business enterprise value in the amount of $47.85 billion (see Exhibit 3.11).

With this last piece of our puzzle we can now utilize the value of the S&R business enterprise as reflected in the value of its invested capital and subtract from that

EXHIBIT 3.11   S&R Business Enterprise Value

BUSINESS ENTERPRISE VALUE	
Common shares outstanding (millions)	2,100
Price @ 12/29	$ 20.40
Common equity value (millions)	$42,840
Long-term debt value (millions)	5,010
	$47,850

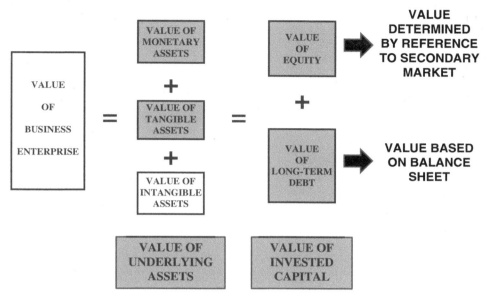

EXHIBIT 3.12   Business Enterprise Equation—Intangible Asset Value

the value of monetary and tangible assets in order to quantify the value of its intangible assets (see Exhibit 3.12).

What remains is for us to make the calculation of the market value of S&R's intangible assets by subtracting the known values of other assets from the total business enterprise value. That calculation is presented on Exhibit 3.13 and indicates that the market value of S&R's intangible assets is $30.42 billion.

We did have an advantage in this situation in that S&R is a public company whose common stock is actively traded on an exchange. Therefore, the information that we needed to calculate the value of S&R's common equity was readily available. If S&R was a closely held company, that is, one in which its common shares were privately held and not actively traded, we would have to perform more extensive analysis in order to come to a conclusion about the market value of its common equity. While this is a more complex undertaking, the means for estimating value for the common stock of closely held companies are well-established and follow the principles that we present for intangible assets and intellectual property. It is beyond the scope of this book to describe those techniques, but there are many sources that the reader can consult for that portion of the task.

Disaggregation   As we focus on identifying the specific economic contribution of intellectual property, we are often confronted with the problem that the data is buried in consolidated financial statements. One of the basic techniques that can be utilized to identify and quantify a specific income stream attributable to intellectual property is the process of disaggregation. At the very least, it can serve as a tool to quantify a range within which one can further analyze. In other words, the total business enterprise must be financially dissected in order to analyze the relevant assets.

EXHIBIT 3.13   S&R Intangible Asset Value

SMITH & RICHEY ENTERPRISES Valuation of Underlying Assets as of 12/2012 ($ millions)		
Current Assets	17,750	
Current Liabilities	13,920	
MONETARY ASSET VALUE	$ 3,830	10.2%
Property, Plant and Equipment, Net		
Land	800	
Buildings and improvements	4,050	
Machinery and equipment	10,450	
Other equipment	1,800	
	17,100	
Less allowance for depreciation	(7,000)	
Net book value	10,100	
TANGIBLE ASSET VALUE	$13,600	36.3%
BUSINESS ENTERPRISE VALUE		
Common shares outstanding (millions)	2,500	
Price @ 12/29	$ 13.00	
Common equity value (millions)	$32,500	
Long-term debt (millions)	5,010	
	$37,510	100.0%
LESS:		
Value of monetary assets	$ 3,830	
Value of tangible assets	13,600	
EQUALS:		
Value of intangible assets	20,080	53.5%

Brand Example   Very few businesses of any size are truly one-product enterprises with a single brand. It is often necessary to segregate business segments and product lines in order to identify the financial characteristics of the subject brand. This is the process of disaggregation, and it is illustrated in Exhibit 3.14.

Building on our example, we assume that S&R is a multiproduct business. The $30.42 billion value of intangibles that we just calculated belongs to the entire enterprise. If our task is to appraise the trademark dedicated to the furniture business segment, we need to first extract the financials of the home products group and then further seek out those of the furniture segment within. We cannot accomplish this without the assistance of our client, S&R. Obviously, this process makes our task more difficult. While we might have access to segment financials, the segment will not be a publicly traded company, so the segment enterprise value will require more effort.

We must be thoughtful in this process and mindful that "the sum of the parts is commensurate with the whole." One can easily imagine that S&R's cosmetic group

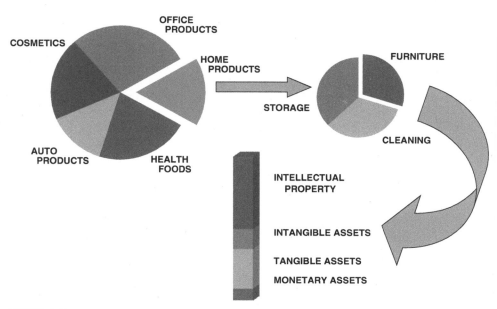

EXHIBIT 3.14 Disaggregating the Business Enterprise

might be highly profitable, very consumer-oriented, and highly brand-dependent. We cannot, therefore, simply divide up S&R's intangibles on some pro rata basis. The cosmetic group brands could well own a disproportionate share of S&R's brand portfolio market value.

Follow the Dollars "Follow the dollars" is an expression relating to one facet of financial analysis—observing the flow of dollars in and out of the balance sheet and income statement of an enterprise. The logic behind this is, of course, that the flow of dollars is in proportion to the amount of business activity. Companies spend money on things that they think are important, and examining sales revenue inflows may tell us something about the risk of the business. If we observe, as an example, heavy expenditures in research and development or in advertising they suggest a lot about the character of the business. On the balance sheet we can observe the amount of tangible asset investment as compared with total assets. This too can give us a hint about the character of the company. A semiconductor company has a high portion of its assets in plant property and equipment because its manufacturing facilities are very high-tech and very expensive to build. Companies in the apparel business can be quite large, but often have very little in the way of tangible assets because they are subcontracting the manufacture of their products.

We previously noted calculations that were made on the financial statements of S&R and those percentage calculations are intended to assist in this type of analysis. These percentages can be used in two ways. First, they can provide a little bit of focus on S&R itself and second they can be extremely useful in comparing the financial performance and activities of S&R with other similar companies for which financial data is available.

As an example we observe that selling, general, and administrative expenses for S&R represent 37.4 percent of its sales revenues. We might conclude that that is a fairly substantial amount and subsequently observe in the notes to the S&R financial statements that most of those charges have to do with distribution and promotion expenses. That would suggest that S&R may be primarily selling its products to retailers rather than the general public. Advertising expenses are relatively modest. In order to confirm this supposition, we would need to gather data from other companies that appear similar to S&R and compare the amount of selling, general, and administrative expenses.

There is more that we can observe from our analysis of S&R. When we calculated the value of intangible assets, the indication was $30.4 million of intangible assets out of the total business enterprise value of $47.9 million. As shown in Exhibit 3.13, the value of intangible assets is 63.6 percent of the total value of the S&R enterprise. We know from studies of large numbers of publicly traded companies worldwide that intangible assets average around 70 percent of the total enterprise value.[4] So S&R is close to the typical aggregation of assets.

If we move back a step in the calculations that we made in Exhibit 3.13, we will recall that our calculation of $47.9 billion of business enterprise value was due in large part to the price of the common shares of S&R in the secondary market. According to conventional investment wisdom, the share price of $20.40 is, in turn, strongly related to S&R's earnings per share of $0.90. That is, a strong increase in earnings per share is likely to enhance the market price of the shares. In effect, we have a circular situation in which earnings improvement results in an increase in value of common stock in the secondary market, which in turn increases the value of the S&R enterprise and, all else equal, increases the portion of that value attributable to intangible assets.

Investors recognize the significance of the intangible assets in the S&R enterprise and the contribution that those assets make to the profitability and growth of the business, and for that reason they're willing to pay more for the shares. This comports with the idea that we presented in Chapter 2 that intangible assets and intellectual property are largely financed by common equity investment rather than debt investment.

Calculating these internal ratios can inform us about S&R if it was our client, or if it was an adversary, or if we are using its financial data as a part of an industry. All of this is useful information as we embark on the task of identifying and quantifying the market value of intangible assets and intellectual property.

NEPTUNE

Neptune is the eighth planet from the sun. It was not discovered by observation, though there were plenty of folks looking at the sky in the 1800s. It was first recognized in 1846 by Berlin astronomer Johann Galle almost exactly where Urbain Le Verrier, a French mathematician, had predicted it would be.

Le Verrier, and others, had observed that Uranus, a visible planet, had an irregular orbit. He calculated that the "perturbation" was caused by the presence of some unknown body and predicted the position and mass of that unseen planet.

In September 1846 Galle aimed his telescope at the expected place and saw Neptune. And so it is with intangible assets and intellectual property. They are invisible to most observers. Yet investors "feel" they are there—why else would they price S&R's common stock above book value? They see their effect and are willing to bet on their presence. Venture capitalists take huge chances and invest large sums in start-ups because they have a positive "gut feeling" about the new company's principals. They are not investing in "bricks & mortar." If they wanted to do that they would open a corner bank. They are betting that the principals can create intangible assets and intellectual property—that is where the money is!

So we know intangibles are there. Our job is to find them, identify them, and estimate their market value. Like astronomers, we look for "perturbations." First, we look in financial statements, then we become detectives and ask questions, and analyze, and ask more questions, and if we are successful the invisible appears. Just like for M. Le Verrier.

TAX ISSUES

While we are on the subject of financial information, we now touch upon some tax issues, primarily international, that it is useful to know about. An extended discussion of international taxation is far beyond the purview of this book. However, we believe that it is important for corporate managers and personnel as well as professionals to have an overall understanding of the intersection between trademarks and taxes in the international arena.

Valuation Precept

A rough rule of thumb: The overarching concept is that whenever property rights, products, services, or money cross national borders there are likely to be tax consequences of one sort or another.

Multinational enterprises (MNEs) continue to expand rapidly and, therefore, their cross-border transactions are also growing and getting the attention of tax collectors worldwide. In these recessive times, governments at every level are seeking to maximize their revenues. In times past, overseas transactions were often limited to building a manufacturing facility. If expansion into a foreign country was more

---

[4] S. Blair and S. M. H. Wallman, *Unseen Wealth: The Value of Corporate Intangible Assets* (Washington, DC: Brookings Institution Press).

complex, the business established was often of a stand-alone nature. Today the business model is likely to be more centralized, with high-value assets and functions centrally controlled and doled out to offshore entities as required. This adds to the complexity of offshore transactions.

Our focus here is on so-called "transfer pricing taxation." Of primary interest are transactions between commonly controlled parties. By that, we refer to transactions between divisions of the same company, parent, and subsidiary, joint venture partners, or perhaps among corporations whose stock is owned by the same party.

The underlying issue is that income tax rates vary from nation to nation. Every corporation is interested in minimizing its tax bill. There is therefore an incentive for a multinational corporation to arrange prices paid for goods and services so that the entities in higher taxed jurisdictions show as little taxable income as possible. A tax collector in that jurisdiction would be understandably dismayed, especially if he or she feels that the transfer price that caused this apparent imbalance in taxable income was unrealistically set.

While we normally think of such transactions as involving component parts, finished goods, or the results of research and development, in most cases, a company's trademarks are a necessary accompaniment to the physical goods being transferred. For a U.S. company, as an example, a wholly owned French subsidiary assembling component parts and selling a finished product would want to do so under the parent corporation's worldwide brands. It is reasonable to expect that the French subsidiary would license that right from the parent since its profitability is enhanced by its ability to market branded rather than unbranded product. Because that payment is a tax deduction in France and because the payment is also taxable income to the U.S. parent, tax collectors on both sides of the Atlantic have some interest.

Arm's Length Standard

One of the keystone principles in transfer pricing enforcement is the *arm's length standard*. That is, taxing authorities compare a disputed transaction with what that transaction would have been had the parties been unrelated. Transfer pricing regulations in the U.S. state: "In determining the true taxable income of a controlled taxpayer, the standard to be applied in every case is that of a taxpayer dealing at arm's length with an uncontrolled taxpayer" (Reg. §1.482-1(b)(1). The OECD Guidelines define the international arm's-length standards as follows:

> *[W]here conditions are made or imposed between two enterprises in their commercial or financial relations which differ from those which would be made between independent enterprises, then any profits which would, but for those conditions, have accrued to one of the enterprises, but, by reason of those conditions, have not so accrued, may be included in the profits of that enterprise and taxed accordingly.*[5]

---

[5] Organisation for Economic Co-operation and Development, *Transfer Pricing Guidelines for Multinational Enterprises and Tax Authorities, Chapter 1.*

Trademarks Included

Transfer pricing regulations in the United States clearly include intangible assets and, more specifically, "trademarks, trade names, or brand names." The OECD Guidelines also specifically include trademarks and trade names and also note the following:

> *Marketing intangible include trademarks and trade names that aid the commercial exploitation of a product or service, customer lists, distribution channels, and unique names, symbols, or pictures that have an important promotional value of the product (§iii) ....*
>
> *The value of marketing intangibles depends upon many factors, including the reputation and credibility of the trade name or the trademark fostered by the quality of goods and services provided ... in the past, the degree of quality control and ongoing research and development ... extent and success of the promotional expenditures incurred to [support] the goods or services ... the value of the market to which the marketing intangibles will provide access (§iv).*[6]

A Typical Transaction

In Exhibit 3.15(A), (B), and (C) are three facilities within the same MNE. Facility A is the headquarters location at which primary research and development takes place and which is the locus of intellectual property ownership.

Some manufacturing is done at location A, and partially completed products are shipped to B, which finishes the products and ships them to C for distribution. A also provides engineering and design services to B and licenses certain manufacturing technology to B as well. A has also licensed to C the right to use its trademarks. Compensation for these goods, services, and intellectual property rights flow back along the supply chain and across national borders. D is a third-party and transactions with it would presumably not be called into question because, being an unrelated third party, they would be arm's length by their very nature. Transactions with D might, however, be of interest since they might lend themselves to a comparison with transactions between B and C.

Additional Considerations

We can expand on the example of Exhibit 3.5 to illustrate similar considerations that deserve a watchful eye within a multinational corporation:

- The trademark license between A and C may have been drawn up without any scrutiny by legal or tax professionals, since it was a "friendly" deal. This might put the trademarks at risk in a purely business sense.
- It could be that there is *no* license between A and C and that the use of the trademarks by C is proceeding under some verbal agreement between managers. This too can put the marks at risk for many reasons (e.g., misuse, lack of quality control).

---

[6] Ibid., chapter 6.

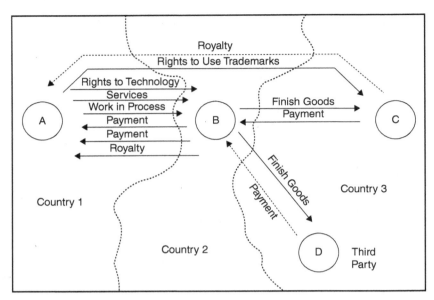

EXHIBIT 3.15   Illustration of Typical Transfer Pricing Transactions
Source: John Wiley & Sons, Inc. Reprinted with permission.

- The issue of *ownership* can come into play in a transfer pricing situation. As an example, the trademarks being licensed to C may in fact be the property of a holding company subsidiary of A, whereas the component parts are the property of a directly owned entity.
- In addition to applying the arm's-length standard, taxing authorities may also examine the extent to which the transactions in question have demonstrable "business purpose" or "economic substance." This means that there is a business reason for the transactions rather than simply tax avoidance.

In general, a transaction that is brought into question will be tested against comparable, arm's length transactions to the extent possible. Sometimes these comparisons are not of specific prices, but for other comparisons of profit levels including those within the taxpayer's organization. Transfer pricing regulations are quite specific about various methods that are acceptable for these tests, and some of them are quite complex.

In the case of a trademark, these more complicated tests are impractical and so most often the testing is against royalty rates in evidence in the marketplace for comparable rights and between comparable parties. Or, as we noted in this chapter, eighteen comparisons can be made between the transaction in question and other external licensing that the taxpayer may have done. In our experience, however, few MNEs have licensed their marks to entities in the same business. Some have licensed their marks as brand extensions but these are generally not sufficiently comparable as a testing mechanism. There are commercial databases of intellectual property transactions available for various types of property, including trademarks. The reader is directed to a more extensive discussion of royalties and the licensing process in Chapter 8.

SUMMARY

There is a wealth of information contained in the financial statements if we know where to look. Of course, financial data is not everything that we need. There certainly is no way that we could competently complete a valuation based exclusively on information taken from financial statements. But financial statements and the information they contain form a very important portion of the information that we described as going into the funnel in Chapter 2. Financial statements don't give us all the answers, but they do point us in fruitful directions.

CHAPTER 4

Trademark Valuation

In Chapter 2, we provided a brief review of the three accepted valuation methods, the cost, market, and income methods. In this chapter, we address each one of these methods individually in much more detail. Because the income method is very often relied upon in the valuation of trademarks, Chapters 5, 6, and 7 continue the discussion of the income method focusing on developing the difficult inputs required (see Exhibit 4.1).

Good valuation practice instructs that all three methods should be employed when it is possible and appropriate. At the very least, the use of each method should be given consideration. It is not uncommon that one or more of the methods may be inappropriate or simply impractical to pursue because of the lack of appropriate factual data. However, in the event that one or more methods are utilized, it remains for the appraiser to reconcile the indications of value from each of the methods because the appraisal task is to arrive at a single conclusion. This reconciliation process is often referred to by professional appraisers as *correlation*.

In the correlation process, the appraiser would consider factors such as:

- The appropriateness of the method used
- The quantity and quality of information available as input to each of the methods used
- The extent to which judgment or alternative assumptions had to be employed
- The sensitivity of the value indication to the various inputs and their relative reliability
- Whether the results of a single method should be relied upon or perhaps some weighting of results is appropriate

Professional valuation standards also instruct us that a competent valuation report should explain the appraiser's consideration of these three basic methods and also explain why they may have been accepted or rejected in arriving at the final value estimate (see Exhibit 4.2).

Valuation Precept

Consider the use of all three valuation methods and be prepared to explain why you rejected or relied on them.

MARKET VALUE

EXHIBIT 4.1 Valuation Methods

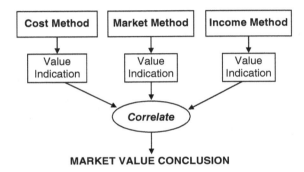

MARKET VALUE CONCLUSION

EXHIBIT 4.2 Correlation of Value Indicators

COST METHOD

The cost method seeks to measure the present value of the future benefits of ownership by quantifying the cost required to replace the future service capability of the subject property. The underlying assumption of this method is that the cost to purchase (or create) new property is commensurate with the economic value of the service that the property can provide during its life. More simply put, when someone decides to purchase or develop a new asset, it is assumed that they have analyzed the cost-benefit relationship to their satisfaction.

While the cost method does not directly consider the amount of economic benefits that can be achieved or the time period over which they might continue, it does, however, require a consideration of economic obsolescence that in turn requires the appraiser decide to what extent future economic benefits will support an investment at the indicated value.

In Exhibit 4.3, we provide the overall schema of the cost method. Observe that there are two paths from the starting point cost estimates to the final conclusion of market value by this method. One starting point is reproduction cost new and another starting point is replacement cost new. These terms were defined in the previous chapter. We remind the reader that reproduction cost new represents the cost to create a replica, while replacement cost new is the cost incurred to obtain an asset with equal utility.

	Reproduction Cost New	or	Replacement Cost New
Less:	Physical Depreciation		Physical Depreciation
Less:	Functional Obsolescence		

Equals:	Replacement Cost Less Depreciation
Less:	Economic Obsolescence
Equals:	MARKET VALUE

EXHIBIT 4.3   Cost Method Schema

The reader is asked to keep in mind that the cost method, as with the other valuation methods we will discuss, is in wide use for all types of property, tangible as well as intangible. Therefore, the reader may recognize certain inputs and relationships in these methods that are not particularly appropriate for intellectual property or trademark assets. We should not, however, summarily dismiss the use of any of these methods in the valuation of the property that is our focus.

Referring back to Exhibit 4.3, the cost approach begins with some form of cost estimate for a new asset, from which deductions must be made because most often we are valuing assets that are not new.

Physical Depreciation

The first adjustment that should be made is to reflect physical depreciation. By that, we refer to simply as "wear and tear." We are really asking ourselves how much of the total service that an asset can provide has been used up at the time of our observation and how much remains. Even the measurement of physical depreciation can have some complexity. As an example, we could assume that an automobile tire under normal conditions will last for 40,000 miles of travel. Under those circumstances, if we observe an automobile tire after 20,000 miles of use, we can expect that physical depreciation would be 50 percent of the 100 percent of total service. If, however, we are observing an automobile tire in service in a hot, dry climate with exposure to intense sunlight, our evaluation of exhausted versus remaining service must also consider the factor of time. So the pattern of decline due to physical depreciation may vary.

Functional Obsolescence

Functional obsolescence (FO) refers to the degree that the subject asset is not "state of the art," or that it may suffer from design or operating deficiencies that reduce its desirability when it is compared with similar assets that may be available in the marketplace. A three-year old cell phone may be in fine condition, and perfectly suitable for making and receiving telephone calls, but it lacks many of the desirable features of a new smartphone.

The reader will recall that the definition of *replacement cost new* (RCN) is premised on the assumption that the asset is being replaced with a new asset that is state of the art at the time of its replacement. For that reason, no deduction for functional obsolescence needs to be made if our starting point is replacement cost new. Reproduction cost new, on the other hand, relates to a replica of the subject property, which would be equivalent to the purchase price of a cell phone that has only the functionality of the three-year old one. Therefore, a deduction has to be made for functional obsolescence. When these deductions are made as appropriate, the result is an estimate of replacement cost less depreciation.

These relationships can also be stated in a formula. If the starting point is reproduction cost new, replacement cost less depreciation is calculated as

$$RCLD = RCN - PD - FO$$

where $RCLD$ = replacement cost less depreciation.
             RCN = reproduction cost new.
             PD = physical depreciation.
             FO = functional obsolescence.

If the starting point is replacement cost new, replacement cost less depreciation is calculated as

$$RCLD = CRN - PD$$

where $RCLD$ = replacement cost less depreciation.
             CRN = cost of replacement new.
             PD = physical depreciation.

You will remember from the previous discussion, replacement cost is not afflicted with functional obsolescence because it presupposes a state-of-the-art property.

We can now complete the equation and describe the full course of the cost approach in determining market value:

$$MV = RCLD - EO$$

where MV = market value.
             $RCLD$ = replacement cost less depreciation.
             EO = economic obsolescence.

Economic Obsolescence

The last ingredient in the cost method is an estimation of the amount of economic obsolescence observed in the property. This is the most difficult input in the cost method. Economic obsolescence is based on the assumption that the subject property is devoted to business use. Therefore, it only achieves full market value when it is capable of a positive contribution to the earnings of the business <u>and</u> when those earnings provide a reasonable rate of return on an investment in the property at its replacement cost less depreciation. We once observed an extensive line of knitting machinery set up for the manufacture of women's hosiery. The equipment was nearly new and was state of the art for its purpose. So, physical and functional obsolescence were minimal. The owner's problem was, however, that this machinery was only capable of producing women's hosiery with a seam. At the time of our observation, panty hose had been introduced and were all the rage. With this drastic market shift, this machinery suffered from substantial economic obsolescence and its market value was severely reduced.

ESTIMATING REPRODUCTION AND REPLACEMENT COST

In the following sections, we will discuss three techniques for estimating replacement and reproduction costs:

- Trended original costs
- Aggregated unit costs
- Unit of production measures

Trended Original Cost

Many companies maintain records of the costs that were incurred to develop intangible assets or to purchase tangible assets. A restatement of these historical costs to current dollars can provide an indication of the total cost that would need to be invested currently in order to reproduce the property. The following example illustrates the use of this method as it might be applied to a computer software system.

In Exhibit 4.4, we have provided a schedule of the historical development costs of this system. We can observe that expenditures began in 2005 with the majority of the development costs being incurred in the following two years. We also observe that, in 2010, some significant costs were incurred as well. It is not unusual for a software system to require modifications during its life. The total original development costs for this particular software system through the end of 2012 are shown to be $838,000.

EXHIBIT 4.4   Historical Development Costs

Year	Original Development Cost
2005	$ 50,000
2006	340,000
2007	178,000
2008	20,000
2009	68,000
2010	131,000
2011	35,000
2012	16,000
	$838,000

EXHIBIT 4.5 Price Index

Year	Price Index
2005	1.09
2006	1.12
2007	1.43
2008	1.66
2009	1.78
2010	1.92
2011	2.05
2012	2.13

The next step is to obtain a price index that tracks the price changes of the major components of the cost to develop a software system. These would primarily be various types of labor and could include hardware costs as well. The U.S. government tracks price changes of many major commodities, labor costs, and manufactured products. Specialized price indexes are also published by private research firms as well as industry associations. An example of such a price index is shown in Exhibit 4.5.

In order to be useful in our arithmetic, we must convert the price index into what we term a translator. We do that by dividing the price index in 2012 by each of the price indexes in the other years. In this way, we calculate a factor that can be multiplied by the original costs of each year and express them in terms of 2012 dollars (see Exhibit 4.6).

We have made that calculation in Exhibit 4.7. The result of that calculation is that the $838,000 of original cost would require an expenditure of $1.3 million in 2012 to finance the same work effort. This is an estimate of reproduction cost and before we use that further in the cost method process we should be confident that we understand the character of the effort that went into the original development.

EXHIBIT 4.6 Calculate the Translator

Year	Price Index	Translator 2012 = 100.0
2005	1.09	1.954
2006	1.12	1.902
2007	1.43	1.490
2008	1.66	1.283
2009	1.78	1.197
2010	1.92	1.109
2011	2.05	1.039
2012	2.13	1.000

EXHIBIT 4.7   Calculate Trended Original Cost

Year	Original Development Cost	Translator 2012 = 1.000	Trended Original Cost
2005	$ 50,000	1.954	$ 97,706
2006	340,000	1.902	646,607
2007	178,000	1.490	265,133
2008	20,000	1.283	25,663
2009	68,000	1.197	81,371
2010	131,000	1.109	145,328
2011	35,000	1.039	36,366
2012	16,000	1.000	16,000
	$838,000		$1,314,174

Valuation Precept

The trended original cost technique always produces *reproduction cost new.*

Aggregated Unit Costs

An alternative method is to calculate replacement cost directly by making an estimate of the individual current costs of replacing the software system with a new one. Using this technique, we estimate the hours of the various employee groups that would be involved in the current development of such a system, multiply those hours by the current hourly rate of salary plus benefits and other overheads and then add the additional overhead costs for such things as facilities, travel, and the use of computer hardware, as well as a profit expectation of an outside contractor. An example of that calculation is shown in Exhibit 4.8, which indicates an estimate of market value of $417,465.

EXHIBIT 4.8   Aggregated Unit Cost Method

	Hours	Rate	Direct Labor	Overhead and Profit	Total Cost
Management specification development	230	$70.25	$ 16,158	125%	$ 36,354
IT project management	420	43.50	18,270	120%	40,194
Computer operations testing	210	23.75	4,988	90%	9,476
Systems analysis	1,375	33.85	46,544	110%	97,742
Programming & testing	3,350	31.50	105,525	110%	221,603
Documentation	180	32.00	5,760	110%	12,096
	5,765		$197,244		$417,465

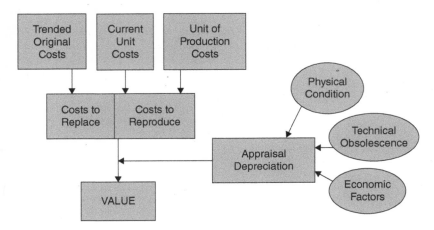

EXHIBIT 4.9   Cost Method
Source: John Wiley & Sons, Inc. Reprinted with permission.

It is important to remember that this amount represents replacement cost because we have assumed in the aggregated unit costs that we are producing a software system with today's programming techniques and hardware and that the system is custom built to meet the current needs of its users.

Unit of Production Measures

There are a number of situations where properties may be uniform enough that rules of thumb are developed among architects, engineers, and designers who are involved in their creation. As an example, we might find rules of thumb that would estimate the number of dollars per seat for a restaurant, the cost per barrel of a modern petroleum refinery, building construction at so many dollars per square foot, or highway construction at so many dollars per mile.

This method, in a sense, crosses over into what we will be discussing later as the market approach (see Exhibit 4.9).

Valuation Precept

The aggregated unit cost and unit of production techniques produce *replacement cost.*

USING THE COST METHOD FOR TRADEMARKS

The reader has probably already generated some doubt about the efficacy of employing the cost method for the valuation of a trademark. One can easily imagine a situation in which there might be a vast disconnect between the cost of developing a trademark and its ultimate market value. An example might be a new product, recently branded, that attracts the attention of a broadcast celebrity or is part of a popular "YouTube" segment. Instant worldwide recognition at little cost!

A more complicated, but more common, situation is that there are a myriad of other factors besides expenditures for design and advertising that drive the success of a brand. We can easily envision a situation in which a trademark such as "iPad" gains value at least in part due to the popularity of the design and technology built into the product itself. The question then arises as to whether any portion of the expenses of research and development should be attributed to the trademark.

Perhaps we should not dismiss the cost method out of hand for intangibles. We previously presented the example of using the cost method to value computer software. We observed that it is not uncommon for companies to set up a project for the creation of a specific software system and therefore its costs tend to be captured fairly accurately by the company's accounting system. In the development of a brand, however, the associated expenses may be strewn throughout the corporate organization and over a long period of time. Both of these factors tend to thwart our ability to gather these costs in a meaningful way to serve as the basis for a calculation of either reproduction or replacement cost as a starting point for the application of the cost method for a trademark.

Trended Original Cost

As noted, one method is a trending of historical costs. The historical costs might include expenditures such as:

- Concept development
- Brainstorming with clients, associates, industry experts, and psychologists
- New brand or brand extension analysis
- Trademark registration in appropriate jurisdictions
- Consulting expenses
- Trademark searches
- A linguistic search to determine the foreign language meaning of possible names
- Preliminary consumer testing
- Market research to study the reaction of consumers, stockholders, company executives, and Wall Street analysts
- Trademark registration in appropriate jurisdictions
- Package designs
- Advertising campaign development
- Commercial planning, scripting, and recording
- Development of branding policy and style standards

One of the obvious complexities here is to determine when actual trademark development began and when it ended. At some point, expenditures for advertising and promotion are also made to sell products or services and may not be exclusively ascribable to brand building.

But presuming that we are able to segregate the historical development costs for the subject trademark, we then apply appropriate price trend factors as described. The result is an estimate of reproduction cost because we would be following in the footsteps of the original creator, whether they were efficient or not.

Aggregated Unit Costs

Another means by which to derive the cost to reproduce a trademark is a direct estimate of the efforts and current costs necessary for creating it. A lack of accurate record keeping (regarding past expenditures) often requires this approach.

This involves a start-from-scratch aggregation of estimates for the hours that will be required by various levels of management and personnel, together with estimates of fees for outside professional assistance. It also would logically include estimates of postregistration advertising and marketing costs to begin to establish the new trademark's market position.

This process yields an indication of replacement cost, since the comparable data reflects current conditions relative to a new mark.

Unit of Production Measures

Information about the costs incurred to establish well-known marks is sometimes available. This data can serve as a guide for trademark values, which have similar fundamental characteristics. Important characteristics for comparison include:

- Size of the market in which the mark competes
- Market share with which the mark is associated
- Price premium on the trademarked products or services
- Advertising support
- Profitability of the product or service with which the mark is associated
- Market research indications of consumer recognition
- Possible trademark extension

If an acceptable comparison exists and the cost to establish a specific trademark is known, then the amount may be useful in estimating an indication of value for the trademark under analysis. Marketing consultants estimate that the national introduction of a newly branded consumer product costs at least $20 million.[1] Information about trademark introductions is often publicized as part of the advertising campaign or is sometimes presented in the annual reports of public companies.

This process yields an indication of replacement cost, since the comparable data reflects current conditions relative to a new mark.

This technique also bears some similarity to the market method of valuation that is discussed in a following section.

Physical Depreciation

Since brands are intangible assets without physical substance, this form of depreciation does not apply.

Functional Obsolescence

We might be tempted to assume that trademarks and brands simply "go on forever" and of course that opinion is strengthened by the fact that the legal property rights

---

[1] Jayne Eastman, "An Innovator's Blueprint," *The Hub Magazine*, January–February 2009.

associated with the trademark do, in fact, last perpetually as long as the associated product or service remains in the marketplace and the appropriate fees are paid. In fact, however, brands can exhibit varying degrees of functional obsolescence. As an example, a brand that is associated with a product or service which is declining in the marketplace would certainly be assumed to exhibit some amount of functional obsolescence.

There are a number of factors that can lead to functional obsolescence in a trademark. Trademarks and logos can be time sensitive in their design and concept and occasionally this needs to be corrected by redesigning. In a more recent example, certain trademarks and brands have been found to be unacceptable in the marketplace because of their relationship to people or ethnic concepts. All of this is discussed in much more detail in Chapter 6, where we discuss the economic life of a brand. The point here is simply that if one elects to use the cost method for the valuation of a trademark, consideration must be given to the possibility that some functional obsolescence exists.

Economic Obsolescence

Even after physical and functional obsolescence are taken into account, the resulting depreciated cost is still not the same as market value. That is, a buyer would not necessarily be willing to pay an amount equal to depreciated cost because of economic reasons. Unless economic benefits can be earned from ownership of a trademark, the value must be relatively low regardless of the amounts originally needed to develop it. The "Duesenberg" automobile brand was well known in the United States during the 1920s and 1930s. This automobile name still has recognition among automobile aficionados and seniors. To create a brand with even this moderate degree of recognition might easily cost millions of dollars. Yet the current ownership of this name is not likely to contribute much in the way of profits. Indeed, the name could be a detriment; association with an old and discontinued product might not inspire consumers in sufficient numbers to justify the risk of attempting to revive such a trademark. The market value of a trademark can therefore be significantly degraded by the economics of the business to which it is devoted. Unique assets such as trademarks may suffer considerably because they have little use outside of a particular business.

In another example, Pfizer Inc's. major cholesterol drug "Lipitor" lost its patent protection towards the end of 2011.[2] Pfizer planned to continue to sell Lipitor but at generic prices directly to patients. Lipitor was the top-selling drug of all time and produced more than $80 billion in sales since its launch in 1997. Obviously, sales revenue to Pfizer from Lipitor as a branded generic version of the original drug will be sharply reduced from the revenues produced during its patent protected years. This is a classic example of the effect of economic obsolescence. Obviously, a potential buyer of the Lipitor brand at this point would take into consideration the reduced future earnings potential vis-à-vis what it once was able to produce.

All of that said, there have been auctions of trademarks that have fallen out of use. Presumably, the buyers made the assumption that the cost of purchase was less than the cost of design, legal, and filing fees for a new mark, or perhaps that the purchased existing mark still carried some of its original cachet. This is an instance where the cost approach for a trademark has some validity.

---

[2] "Lipitor," Registration No. 2,074,561, owned by Pfizer Ireland Pharmaceuticals.

POST-ITS

We are all aware of the "Post-it"[3] brand of reattachable adhesive paper notes. The brand is owned by 3M Corporation and this product and brand represents a dramatic example of the shortcomings of the cost method for valuing intellectual property. The essence of the Post-it product is a pressure sensitive adhesive that was invented essentially by accident in 1968. It was not until 1974 when a colleague of the inventor, again by happenstance, came up with a way to exploit this adhesive technology. The concept of adhesive backed slips of paper was originally marketed three years later. The concept was slow to catch on but the product was launched in the United States in 1980. Of course, this product, as well as the many related products that grew under the Post-it brand umbrella, have been an exceptional source of sales and profits for the 3M Corporation. Quite obviously, any calculation of the cost to develop this brand has no relation to its value.

We were also interested to note that in a recent case before the U.S. Bankruptcy Court for the Eastern District of Pennsylvania, testimony was given about the market value of technology for an automated system for use in the high-speed printing industry. One of the appraisers concluded a market value based upon the use of the cost method. The expert opined that the value of the technology was equal to its development cost. In response the court said, "the absurdity of this statement is stunning."[4] The court also opined that the cost method was a "strikingly inappropriate method" with which to determine the market value of unique technology. While this is not a brand-related case, it emphasizes, for intellectual property, that there can be (at least in this court's view) an extreme disconnect between cost and market value.

Cost Method Summary

While the cost method is well developed and has been in use for decades, readers can observe for themselves that it is clearly most applicable for tangible assets and intangibles such as computer software, some customer-based intangibles, and an assembled workforce. Generally speaking, it is not a method that can be relied on for intellectual property such as trademarks.

MARKET METHOD

The market approach is attractive because it takes the analyst right to the "bottom line" of market value. The assumption is that other buyers of comparable property were willing, had knowledge of all relevant facts, and struck a deal that was fair and, therefore, represented market value at the time of the transaction and for that

---

[3] "Post-it," Registration No. 1,046,353, owned by 3M Company Corp.
[4] *In re Scheffler*, 471 B.R. 464, 481 (Bankr. E.D. Pa. 2012).

particular property. Alternatively, one could say that both buyer and seller had made a judgment about the present value, at the time of the transaction, of the future benefits of ownership. In essence, the market measures and adjusts for all forms of appraisal depreciation (physical, functional, and economic) in a single step without necessarily addressing them individually.

The market method is ideally based upon an analysis of relevant transactions:

- Of comparable property
- Between unrelated parties
- Contemporaneous to the valuation date
- In an active market

Comparable Property

We customarily use the market method in the valuation of our homes and our automobiles. The reason for this is that there is a fairly high degree of comparability among those properties. There is also an active enough market to wash out differences that might occur because of unusual transactions.

Transactions involving individual trademarks are, however, infrequent. When they do occur, their terms are often unique or not publicly disclosed. The most difficult aspect of the market method as it applies to trademarks is therefore comparability. In fact, one could argue that the IP legal system has developed with the objective of *preventing* comparability, at least to the extent of sensory appearance. About as close as we can come is similarity of product, service, company, or business segment.

Even if we are aware of specific information for a trademark transaction, the price at which the trademark exchanged will likely have little bearing on the value of other trademarks unless positive comparability exists.

The value of a business enterprise, including all of the tangible and intangible assets, is greatly influenced by the industry in which it operates. Exogenous influences, such as industry cycles and general economic trends, can delimit the value of business enterprises and their trademarks.

If we are using market transactions to serve as the basis for an indication of value, it is most useful if they represent transactions within the same industry, subject to the same exogenous influences and investment risks. If a cosmetic trademark were sold, the price at which the transaction took place might be a good indication of the value of other cosmetic trademarks. A trademark exchanged in the automobile industry would be of little use in this case.

Again, profitability is also a fundamental in the value of any asset. Even market transactions involving trademarks in the same industry might not be reasonably comparable unless there was some comparability between their profit contribution to their respective enterprises.

Market share is often associated with profitability and a substantial market share would be expected to be influential in the value of a trademark. Therefore, we would look for some comparability in market share in utilizing this technique to obtain an indication of value for a trademark.

An industry in which there are significant barriers to entry is quite different, from a trademark value standpoint, from one in which that condition does not exist. The purchase of an existing trademark in such an industry would be a much more attractive alternative than going to the expense of creating a new trademark to enter this type of industry situation.

Growth prospects are also directly related to value. This is because a growing income stream is more valuable than a flat or declining income stream. A trademark associated with a growing income stream would be more valuable, all else being equal.

When market transactions of trademarks exist that have similar characteristics to the trademark being appraised, a direct application of the market approach is possible. When a trademark has been exchanged as part of a portfolio of assets, then an allocation of the purchase price among the assets is required in order to identify the amount that might be specifically attributable to the trademark.

Unrelated Parties

Obviously, we are seeking transactions in which there are no special conditions that might have influenced the negotiated price. When the buyer and seller are related in some way, we cannot be sure of the conditions of sale. Another way of describing this situation would be that we are seeking transactions that are at "arm's length."

Contemporaneous

In the previous chapter, we noted the inescapable fact that value changes with time. That fact, of course, influences the prices emanating from transactions that we might seek in using the market method. Just as we would hesitate to use the selling price of a home in a 1997 transaction for a valuation today, we must be sensitive to the objective of locating transactions that are as contemporaneous as possible to the "as of date" of an appraisal.

Active Market

The ideal situation is to have a number of property exchanges to use in this analysis. One sale does not make a market. There are, for example, publicly traded common stocks in which only a few shares are traded in a year. Their exchange price has much less validity as a measure of their value than, for instance, Microsoft stock, in which thousands of shares are traded each day. All the other requisites except activity are there. Obviously, there is not an active market in trademark rights.

Public Market   To be useful, the exchange consideration must be known or discoverable. The prices of common stock in the primary exchanges are known in minute detail. For other types of property, it becomes more and more difficult to discover the exchange price. Even with real estate, the published price may be misleading due to financing arrangements between buyer and seller that are not made public. Transactions between businesses, such as the sale of a plant, product line, or subsidiary may be very difficult or impossible to evaluate because competitive pressure motivates the participants to keep the details confidential, and there is a myriad of other considerations that can be ancillary to the primary transaction, but which can affect it.

Making Adjustments

The best of all worlds for an appraiser is to find, for a subject property, an arm's length sale of an exact replica property, located across the street, and made the day before the appraisal! Unfortunately, this does not happen with enough regularity to eliminate the need to make adjustments when comparable sales are not exactly comparable. Real estate appraisers continually grapple with the problem of quantifying differences in property, so that the location, amenities, zoning, size, shape, and topography of comparable sales can be equated to the subject so as to provide an indication of value. Analysts using this approach for other types of property have the same challenge, but comparability tends to be more obvious—one either has it or not—and there are fewer nuances. This is probably a near impossible exercise with respect to trademarks.

Adjustments for Time Sometimes it is necessary to utilize sale information that is not contemporaneous with the appraisal. In this case, the appraiser must adjust for price changes over time, and this may necessitate a separate study of changes in property value in the subject area during a recent period of time so as to develop some specialized indexes to use in the adjustment process.

Market Method Summary

The overall schema of the market method is shown Exhibit 4.10. This method is very effective and can provide strong support for a market value opinion when the proper conditions are present, the keystone of which is an active market.

We have all been reminded of this condition as we experienced the recent economic recession. One would think that the market value of financial assets such as loans, bonds, and other financial instruments would be easily determined using the market method. We discovered, however, that many financial instruments, because of their design and murky collateral, had such a thin (i.e., small) market that this method fell far short. The difficulty of realistically reflecting the value of these instruments on the financial statements of their owners led to the emergence of some of the new accounting standards that we mentioned previously.

When an active market disappears, so does this otherwise reliable method.

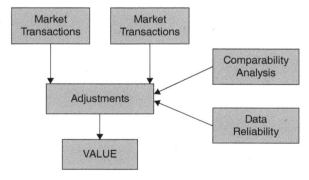

EXHIBIT 4.10 Market Value
Source: John Wiley & Sons, Inc. Reprinted with permission.

USING THE MARKET METHOD FOR TRADEMARKS

In a search for data on trademark and domain name sales, RoyaltySource[5] supplied us with the sampling of transactions listed as follows:

- Purchase of the U.S. rights to the "DHL" trademark for 15 years by Lufthansa German Airlines, Japan Air Lines, and Nissho Iwai in 1997. Price reported was $20 million.[6]
- Purchase of seven liquor trademarks by American Brands, Inc., from Seagram Company for $372.5 million. The marks included "Calvert Gin," "Calvert Extra American Whiskey," "Kessler American Blended Whiskey," "Leroux Cocktails," "Lord Calvert Canadian Whiskey," "Ronrico Rum," and "Wolfschmidt Vodka."
- Sale of the "Florsheim" trademark for footwear to the Weyco Group, Inc., in May 2002, for $9.8 million following bankruptcy.
- Sale of the "Gloria Vanderbilt" trademark by Murjani in 1988 for $15 million to Gitano. Reportedly $12 million was for the U.S. rights and $3 million for the Canadian and other foreign rights.
- Sale of the "Speedo" swimwear trademark by Linter Group to Pentland Group of Australia in 1990 for Aus$37.5 million.
- Purchase of the "Berghoff" beer brand for $1.2 million, by the Joseph Huber Brewing Co., of Monroe, WI, in September 1994. Reports indicated it may have been a distressed sale.
- Sale of the "Dexatrim," "Sportscreme," and four other over-the-counter drug brands for a reported price of $95 million by Thompson Medical Company to Chattem Inc. in November 1998. The brand's annual sales were reported at $55 million.
- The "Rolls-Royce" trademark rights were purchased in 1998 by Bayerische Moteren Werke AG (BMW) for $66 million.
- Pillsbury Company in January 1999 was reported to be selling its "Underwood" meat spread and "B&M" baked bean brands, plus four others to B&G Foods Inc. for $192 million.
- Purchase by National Airlines of the "National Airlines" trademark from Pan American World Airways in 1998 for $175,000.
- Purchase from an individual by Bank of America of the "Loans.com" domain name for $3 million in February 2000.
- Purchase of the "Bingo.com" domain name by Bingo.com, Inc. in January 1999 for $1.1 million.
- Purchase by Marc Ostrofsky of "Business.com" domain name from Business Systems International of London in 1997 for $150,000.
- Sale by Marc Ostrofsky of "Business.com" to Ecompanies Inc., in 1999 for $7,500,000.
- Purchase by Wine.com of the domain name "Wine.com" from Virtualvineyard.com in 1999 for $3,000,000.

---

[5] RoyaltySource.com is a supplier of IP sales and licensing data. It is a division of AUS, Inc., Mt. Laurel, NJ.
[6] "DHL," Registration No. 1,398,896, owned by Deutsche Post AG Corp.

- Sale by Wine.com of "Wine.com" to Evineyard.com in 2001 for $9,000,000 (including 210,000 customer list).
- In 2001, Planetrx.com sold 26 health-related URLs to several pharmaceutical companies for a total of $2,000,000, at individual prices ranging from $50,000 to $250,000.

By observing these illustrative transactions, one can appreciate the difficulty of applying the market method in a valuation of brands. A number of these transactions arose out of bankruptcy proceedings. That leaves one to question whether the prices reflect willing-buyer, willing-seller transactions. We can also observe that, in a number of cases, a family of brands was sold and we are left with the task of attempting to allocate the price to individual brands. Quite obvious is the fact that the prices exhibit a very wide range. We can also observe that some of the domain name sales were paired transactions. These were during a period when entrepreneurs obtained domain names in order to resell them to the trademark owners. Again we have to question whether the price represents market value as we have defined it.

We are also aware of trademark auctions that have been held recently. One such auction was sponsored by Racebrook Marketing Concepts, LLC in December 2012.[7] This organization reportedly offered 170 trademarks at this auction. In subsequent reports by others, these sales included:

- "Meister Brau" beer, $32,500
- "Victrola" phonograph records, $1,000
- "Linen Closet," $2,000
- "Computer City" $2,000
- "Financial Corporation of America," $2,000
- "General Cinema," $1,000
- "Shearson" brokerage firm, $45,000[8]

What can we make of this data? Presumably these trademarks were sold under an "Intent to Use" registration. Under that form of registration, the buyer must begin commercial use of the trademark within a two-year period or the rights will lapse. In addition, the buyer will have to renew the ITU registration every six months and may be asked to prove a meaningful intent to commercialize the trademark to ensure that it is not being purchased simply to "tie up" the mark. So, there are some very specific IP rights being purchased here and those rights fall considerably short of the complete ownership bundle of rights. And, even if all goes well, the new owner will incur some time and cost to perfect full trademark registration.

In terms of market value, these auction prices are analogous to the newly registered trademark that we discussed in Chapter 1 that was associated with our fledgling "yellow lawnmower" business. Assuming that the buyers fully intend to use the marks in commerce, these auction purchases represent a potential expense saving,

---

[7] See www.trademarkauctioninfo.com.
[8] See Bruce Watson, "Psst! Wanna Buy an Old Brand? Nostalgia Goes for Bargain Prices at Auction," *Daily Finance*, January 6, 2011, www.dailyfinance.com/2011/01/06/auction-trademark-dead-brands-nostalgia-bargain/.

in that some of the trademark design and registration process has already been accomplished. There might also be an expense saving of some magnitude if the dregs of some positive brand attributes once connected to these trademarks when they were in the marketplace are still present. This could conceivably speed time to market and enhance the effectiveness of these marks, if properly exploited. There are many "ifs" associated with these auction trademarks, so these prices need to be used with caution for valuation purposes.

Securitization

In 1993, Calvin Klein Inc. borrowed $58 million secured by its royalty stream from the licensing of its fragrances. Four years later, David Bowie securitized a loan of $55 million with 10 years of future royalties from his music catalog. Since then, companies such as Bill Blass (apparel), Triarc (Arby's restaurants), Dream Works SKG, and Vivendi Universal (motion pictures) have securitized financing supported by trademarks and film catalogs. There have also been securitizations of drug patent royalty streams, but patents as collateral have recently lost popularity because of the increased litigation exposure. So, copyrights and trademarks remain the collateral of choice. And, of course, the emphasis is on royalty streams of IP that has a track record of steady success in the market place.

One might look to these transactions as indications of the market value of the underlying intellectual property (IP) assets involved. It is important, however, to examine carefully the IP rights that these securitized amounts represent. True, the securitized amount represents someone's judgment of the present value of an income stream. But does that income stream necessarily represent the total economic benefit attributable to the intellectual property? Is there a time or territorial limit on the underlying royalty stream? Does the owner retain some exploitation rights? A typical IP securitization is supported by a portfolio of works in order to reduce risk to the lender and make the package more attractive. This presents the comparability problem noted when a group of trademarks or domain names is sold in a single transaction.

A license divides the economic benefit between licensor and licensee. A capitalization of only a portion of the income attributable to an asset only captures a portion of its value. If we want to use one of these transactions as an indicator of market value, we must satisfy ourselves that the income stream that supports the securitization represents all of the income that can be reasonably expected from exploiting the intellectual property.

A Market Method Variant

As homebuyers in a previous example, we might be uncomfortable with the inexactness of our evaluation of the benefits of home ownership. We might seek to make the process more "scientific" by devising a scoring system to rate the home's features and benefits. While such a system has the implication of precision, it would not assist us in coming up with an offering price. In other words, our scoring system would not turn features into dollars. Only if we took the time and trouble to score many houses and then wait to see what their selling price was, could we test our scoring system against actual market prices. Even if scores and prices bore some relationship, we would still only have a glimpse of a valuation system for some specific area and for some specific time.

For the same reasons, we caution against the temptation to rely on some subjective scoring system to value brands. It is tempting, to be sure, because there are so many varied aspects of a brand that make it attractive or unattractive, powerful or less powerful, long lived, or short lived. And a scoring scheme could be devised to rate these attributes. But, in the end, with such a system we still don't have a logical and explainable connection between the results of some scoring system and a dollar amount, which is the objective of a valuation. Therefore, we are faced with the task of expressing the future benefits of brand ownership in terms of dollars because we have recognized tools to restate the future dollar expectations into a current price in a logical and explainable way. Scoring and rating systems can be useful as a checklist to *evaluate or compare* brands, but they lack the needed direct connection to dollars required by a valuation method, in our view.

INCOME METHOD

The income method is directly related to one of the definitions of market value that we provided previously: Market value is equal to the present value of the future economic benefits of ownership.

While this is a simple statement, its meaning may not be intuitively obvious to many readers. We also previously emphasized the fact that every valuation is based upon future events. Let us observe that future in a more familiar setting.

When we buy a home, we buy it with the expectation that it will provide shelter to our family over some future period. Our expectation has many elements. The shelter part is obvious, but we may also think about the quality of schools, space for our pet, the prestige of a grand home, its future market value, or the desirability of a quiet neighborhood. We typically put all of these judgments together in a highly subjective process to form our opinion as to what we might be willing to pay for the home. The price that we might agree upon is, in essence, the "present value" of what we judge the future benefits of home ownership will be.

When we buy an automobile, we have an expectation about the transportation that it will provide to our family in the future. Again, that expectation has many parts to it, subjective and otherwise, but that is what governs what we would be willing to pay for that future benefit.

When we purchase a common share of the Coca-Cola Company stock, what do we expect the future benefit to be? As this is written, that share would cost around $40. Coca-Cola has been paying a dividend for a long time and currently it is about $1 annually. Our expectation is that Coca-Cola will continue to grow and be successful, and that the price of its common shares will increase as a result. At some future time, we can sell our share for more than we paid. Along the way we will receive dividends. So the gain on the sale plus dividends is the future economic benefit. Others in the market have judged that the present value of that benefit is $40. If we agree, we buy the share. If we think the present value is less than $40, we don't buy. If we think the present value is higher than $40, we buy two shares. Unlike our home and our car, this is a purely dollar-based decision.

Of course, we are here discussing the valuation of IP assets that are devoted to a business enterprise. The future service that those assets will provide to the enterprise cannot be simply described as "shelter" or "transportation." Nor are IP assets normally purchased with resale in mind, as a share of capital stock. Yet the future economic benefit must be described in terms of dollars because these assets must pay for their keep with some dollar benefit to the enterprise.

But those dollars are going to be received by the enterprise owner in the future, or at least that is the expectation. When the future service is in terms of dollars, it's very difficult, if not impossible, to make a price judgment on a subjective, intuitive basis as does a home or auto buyer. We therefore look to financial tools to assist us in coming to an opinion about the present value of those future dollar benefits.

We must also remember that those future dollar benefits are an *expectation*. Like all expectations, the future dollars may not materialize as we plan. They may not materialize at all, they may not materialize when we expect them, they may not materialize how we expect them, and they might also materialize in much greater abundance than we expect. We therefore need to make judgments about the likelihood of various outcomes and we need a tool to turn those expectations into a current day price that makes sense to us as an investment.

This is what the income method is all about.

Valuation Precept

Readers who are not familiar with the concept of present value or the mathematics of basic investment theory can refer to the discussion in Appendix A that covers these basic principles in detail.

Mathematics of the Income Method

In Appendix A, we introduce three mathematical formulas for the calculation of present value. Here, we are going to put some numbers with those formulas to illustrate, in its simplest form, the use of the income method.

Perpetuity   In Exhibit 4.11, we have shown the simplest formula for direct capitalization. Use of this formula is indicated when the relevant income is expected to last, unchanged, into perpetuity. As we noted, any estimate of future financial benefit has some risk associated with it. In the present value formulations, this risk is reflected as a percentage. A low percentage is indicative of low risk and a high percentage reflects the expectation of high risk. In subsequent chapters, we examine the concept of risk and its quantification in more detail. For now, we can accept the examples as they are.

Exhibit 4.11 is a calculation of the present value of a calculated amount of income. Assume that this example represents the financial expectations of a brand. In this example, we expect that the brand is responsible for $1,000 of revenue in each year into perpetuity. All of that does not go into our pocket, however, because we will incur a variety of expenses to maintain and grow this revenue that is attributable to the brand. These expenses are subtracted from the revenue to indicate that we will realize $250 per year in future economic benefit from the exploitation of the subject brand.

$$PV = \frac{INCOME\ (\$)}{RISK\ RATE\ (\%)}$$

Revenues	$1,000
Expenses	750
Income	$250
Risk rate	15%
Present Value	$1,667

EXHIBIT 4.11 Direct Capitalization

We recognize that our estimates of future economic benefit may in fact not be realized and, of course, perpetuity is a very long time. Our judgment is that the risk of realizing our expectations is reasonably reflected in an amount of 15 percent. Using these amounts, the present value formula results in the calculation of present value in the amount of $1,667. Stated in terms of a transaction, we can say that we would be willing to pay $1,667 for the ownership of this brand, which we expect to produce $250 annually in economic benefit into perpetuity.

We should recognize that this presents an unrealistic picture as it applies to the value of a brand. The economic benefit of any brand is in the end driven by market forces acting on the success of some product or service. The likelihood of unchanging economic benefit reaching into the distant future is highly unlikely.

Steady Growth In Exhibit 4.12, we introduce the additional complexity of growth. That is, we expect the income of $250 per year from the brand to grow in an amount of 3 percent annually. Again, this calculation assumes that the income stream continues into perpetuity. Keeping the same 15 percent estimate of risk, this calculation yields a present value of $2,146.

This form of capitalization offers a partial solution by permitting a consideration of growth, but again, that growth estimate cannot vary.

Discounting In the third present value formula discussed in Appendix A, the calculations for each year in the future are separate. This formula, shown in Exhibit 4.13, in essence presents a series of individual discrete period present value calculations, which

$$PV = \frac{INCOME \times (1 + Growth\ Rate)}{(Rate - Growth\ Rate)}$$

Revenues	$1,000
Expenses	750
Income	$250
Risk rate	15%
Growth Rate	3%
Present Value	$2,146

EXHIBIT 4.12 Direct Capitalization with Growth

$$PV = \frac{\text{INCOME 1}}{(1 + \text{Rate})} + \frac{\text{INCOME 2}}{(1 + \text{Rate})^2} + \frac{\text{INCOME 3}}{(1 + \text{Rate})^3} + \ \ldots$$

Revenues	$1,000	$1,020	$1,061	$1,124	$1,214	$1,336	$1,536	$1,459	$1,168	$701
Expenses	750	765	796	843	911	1,002	1,152	1,095	876	525
Income	$250	$255	$265	$281	$304	$334	$384	$365	$292	$175
Risk rate	15%									
Present Value	$217	$193	$174	$161	$151	$144	$144	$119	$83	$43
Total Present Value	$1,429									

EXHIBIT 4.13   Discounting

are then added together. This formula is useful because, in the real world, the economic benefit produced by any form of intellectual property, including a brand, is rarely constant year to year and rarely does it exhibit a steady growth or decline pattern.

In Exhibit 4.13, one can observe that the revenue in the amount of $1,000 in the first period grows in varying amounts over the next periods and towards the end begins to decline. This is not an unusual pattern for income attributable to IP or intangible assets. In our calculations shown in Exhibit 4.13, expenses have remained constant as a percentage of the revenue stream and the net benefit for each year is calculated as before. We retained the same 15 percent risk rate in this calculation and using the formula calculated the present value of the net benefit each of the 10 periods and summed them to be $1,429.

This is a simplified example of a *discounted cash flow* (DCF) calculation, the most frequently used tool in valuation. The "cash flow" portion of that term needs some explanation and that will be provided in Chapter 6.

In actual IP valuation practice, this is the formula that is utilized nearly all of the time. This is because the expectation is that the net benefit from a brand is rarely smooth and easily predictable, nor is it expected to remain in perpetuity. This formula therefore represents the most realistic picture of the present value of future economic benefits of ownership, which is what we seek.

The reader may recall a discussion in Chapter 2 regarding how a valuation proceeds in the overall. We pointed out in that discussion that the process can be likened to a funnel, in that a massive amount of information is gathered and analyzed to extract the essential four ingredients. We now can see what those ingredients are.

We can also observe at this point that the mathematics involved in the calculation of present value is not overly complex or mysterious.

We believe that the reader can now agree with our previous statement that "the arithmetic is easy, it's the inputs that are hard." Even in the simple example shown in Exhibit 4.13, one can well imagine the work effort that went into a 10-year forecast of revenue attributable to a brand. It required us to address such questions as:

- What is the revenue forecast for the entire business that owns the brand?
- How much of that total revenue is logically attributable to the existence of the subject brand?

- What will be the expenses incurred to maintain whatever income stream we have forecast?
- What is the likelihood that our forecast will come true?
- What are all the positives and negatives that could affect our forecast in the future?
- Should our forecasts go beyond 10 years?
- Is our starting point revenue of $1,000 for the first year reasonable?

Valuation Precept

To utilize the Income Method there are FOUR estimates we must make about the future economic benefit:

- Its AMOUNT
- Its DURATION
- The PATTERN of its receipt
- The RISK that the amount, duration, and pattern won't happen as we forecast

It is helpful to understand the overall relationships of these for inputs. From practical experience or from analyzing the preceding mathematical formulas, we can observe that:

- It is quite obvious that the greater the amount of economic benefits, the larger its present value.
- The longer the duration of the economic benefits, the greater its present value.

Not as obvious, perhaps, the *pattern* of receiving the future economic benefits is quite important in its impact on present value. An economic benefit to be received in the near term has a much greater present value than the same benefit that will not appear for some time.

The greater the *risk* that the forecasts of the amount, duration, and pattern, of receiving the economic benefits will not materialize as planned, the lower will be the present value. Remember that risk is expressed in a single percentage intended to reflect all of the business, economic, and regulatory conditions associated with exploiting the property in achieving the expected future economic benefit. From this point on in our discussions, we will be referring to this risk percentage as the *discount rate*.

Income Method Summary

The income method is based on well-known investment principles that have been with us for a long time. It is a method that is extensively relied upon by appraisers because it is founded on financial principles that are utilized every day in business decisions. Our dependence on this method, however, does not make it easier to use. It requires careful investigation and analysis to extract the necessary inputs for the income method. And there really are no shortcuts.

USING THE INCOME METHOD FOR TRADEMARKS

As with other forms of intellectual property, we rely heavily on some form of the income method to value brands. And unlike other forms of intellectual property, the development of the necessary inputs is more difficult. A patent usually has a much more narrow, concentrated effect within an enterprise. Its contribution is more visible. The effect of a brand, however, is distributed within the enterprise and is therefore more difficult to locate and quantify.

Trademarks are but one of an array of monetary, tangible, and intangible assets that make up the portfolio of a business enterprise. We must remember that the earnings of the business enterprise are attributable to *all constituents* of that asset portfolio. We must be very careful that the income stream that we choose to ascribe to a brand does not, in fact, usurp income for which other assets are responsible.

As an example, we could consider this difficulty in the context of a large regional shopping mall. The mall is itself a business enterprise, organized for the purpose of renting space to retailers of goods and services. And the mall has a brand of its own. If we were charged with the task of appraising the mall's brand, we would have to ask ourselves whether the patronage that drives the mall's success is due to the mall's brand or the brands of the retailers therein. Mall shoppers sometimes travel considerable distances. Do they make this effort because of a particular retailer or one of the "anchors?" Do they shop there because of the mall's location? Is it because they have heard about the attractiveness of the mall? What would happen to the mall business if it changed its name? What would happen to the mall business if the population of retailers changed significantly?

These are difficult questions to answer and the next chapters of this book will concentrate on in-depth discussions of the analysis tools that are available to develop these difficult inputs for the income method.

SUMMARY

This chapter presents the three well-accepted methods for valuing any type of property. We believe that these are the only three methods and that methods with other names that one may encounter in articles or regulations are, in fact, simply permutations of the cost, market, and income methods that we have described.

Since this book is focused on the valuation of trademarks, we evaluated each of these methods in that light. Both the cost method and the market method, while they are individually excellent for appraising other types of assets, have significant deficiencies when it comes to trademarks and brands. So we encourage you to concentrate on the income method. Because its application is complex, we are going to continue to expand our discussion of the income method in the coming chapters.

CHAPTER 5

Trademark Economic Benefit

In the previous chapter, we introduced the mathematics of the income method, which are based upon the principle that market value is equal to the present value of the future economic benefits of ownership. In this chapter and the next, we discuss the techniques and tools that can be employed to estimate the essential inputs to the income method. The reader will recall the following from the previous chapter:

> To *utilize the income method, there are four estimates we must make about the future economic benefit:*
>
> 1. *Its amount*
> 2. *Its duration*
> 3. *The pattern of its receipt*
> 4. *The risk that the amount, duration, and pattern won't happen as we forecast*

Properly done, these are four aces—a sure winner. Carelessly done, they are more like the Four Horsemen.

In this chapter we will address the first of these four elements—the amount of future economic benefit.

FUTURE ECONOMIC BENEFIT

Why do we use the term *economic benefit* instead of "earnings" or "profits?" Yes, at the end of the day we are seeking the amount of profit that can be ascribed to an aggregation of brand elements and a trademark. We do not, however, want to direct the investigation to focus solely on financial data and performance. Economic benefit can come in many forms and it is essential in our investigation to "leave no stone unturned." As an example, a strong brand can serve as an economic barrier to competition. Yes, ultimately that should result in higher profits than otherwise but our investigation begins by discovering a brand characteristic that is not, at the beginning, expressed in terms of dollars.

We also need to recognize that an economic benefit flowing from a trademark is subject to continual change. In a competitive and mature market, profits are eventually driven downward to the lowest level at which a fair return can still be extracted. Competitors are quick to recognize and enter high profit markets. At times, when supply exceeds demand, the resulting reduction in selling prices can depress the profitability of an entire industry. The essential point is that we cannot simply focus on profits at the outset, we need to understand the drivers of those profits as well. Therefore, we use the more general term of economic benefit in order to stimulate our investigation in the broadest possible way.

However one defines it, economic benefit arises from successful exploitation. As we noted in a previous chapter, without successful exploitation or the reasonable expectation of it, there is no market value.

Brand Exploitation

The term *exploitation* can have a rather negative connotation, in the sense of taking advantage of something or someone for one's own ends. However, it also means to use or develop fully, as for profit or advantage, and it is in this sense that we refer to brand exploitation.

A trademark could be likened to a fruit-bearing tree. After planting as a seed, it is tended, fertilized, and watered with advertising and the support of high-quality products or services. It is sprayed to protect it from disease, predatory insects, and marketplace competition. As it matures, it begins to bear fruit and be productive on its own. Its obvious exploitation is by selling the fruit. If its fruit finds eager acceptance in the market, then the owner will be very attentive in nurturing the tree, raising more of the same type of tree and, perhaps, looking for other ways to exploit it. Seedlings from the tree can be sold. Portions of it can be grafted onto other trees to create new hybrids. This begins to sound like licensing and brand extension, which we will discuss.

Not all of these experiments will be successful. A grafting of our orange tree to a grapefruit tree might work very well, but attempting to create an orange-fig hybrid could be a failure because we could not obtain fruit or, perhaps, because the fruit was rejected by our customers. Will that rejection cause customers to become disenchanted with our original orange product?

Buyers of our seedlings may be very clever in nurturing them and developing new strains that produce fruit better than ours. Success in the marketplace breeds competition. We need to be ever attentive that our tree stays healthy and fruit bearing, so that we continue to have a place at the market.

Lest we conclude that trademark exploitation has only reached its zenith in modern times, we pass along this chronology of the venerable "Quaker Oats" brand, now one of many famous trademarks of PepsiCo: "[T]he Quaker symbol was given commercial form in 1877 when the Quaker Mill Company registered as a trademark the 'figure of a man in Quaker garb' ...."[1]

By 1893, under the direction of Henry Parsons Crowell, a marketing pioneer:

The Quaker Oats trademark blazed from the side of buildings, illuminated billboards at eye-catching vantage points ... caught the gaze of streetcar riders from car cards ... and missionary exhortations on the merits of Quaker were printed on the reverse side of the Sunday bulletins in score of city churches ....[2]

---

[1] Arthur F. Marquette, *Brands, Trademarks and Goodwill*, (New York: McGraw-Hill, 1967), 31.
[2] Marquette, 49.

The Quaker Oats story illustrates one form of exploitation; but exploitation comes in all shapes and sizes and, in order to evaluate brand exploitation potential, it is useful to be exposed to some of the means of exploitation and their characteristics.

There is a valuation concept, critical to the appraisal of property such as land, called the theory of highest, best, and most profitable use. This concept can help guide our thinking about brand exploitation. The theory is that property should be valued as if available for its highest and best use, *even if that is not its present use.* Highest and best use is defined "as the available use and program of future utilization that produces the highest present value."[3] If we were appraising an acre of land adjacent to the boardwalk in Atlantic City, New Jersey, we would be seriously in error if we valued the land as a farm. The highest and best use of that acre of land (i.e., the use that would produce the highest return on investment) is obvious by observing what is next door!

In a trademark example, let us assume that we own the trademark "MONEY" (of course, being a word of our language, it is not a trademark possibility, but it is a good example). We can further assume that we are using this trademark on our brand of chewing gum. It is quite clear, however, that a trademark such as MONEY could be applicable to a host of products and services. When we are estimating the future economic benefits of exploiting the MONEY trademark, we should not therefore limit our investigation to the economic benefit within our chewing gum business but also investigate all other *reasonable* exploitations. Yes, *reasonable* is a qualitative judgment. Would it be reasonable to exploit the MONEY brand on a budgeting app

---

[3] American Institute of Real Estate Appraisers, *The Appraisal of Real Estate*, 7th ed. (Chicago: 1978), 45.

for a mobile device? Yes. Does it make sense to use it for a line of luggage? No. Any valuation is replete with judgments.

In subsequent sections, we will investigate the quantification of trademark value by using present value techniques. Before doing so, however, we should explore the range of exploitation possibilities for trademarks and understand how to apply the concept of highest and best use when the time comes.

Primary Exploitation

Primary exploitation is the use of the mark on the original product or service on which it was built and with which it was first associated. This is the original "tree," to use the analogy. The "Arm & Hammer" brand is an example.[4] This well-known trademark, said to date from the 1860s, was built on a baking soda product. Some brands never their leave their primary role if the underlying product or service is timeless as is baking soda. Other brands never move outside their primary exploitation because they are narrowly focused.

The relationships between brands and the trademarks around which they are constructed can, in a large organization, become extremely complicated because the company's brand exploitations become interconnected. So complicated, in fact, that the valuation task can appear insurmountable. In fact, we believe the valuation task can be more straightforward than that of a marketer attempting to design new strategies or measure the old ones. As valuers, we only need to follow the dollars. We do not need to understand all of the crosscurrents of influence that are producing those dollars.

As an example, let us observe a small manageable enterprise—General Motors (GM). Its brands can be thought of as a pyramid and "GM" is the trademark at the top of the pyramid.[5] It is the parent brand of a large family of trademarks encompassing not only those for automobiles, but also those for trucks, financial

---

[4] "Arm & Hammer," Registration No. 47,947, owned by Church & Dwight Co., Inc.
[5] "GM," Registration No. 271,167, owned by General Motors.

services, parts, and a whole host of other manufactured products. The "Buick" brand is one of the automobile brands.[6] It, in turn, is an umbrella brand for several automobile models, such as "Enclave," "Verano," and "Regal." We can build this pyramid almost endlessly, for there are accessories, car care products, ball caps, golf shirts, replicas of old dealer signs, and toy vehicles, all bearing some trademark or other in the General Motors family. Some of these brands are being exploited by GM, others by licensees. The exploitation of these many brands has an effect on the others, to some greater or lesser degree. The influence can be negative or positive (or neutral).

A valuation task may seem simpler if we start at either the top or bottom of the pyramid. We could begin with the value of General Motors as a whole and from there estimate the value of the whole body of GM trademarks. In that value, we would have captured all of the good things (from an economic standpoint) and all of the bad things. We would have reflected all of the interrelated effects.

At the bottom, we could analyze the income-producing capability of the ball cap business, which would probably be that of a licensee. That would be a straightforward process, focused on the stream of royalty income to GM. In the center section of the pyramid, the small income streams are becoming creeks are becoming small rivers are becoming tributaries are becoming rivers of income flowing into the General Motors lake. When we measure the income (and therefore the value) at any point, we are quantifying all the positive and negative effects below it. As an example, suppose the ball cap licensee is paying royalties that contribute to the overall earnings of the corporation. Suppose, however, one Buick ball cap purchaser was unhappy with its quality and, because of that, purchased a Pontiac instead of a Buick. When we valued the Buick brand, we would (theoretically) observe the effect on earnings of that one unsold automobile, and the effect would be felt in the value of the Buick brand. So, while we might not be aware of this specific occurrence, we will catch up with its effect somewhere in the chain of earnings.

The essence of this technique is that we treat each brand exploitation as a business enterprise (see Exhibit 5.1).

It should be obvious that the value of a business enterprise, absent unusual circumstances, is equal to the sum of the values of its constituent parts.[7] If our task is to value one of the parts, we start with the value of the whole and allocate values to the parts until we are able to extract the value of the one we are interested in. Alternatively, we can build up the values from the bottom of the pyramid, as long as we correlate the resulting values with that of the whole. The same process governs a trademark valuation in one of these complex organizations. Exhibit 5.2 illustrates the parent-subordinate relationships in terms of brands.

The reader should keep in mind that in order to maintain simplicity, each block on this diagram is shown as a trademark. Actually, each block is comprised of several types of assets that represent the portfolio within a business enterprise and that were described in Chapter 2.

---

[6] "Buick," Registration No. 511,603, owned by General Motors.

[7] For the purpose of this discussion, we ignore premiums sometimes paid when businesses are acquired. Such premiums can be a reflection of assets undervalued (by investors), a payment for control over the exploitation of those assets, or a payment to overcome investor inertia.

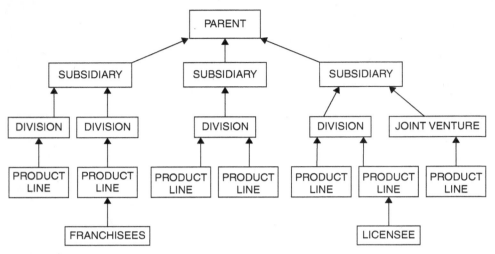

EXHIBIT 5.1   Consolidation of Business Enterprise Values
Source: John Wiley & Sons, Inc. Reprinted with permission.

Secondary Exploitation

We use the term *secondary exploitation* to refer to any exploitation that is beyond the mainstream, original product or service. Our original tree, if you will. Secondary exploitation takes many forms and can be accomplished by the trademark owner or by others to whom the owner has granted specific rights. From a legal standpoint, we suppose, all trademark exploitation is by the trademark owner because of the neces-

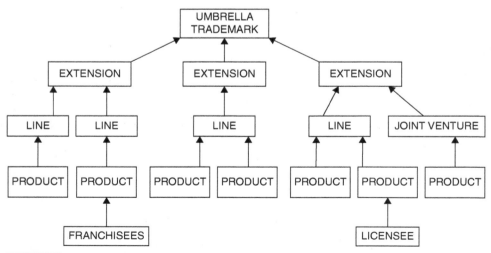

EXHIBIT 5.2   Consolidation of Brand Values
Source: John Wiley & Sons, Inc. Reprinted with permission.

sity for the owner to continually exert quality control over the products or services that bear his mark. A patent or proprietary technology could be licensed to another (perhaps even with sublicense rights), and the owner might have no further contact with the licensee or the products that ultimately use it, other than to perhaps audit the transaction from a financial point of view.

Successful secondary exploitation requires a mark that has firmly established itself and has a strong "persona." With that prerequisite, a trademark is less likely to be damaged by a secondary exploitation that fails. A new or weak trademark that is extensively exploited in faintly related products or services raise the question, "What does this mark stand for?" There have been cases of this with celebrity endorsements that ranged far and wide over products and services to the extent that the brand became quite diluted because it was unclear what qualities and brand personality it represented.

An example of successful secondary exploitation takes us back to the Arm & Hammer brand. That brand has been successfully extended by the Church & White Company and its licensees to household deodorizers, laundry detergent, toothpaste and whitening systems, and pet care products, among others. These brand extensions were enabled because of the baking soda's ancillary attribute as a deodorizing agent for refrigerators. Being associated with that niche enabled brand extensions into related product lines.

Trademark extension refers to the use of a mark in a new class of product or service. New, that is, with respect to the product or service on which it has already become known. An extension can be a small step, from bar soap to a laundry detergent, for example, or a major move, such as using a corporate mark on footwear. As Kapferer notes, there is always "stress on the brand" in an extension.[8] Customers will readily accept some extensions and reject others. The rejection can affect not only the extended product or service, but also the core brand itself and this potential is the marketer's nightmare.

Two American icons—"Aunt Jemima"[9] and "Betty Crocker"[10]—are exemplary instances of successful brand extensions. The Aunt Jemima brand began over 100 years ago as a pancake and waffle mix. Today, this fictional cook presents several

---

[8] Jean-Noel Kapferer, *Strategic Brand Management* (London: Kogan Page Limited, 1992), 91.

[9] "Aunt Jemima," Registration No. 1,575,365, owned by The Quaker Oats Company.

[10] "Betty Crocker," Registration No. 945,806, owned by the General Mills Corp.

kinds of pancake mixes, as well as coffee cake and cornbread mixes and self-rising flour, together with companion syrup products.

Betty Crocker began life in the 1920s as another mythical cook who responded to baking questions posed by customers of the then Washburn Crosby Company in Minneapolis. Today, she is the endorser of a host of products including "Bac-Os," "Hamburger Helper," "Potato Buds," "Homestyle Stuffing," and many prepared cake mixes and frosting products. And she is still answering customer questions for General Mills Company as well as publishing cookbooks.

The potential economic benefit of brand extension is plain. In choosing a brand extension strategy rather than the introduction of an entirely new brand, companies hope to reduce the cost of the endeavor. Cost reduction can be realized in several ways:

- Reduced time from concept to market
- Reduced advertising and promotion costs due to the influence of the parent brand
- Quicker market penetration
- Potential enhancement to the parent brand by increasing its "reach"
- Expand the parent brand beyond its core constituency

Not all brand extensions are linked as closely to the parent brand as are those of Aunt Jemima and Betty Crocker mentioned before. Caterpillar is a very well-known global manufacturer of construction machinery and other heavy equipment. The company successfully introduced a line of gifts and apparel including boots, shoes, shirts, scale models, toys, watches, hats, and jackets for both men and women. The success of this strategy seems to play on an interesting aspect of the "CAT" brand's cachet.[11]

---

[11] "CAT," Registration No. 778,638, owner by Caterpillar Tractor Co.

CAT®

While Caterpillar was successful in an extension that was rather a long reach, not all brand extensions turn out to be so successful. As an example, "Ben-Gay," a well-known U.S. brand of analgesic cream made the decision to introduce Ben-Gay branded aspirin and that extension was abandoned because of lack of marketplace acceptance. The well-known women's magazine, Cosmopolitan, introduced "Cosmopolitan Yogurt" and, again, this was too much of a stretch for the marketplace to accept. The same fate befell "Colgate Kitchen Entrées," "Pond's Toothpaste," and "Lifesavers Soda."

The essential point for our purposes here is that secondary exploitation strategies contain some risk. And the risk is greater than for primary exploitation by the brand owner. This element of risk is something that we must recognize if we choose to include brand extension strategies in our quantification of future economic benefit in a valuation.

In Chapter 6, we will include a discussion of how the aspect of risk is reflected in a valuation. In the sections that follow, we discuss some of the analytic tools that companies use to evaluate a brand extension strategy.

Trademark licensing is discussed in more detail in a subsequent chapter. Here, we simply note that licensing is an important form of secondary exploitation. In essence, it is a secondary exploitation undertaken by someone other than the brand owner. We typically judge it to be more risky than in the secondary exploitations discussed. This is because control of the licensee is not as close and immediate. As an example, if the brand owner decides that a licensee's exploitation is not sufficiently successful in the marketplace, it may be more difficult to withdraw it. From the exploitation perspective, however, licensing can achieve several objectives:

- It can enhance company value by increasing exposure to important constituencies, and build brand equity by increasing its exposure in the marketplace.
- It can provide a source of otherwise unavailable income.
- It can be a tactical move in an expansion or redirection strategy.

Conclusion

The economic underpinnings of brand extension lie in achieving growth and improving the rate of profitability. Having established a strong brand through successful primary exploitation, it is management's responsibility to fully exploit it. The market position of the primary brand may be such that further growth can only be achieved at great expense. On the other hand, brand extensions may be a less expensive way to ride on the coattails of the primary brand, and the company will receive more than otherwise for its advertising dollars.

Often a brand extension is an economical and relatively transparent way to update a product or service, or to make changes in its make up without causing too many ripples in the consumer world. If consumers want "fat-free," "sugar-free," or "low-salt," a brand extension can achieve this. If the government decrees "no more lead/preservatives/dye," a brand extension can facilitate compliance with minimal market disruption.

QUANTIFYING ECONOMIC BENEFIT

Our purpose in classifying brand exploitation as primary or secondary is to facilitate a discussion about how the nature of trademark exploitation relates to techniques for estimating future economic benefit. That is, understanding the means of exploitation will help lead us to identify an appropriate way to quantify future economic benefit in terms of dollars.

We must remember that the economic benefit of brand exploitation is a *net* number, just like the bottom line earnings of the enterprise. There are expenses involved in brand exploitation, but the expectation is that enhanced sales revenues will exceed them and result in positive earnings. Therefore, we can look to both sales revenue and expense levels in our search for economic benefit.

Valuation Precept
To have value, intellectual property rights must bring a reasonable expectation that they will (1) enhance future revenues, (2) reduce future expenses, or (3) both.

Revenue Enhancers

Successful brand exploitation can produce enhanced revenues in many different ways:

- Permit premium pricing
- Increase market share
- Enable the introduction of new products or services
- Extend product life in the marketplace
- Accelerate time-to-market
- Ease market penetration
- Increased growth rate
- Provide versatility for product extensions and/or licensing

Expense Reducers

A successful brand exploitation can also have the effect of reducing business expenses, although it may be more difficult to discover these reductions than it is to observe the ways in which a brand enhances revenues:

- Relieves the owner of the cost to create
- Provides purchasing power
- Provides economies of scale
- Reduces advertising and promotion costs

A NEW VISTA

In our search for economic benefit attributable to successful trademark exploitation, we must be very careful that an economic benefit that we discover is in fact solidly attributable to the brand in question.

As an example, five years ago Microsoft released its "Windows Vista" operating system.[12] If, after that, we had had the assignment of estimating the market value of the Vista brand, we might well have analyzed the sales and expenses associated with the Vista product line. It is likely that we would have discovered a positive economic benefit to the Microsoft enterprise. We might also have discovered that the Vista operating system was not overwhelmingly popular. We would then have to ask ourselves the question as to whether the positive economic benefit we observed was in fact due to the Vista brand or whether it was simply because that brand had been introduced under the very powerful Microsoft brand umbrella. With hindsight—observing that the Vista operating system was rather promptly replaced by Windows 7—we would have been correct to ascribe the positive economic benefit to the Microsoft brand.

The remainder of this chapter presents specific techniques for the calculation of the future economic benefit of brand exploitation. The particular technique to be chosen will depend on the way that a brand is being exploited or the ways in which it could be exploited. The technique chosen will also be dependent on the information available and its reliability. These techniques are separated into two groups—direct techniques and indirect techniques.

A HIGH-VOLUME QUESTION

We must be just as careful in ascribing expense reductions so that we have some assurance that they are in fact attributable to the subject trademark. As an example, if we were valuing the McDonald's brand our analysis might reveal that the average price that McDonald's Corp. pays for ground beef is something less than what most other wholesale buyers pay.

Wal-Mart Corporation has the reputation of being able to purchase goods at lower cost than many other retailers. Passing along some portion of these savings to customers is part of the company's business model.

In both of these cases high volume purchases result in lower costs. Is that expense reducing economic benefit attributable to the McDonald's or Wal-Mart brands?

We leave that question for you to ponder.

---

[12] "Windows Vista," Registration No. 3,551,892, owned by Microsoft Corporation.

DIRECT TECHNIQUES

Direct techniques are those in which we are able to make specific calculations based on specific subject—related data.

Premium Pricing

When above-average profits are generated on a consistent basis, intangible assets or intellectual properties are likely responsible. Sometimes intellectual property contributes by commanding a premium selling price on a consistent basis regardless of competitor actions. Well-recognized trademarks are good examples. If this enhanced market demand for the product or service is brought about by the magnetism of the trademark, then the income stream represented by the premium price can be attributed to this asset.

While the underlying concept and the apparent economic theories make sense, we must be careful with this technique. The potential pitfall is the question of whether we can ascribe the entire premium price to the trademark. Is a "Rolex" watch really the same as a "Brand X" watch, or a "Mercedes-Benz" automobile the same as another brand of automobile? When we say "the same as," we refer to performance, reliability, longevity, technological advancement, and the like. Few brands are able to sustain a premium price position on trademark alone for long. Something else must be there, embodied in the product or service in order to sustain this element of leadership. If this latter is true, then perhaps we cannot ascribe the entire premium price as the economic benefit attributable to the trademark.

This caveat aside, how is this future economic benefit calculated? Exhibit 5.3 illustrates.

EXHIBIT 5.3   Premium Pricing Technique

	1	2	3	4	5	TOTAL
S & R Enterprises						
SALES OF PREMIUM PRICED PRODUCT						
Unit Sales Forecast (millions)	12,410	12,530	13,454	13,896	14,458	
Price per Unit	2.49	2.49	2.49	2.49	2.49	
Sales Revenue (millions)	$30,900	$31,200	$33,500	$34,600	$36,000	$166,200
S & R Enterprises						
WITH GENERIC PRODUCT PRICING						
Unit Sales Forecast	12,410	12,530	13,454	13,896	14,458	
Price per Unit	2.19	2.19	2.19	2.19	2.19	
Sales Revenue	$27,177	$27,441	$29,464	$30,431	$31,663	$146,176
REVENUE ATTRIBUTABLE TO IP	$ 3,723	$ 3,759	$ 4,036	$ 4,169	$ 4,337	$ 20,024

EXHIBIT 5.4 Alternative Premium Pricing Technique

	1	2	3	4	5	TOTAL
S & R Enterprises						
SALES @ PREMIUM PRICE INCREMENT						
Unit Sales Forecast	12,410	12,530	13,454	13,898	14,455	
Premium price component ($2.49-2.19=$0.30)	0.30	0.30	0.30	0.30	0.30	
REVENUE ATTRIBUTABLE TO IP	$3,723	$3,759	$4,036	$4,169	$4,337	$20,024

In this case, we have calculated the difference (over a five-year period) between the forecasted sales revenue of Smith & Richey (S&R) Enterprises' premium price product or service and that of a generic or similar but lower priced product or service. We did this by repricing S&R's forecast using the lower price offered by others. The assumption is that both scenarios reflect the same quantity of goods or services. The excess income of S&R, with the premium priced product or service is $20,024, and this is the future economic benefit attributable to the trademark in question, at least for the five-year period calculated.[13] The generic price level could also be a typical price of several companies grouped together.

We can also make this calculation in an alternative way. We would obtain the same quantitative result if we were to compare the unit prices ($2.49 vs. $2.19) and multiply the difference by S&R's sales quantity (see Exhibit 5.4).

As we previously noted, success in business attracts competitors. The enhanced earnings that ought to result from premium pricing are just such an attraction and we must consider the possibility that a premium price advantage can erode. An examination of S&R's previous experiences in the marketplace might inform us about the likelihood of that happening in the future.

Have we calculated the income attributable to S&R's trademark correctly? Perhaps not. After all, the generic (or typical companies) may have a trademark that contributes to their ability to charge the price they do. A portion of their $2.19 selling price may be attributable to their brands. That amount plus the $.30 price advantage we calculated might better reflect the contribution of the S&R trademark. Therefore, we may be understating the value of S&R's mark by using this method. It would be more accurate if we had compared its price to the price of a company that had <u>no</u> trademarks, such as a contract manufacturer, but this information is not always available. We will touch on that in the following pages.

---

[13] Readers are advised that these calculations, as well as others in the book, may not precisely add up due to rounding. The five-year time frame that we used here for illustrative purposes is arbitrary and in real life should be based upon facts and circumstances.

Licensing Income

We might be fortunate enough to encounter a situation in which our client, S&R, has licensed the mark to others. Assuming that there is incoming revenue from royalties, we would have an identifiable income stream with which to work.

Whatever the amount of royalty revenue, that is not itself equal to the income attributable to the trademark to be appraised. The future economic benefit is the *net* of royalty revenue and the expenses associated with receiving the royalty revenue. There are administrative expenses (remember that a trademark owner must monitor product quality and use of the mark), perhaps collection expenses, and the expenses associated with performing an audit of the licensee's business to ensure that the proper royalties are being remitted.

If the trademark owner is also making use of the mark, there will be at least two income streams to seek. In Chapter 8, this is discussed at greater length.

"But for" Logic

In our quest for a brand's economic benefit, evidence of a premium price or an established trademark license is the "low hanging fruit." That information is usually readily apparent and unambiguous. But trademark licensing is not very common and there are many instances of very valuable brands in a marketplace free of premium pricing. So we need other tools.

In our Chapter 3 discussion about using financial data, we suggested the technique of "following the dollars." That is, we can look elsewhere in financial data for evidence of income attributable to a brand. When found, the typical technique for isolating the income involves subtracting some sort of benchmark value or income from that of the subject company in order to estimate the amount of income or value attributable to the trademark. In theory, it is a sound method. In practice, it may be difficult to apply, especially when the benchmark is taken from other companies in the marketplace.

As an example, suppose we are trying to value the trademark of a company, and we have valued the enterprise at $10 million. If we could find a comparable company that has no trademark, and it has a value of $8 million, then we can conclude that the trademark has a value of $2 million. Or, if our subject company generates debt-free cash flow of $1.2 million annually, and a comparable company with no trademark generates $1 million, we can capitalize the difference, say at 10 percent and conclude a value for the trademark of $2 million ($200,000/.10). On the surface, the theory seems fine. But where do we find a comparable company with no trademark? To make this work, we need a company that has the same mix of monetary, tangible, and intangible assets as our subject and that also lacks the one asset that the subject has—the trademark.

Finding such a company is not always easy. Even producers of generic products or contract manufacturers may have important intangible assets associated with them (i.e., a long-term contract to supply a retailer with house-branded products, distributor networks, and supplier relationships). If the benchmark is faulty, then the residual income and value are faulty as well. Taking this a step further, suppose our search reveals a comparable company with no trademark whose value and cash flow are the same or more than our subject. Does this mandate that the trademark of our subject has no value? The earnings of our subject might be less than otherwise (or those of the comparable might be more) for a host of reasons unrelated to the relative contribution of the trademark.

It can also be useful to use a permutation of this subtraction logic within the subject company. One might ask the question—what would the effect on the company be if the subject trademark were declared invalid or if a court injunction prohibited its further use? We are, in effect, "assuming away" the subject brand in order to gain some insight into its relative contribution. This is a much more subjective exercise, and it may not lead to a specific dollar value, but it can be useful as a means to make a general evaluation of potential value. We could also assume away a specific brand within a multibranded enterprise as a way to measure its market value. One would need to remove the revenues and expenses associated with the subject brand and also consider the value of other assets, monetary and tangible, to the extent that they are dedicated to the subject brand. The difference between the value of the enterprise with and without this brand would provide an indication of its value.

Cost Savings

When above-average profits are earned on a consistent basis, some form of intellectual property is often responsible. While cost savings are typically associated with the exploitation of technology—related intellectual property, we previously noted that it is possible for a strong brand to produce cost savings for its owner by reducing business expenses over what they would otherwise be. We cited the possible examples of McDonald's Corp. and Wal-Mart Corporation.

We can "follow the dollars" at any point in the financial statements that are appropriate, and this example is at the gross profit level. We cannot always make a judgment about the presence or absence of intangible assets or intellectual property by observing just the gross profit performance of the subject company. We must make this observation in comparison with other companies that we feel are not similarly blessed. If our example, Smith & Richey Enterprises, is in the food industry, we would select a group of so-called private label manufacturers that manufacture food products to the specifications of others and sell their products with the brands of their customers. One would expect that the gross profit of our branded company would be higher than that of the contract manufacturers. This might be due to premium pricing of the products with well-known brands. This also might be due to the economies of scale that the branded manufacturers enjoy because of their market strength and claim on retail shelf space generated by their strong brands.

We would probably observe from our calculation of the difference in gross margins that the average gross profit margin for a branded company is significantly higher than that of the private label companies. We must recognize, however, that companies with well-known brands do not reap their benefits entirely without cost. There is a continuous need to support these brands with advertising and promotional activities. We therefore should adjust the gross margin calculations by subtracting the percentage amounts of selling, general, and administrative expenses.

On an adjusted basis, we would probably discover that the difference in gross margin between the two groups is smaller than we first calculated. It is important to remember that this is a shortcut method and does not specifically address the differences that may exist in the complementary assets that the two company groups may employ. It also does not specifically identify the assets that give rise to the difference, be they brand or other. This is, however, a very useful method to identify the order of magnitude of intangible assets and intellectual property that is contributing to an earnings advantage.

Cost saving benefits can be elusive when we search for them and can be difficult to attribute. As an example, there are consumer products that, because of strong and sustained demand, simply must be on the shelves of a retailer. Thus, the manufacturer of these products enjoys lower selling costs than otherwise. Can this cost benefit be attributed to the brand (trademark)? Can it be attributed to a unique formula or patented feature?

Production Cost Saving   Exhibit 5.5 illustrates a calculation of economic benefit attributable to production cost saving. Production costs are embedded in the cost of goods sold of S&R and it enjoys a gross profit margin of 66.67 percent, in contrast to the 63.01 percent observed for a group of comparable companies in the same industry. This difference enhances the company's gross profit by $65.0 million over the five-year period shown.

The contribution to earnings of intellectual property is at times subtle. Even when active contributions to earnings are not present, intellectual property can provide a company with above-average profits. A dominant position in a market allows a company to enjoy large sales volume on a consistent basis. Manufacturing and operating synergies can then enhance profits. Very often costs are saved just from operating efficiencies associated with large-scale production. This, however, is possible only because of passive intellectual property.

When large and reliable amounts of production volume consistently go through an organization, synergistic advantages are possible, and they generally lead to enhanced profits. Some of the typical synergies associated with large production volumes include:

- Raw materials can be purchased at large-order discounts. Suppliers are likely to offer discounts to customers that place large orders. A cost savings is the result.
- Manufacturing efficiencies can be introduced throughout each step of the process.
- Selling expenses might be more controllable with fewer salespeople covering large accounts.
- Retail efficiencies can include special arrangements with distributors or discounts in the purchase of shelf space at retailers.
- Regulation and compliance costs can be spread over a larger production base along with other fixed overhead costs.
- Large volumes can allow companies to provide utility companies with guaranteed energy purchases that could be obtained at a bulk rate discount.

Each synergistic benefit combines to provide enhanced profits that are made possible by market-dominating intellectual property, such as a trademark, though we again must be very careful here that Fancy's advantage does not arise from some unique manufacturing technology that it employs to reduce manufacturing costs.

EXHIBIT 5.5 Production Cost Saving Measured by Gross Profit

	1	2	3	4	5	TOTAL
S & R Enterprises						
Unit Sales Forecast (millions)	12,410	12,530	13,454	13,896	14,458	
Price per Unit	2.19	2.19	2.19	2.19	2.19	
Sales Revenue	$ 27,178	$ 27,441	$ 29,464	$ 30,432	$ 31,663	$ 146,178
Cost of Goods Sold PER UNIT	0.73	0.73	0.73	0.73	0.73	
Cost of Goods Sold	9,059	9,147	9,821	10,144	10,554	
Gross Profit	$ 18,119	$ 18,294	$ 19,643	$ 20,288	$ 21,109	$ 97,452
Gross profit margin						66.67%
COMPARABLE COMPANY GROUP						
Unit Sales Forecast	750,000	780,000	811,200	843,648	877,394	
Price per Unit	2.19	2.19	2.19	2.19	2.19	
Sales Revenue	$1,642,500	$1,708,200	$1,776,528	$1,847,589	$1,921,493	$8,896,310
Cost of Goods Sold PER UNIT	0.81	0.81	0.81	0.81	0.81	
Cost of Goods Sold	607,500	631,800	657,072	683,355	710,689	
Gross Profit	$1,035,000	$1,076,400	$1,119,456	$1,164,234	$1,210,804	$5,605,894
Gross profit margin						63.01%
S & R Enterprises						
Sales Revenue	$ 328,500	$ 341,640	$ 355,306	$ 369,518	$ 384,299	$1,779,262
Cost of Goods Sold ADVANTAGE	3.65%	3.65%	3.65%	3.65%	3.65%	
GROSS PROFIT ATTRIBUTABLE TO IP	$ 12,000	$ 12,480	$ 12,979	$ 13,498	$ 14,038	$ 64,996

We then ask the question whether this comparison of gross margin captures all of the trademark advantage. A really strong trademark should also bring some increased profitability due to a reduced need for promotion expenses and, perhaps, even sales expense. These are not expenses included in cost of goods sold and so, perhaps, we should give some consideration to advantages even further down in the income statement.

One way to do this is to compare the operating profit levels of S&R with that of a comparable group (CG). This will recognize the selling, general, and administrative expense experienced by these businesses and, if there are advantages to S&R, it will become obvious (see Exhibit 5.6).

As this schedule shows, S&R's financial performance is better than CG by virtue of its lower selling, general, and administrative costs. Its operating profit, expressed as a percentage of sales revenue, is 33.28 percent, contrasted with CG's 30.68 percent. This translates to an income advantage that *may* be attributable to S&R's of $4.3 million ((.3328 − .3068) × $166.2 million).

In this way we are attempting to capture all of the income that may be attributable to S&R's trademark, wherever its source in financial reports. Of course, the broader the measure, the more careful we must be that there are not other, extraneous causes or influences which give rise to the differences that we observe.

Comparable Return on Assets Technique

Another broad measure is to compare returns on a company's assets. A return higher than that of a properly selected peer group is an indicator of an asset performing unusually well. If we are comfortable that we have isolated this performance to a trademark, then that indicator can lead to trademark value.

Some additional financial concepts need to be introduced in order to make the following discussion more meaningful. These are cash flow, assets employed, and certain rates of return.

Cash flow is very important in the valuation of a business or its assets. *Net cash flow*, or *free cash flow*, is the amount of cash remaining after reinvestment in the business to sustain operations or to fund growth. Net cash flow represents money available for any use to which the owners wish to apply it. If we calculate the present value of all future net cash flow that a business is capable of producing, we have calculated the value of the enterprise.

We can observe from Exhibit 5.7 how net cash flow is calculated for one year's results of operations, in this case for S&R. The calculation begins with after-tax net income before extraordinary items. Extraordinary items are eliminated from the net cash flow calculation because by definition they are financial events that are not expected to happen again. Depreciation expense is added back because it is a non-cash expense (no business funds are actually paid to outsiders), and because it represents the "return of" element of investment, and it should therefore be a component of cash flow. Net income plus depreciation is called by some, *gross cash flow*.

As noted previously, net cash is the amount available to the owners of a business after consideration of the finances necessary to assure continuation and growth of the enterprise. This consideration focuses on two primary areas. First, if the company's sales are going to grow, inventories and accounts receivable will also grow. Thus, monetary assets will grow, and some of the gross cash flow will need to be invested

EXHIBIT 5.6 Operating Profit Comparison

	1	2	3	4	5	TOTAL
S & R Enterprises						
Unit Sales Forecast (millions)	12,410	12,530	13,454	13,896	14,458	
Price per Unit	2.49	2.49	2.49	2.49	2.49	
Sales Revenue	$ 30,901	$ 31,200	$ 33,500	$ 34,601	$ 36,000	$ 166,203
Cost of Goods Sold PER UNIT	0.73	0.73	0.73	0.73	0.73	
Cost of Goods Sold	9,059	9,147	9,821	10,144	10,554	
Gross Profit	$ 21,842	$ 22,053	$ 23,679	$ 24,457	$ 25,446	
Selling, General & Administrative Expense	11,557	11,669	12,529	12,941	13,464	
Operating Profit	$ 10,285	$ 10,384	$ 11,150	$ 11,516	$ 11,982	$ 55,317
Operating profit margin						33.28%
COMPARABLE COMPANY GROUP						
Unit Sales Forecast	750,000	780,000	811,200	843,648	877,394	
Price per Unit	2.49	2.49	2.49	2.49	2.49	
Sales Revenue	$1,867,500	$1,942,200	$2,019,888	$2,100,684	$2,184,711	$10,114,982
Cost of Goods Sold PER UNIT	0.73	0.73	0.73	0.73	0.73	
Cost of Goods Sold	547,500	569,400	592,176	615,863	640,498	
Gross Profit	$1,320,000	$1,372,800	$1,427,712	$1,484,820	$1,544,213	
Selling, General & Administrative Expense	747,000	776,880	807,955	840,273	873,884	
Operating Profit	$ 573,000	$ 595,920	$ 619,757	$ 644,547	$ 670,329	$ 3,103,553
Operating profit margin						30.68%
S & R Enterprises						
Sales Revenue	$ 30,901	$ 31,200	$ 33,500	$ 34,601	$ 36,000	$ 166,203
Operating Profit ADVANTAGE	2.60%	2.60%	2.60%	2.60%	2.60%	
GROSS PROFIT ATTRIBUTABLE TO IP	$ 803	$ 811	$ 871	$ 900	$ 936	$ 4,321

EXHIBIT 5.7   S&R Calculation of Net Cash Flow and Rate of Return on Book Assets Employed

NET CASH FLOW	
Net income before extraordinary items	$4,257
PLUS depreciation expense	900
LESS additions to working capital	180
LESS capital expenditures	600
	4,377
ASSETS EMPLOYED	
Current assets	17,750
Current liabilities	13,920
Net working capital	3,830
Property, plant and equipment at cost	17,100
Net property, plant and equipment	10,100
Average	13,600
Assets Employed Per Books	17,430
RATE OF RETURN ON BOOK ASSETS EMPLOYED	
Net cash flow	4,377
DIVIDED BY Book Assets Employed	17,430
	25.1%

there. Second, capital investments may be required to replace or add to buildings and equipment or other assets of a capital nature.

Therefore, it is necessary to estimate the amount of investment that will be required to meet these needs, and subtract it from gross cash flow. That is reflected in Exhibit 5.7. Since we will be using such a calculation for valuing trademarks, another element should be considered. Advertising expenditures build a trademark just as capital expenditures build a plant. Should we not consider this in the conversion from gross to net cash flow? The answer is yes, and this is probably best done by examining the amount of after-tax net income. Advertising expense has been deducted in arriving at that amount, and is therefore effectively removed from cash flow. If, however, existing advertising expenditures are not sufficient to support the forecasted growth, or if the brand is being "milked" without adequate support, then some downward adjustment should be made to reflect the additional amount of investment that might be required.

The calculation shown for "Rate of Return on Book Assets Employed" is not based on an accounting convention but is a calculation of ours used for a specific purpose. Others might calculate this amount differently. The precise method of calculation is not critical, as we will be using this amount to compare companies and groups, and the critical element is to be consistent in the comparison. There are a number of reasons to obtain this amount. If we want to know, as an example, whether we are receiving a reasonable return on our investment in a business, we need to know the amount of that investment. More precisely, we should know the *value* (rather than the cost) of that investment, which is why we make this calculation as we do. Two of the asset classifications, which comprise the business, are monetary and tangible assets. We estimate the value of monetary assets from their carrying amount on the company's balance sheet, subtracting current liabilities from current assets. This is a reasonable assumption because, as we understand financial reporting standards, the constituent accounting entries are scrutinized continually as to whether the amounts are "realizable" and properly reflect financial reality.

We have estimated the value of tangible assets by computing the average of gross and net book cost of plant, property, and equipment. The derivation of these two accounting measures was discussed in Chapter 3. This is a crude measure, but one that, in our experience from observing hundreds of fixed asset appraisals over the years, is reasonable.

We calculate the overall return on the monetary and tangible assets employed as shown in Exhibit 5.8, by dividing net cash flow by the value of book assets employed.

With this brief background in accounting basics we can discuss some additional techniques for estimating the future economic benefit attributable to a trademark.

In Exhibit 5.7, we observed that S&R's return on book assets is 25.1 percent. In this exhibit, we are comparing that performance with that of a group of contract manufacturing companies. The Contract Manufacturing Group (CMG) earns 21.0 percent. If we force S&R's return to the level of CG, its net cash flow would be $717 million lower than it is (.251 − .210) × $4,377 million). This is an indication of the income, as represented by net cash flow, produced by S&R's trademark, at the current time.

Readers are reminded that all of these calculations have as their objective the estimation of some level of *income* attributable to a trademark. They are not calculating *value*.

EXHIBIT 5.8 Comparable Return on Assets Technique

S & R Enterprises	Actual	Pro Forma	Difference
Monetary Assets	3,830	3,830	
Tangible Assets	13,600	13,600	
Assets Employed Per Books	17,430	17,430	
Net Cash Flow	4,377	3,660	717
Rate of Return on Book Assets Employed	25.1%	21.0%	
CONTRACT MFG. GROUP			
SALES OF GENERIC PRODUCT			
Monetary Assets (Net Working Capital)	20,000		
Tangible Assets	130,000		
Assets Employed Per Books	150,000		
Net Cash Flow	31,500		
Rate of Return on Book Assets Employed	21.0%		

Groups and Comparability   The concept of using comparable company data for the valuation process comes from the basic market approach. We first seek a transaction identical to that which we are studying. If none is available (which is most often the case), then we look for reasonably similar transactions. If our task is to appraise a home, we seek information from the sales of homes that are reasonably similar to our subject. If we are valuing common stock, then we investigate the sales of common stock of similar companies.

In the examples shown, we use the financial performance of similar companies as a benchmark. What we are really using is the financial results of the transactions between similar companies and *their* customers. That is, we may have hypothesized that our subject company (by virtue of its trademarks) receives a premium price for its product or service. We test this hypothesis by comparing the financial performance of our subject with that of a group of similar companies. If the hypothesis appears to hold, then we use the same technique to quantify the difference. This difference becomes an input to the valuation process.

All of this hinges on the analysis of *comparable* companies, and that, in turn, depends on defining comparability for the purpose we seek. This is rather important for the task. As guidance in this task, we provide some discussions on comparability standards from other sources. Taken together, they provide a general checklist of criteria. Not all of these are appropriate in every case or are practical to employ. Determining comparability is constrained by the information available. Much of the information that we might want about companies deemed comparable is proprietary data and not publically available. We simply must do the best we can with the information that is available and relevant to a particular case.

A number of years ago, faced with controversy about the value of the common stock of closely held (not traded on an exchange) companies, the IRS developed Revenue Ruling 59–60, which identified guidelines for the appraiser to use in beginning the comparability analysis:

- The nature of the business and the history of the enterprise from its inception
- The economic outlook in general and the condition and outlook of the specific industry
- The book value of stock and the financial condition of the business
- The earning capacity of the company
- The company's dividend paying history and its capacity to pay dividends in the future
- Whether or not the enterprise has goodwill or other intangible vale
- Sales of the common stock and the size of the block to be valued
- The market price of stocks of corporations engaged in the same, or similar, lines of business having their stocks actively traded in a free and open market, either on an exchange or over the counter

Obviously, these standards apply specifically to the valuation of common stock. They also point out the necessity of knowing about the subject company, its business, and its relationship to its industry and the economy as a whole. They are not presented because they are a definitive standard, but because they represent a proven and succinct enumeration of factors to consider.

More recently, our tax collectors and our legislative representatives have been heard again on this subject. This time the subject was intracompany transfer pricing.

This subject is covered elsewhere, but we touch on it here because it is another situation in which we reach out to "comparable company data" in order to provide a benchmark. The essential question is whether the sales of goods and/or services within a company comport with arm's length transactions elsewhere in the business world. To discover the answer, we are told that we should make a study of "arm's length transactions" and compare them to our subject. This is not unlike our task here, but not every consideration is relevant to the same degree.

Federal tax regulations deal with comparability in a way that is more to the point (we have substituted language that is more meaningful to our subject):

> *In order to be considered comparable to [our subject], the [comparable] transaction need not be identical ... but must be sufficiently similar that it provides a reliable measure of an arm's length result.*
>
> *Factors for determining comparability include the following: Functions, Contractual terms, Risks, Economic conditions, and property or services.*[14]

Functions   What are the parties doing? We need to compare their:

- Advertising and promotion
- Research and development
- Product design and engineering
- Manufacturing, production, and process engineering
- Product fabrication, extraction, and assembly
- Purchasing and materials management
- Marketing and distribution functions, including inventory management, warranty administration, and positioning.

Do you recall our admonition to investigate whether the apparent financial advantage of our subject company (ostensibly provided by our trademark) was due to another production element and *not* the trademark? This is the analysis that must be done to cover that base.

Contractual Terms   Is the way that our subject does business the same as the supposed comparables? We are attempting to use the sales of comparable companies as benchmarks, but are those transactions really comparable? We are selling our product with a lifetime warranty and other companies are not. Is our higher price due to the warranty or our trademark? We need to investigate:

- The form of consideration charged or paid.
- Sales or purchase volume.
- The scope and terms of warranties provided.
- Rights to updates, revisions, or modifications.
- Collateral transactions or ongoing business relationships between buyer and seller.

---

[14] 26 C.F.R. § 1.482–1.

Risks   To be comparable, companies or transactions should be subject to a similar degree of risk, including:

- Market risks, including fluctuations in cost, demand, pricing, and inventory levels
- Risks associated with the success or failure of research and development
- Financial risks, including fluctuations in foreign currency rates of exchange and interest rates
- Credit and collection risks
- Product liability risks
- General business risks related to the ownership of property

Economic Conditions   The economic conditions surrounding or affecting the companies or transactions should also be similar and consideration should be given to:

- The similarity of geographic markets
- The relative size of markets and their stage of development
- The level of market (wholesale, retail, etc.)
- Relative market shares
- Location-specific cost of the factors of production
- Extent of competition in the markets
- The economic condition of the industry (contracting, expanding, etc.)

Property or Services   To be considered comparable, the property or services that are the subject of a supposed comparable transaction should be similar. This seems obvious, but because of the unique nature of trademarks, there are often few, if any, similar transactions to study. Therefore, the temptation exists to widen the application of this comparability standard. This can be acceptable as long as it is done with an understanding of the deterioration in the quality of the analysis that will result.

Investment Rate of Return Technique

In the comparable return on assets technique described in the previous section, we contrasted the financial performance of the subject against a group of comparable companies. We can also use this same basic technique without using the comparable company financial profile, but rather using rates of return from market comparable companies. This methodology is best understood by starting with some fundamentals.

From previous chapters we know that the total earnings of a business enterprise are derived from the exploitation of the assets that comprise it. Therefore:

$$E_t = E_{wc} + E_{fa} + E_{iaip}$$

where E_t = total earnings of the enterprise.
   E_{wc} = earnings attributable to net working capital.
   E_{fa} = earnings attributable to fixed assets.
   E_{iaip} = earnings attributable to intangible assets and intellectual property.

We also know that earnings attributable to intangible assets derive from the contribution of typically commodity-like intangibles (such as software, an assembled workforce, and other elements of a going concern) and from intellectual property (which is unique and likely to be the driving force behind enhanced earnings):

$$E_{iaip} = E_{ia} + E_{ip}$$

where E_{ia} = earnings attributable to intangible assets.
E_{ip} = earnings attributable to intellectual property.

Our objective is to isolate the income attributable to trademarks, so the next step can be expressed as

$$E_{ip} = E_t - (E_{wc} + E_{fa} + E_{ia})$$

The distribution of earnings among asset classifications is primarily driven by the value of the assets and their relative risk. It is a tempting shortcut to consider allocating the total income of the business to assets simply on the basis of their relative value. This does not, however, recognize the very important element of relative risk. Assets are investments, and that must be continually kept in mind.

We can then use this concept to estimate the values of E_t, E_{wc}, E_{fa}, and E_{iaip}. We introduce market-based rates of return at this point, and the reader is directed to Appendix C wherein this subject is presented in some detail. This interruption is not necessary, however, if one is willing to temporarily accept the relative rates of return used in the following example:

EXHIBIT 5.9   Allocating Income Among Assets

ASSET CATEGORY	ASSET VALUE ($ 000's)	RETURNS REQUIRED	AMOUNT OF RETURN ($ 000's)
NET WORKING CAPITAL	3,830	2.7%	103
TANGIBLE ASSETS	13,600	5.7%	775
INTANGIBLE ASSETS	5,000	12.0%	600
INTELLECTUAL PROPERTY	15,080	18.0%	2,714
TOTAL	37,510	11.2%	4,193
TECHNOLOGY IP	5,000	25.0%	1,250
TRADEMARKS	10,080	14.5%	1,462
	15,080	18.0%	2,712

On the upper portion of Exhibit 5.9 we have calculated income attributable to intellectual property in the amount of $2,714 million. Note that the total amount of income allocated to assets is $4,234 million, or approximately the same as the net cash flow calculated in Exhibit 5.8 for S&R. We ask the reader to accept the values for asset classifications as shown. We will later illustrate how this model can deal with more than one unknown factor, but we wish to concentrate on the income attribution at this point. The $2,714 million of income is attributable to all intellectual property, of course, and a further distribution of income is necessary in order to isolate that which can be ascribed to trademarks alone. This can be done following the same principles presented for the other asset classes and is shown on the lower part of the Exhibit 5.8.

In this calculation we have allocated the $2,714 million among the intellectual property assets, and conclude that $1,462 million is allocable to trademarks. Please note that, in doing so, we have insured that the overall return for intellectual property of 18 percent is maintained, as well as the overall intellectual property value of $37,510 million.

Discounted Cash Flow Technique

The discounted cash flow model is a permutation of that described, but the enterprise income to be allocated is directly driven by the elements of an income statement (see Exhibit 5.10).

EXHIBIT 5.10   Discounted Cash Flow Technique

SMITH & RICHEY ENTERPRISES
Consolidated Statement of Earnings
($ millions)

Year ended December 31,	2012	%
Net Operating Revenues	$30,900	100.0
Cost of Goods Sold	14,500	46.9
Gross Profit	16,400	53.1
Selling, general and administrative expenses	9,000	29.1
Other operating charges	275	0.9
	9,275	30.0
Operating Income	7,125	23.1
Interest income	340	1.1
Interest expense	450	1.5
Other income — net	80	0.3
Income before income taxes	7,095	23.0
Income taxes	2,838	9.2
Net income	$ 4,257	13.8

EXHIBIT 5.10   (*Continued*)

Year ended December 31,	2012	%
CALCULATE NET CASH FLOW		
Add: Extraordinary items to normalize	0	(see Exhibit 5.7)
Add: Depreciation expense	900	(see Exhibit 5.9)
Subtract: Additions to Working Capital	180	(see Exhibit 5.9)
Subtract: Capital expenditures	600	(see Exhibit 5.9)
	$ 4,377	
LESS RETURNS REQUIRED ON OTHER ASSETS		
Net working capital	103	(see Exhibit 5.9)
Tangible assets	775	(see Exhibit 5.11)
Intangible assets	600	(see Exhibit 5.11)
	$ 1,478	
ALLOCABLE TO INTELLECTUAL PROPERTY	$ 2,899	

The advantage of this model is that what-if questions can be addressed relative to income or expense items that may vary, and their effect on income attributable to intellectual property can be immediately observed. In a following chapter, we will present another effective use of this model to estimate reasonable royalty rates.

In Exhibit 5.10, we have used rates of return that are current yields. We have done this for simplicity and to illustrate a technique, while recognizing that in some cases a growth component might be removed from such rates of return.

INDIRECT TECHNIQUES

Indirect techniques rely on the use of more subjective inputs in the use of surrogate models.

Relief-from-Royalty Technique

The relief-from-royalty technique is the most commonly used method for valuing trademarks. It is the most commonly used technique not because it is the best method but rather because it is the easiest. It is based on the concept that a company that owns a trademark does not have to license in a mark and therefore is relieved of the necessity of paying a royalty. The amount of that nonexistent payment is used as a surrogate for the income attributable to the owned trademark, and a calculation of the after-tax present value can proceed.

The royalty used in this type of calculation is best taken from the market—that is, from other licensing transactions. A less reliable technique is to use rules of thumb in the relevant industry, and there is nothing to prevent judgment being exercised if the subject property is sufficiently different from the available data.

We caution users of this technique that the relief-from-royalty income stream may represent only a portion of the economic benefit attributable to the asset being appraised. That is, one must be attentive to the license terms that give rise to a royalty rate taken from the "market." If those license terms transfer only a portion of the full rights of ownership (the licensor retains the right to exploit the intellectual property for itself), then the payment for those limited rights (royalty) may not be an adequate surrogate for the full economic benefits of ownership.

In an example from the world of real estate, assume that a building owner occupies one-half of the structure and leases the remainder to another. A capitalization of the rental income obviously would not be an appropriate indication of value for the entire building because the rental income is not representative of the income potential of the entire building. To be sure, the rental income from that tenant might be a very good indication of market rental rates (i.e., $ per square foot), but it is not

---

A VIEW FROM THE BENCH

This limitation of the method recently received judicial notice in a decision of the U.S. Second Circuit Court of Appeals in the matter of a U.S. Tax Court decision relating to Nestle Holdings, Inc. Experts for both the taxpayer and the IRS utilized the relief-from-royalty method in the valuation of trademarks. The Second Circuit, however, was not persuaded that the resulting values were appropriate, commenting:

> *In our view, the relief-from-royalty method necessarily undervalues trademarks. ... Royalty models are generally employed to estimate an infringer's profit from its misuse of a patent or trademark. ... However, use of a royalty model in the case of a sale is not appropriate because it is the fair market value of a trademark, not the cost of its use, that is at issue. A relief-from-royalty model fails to capture the value of all of the rights of ownership, such as the power to determine when and where a mark may be used, or moving a mark into or out of product lines. It does not even capture the economic benefit in excess of royalty payments that a licensee generally derives from using a mark. Ownership of a mark is more valuable than a license because ownership carries with it the power and incentive both to put the mark to its most valued use and to increase its value. A licensee cannot put the mark to uses beyond the temporal or other limitations of a license and has no reason to take steps to increase the value of a mark where the increased value will be realized by the owner. The Commissioner's view, therefore, fundamentally misunderstands the nature of trademarks and the reasons why the law provides for exclusive rights of ownership in a mark. Given the shortcomings of the relief-from-royalty methodology, the Tax Court erred when it adopted the Commissioner's trademark valuations. The Tax Court is instructed to examine alternate methods of determining the fair market value of the trademarks in question.[15]*

---

[15] *Nestle Holdings, Inc. v. C.I.R.*, 152 F.3d 83, 88 (2d Cir. 1998).

necessarily proper for valuation purposes if the objective is to appraise the entire building.

It is helpful, in the understanding of property rights and the role of the royalty, to examine the basic aspects of the licensing process. By means of a contract (license), the owner of intellectual property (licensor) rents some of the total bundle of rights to another (licensee). The licensee typically pays for those rights by means of a royalty. If we add the value of the licensor's rights to those of the licensee, we would capture all of the intellectual property value.

If we use an income approach to value intellectual property and wish to use a market royalty rate as a surrogate for the income attributable to the asset we must capitalize both the income realized from the licensor's exploitation of the mark, and the income attributable to the property from the licensee's exploitation. This latter is not necessarily the amount of royalty being paid by the licensee. The essential point is that we need to consider all of the potential income streams that may be associated with licensed intellectual property and understand which streams belong to whom (see Exhibit 5.11).

The value of all of the rights in the intellectual property would be obtained by capitalizing the income streams A and B. What is the income C that is the royalty payment? It is a portion of income B, and a capitalization of it would be representative of the value of the license contract to the licensor. If our task were to value the licensor's rights in the intellectual property, we would capitalize income streams A and C. If we were to value the licensee's rights in the intellectual property, we would capitalize income stream B less the royalty expense C. It is apparent that there is some overlap here, and one must carefully define the asset to be valued and also carefully define the income associated with that asset before proceeding.

The situation could be even more complicated if the trademark owner did not directly exploit it, but instead licensed it to others, with perhaps even master licensees

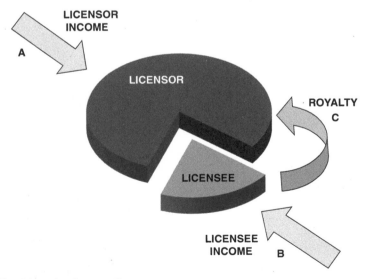

EXHIBIT 5.11   Licensing Income Streams

and sublicensees, as in the case of a franchise. There would be many income streams to consider, depending on the specific rights being valued.

Royalty rate information can be very useful to the financial analyst and the appraiser. As with any data from the marketplace or about comparable transactions, one must be sensitive to the terms of the transaction and to the nature of the property rights involved. With this, one is prepared to judge whether such information is an appropriate benchmark.

Russell Parr emphasizes the care with which this technique should be employed. His focus is on using royalty rates from the market in infringement analyses, but the very same caveats apply:

> *Indications of reasonable royalties can sometimes be derived from market transactions but extremely careful analysis is required. The amount at which independent parties licensed similar intellectual property can sometimes provide an indication for a reasonable royalty. ... Market transactions considered useful for deriving reasonable royalties are usually between unrelated parties where intellectual property is the focal point of the deal.*
>
> *Establishing reasonable royalties for calculating infringement damages is often accomplished by looking at the royalty terms specified in licenses involving similar intellectual property. Many aspects of the license agreement must be analyzed for the royalty provision to be a useful proxy. In a perfect world a useful proxy license for establishing infringement damages would:*
>
> 1. *not be an internal license between a parent corporation and a subsidiary;*
> 2. *have been negotiated at a date that is relevant to the date at which infringement damages are being fixed;*
> 3. *have been negotiated between two independent parties, neither of which were compelled to complete the transaction because of financial distress;*
> 4. *involve similar intellectual property licensed for use in the same industry in which the infringement took place;*
> 5. *transfer license rights for use of similar intellectual property into a country having similar economic conditions as the country in which infringement has occurred;*
> 6. *involve similar intellectual property with similar remaining life characteristics;*
> 7. *require similar complementary asset investment requirements for commercial exploitation;*
> 8. *specify royalty terms that are not clouded by non-monetary components of compensation;*
> 9. *include comparable aspects of exclusivity;*
> 10. *include royalty terms that were freely negotiated and unencumbered by governmental regulations;*
> 11. *specify royalty terms that are not clouded by undefined amounts that are indirectly attributed for technical assistance compensation;*
> 12. *involve unrelated parties that are truly independent, having negotiated the proxy royalty terms at arm's length.*

> *Many aspects of a license agreement must be analyzed before a license can be relied on as a proxy for establishing infringement damages. ... Utilizing the royalty terms of similar license agreements, involving similar intellectual property, as a proxy for infringement damages is a rational way to proceed but is extremely difficult to successfully implement.*[16]

If one has a royalty rate that is appropriately comparable for this purpose, Exhibit 5.12 shows how the calculation is made:

EXHIBIT 5.12 Relief from Royalty Income Stream

	1	2	3	4	5	TOTAL
S & R Enterprises						
Sales Revenue (millions)	30,900	31,200	33,500	34,600	36,000	166,200
Trademark Royalty Rate	8%	8%	8%	8%	8%	
Income Attributable to Trademark	2,472	2,496	2,680	2,768	2,880	13,296

SUMMARY

The foundation of trademark value is successful exploitation. The keystone of brand valuation is therefore a solid understanding of the range of exploitation possibilities. This information can only be gleaned by hands-on investigation. Armed with this information, we are prepared to quantify the future economic benefits of ownership. The essence of this task can be illustrated by a series of questions:

- What does this brand *now* do for its owner?
- What *could* this brand do for its owner?
- Does this brand enhance revenues?
- Does this brand reduce expenses?

The answers to these questions give the valuation a direction that leads us to the use of one or two of several available tools that can quantify the future economic benefits of ownership in terms of dollars.

---

[16] Russell L. Parr, *Intellectual Property Infringement Damages*, (Hoboken, NJ: John Wiley & Sons, Inc., 1993), 181.

CHAPTER 6

Income Method

Economic Life and Risk

Market value is equal to the present value of the future economic benefits of ownership. The income method specifically addresses this equation, and requires four inputs that describe the nature of future economic benefit:

1. Its *amount*
2. Its *duration*
3. The *pattern* of its receipt
4. The *risk* that the amount, duration, and pattern won't happen as we forecast

The previous chapter presented techniques with which we can estimate the amount of future economic benefit. This chapter discusses the remaining three inputs to the income method—the duration, pattern, and risk elements of future economic benefit. These add specific parameters to the estimated amount of future economic benefit.

Conventional wisdom holds that trademarks are timeless and eternal as the flag-bearers of brands that last forever. There seems to be ample evidence of that. Some of the best-known brands in the world today were also the best known decades ago. It is hard to imagine that there is a single living person (at least in the United States) that has not been aware of Heinz brand ketchup or Coca-Cola beverage since their earliest memory.

In spite of that, we must question this conventional wisdom because it is clear that even the best-recognized trademarks must be maintained continually by advertising and by being associated with a product or service that continues to find favor with the buying public. The life of a brand can end if it is so closely identified with a product or service that is rejected in the market place that it cannot be redeployed. A brand can be misused by unwise extension to inappropriate or poor-quality products and its value thereby degraded. There are, too, totally external factors that can spell the demise of a brand.

So we must recognize that brands are not impervious to market forces or other events that can strip them of their economic viability, however long their legal existence can be. Even their legal existence is limited by a "use it or lose it" requirement. These factors must be recognized in any valuation process and this chapter is devoted to a discussion of the market forces, events, and risks that can affect future economic benefit and, therefore, the market value of a trademark.

DEFINING ECONOMIC LIFE

If we are going to base our market value estimate, at least in part, on "economic life," we need to be clear about what we mean by that, and it may not be as obvious as it appears. Just as "value" is a term with many meanings, so is "life."

As an example, if we were asked to opine about the expected life of our automobile, how would we respond? One difficulty arises because our car is made up of many parts. How do we deal with the facts that the tires might last two years, while the brakes might not need replacing for five, and then there are the engine, lights, CD player, and so forth. We might answer the question based on our plan to trade in the car in six years, or when the odometer reads 150,000 miles. Or we might be planning to retire our worn-out car to the backyard and use it as a chicken coop, in which case it might last 20 years. We must decide what constitutes the end of life for our purposes.

The income method is based on *economic life,* which is the period during which it is profitable to use an asset. Economic life ends when it is either:

- No longer profitable to use an asset (the future economic benefits are used up)
- More profitable to use another asset.

This is quite different from the *service life* of an asset, which is the period from its installation (or beginning of use) to the date of its retirement (or the end of use), irrespective of its earning capability along the way. Service life has more meaning for tangible assets than for trademarks. It is, however, a common term used by valuation professionals. Others, such as accounting and tax authorities have expressed opinions on lives of property, including trademarks, for a number of purposes. Some knowledge of these helps to put our definition of economic life into perspective.

Legal or Legislated Lives

For years, schedules of suggested or required lives for the calculation of depreciation (capital recovery) have been a part of the U.S. Internal Revenue Code. These were once realistic estimates of typical economic life of various types of property and became part of tax legislation in order to reduce controversy between the government and taxpayers since depreciation is a tax deductible expense. Legislators soon realized, however, that changing these lives (and depreciation methods as well) was a relatively uncontroversial way to alter the effective tax rates of corporations and it came to be seen as a tool with which to manage a section of the economy. Property lives for tax depreciation, therefore, have been often changed and they now bear no resemblance to realistic economic lives of property.

Federal and state income tax codes in the United States treated trademarks similarly to goodwill, and did not permit their amortization.[1] On this basis, tax regulations assumed an effective economic life for trademarks in perpetuity. More recently, the Internal Revenue Code has been modified to suggest amortization of trademarks

---

[1] *Amortization* is the term used to describe capital recovery of intangible asset investment. *Depreciation* applies to capital recovery of tangible assets.

(as well as other intangible assets) over a period of 15 years. As with the accounting conventions, this is a legislated life, intended to eliminate what has been a long standing series of disputes between taxpayers and the Internal Revenue Service (IRS). We cannot take it as a true indication of economic life.

Financial Reporting Standards

In Chapter 3, we discussed the circumstances under which trademarks acquired as part of a business combination are subject to amortization for accounting purposes. Typically, the cost of developing and registering a trademark is treated as an expense, and so trademarks, as self-created assets, do not appear on a balance sheet. When they are acquired as part of a business combination, however, they might become classified as an asset and so appear.

When intangible assets are subject to amortization, the issue of *useful life* arises as the basis on which to calculate it:

Useful life is:

(a) the period over which an asset is expected to be available for use by an entity; or (b) the number of production or similar units expected to be obtained from the asset by an entity. . . .

An entity shall assess whether the useful life of an intangible asset is finite or indefinite and, if finite, the length of, or number of production or similar units constituting, that useful life. . . .

An intangible asset shall be regarded by the entity as having an indefinite useful life when, based on an analysis of all of the relevant factors, there is no foreseeable limit to the period over which the asset is expected to generate net cash inflows for the entity.[2]

So following an acquisition that includes trademarks, management must decide whether their useful life is finite or indefinite. If finite, the decision remains as to an appropriate useful life and the pattern of its decline:

The amortisation method used shall reflect the pattern in which the asset's future economic benefits are expected to be consumed by the entity. . . .

If that pattern cannot be determined reliably, the straight-line method shall be used.[3]

An accounting principle of a previous time contained a rather comprehensive list of factors to be considered in estimating an appropriate useful life:

- Legal, regulatory, or contractual provisions may limit the maximum useful life.
- Provisions for renewal or extension may alter a specified limit on useful life.
- Effects of obsolescence, demand, competition, and other economic factors may reduce a useful life.

---

[2] International Accounting Standards (IAS) 38 – Intangible Assets.
[3] Ibid.

- A useful life may parallel the service life expectancies of individuals or groups of employees.
- Expected actions of competitors and others may restrict present competitive advantages.
- An apparently unlimited useful life may in fact be indefinite and benefits cannot be reasonably projected.[4]

We must remember, however, that these pronouncements as to economic life of intangible assets (including trademarks) are accounting conventions. While their objective is to truly reflect the actual economic life of assets acquired, accounting practice is rooted in the dichotomy of recognizing intangibles as assets some of the time and not at others, and also in a basic conservatism. In our experience, accountants in the United States, under the watchful eye of the Securities and Exchange Commission (SEC), wish to get intangible assets off the balance sheet as soon as possible and to avoid the possibility of an apparent overstatement of earnings. On the other hand, corporate managers have an incentive to adopt long lives to keep amortization expense lower than otherwise, so reported earnings will be higher, though that incentive does not seem to be overpowering in the upcoming data shown.

We extracted from the RoyaltySource database of *purchase price allocations* (PPAs) the following selection of industries most active in *merger and acquisition* (M&A) activities recently. There are 547 acquisitions represented in this data. For each, we have shown the brand assets to which allocations were made and we can also observe the years of useful life assigned to the various asset classes. (see Exhibit 6.1).

We can observe several things from this exhibit. First, we note that the corporate managers responsible for the preparation of financial statements have used three descriptors for brand assets. This is probably due to some confusion about trademark assets as we discussed in Chapter 1. While there are some guidelines in financial reporting standards, corporate managements are free to select their own description of the assets acquired. We also observe that in the 13 acquisitions involving commercial banks, there was no allocation of purchase price to trademark assets. Undoubtedly, the acquired banks did have trademarks, but it is probably safe to assume that the acquiring organizations planned to combine the acquired banking organizations into their own. Under such a plan to abandon existing trademarks, none of the purchase price would be allocated to such assets.

We can also observe that the remaining useful lives, which will be used for calculating amortization, are often very short and far short of the legal life for such assets. Again, this is probably due to plans of the acquiring company to bring the acquired products or services into its own brand structure.

In only four acquisitions was an indefinite life assigned.

While compliance with financial reporting standards or tax regulations produces occasional data about trademark values and useful lives, we should be judicious about its use. As with other comparable data, we need to understand what it is, where it comes from, and the extent to which it may or may not be applicable to the facts and circumstances of our evaluation task.

---

[4] Accounting Principles Board, APB Opinion No. 17, "Intangible Assets" (1970).

EXHIBIT 6.1   Example of Useful Lives Assigned in Purchase Price Allocations

	TRADE NAME		BRAND NAME		TRADE MARK	
	Low	High	Low	High	Low	High
Computer Programming, Data Processing, And Other Computer Related Services	0.2	15.0	4.0	10.0	1.0	30.0
Miscellaneous Business Services	1.0	15.0			1.5	indef
Electronic Components And Accessories	3.5	8.0			3.0	10.0
Surgical, Medical, And Dental Instruments And Supplies	5.0	23.0	10.0	12.0	8.0	indef
Communications Equipment	3.7	indef			1.5	23.0
Laboratory Apparatus And Analytical, Optical, Measuring, and Controlling Instruments	1.0	20.0	8.0	8.0	10.0	10.0
Management And Public Relations Services	5.0	10.0	10.0	10.0	1.0	indef
Drugs	10.0	37.0			5.0	20.0
Computer And Office Equipment	2.5	4.5	5.0	5.0	4.9	16.0
Commercial Banks (NO ALLOCATIONS TO TMs)						
AVERAGE Excluding "indef"	3.5	16.6	7.4	9.0	4.0	18.2

Legal/Contractual Life

The economic life of tangible assets is commonly not affected by legal or contract terms. These assets belong to the business and remain in place for as long as management decides. However, many intangible assets as well as intellectual property do have a recognized legal or contractual life. These include:

- Patents
- Copyrights
- Trademarks (to the extent of renewal terms and acts necessary to retain their rights)
- Leases
- Supply or distribution contracts
- Subscriptions
- Mortgages, or other loan agreements
- License agreements
- Franchise agreements

Indefinite Economic Life

Most intangible assets and intellectual property have an economic life undefined by law or contractual terms. Therefore, these assets first must be analyzed in order to determine whether legal or contract terms will be controlling with respect to their remaining economic life. In many cases, economic life is shorter than legal life. The effectiveness of a patent may be ended before its 20-year legal life. An unexpired patent may be made obsolete by advancing technology or because the product in which it was used has lost its place in the market. It is not at all uncommon in the semiconductor industry for innovations to be held as trade secrets rather than patented technology. The reason is that innovations become obsolete before a patent could be issued and to incur the expense of patent prosecution makes no sense.

Alternatively, the economic life of a magazine subscription or consumer loan contract may be longer than its (legal) contract life if there is a history of renewals. In our experience, most often the legal or contractual life is not controlling with respect to the economic life of intangible assets and intellectual property. The economic life of these assets depends on their response to a host of outside forces that must be measured by their overall influence or by analyzing the individual forces.

TRADEMARK ECONOMIC LIFE AND PATTERN

In the previous chapter, we discussed the quantification of the *amount* of economic benefit ingredient in the income method for valuation. The *duration* of economic benefit and the *pattern* by which it will be received are important parameters and have a substantial effect on a present value calculation. Present value is discussed at length in Appendix A. The longer the duration of future economic benefit the higher will be the value of the underlying asset. When the economic benefit is received sooner rather than later, that pattern also results in a higher value.

Because the duration and pattern are so closely related, our subsequent discussion will combine these two parameters.

Perpetuity Hypothesis

One way to approach the analysis of duration and pattern is to adopt the hypothesis that the subject brand will produce economic benefits in perpetuity. This assumes that everything proper will be done to maintain legal trademark rights and that the underlying product or service brand attributes will continue to be successful in the marketplace for as far as the eye can see.

The next step is to analyze the facts and circumstances in order to test whether they support that hypothesis. This way of thinking forces us to identify conditions that might shorten economic life or change its pattern and guides us to ask the proper questions, such as:

- Where in the underlying product life cycle are we?
- Where along the spectrum from commodity-like brands to consumer/entertainment are we?
- Is this an umbrella brand or a specific product/service brand?
- What is the size and nature of the competition?
- What has been the historical behavior of the brand?
- How versatile is the brand?
- Is the brand being supported sufficiently?

Look to the End-User

We have found, in this analysis, that it is very useful to direct some attention to the end user of the product or service that a brand represents. We say this because it is sometimes easy to become fixated on a product itself and its brand attributes to the exclusion of the needs and wants of the marketplace. As an example, "this is the best quality laundry soap bar on the planet, it is fragrant, extremely effective, it is priced very competitively and it has been around for years." With those attributes this brand ought to last forever. But what if households are beginning to switch to laundry soap in powdered form and competitors are beginning to experiment with liquids?

Looking through to the final ultimate user of a product or service can help us gain some understanding of the factors that could affect the length or shape of its remaining economic life.

This concept of looking through to the end-user is also helpful when estimating the future economic benefit. Why is the end-user buying? We might think that the buyer of a celebrity-brand shirt is purchasing for the "feel-good prestige" of the prominent trademark, when actually it is the tailoring and the pearl buttons!

Functional Obsolescence

This refers to the degree to which an asset can perform its intended functions vis-à-vis another newer, perhaps technologically superior asset.

Trademarks themselves do not suffer from functional obsolescence due to advancing technology, but perhaps they do from form or style. The passage of time can produce this type of functional obsolescence in a trademark. Trademark owners are continually updating their look, using different typefaces, and restyled logos. The essence of the mark stays the same; it is only freshened to reflect changing styles. As a

---

COLOR FILM

Kodak's "Kodachrome" color film was introduced in 1935 and became the "gold standard" in its rendition of color and sharpness. However, Kodak ceased production of Kodachrome after over 70 years of building this well-known brand. It is likely that photographers using Kodachrome film maintained their loyalty and appreciation of its attributes right up to the day that Kodak announced that it would be discontinued. In fact, we know photographers who refrigerated all that they could buy of Kodachrome film in order to continue to enjoy its quality. In the few years before its demise, if we had spoken to satisfied Kodachrome photographers they would probably not have told us that they expected its imminent demise. We would have had to observe the totality of the photographic market place in order to see the threat of the oncoming digital age. This illustrates the importance of looking through to the end-user marketplace when we are estimating economic remaining life.

business adds brands to a family, or repositions brands or product lines, trademarks may be restyled to create, retain or strengthen a "family" look

In Chapter 5 we mentioned Betty Crocker and the many brands marketed under her umbrella image. We can observe that there have been many changes to that image over the years to update her appearance. We can also observe the same freshening of a mark such as Kodak's primary logo.

1936   1955   1965   1968

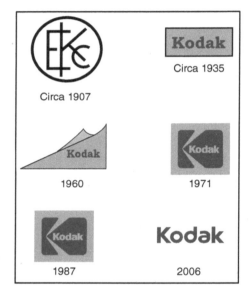

Secondary Turnover   In Chapter 5 we discussed the relationship between a parent brand, such as General Motors, one of its secondary brands, Buick automobiles, and Enclave for a particular model in the Buick line. We have observed that slogans, words, or symbols that are used subordinately to a primary trademark tend to have finite lives. It seems to us a logical assumption that the lifespan of a subordinate brand would be shorter than that of the parent because there are far more life—influencing factors at the specific product level than there are at the overall corporate level.

Economic Obsolescence

Economic obsolescence reflects the effect on market value of factors outside of the brand itself. Property devoted to business use achieves full market value only when it is capable of contributing to the earnings of that business and when those earnings provide a reasonable rate of return on all business assets. So the market value of a brand is dependent to some degree on factors that arise entirely outside of its own particular circumstances. The market value of an asset can be significantly degraded by the economics of the business to which it is devoted. The extent to which it is degraded depends on the type of asset.

Unique assets (such as intangible assets and intellectual property) may suffer considerably because they have little use outside of the particular business. Other assets that have general use may only suffer in value to the extent of the costs that would be incurred to remove them from the business and transport and install them in a new business and location for use in a more profitable industry.

For example, assume the existence of a restaurant under three different scenarios. The restaurant has been in operation at the same location for 20 years. The three scenarios are:

1. The owner is doing well in the business but desires to sell the enterprise because he wants to retire. Result: The owner is selling a going business with earnings that are adequate to justify an investment by a purchaser equal to the current market value of the land and building plus the value of the trademark and other intangible assets. The market value of the enterprise assets might be $800,000.
2. The owner is making very little in this business and wants to liquidate in order to invest the proceeds elsewhere. Result: The owner is offering a marginal business. A potential buyer may be one who feels that he or she could be successful by more efficient operation, or one who will convert the location to another type of operation. In this case, the buyer is interested in the physical property and will not consider any intangible assets such as the trademark to have significant value. Such a buyer might also reduce the offering price by the cost to convert to a new restaurant concept. The market value might be $500,000.
3. The owner is losing money and the location is no longer suitable for restaurant operation. Result: The owner will have to offer the location to an alternate user. The price would likely equal the market value of the land plus any value that might exist in the building for other uses. In an extreme case, the building might have no value, or the value of the deal might be reduced by the cost of removing the improvements in order to clear the land for other use. The value of the trademark and other intangible assets would be zero. The market value of the asset package might be $250,000.

The difference between these three scenarios is the earning power of the assets being offered for sale. The physical depreciation and functional obsolescence present in the fixed assets is the same in each case. Economic obsolescence is the determinate of value. If business property is incapable of earning a reasonable return on an investment at its presumed fair market value in continued use, then the fair market value will be based, at least in part, on a liquidation premise. Under this assumption, intangible assets may have little, if any, value. Thus, we are continually reminded that the fair market value of a business and individual assets within that business are dependent on their earning power. There is an indestructible link between the fair market value of business property and its earning power.

The Kodachrome example is also an illustration of economic obsolescence. Up until the day it was discontinued, Kodachrome continued to fulfill its "brand

AN ECONOMIC ROLLERCOASTER

"Snapple" iced tea was introduced in the late 1980s by Unadulterated Food Products, Inc., founded in 1972 by three friends in Brooklyn, NY. It is probably a good thing that the founders did not assign the original company name to their products. Snapple sales rose to $674 million by 1994 and the company was acquired by Quaker Oats Co. for $1.7 billion. The brand did not fare particularly well as part of Quaker Oats's beverage brands, however, and Snapple was sold to Triarc in 1997 for $309 million. The brand was subsequently sold again and is now one of the 50 brands of the Dr. Pepper Snapple Group Inc.[5]

An interesting ride for this popular beverage brand.

promise". The trademark and its brand attributes were all in place and in good condition. The brand was overcome by a technological tsunami about which nothing could be done. Any economic rescue had to be undertaken at a level higher than that of an individual product.

With this background, we can examine the factors that lead to economic obsolescence in trademarks or brands. By understanding these factors we equip ourselves to estimate their economic life. We are not attempting to invent new forms of obsolescence. These are simply a ready means of identifying some of its causes. We view these as subsets of economic obsolescence as it has been previously defined.

Event Obsolescence

We use this term to describe potential life-shortening events that can cause trademark value reductions caused by business transactions or events that are outside the course of normal trademark life activities.

Product Quality The product-tampering episode involving "Tylenol," the popular acetaminophen pain reliever, could have been a life-threatening event for that trademark had Johnson & Johnson management not reacted in timely and effective fashion.

Mergers & Insolvency The bankruptcies of Macy's and Western Union might have severely "dented" or even ended the economic lives of those venerable trademarks, but they proceeded fairly rapidly and caused no appreciable damage. The specific effects of bankruptcy are discussed in Chapter 10.

Not every merger goes well. Not every acquirer of a business considers the value of its underlying assets (including trademarks) to be the same as their former owner. Tangible assets, intangibles, and brands are sometimes sold off after an acquisition

---

[5] Stephen Miller, "Snapple Guy's Overnight Success Took Decades," *Wall Street Journal*, May 23, 2013, B1. See also http://www.drpeppersnapplegroup.com/brands/.

to help pay down debt. They do not always find a good home. At times, brands that are not in the new company's mainstream are allowed to languish. Some brands may simply disappear in the merger process.

American Machine & Foundry Co. was founded in 1900. In the merger-mad 1960s, it joined the fray and acquired several recreation and leisure equipment companies such as Alcort, Inc. (sailboats), Head Ski Co., Inc., and the Marine Division of North American Rockwell Corp. Harley-Davidson, the makers of iconic American motorcycles, was acquired in 1969. The American Machine & Foundry Co. name was changed to AMF Incorporated in 1970. Diverse and acquisitive, AMF probably did not give Harley-Davidson the attention it needed at the time, the business cultures of Milwaukee, where Harley-Davidson was based, and AMF in New York did not merge as smoothly as the two legal entities did and AMF concentrated on bringing its mass production skills to Harley-Davidson.

The overall result was that Harley-Davidson motorcycles suffered in the marketplace from the double effect of poor quality and Japanese competition. Its trademarks suffered as they would be expected to from those pressures, and, in addition, counterfeiters and knock-off artists enjoyed the corporate inattention. As then-CFO Timothy K. Hoelter described it, "There was a very strong risk back then that the Harley-Davidson trademark would go the way of Escalator and Aspirin because it was being used by unauthorized people with abandon."[6]

In 1981, AMF sold Harley-Davidson to its management and the company embarked on a program to improve quality, rejuvenate its image, and to enforce its trademarks. Sales grew to $1.2 billion by 1994, with sales of 92 thousand units. In 2012, sales were $4.9 billion on 248 thousand units, of which 87 thousand were overseas. This is a real success story in brand rescue. But there is also the story of brand deterioration behind it. It *can* happen.

Generic*ness* If a trademark is judged to have become part of everyday language, its legal protection can be lost if challenged. This is discussed in more detail in Chapter 1. It is a threat that is not such a remote possibility. Every trademark owner strives to have his or her brand on the lips of everyone in the relevant market. The more successful these efforts are, the greater is the likelihood of the brand tipping over into common usage. We offer several cases in point:

- In *Firefly Digital Inc. v. Google Inc.* the court held that "Gadget" and "Website Gadget," both Firefly trademarks, are generic. The court considered several factors in its genericness analysis, including: "uncontested generic use by competitors, generic use by the plaintiff, dictionary definitions, media usage, testimony of persons in the trade and consumer surveys."[7]
- In *Miller's Ale House, Inc. v. Boynton Carolina Ale House, LLC* the court reaffirmed that "Ale House" is generic and held that because the plaintiff knew of the term's genericness, it was liable for attorney's fees for filing an infringement claim.[8]

---

[6] *Corporate Legal Times* 6, no. 51 (February 1996). Hoelter was referring to the possibility of the Harley-Davidson trademarks becoming generic.

[7] *Firefly Digital Inc. v. Google Inc.*, CIV.A. 10-0133, 2011 WL 4454909 (W.D. La. Sept. 23, 2011).

[8] *Miller's Ale House, Inc. v. Boynton Carolina Ale House, LLC*, 09-80918-CIV, 2011 WL 855276 (S.D. Fla. Mar. 9, 2011).

■ In *Hershey Co. v. Promotion in Motion, Inc.* Hershey Co. was fortunate in that the court held that Hershey's "Kisses" trademark survives a genericness analysis. The court considered numerous factors, including public opinion surveys, licensing, and private labeling, but made its decision primarily based on the public perception revealed in the surveys.[9]

Technological/Product Obsolescence

We read that chip manufacturers now have several generations of integrated circuits under development simultaneously, in order to shorten their time to market. The computer we are working on therefore becomes obsolete by the minute. What of the trademarks that go with these technologically decaying products? It all depends on what we mean by "go with." As with genericness, the brand owner faces a two-edged sword. After striving to have a trademark inextricably linked with a particular product or service so that its purchase is a mindless affair, the owner can only watch helplessly as the trademark goes to oblivion with the technologically obsolete product. Of course some trademarks are associated with products or services that can gracefully slide from technology to technology and they do the same. Some trademarks are positioned so that they can even move across rather wide technology gaps, and these are the ones that seem to live on and on. The IBM trademark has successfully bridged the technology gap from punched card processing to mainframes to services. Fifteen years ago, when the first edition of this book was written, we wondered how the "ThinkPad" laptop computer brand (then IBM's) would fare, being so closely associated with a high-tech, fast-moving product. "Its product focus is narrower" we noted then, "and perhaps notebook computers will evolve into hand-held devices into which we speak and that trademark will no longer be appropriate and will not be able to bridge this gap. Time will tell." As it happens, IBM sold its laptop product line to Lenovo, and Lenovo opted to continue the ThinkPad brand, linking it with its own.

Closely linking brand to product does not necessarily mandate a shorter economic life for the brand. In some cases the effect is just the opposite as illustrated by the example on the next page.

The Gore-Tex example situation is not unlike Intel Corp.'s "Intel Inside" trademark that we see on our personal computers. It alerts us to a brand that would otherwise be buried unknown inside the device. Presumably, if we are happy with the device, Intel Corp. enjoys some enhancement to its own brand.

Pfizer Inc. is a manufacturer of the cholesterol fighter Lipitor which was the top-selling drug of all time. Lipitor is effective and it built a very strong brand reputation during its period of patent protection. Pfizer's strategy now is to continue to sell Lipitor as a prescription as well as over-the-counter pharmaceutical, using the brand's reputation to soften what is often an abrupt drop in sales following the expiration of the patent.

---

[9] *Hershey Co. v. Promotion in Motion, Inc.*, CIV.A. 07-1601 SDW, 2011 WL 5508481 (D.N.J. Nov. 7, 2011).

TECHNOLOGY/TRADEMARK SYMBIOSIS

In 1958, Wilbur Lee Gore and his wife founded a company in order to develop a process for insulating electric wires. About 10 years later, his son, then working for the company, perfected the means to manufacture a waterproof, breathable plastic fabric. They called it "Gore-Tex." Its first application was as a wound dressing. Sometime after that, this fabric came to the notice of apparel manufacturers. They discovered that, for waterproof outerwear, the material had the unique property of shedding water while allowing the garment to breathe. These garments were much more comfortable than the impermeable rainwear then available.

Gore's company, W. L. Gore and Associates, Inc., is still in existence manufacturing Gore-Tex. Its underlying patent protection has long ago expired and there are competitive films on the market. Mr. Gore, however, was an astute businessman. When he agreed to sell his Gore-Tex film to apparel manufacturers, he required them to notify retail purchasers that the garment included Gore-Tex. This was done by means of a "hang-tag" on each garment. In doing so, the buying public became aware of this new material that otherwise would have been hidden and unknown inside a jacket or coat. We became educated to look for Gore-Tex products because they were effective. The Gore-Tex brand extended the economic life of the manufactured product far beyond what it otherwise would have been.

Exhibit 6.2 illustrates graphically this concept of employing a combination of IP to extend the economic life of a market position.

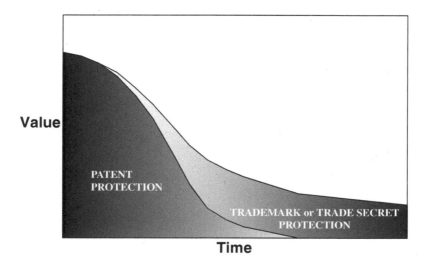

EXHIBIT 6.2   Technology/Trademark Life Extension

Cultural Obsolescence

Several years ago a controversy arose over the sale of "Crazy Horse" malt liquor in several states. A leader of the Oglala Sioux, the historical Crazy Horse was opposed to drinking alcohol, and his descendants protested the use of this trademark on beer. This is one of many such controversies over the use of Native American images and names as trademarks. It is an example of our increasing sensitivity to points of view as well as religious, ethnic, and gender-related issues. Trademarks must be catchy, trendy, bright, arresting, attractive, and versatile, yet politically neutral. This is not always easy.

Then too, there are environmental and health issues to contend with. Labeling a can of paint as produced by the Acme Lead Company would not be a good idea, no matter how safe the contents. We don't wear watches with "radium dials" anymore, either, even though the necessary fluorescence may not have been produced by radium anyway. Does the fact that "Marlboro" cigarettes now have to display the Surgeon General's health warning diminish the power of that trademark?

Today, a trademark *must* have internationality. That is, it must be at home in all the world's languages because the markets are without national boundaries. It must also be in tune with the world's cultures and customs or, at least. not be in conflict with them. Last year, Qiodan Sports Co. of Beijing was sued by Michael Jordon, celebrity and basketball star for using his name in marketing. The basis: the company's name "Qiodan" is pronounced "cheow-DAN" in Mandarin. Mr. Jordan felt that was too close to his name, and the issue was further complicated by Qiodan's logo having some similarity to Mr. Jordan's "Jumpman" logo.[10]

Language presents an ever present problem in the world of brands. Worldwide IKEA uses Swedish names for many of its products. It discovered that some of these, when pronounced by Thai employees in its Bangkok store, sounded like rude Thai words. A bit of training ensued to solve the problem.[11]

When a trademark has some characteristic that is counter to our changing cultural mores, or becomes caught in a controversy, its life may be in danger. If the owner cannot modify it to ameliorate its undesirable characteristics, or if the product or service with which it is inextricably identified simply "has to go," then it may have to be abandoned.

Forecasting

All valuations are forward looking. We are interested in the past only when we conclude that some past behavior or performance is indicative of the future. Otherwise our focus is entirely ahead. Valuations are also made as of a specific point in time, so presumably at that moment we are standing somewhere between the time when the brand started and the time of its demise.

---

[10] Laurie Burkitt, "In China, Air cheow-DAN Cries Foul," *Wall Street Journal*, February 24, 2012, B4.

[11] James Hookway, "IKEA's Product Names Make Shoppers Blush in Thailand," *Wall Street Journal*, June 5, 2012, A1.

However, simply knowing the age of an asset and making a forecast of how long that asset will continue to exist is not enough information to calculate its value. Expanding on our previous example about our automobile, let us assume that our car is three years old and that we expect to continue using it for five years. That information is not sufficient for us to estimate its current value. When the car was new it could dependably do anything that we asked of it. As our car approaches its eighth year it will no doubt be less dependable and perhaps functionally impaired because a window cannot be opened or the air-conditioning does not work properly. So the amount of service that our car can provide does not necessarily change in lockstep with the passage of time. For valuation purposes we are more interested in the quantity and quality of the service that the car can provide or, in the case of a brand, the amount of economic benefit that it can produce. We can illustrate this concept in Exhibit 6.3.

In Exhibit 6.3, the dotted line represents the point at which we are making a valuation. Let us assume that the age of the subject asset is three years and the expected remaining life is five years. The future economic benefit to be provided by the asset is represented by the area under the curve to the right of the valuation point. The economic benefit that the asset has produced prior to our valuation is represented by the area under the curve to the left of the measurement point. In this diagram, these two areas appear to be about equal. So we would conclude that this asset is at midlife in terms of the total economic benefit it can provide. Yet chronologically it has lived only three-eighths of its life.

This illustration also indicates that we expect the future decline to occur on a "straight-line" path. Actual facts and circumstances are rarely this regular. More common patterns of economic life decline are shown in Exhibit 6.4(A), (B), and (C).

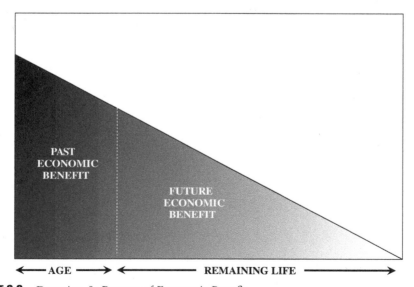

EXHIBIT 6.3 Duration & Pattern of Economic Benefit

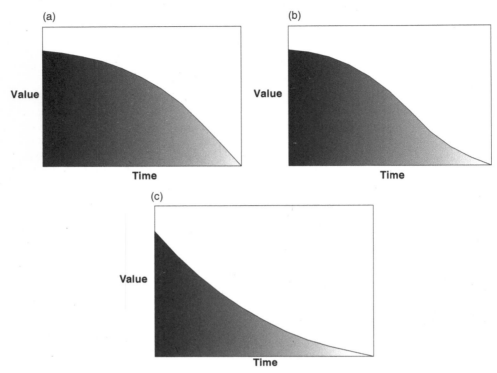

EXHIBIT 6.4   Typical Economic Life Patterns

These economic life patterns are typical for assets that begin their life at 100 percent value. As an example, a printing press, once it is installed and run in, is at its highest value and that value will only decline.[12] The pattern shown in Exhibit 6.4(A) is typical for a tangible asset whose economic life is primarily controlled by physical deterioration. The pattern shown in (B) is typical for the same type of asset, when the effects of functional and economic obsolescence are felt later in its life. The pattern shown in (C) is often exhibited by intangible assets, such as customer relationships, mortgage accounts, or an assembled workforce, where there is some degree of "infant mortality."

When we appraise these types of assets we are only dealing with the decline side of economic life. Because of their nature, when we come upon tangible and intangible assets of these types, we know that the market value is not at all likely to increase. Therefore, we are focused on the expected shape of their value decline.

SURVIVOR CURVES AND STUDIES OF HISTORICAL LIFE

In 1935, what was then the Iowa Engineering Experiment Station of Iowa State University published Bulletin 125, *Statistical Analysis of Industrial Property Retirements*.

---

[12] A tangible asset can, in rare cases, increase in market value due to scarcity.

This bulletin is regarded by many as the seminal work in this field. In the 1967 edition, Professor Harold A. Cowles wrote:

> *By observation and classification of the ages at death of hundreds of thousands of people, actuaries have built up mortality tables by which the average life of humans and the expectancy of life at any age can be determined accurately. Similarly, engineers and industrial statisticians have assembled the life histories and ages at retirement of many types of industrial property units from which they are enabled to forecast the probable lives of similar units still remaining in service. The estimate of life expectancy for a single unit or a small group of units may be in considerable error. However, the probability of error is reduced when the service conditions of the property are taken into consideration and evaluated by engineers of expert judgment in these matters, the estimate being revised from time to time as the life history of the property unfolds.*[13]

One of the results of that analysis has been to provide a number of techniques that can be utilized in the determination of the economic life of assets. This is also true for estimating the economic life of certain types of intellectual property. All of these techniques have a common basis, however:

> *The estimation of expected remaining service lives of industrial property has always been and will continue to be based upon the considered judgment of the engineer or the technically competent estimator. Judgment is exercised through a consideration of what is known about the past and the present life characteristics, and how they will be influenced by expected future conditions. It is significant to note that the starting point of the estimation is knowledge of past experience.*[14]

Retirement data for a group of property units are analyzed in order to develop a survivor curve that graphically depicts the duration and pattern of the group's life expectancy. The ordinate to the curve indicates the percentage (or number) of the original group surviving. The abscissa indicates the passage of time. Exhibit 6.5 shows a typical survivor curve.

The survivor curve itself is a reverse S-shape. In this case, it illustrates that, for a group of units, retirements are few at the beginning of life. As age increases, retirements become more frequent (the curve slopes more steeply). Toward the end of life, retirements are again less frequent. If one were to plot the frequency of retirements, a bell-shaped curve would result.

The total area under the curve represents the amount of service that would be rendered by the entire group of property units during its life.

The average service life is the area under the curve divided by 100 percent, expressed in percent years. In Exhibit 6.4, this is the distance A, or 10 years, for the group at age zero. The horizontal distance between the survivor and remaining life curves is the remaining life (shown as distance C).

---

[13] Winfrey Robley, *Statistical Analysis of Industrial Property Retirements* (Ames, IA: Engineering Research Institute, Iowa State University, 1967), 1.

[14] Ibid., 2.

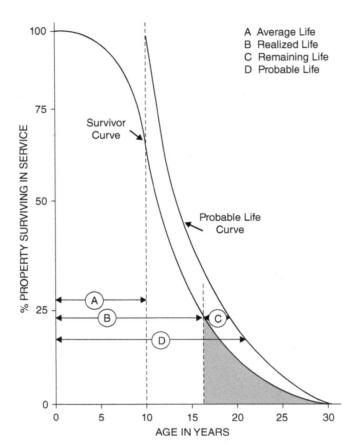

EXHIBIT 6.5 Typical Survivor Curve

Source: John Wiley & Sons, Inc. Reprinted with permission.

For a group of property units with an age of 16 years (shown at the distance B), the remaining service is represented by the shaded area.

The survivor curve represents both the duration and pattern of service life for a group of property units. It is derived from detailed historical retirement and survival data of the group of units being analyzed. It is important to note that while we study survival patterns as a function of age, age alone is not the cause of retirement. Age is simply the scale by which we measure the effects of retirement forces that can be as divergent as wear and tear, customer dissatisfaction, or changing business requirements.

Even though this discussion centers upon tangible assets and certain types of intangible property, it is not irrelevant to our discussion of intellectual property and, in particular, brands.[15] We should remember that a brand represents the trademark

---

[15] For a more complete discussion of survivor curve methods and derivation, reference is available in Gordon V. Smith and Russell L. Parr, *Valuation of Intellectual Property and Intangible Assets,* 3rd ed. (New York: John Wiley & Sons, Inc.), 214–219.

and attributes of a particular product or service. Brands that are tightly connected to a product or service may well behave in a similar fashion to tangible assets and physical products. That is, if we observe that the sales of such a product or service are in decline, the future pattern of that decline might well be similar to survivor curves of tangible assets.

There are also situations in which our analysis convinces us that the subject brand is fully mature and that there are conditions on the horizon that will contribute to its decline. In that situation, then, studies of asset survival could be useful.

Survivor Curves and Brands

Intellectual property by itself is, however, quite a different situation. Intellectual property rights often begin life at negligible value, not "full value". This is especially true of brands as we have discussed and illustrated in previous chapters. Intellectual property rights constitute or at least support products and services that live or die according to the vagaries of the market place which can take us in an upward direction. For this reason, we cannot simply focus on the decline side of the economic life pattern; we must consider the growth side as well.

FORECASTING GROWTH

Future economic benefit is represented by debt-free net cash flow that can be reasonably expected to result from brand exploitation. That is the income stream that can be capitalized to indicate the present value of future economic benefit, or market value. In order to arrive at the debt-free net cash flow "bottom line" we need to start at the sales revenue "top line" and reflect expenses in between. Most of us are better at forecasting expenses than we are at forecasting sales revenue. This is probably because we are more likely to understand the components of expense (human effort, capital expenditures, and financing costs) than we are to understand the workings of the "market" from which sales revenue will ultimately come.

We are therefore going to focus on the forecasting of sales revenue. Therefore, the methods and techniques we are about to discuss should be interpreted as applying to the derivation of sales revenue.

Direct Estimates

In this situation, we consider all of the facts that we can discover that might affect the subject brand during its economic future, and reflect that consideration either in the form of specific sales estimates for future periods or some overall growth pattern. This approach could also be called an expert consensus methodology, where there is only one expert. A more sophisticated version of this approach would be to aggregate the results of educated guesses by other experts in the relevant field.

While this technique could result in discrete estimates for each year, it is common to express opinions about sales forecasts in terms of a growth rate, or more mathematically, a *compound annual growth rate* (CAGR). This calculation requires a beginning value that is multiplied by (1 + rate), as is each year's amount that follows. This is illustrated in Exhibit 6.6.

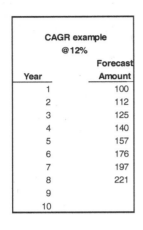

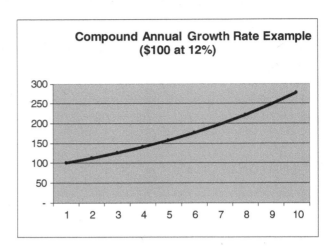

EXHIBIT 6.6   Compound Annual Growth Rate Example

The annual growth rate can be changed during the series if the expected future conditions warrant it (i.e., annual growth rate low for the first three years, higher for the next eight years, and then low again for subsequent years). This not too common in our experience, but it can be done (see Exhibit 6.7).

Extrapolation of Historical Data

A very commonly used forecasting method is to extrapolate patterns of historical growth. The more information about historical growth that is available, the better

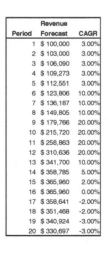

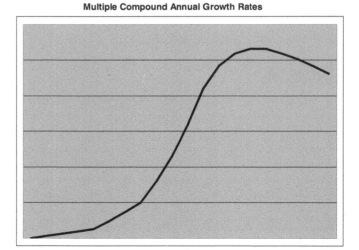

EXHIBIT 6.7   Varying Compound Annual Growth Rate Example

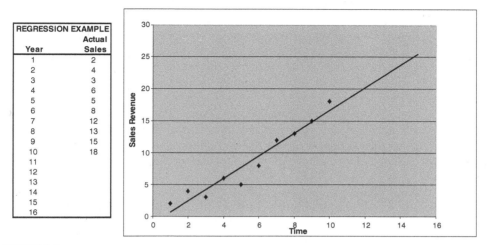

REGRESSION EXAMPLE	
Year	Actual Sales
1	2
2	4
3	3
4	6
5	5
6	8
7	12
8	13
9	15
10	18
11	
12	
13	
14	
15	
16	

EXHIBIT 6.8   Example Extrapolation of Historical Data Using Linear Regression

the forecast is likely to be. As an example, financial analysts attempting to forecast the growth of indexes reflecting the movement of the United States stock market have available many years of historical growth patterns to observe. A more difficult prediction would be the behavior of the stock market during periods of official recession because historical data would be in segments separated by years.

This hindrance often arises in the valuation of intellectual property in that actual historical data is difficult to come by and may lack comparability to the forecasting problem. In many cases, in fact, there is no historical data to utilize as a guideline because the subject intellectual property has no history and is unlike anything that has come before.

When historical data is available, however, extrapolating it can be a strong forecasting tool. Fortunately, for our purposes, the necessity for appraising a brand-new trademark is rare so most often there is at least some history of brand sales data with which to work. There are many methods available for this analysis and extrapolation. One of the least complex is some form of regression analysis in which a line, mathematically judged to be the "best fit" is drawn through the actual data and extended. An example of this is shown in Exhibit 6.8.

In this very simple example, the line drawn through the actual data has been mathematically judged to be the best representation of it. Its extension beyond the actual data points represents a forecast of the future for this data set. If we consider this data set to be comparable to our subject, then we can utilize the slope of the line to forecast from our subject's starting point. There are a number of sources from which readers can expand their knowledge of techniques to analyze and extrapolate historical data.[16]

---

[16] See, for example, Spyros G. Makridakis, *Forecasting Methods and Applications*, 3rd ed. (New York: John Wiley & Sons, Inc., 1998).

Surrogate Data

The use of surrogate growth patterns takes some elements from the extrapolation discussion just mentioned and the upcoming model discussion. This technique begins with research to discover historical growth patterns of brands that we judge to be comparable to our subject. If, as an example, we are trying to forecast future sales revenue for a recently—introduced tablet computer, we would certainly gather data about the past sales of the several tablet computers that have been in the marketplace. To be usable, the surrogate growth data needs to be matched against some mathematical expression, such as a *compound annual growth rate* (CAGR) or index number calculation, that can be applied to the estimated starting point of the subject brand sales.

As with any reliance on the historical data, we need to be confident that there are no unusual circumstances reflected in the historical data. As an example, we might be guarded about using historical data for the very first tablet computer introduced to the market. Sales data for subsequent market entrants might be more suitable for our purposes.

Model Growth Patterns

Models can take a variety of forms, but they all attempt to emulate conditions from the real world and actual data. Since our focus is the forecasting of sales revenue, we are led to the S-shape, or sigmoidal, family of curves. These curves, a sample of which is shown as Exhibit 6.9, graphically represent the typical stages in the life of a product.

Product life cycle theory assumes that the diffusion of a product into the economy follows a pattern containing four stages: (1) introduction, (2) growth, (3) maturity, and (4) decline.

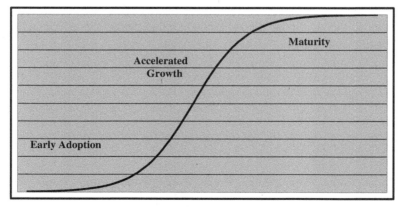

EXHIBIT 6.9   Classic Growth Pattern

S-CURVES IN GENERAL

These curves are not just applicable when one must start with zero, as in the case of embryonic technology.[17] If a brand is in the early stage of commercialization, where there is some sales data—that data can be matched against curve points—and the best-fit curve selected. That curve can then be used to forecast the ensuing growth.

The use of s-curves is a viable alternative to forecasting on the basis of a CAGR or straight-line extrapolation because of the evidence that the s-curve shape most often fits the growth pattern of the real world.

The time period over which this pattern is completed varies significantly by industry and product. Its span can be as little as months or as long as a decade. During the introductory stage, sales volume is usually low, and the product or service is highly priced. Consumers are not well informed as to the benefits associated with a new product, and a process of education is required. Once proven, the product or service gains acceptance, and more sales volume is generated. Manufacturing techniques can be improved as economies of scale from larger production volumes are achieved. These cost reductions can allow a lower selling price that helps to further expand the market. If the product is patented (e.g., the pharmaceutical industry), above-average profits can be protected from the encroachment of competitors. Without patent protection, pricing pressure during the growth stage may deteriorate the above-average profit margins that are enjoyed during the introductory stages. At maturity, the overall market for the product or service is well established, and further penetration by the industry producers is slow. Pricing pressures may become significant. Decline can begin as advances in technology introduce new product and service offerings that erode the demand for the established product. Pricing pressure and reduced demand for the product can cause the product or service to assume the characteristics of a commodity.

From this understanding of the classic S-curve shape of technology development, we learn that there are permutations of this curve type that have been developed from actual observations. These can be a basis on which to make forecasts, if we combine their use with the knowledge we accumulated in the fact-finding stage. The following sections discuss these type S-curves and their characteristics.

Gompertz Model

The Gompertz model is often referred to as a mortality model because its creator, Benjamin Gompertz, an English demographer, developed the curve after studying the mortality rate of a human population. In his analysis, he observed that the mortality rate of a population grew exponentially as the age of the population increased. The Gompertz model is defined by the equation shown in Exhibit 6.10.

The lateral position of the Gompertz curve can be adjusted by changing the value a (location coefficient), and the shape can be adjusted by varying s (market shape factor). For low values of s, the curve rises gradually. As the value of s is increased, the curves rise more abruptly to the maximum penetration.

---

[17] A discussion of this forecasting technique is provided in Appendix D.

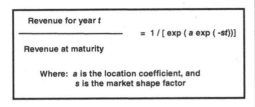

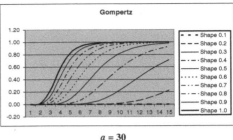

$$\frac{\text{Revenue for year } t}{\text{Revenue at maturity}} = 1 / [\exp(a \exp(-st))]$$

Where: a is the location coefficient, and
s is the market shape factor

$$a = 30$$

EXHIBIT 6.10   Gompertz Model

The Gompertz Model is often used to forecast market penetration of branded technologies that are replacing an older branded technology without a significant clear-cut advantage. These situations are primarily driven by the demise of an existing product or service, hence the association with mortality.

Fisher-Pry Model

The Fisher-Pry model, originally reported by John Fisher and Robert Pry in 1971, is based on what they called a "substitution model of technological change." Its authors felt that this curve was representative of the pattern when one technology replaced another, due to clear-cut economic advantages of the new, such as when open hearth steelmaking replaced the Bessemer process. The formula and examples for the Fisher-Pry model are shown in Exhibit 6.11.

Again, there are two primary inputs to this equation. The first (t_{50}) is the year in which 50 percent market penetration is reached, and the second (s) is a market shape factor. Intuitively, changing the year in which 50 percent penetration occurs will shift the curve horizontally. The effect of the market shape factor is to produce a much steeper curve for high values and a much gentler curve for low values.

Most feel that the Fisher-Pry model is appropriate to represent the growth of a technically advanced product in which the product is diffused into the marketplace, starting out as an unproven technology and growing as early buyers report success and as the mechanisms to support the product are enhanced.

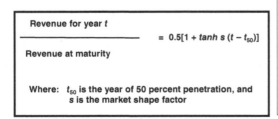

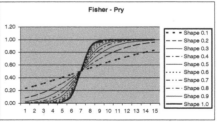

$$\frac{\text{Revenue for year } t}{\text{Revenue at maturity}} = 0.5[1 + \tanh s\,(t - t_{50})]$$

Where: t_{50} is the year of 50 percent penetration, and
s is the market shape factor

$$t_{50} = 7$$

EXHIBIT 6.11   Fisher-Pry Model

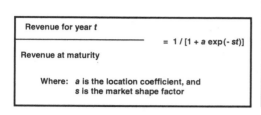

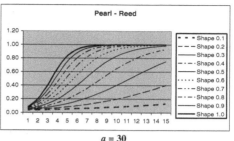

$a = 30$

EXHIBIT 6.12   Pearl-Reed Model

Pearl-Reed Model

A third S-curve model is similar mathematically to the Fisher-Pry model, but produces a somewhat different curve which is similar to the Gompertz curves in that the curves developed using various location coefficient and market shape factor inputs do not cross one another, but all start out at a common point. Those with a high market shape factor rise rapidly, and those with a high location coefficient shift more to the right. Examples of the Pearl-Reed curves are shown in Exhibit 6.12.

Bass Model

The Bass model is based on diffusion theory which reflects how information is disbursed within a society. Humans rely on media as well as interpersonal communication to learn about new products and services available. People vary considerably in the extent to which they rely on one or the other of these information sources. A diffusion model attempts to exemplify the cumulative percentage of a potential market that has been absorbed by the initial purchase of a new product. As with other S-curve models, we expect that new product sales begin to grow at a slow rate, then at a very rapid rate, following which the rate of growth tapers off and perhaps even declines with time. The Bass model, as with other S-curve models, is a single-purchase model, used to forecast the sales of products that are typically bought just once or infrequently, such as consumer durable goods. It is not intended to forecast the sales of repeat purchases (such as a new toothpaste product) that can drive a very rapid growth of sales volume if the initial purchase is successful in the eyes of the buyer.

The Bass model combines the innovation model and imitation model of Fisher-Pry and was designed to be a forecasting model to be used prior to the introduction of a new product and has, in fact, been widely used by major corporations for that purpose. The mathematics and examples of the model are shown in Exhibit 6.13.

The values for the p and q coefficients are not intuitively obvious but due to the widespread use of this curve, a literature search will reveal a large amount of empirical data that has been gathered relating the coefficients with types of products. The p is the coefficient of innovation, or the likelihood that an individual will start using a product because of media communication. The q is the coefficient of imitation, reflecting the likelihood of an individual starting to use a product because of interpersonal communication.

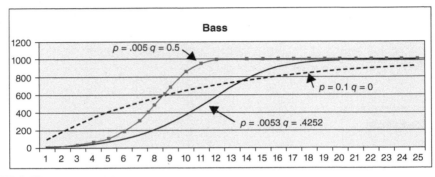

$$Q_3 = (((p + q^*(A/M))^*(M-A)))$$

Where: Q_3 = number of adopters or unit sales at time t
p = coefficient of innovation
q = coefficient of imitation
M = market size, or ultimate number of adopters or unit sales
A = cumulative number of adopters or unit sales to date

EXHIBIT 6.13   Bass Model

The reader is referred to a more complete discussion of the Bass Model, contained in Appendix D, which was researched and written by Richard A. Michelfelder and Maureen Morrin of Rutgers University.

Economic Life and Pattern Summary

To summarize this section:

- Economic life is the period during which it is profitable to use an asset.
- Economic life ends when (1) it is no longer profitable to use an asset (the future economic benefits are used up); or (2) when it is more profitable to use another asset.
- The pattern of economic life is critical because economic benefit to be received sooner increases value and economic benefit to be received later diminishes value.
- Unless the perpetual hypothesis is clearly supportable, "what goes up must come down." There are forecasting tools to help us quantify our opinions about the shape of the upward path as well as that of the downward path.

ELEMENTS OF RISK

In the previous chapter, we discussed analysis tools that can enable us to refine an estimate of the amount of economic benefit that could reasonably be expected from the exploitation of a brand. In the first part of this chapter, we discussed techniques that can be used to estimate the economic life and pattern by which those economic benefits may be realized. So we have covered the first three of the "big four" ingredients to the income method. The final ingredient is a quantification of risk.

Investors speak of "risk premium" as the added amount of return that they demand for assuming risk in excess of real interest, in a risk-free investment when there is the possibility of loss or an anticipated variability in earnings. One might say that the future is always an unknown, but we have to make a judgment about just how great we think the great unknown really is.

Our previous discussions have prepared us for the realization that an investment in a brand, like any other form of intellectual property, is not without risk. So, the task at hand is to come to an opinion about the risk premium that ought to be associated with an investment in the brand we are appraising. The risk premium is the added amount of return that investors demand for the assumption of risk in excess of real interest in a risk-free investment when there is the possibility of loss or anticipated variability in earnings.

Again, we are putting ourselves in the position of a virtual buyer who has carefully evaluated the future economic benefit of owning the subject brand and we have come to a conclusion and our best estimate as to how long that economic benefit will last and the pattern by which we expect to receive it. Some of the risks associated with the realization of economic benefit involve the following questions:

- Will it grow to the level that is expected?
- Will it last as long as expected?
- Will it be more volatile than expected?
- Does it require large increments of investment?
- Will it stop sooner than is expected?
- Will it start later than expected?

When most of us consider risk, we think in qualitative terms and rarely attempt to quantify it. With respect to our investments, however, we are forced by the marketplace to quantify risk. The market tells us what interest rate we will pay for a mortgage and what rate of return we might expect from buying a mutual fund, but we must reconcile those numbers with our subjective opinions about our risk tolerance. The previous discussion about the economic life of brands is really a subjective presentation of risk elements. We now need to use some investment theory to assist in quantifying those elements.

To begin our discussion of risk, we refer our readers back to the concept of the business enterprise as a *portfolio* of assets. This was introduced in Chapter 1, and we touched the idea that assets in the portfolio have different risks associated with their ownership. This concept is further discussed in the latter sections of Appendix C, and also in the bankruptcy discussion in Chapter 10. If readers are unfamiliar with the financial principles of investment risk, we suggest a reading of Appendix C before moving on. Generally speaking, there is a progression of risk, from low to high, in moving from monetary assets to tangible assets to intangible assets (including trademarks).

PIPE DREAMS

We were once engaged to value the inventory of an industrial distributorship. This inventory formed a significant part of the monetary assets of that business enterprise. The valuation was required because the company was in financial difficulty. The inventory told us why. It was comprised of every possible type of fitting of every possible size of very high quality stainless steel pipe. This pipe was designed to be used in a nuclear power plant, and this distributor had stocked up for a good deal of power plant construction that was never to occur. So monetary assets, while they may be liquid and versatile (in this case the pipe was salable for many uses) but the price would be severely reduced. The more ordinary uses for this pipe did not require the extreme quality and the price likely to be realized (current liquidation value) would be far lower than cost. Generally, however, monetary assets are the least risky within the business enterprise.

Monetary assets are considered to be the least risky assets in the business enterprise portfolio because they are versatile, liquid assets. While this is most generally true, the reader is cautioned not to accept this as an absolute.

Tangible assets are considered to be moderately risky for the reasons cited elsewhere, but again the reader is cautioned. The more narrowly defined is the use of tangible assets, the more risky is their ownership.

The risk associated with the ownership of intangible assets is generally the highest of the three asset classes, because intangibles are not very liquid or versatile outside of the business in which they were created. In addition, the range of ownership risk for intangible assets is much wider, and can even overlap that of monetary or tangible assets in an extreme case. This is caused by the disparity in the characteristics of the various types of intangible assets.

There is a relationship, however, between the risk of an investment in a business enterprise and the relative risks associated with the assets that comprise it. In Appendix C, we discuss the various means for quantifying the risk of a business enterprise. These techniques are based on an analysis of past actions of investors in the market.

SKATING ANYONE?

Picture the construction of an electron accelerator, built of heavy concrete, underground, in the form of a circle, a couple of hundred yards in diameter. If the need for electron acceleration research disappears, what would anyone do with such a structure? Perhaps convert it into a very inefficient underground water tank (or roller skating rink?).

If our task is to value an entire business, these techniques can provide us with the market benchmarks for doing so. These techniques allow us to calculate a *weighted average cost of capital* (WACC) which is a rate of return indicative of the investment risk associated with the ownership of an entire business.

Our present task is to relate such an overall rate of return to the appropriate rates of return for the individual assets that comprise the business, such as a trademark. Appendix C provides some benchmarks for rates of return applicable to monetary and tangible assets, and we will use them in this discussion without further comment, except to remind the reader that these also must be critically examined in the light of the previous discussion.

Rates of return for intangible assets must be calculated. Generally speaking, we cannot go to third-party market transactions in order to directly estimate return requirements for these assets.[18] We can only do that with any reasonable degree of precision for the entire business. We are not left completely without guidance in this endeavor, however, because we know the relative risk of the whole enterprise from its WACC. We can also calculate the value of the entire business enterprise. So we know about the whole, and about *some* of its parts, and we know that the *sum* of the parts must be commensurate with the whole.

The WACC is the return that must be realized by the business in order to satisfy the requirements of investors in the debt and equity of this business. Hence the name "cost of capital." The cost of debt is the after-tax amount of interest that the company must pay on its borrowings (after-tax because interest expense is a deduction from income taxes). The cost of equity capital is the amount of earnings that the company must produce in order to maintain the value of its capital stock in the marketplace. Weighting these two capital costs in combination produces the WACC. Since we know that the value of debt plus equity is the same as the value of the business's underlying assets, the return required on the portfolio of underlying assets is equal to the WACC.

You can also refer to Appendix C (Exhibits C.1 and C.2). We can now move a step further and allocate the WACC to individual assets within the intangible classification (see Exhibit 6.14).

We see that, given the same relative values of the three asset classes, the required rates of return for "Computer Software," "Assembled Workforce," "Patented Technology," and "Brands" are 11.0 percent, 13.0 percent, 25 percent, and 14.5 percent, respectively. Within the intangible asset classification, we have judged software to be the least risky and patented technology to be the most risky. This is where we must begin to exercise the judgment that was developed in the previous section about economic life. In order to do that, it is quite obvious that we need to look to the nature of the enterprise as a whole, and at the nature of the other assets that comprise it, in order to gauge their possible effect on the risk of the brand asset.

If the relative values of the asset classifications is changed, the return requirements for individual assets changes as well (see Exhibit 6.15).

---

[18] This is not to say that business people and investors have no opinion about return requirements for these types of asset. Business people making decisions as to whether to invest in the development of these assets for their own enterprises may use "hurdle rate" or other benchmarks in that decision-making. Venture capitalist rate of return are arguably risk-return measures for early stage intangible assets rather than mature and proven intangible assets or intellectual property.

EXHIBIT 6.14   Allocating WACC among Assets

ASSET CATEGORY	ASSET VALUE ($ MILLIONS)	PERCENT OF ENTERPRISE VALUE	RETURNS REQUIRED	WEIGHTED AVERAGE COST OF CAPITAL
NET WORKING CAPITAL	3,830	10.2%	2.7%	0.3%
TANGIBLE ASSETS	13,600	36.3%	5.7%	2.1%
INTANGIBLE ASSETS				
Computer Software	2,000	5.3%	11.0%	0.6%
Assembled Workforce	3,000	8.0%	13.0%	1.0%
Patented Technology	5,000	13.3%	25.0%	3.3%
Brands	10,080	26.9%	14.5%	3.9%
TOTAL	37510.0	100.0		11.2%

In this case, if value shifts from net working capital to tangible assets, the required return for trademarks moves from 14.5 percent to 14.0 percent, everything else held constant.

It may seem that this is an exercise in several unknowns which, with the help of spreadsheet technology, can be made to come out any way one chooses. This is not the case, however, and there are implicit checks and balances built in to the procedure, governed by "investment common sense."

EXHIBIT 6.15   Alternative Allocation of WACC among Assets

ASSET CATEGORY	ASSET VALUE ($ MILLIONS)	PERCENT OF ENTERPRISE VALUE	RETURNS REQUIRED	WEIGHTED AVERAGE COST OF CAPITAL
NET WORKING CAPITAL	2,000	5.3%	2.7%	0.1%
TANGIBLE ASSETS	15,430	41.1%	5.7%	2.3%
INTANGIBLE ASSETS				
Computer Software	2,000	5.3%	11.0%	0.6%
Assembled Workforce	3,000	8.0%	13.0%	1.0%
Patented Technology	5,000	13.3%	25.0%	3.3%
Brands	10,080	26.9%	14.0%	3.8%
TOTAL	37,510	100.0		11.2%

If, as an example, the values shifted among assets in such a way that a 40 percent return was required on the brand value, our common sense alarm should begin to sound. Why is the risk associated with the trademark asset so much higher than that of the business as a whole? The answer might be that the mark has been challenged in litigation, the outcome of which is in question. Other answers are not so satisfying. If the business represents a speculative extension of the trademark to a new and untested product or service, then the entire business would have a higher risk rate, and all of the assets would be subject to higher risk requirements.

If values shifted among assets in such a way that the trademark asset required a 5 percent rate of return, alarm bells would again sound. Can a trademark be as versatile and liquid as cash? Unlikely.

This sort of incongruity triggers a reanalysis:

- Is the business enterprise value in error?
- Is the enterprise WACC in error?
- Is the group of comparable companies used as the benchmark really comparable?
- Are the asset values correct?
- Are there assets inadvertently omitted?
- Have elements of obsolescence been overlooked or improperly estimated?

We also must remember that some assets within the enterprise will have been valued using cost or market approaches which are exogenous to this process. Their values help to reduce the number of unknowns, though they are subject to reevaluation if the parts do not fit.

Coming to an opinion about an appropriate discount rate for a brand may seem like a daunting task. We suggest, however, that an analysis of the weighted average cost of capital we have just illustrated can be a useful place to start. It has the advantage of ensuring that all of the pieces fit together. Based on our previous discussions, it becomes clearer that a discount rate for a brand will be closer to the required rate of return for equity than for debt, because, as we earlier pointed out, brands and other intellectual property are typically created with equity capital.

We have often found it useful to begin with the cost of equity of the company owning the brand and then to list all of the factors from our investigation that might increase the brand's risk of exploitation and then to list all those factors that would contribute to a lower risk profile. In addition, one can look toward the outer ends of the range of risk. Is this a brand that is so long-lived and strong that its risk is akin to the risk of the company's entire portfolio of assets (e.g., its WACC)? Or is this a fledgling brand in such a risky environment that it should take on the risk profile of venture capital? A discount rate for a brand at either one of these extremes would be very rare.

Appraisers of commercial real estate can often "back into" the discount rate implicit in market transactions. Readers will see, if they refer to Appendix A, that if the amount, duration, and pattern of net cash flow is known and if the present value is known (transaction price), then the discount rate can be calculated. So, if there are market transactions of commercial property, often future net cash flow can be estimated reasonably accurately and some indication of the discount rate in the buyer's mind can be extracted. Unfortunately, that level of information is not readily ascertainable in the case of brand sales.

At the end of the day, however, it is clear that the selection of a discount rate is an opinion based on subjective measures.

The Many Faces of Risk

Many of us are risk-averse. We tend to look at things through the wrong end of the telescope and tend toward conservatism, especially when making estimates about the future. We have found that this is especially true when a valuation result is going to be used in decision making relative to a substantial business investment, or when it will be subject to review in some adversarial atmosphere.

If the reader will think back over this chapter and the previous one, you will clearly observe that each of the four income method ingredients can be made to significantly alter the outcome in a valuation. In many ways, the many factors that we described that can alter the amount of future economic benefit, it's remaining life, and the pattern by which it will be received are, in fact, elements of risk. If, as an example, we observe a strong possibility of unforeseen negative outcomes or are simply motivated toward conservatism in a given situation, we could reflect that in several ways:

- We could reduce the total amount of future economic benefit to the lowest reasonable estimate.
- We could truncate the estimate of remaining economic life.
- We could push the realization of economic benefit farther into the future.
- We could increase the risk rate.

Finally, we would like to call the reader's attention to Appendix E., a paper by our colleague William Murphy entitled "Dealing with Uncertainty and Immeasurables in Trademark Asset Valuation." This is a very comprehensive yet readable discussion of some sophisticated techniques for quantifying risk in a trademark valuation.

DON'T DOUBLE COUNT RISK

Our belief is that it is better to concentrate on the risk-rate ingredient to portray our opinions about the future, whether positive or negative. Let the *amount* of future economic benefit, its remaining *economic life*, and its *pattern* of receipt reflect our best, reasoned judgment, unaffected, as best we can, by optimism or pessimism.

SUMMARY

This chapter's highlights include:

- Economic life is the period during which it is profitable to use an asset. Economic life ends when is either:
  - No longer profitable to use an asset (the future economic benefits are used up)
  - More profitable to use another asset
- Valuations are forward-looking and the forecasting task is inescapable.
- There are many recognized tools and exogenous data that can assist in forecasting.
- Each asset comprising a business enterprise has its own risk profile.
- The essence of the risk ingredient is a judgment about the likelihood of our forecast coming true.
- Don't double-count risk. Once is enough.

CHAPTER 7

The Income Method

Putting It All Together

Now that we have in hand the means by which to estimate the four ingredients of the income method, we can examine various examples of how those ingredients come together to calculate the present value of future economic benefit.

In Chapter 4, we discussed the use of the cost and market methods for valuing trademarks. While we do not rule out the possibility of relying on those methods, our experience tells us that we will find few situations in which they are appropriate. Therefore in Chapters 5 and 6 we concentrated on the income method, and this chapter completes that discussion.

TRADEMARK VALUATION BY RESIDUAL

Perhaps the most straightforward trademark valuation, given the principles described in Chapters 2 and 3, is by a residual approach. This could be described mathematically as:

$$V_{tm} = V_{be} - V_m - V_t - V_{ia}$$

where V_{tm} = the value of trademarks.
V_{be} = the value of the business enterprise.
V_m = the value of monetary assets.
V_t = the value of tangible assets.
V_{ia} = the value of other identified intangible assets.

The strength of this method is its simplicity and ease of understanding. Its weakness is the quantification of the asset values to be subtracted from that of the business enterprise. One must be comfortable that all such assets have been identified and reasonably valued and that the residual value is therefore truly representative of trademark value alone.

Valuation Using a Premium Price

In Exhibits 5.3 and 5.4, there was a calculation of income attributable to a trademark. The basis of the income estimate was a premium price attained in the marketplace

EXHIBIT 7.1   Trademark Valuation—Premium Price Advantage

	1	2	3	4	5	TOTAL
S & R Enterprises						
SALES OF PREMIUM PRICED PRODUCT						
Unit Sales Forecast (millions)	12,410	12,530	13,454	13,896	14,458	
Price per Unit	2.49	2.49	2.49	2.49	2.49	
Sales Revenue (millions)	$30,900	$31,200	$33,500	$34,600	$36,000	$166,200
S & R Enterprises						
WITH GENERIC PRODUCT PRICING						
Unit Sales Forecast	12,410	12,530	13,454	13,896	14,458	
Price per Unit	2.19	2.19	2.19	2.19	2.19	
Sales Revenue	$27,177	$27,441	$29,464	$30,431	$31,663	$146,176
REVENUE ATTRIBUTABLE TO IP	$ 3,723	$ 3,759	$ 4,036	$ 4,169	$ 4,337	$ 20,024
INCOME ATTRIBUTABLE TO TRADEMARK	$ 3,723	$ 3,759	$ 4,036	$ 4,169	$ 4,337	
Less: Income Taxes	1,489	1,504	1,614	1,667	1,735	
After-tax Income Attributable to Trademark	$ 2,234	$ 2,255	$ 2,422	$ 2,501	$ 2,602	
Present Value of After-Tax Income	$ 2,092	$ 1,853	$ 1,745	$ 1,581	$ 1,443	
Total Present Value	$ 8,715					

by the subject trademarked goods or services. This trademark can be valued by calculating the present value of the income attributable to it. See Exhibit 7.1.

This is a straightforward discounting of five years of after-tax income attributable to the premium price advantage. This calculation indicates a market value of $8,715.

There are several very important assumptions implicit in this example:

- The premium price advantage will go right to "the bottom line." That is, every dollar of price advantage will increase pretax income by one dollar. This may not be true in every case. A product or service with a premium price may have to be supported with greater than otherwise product manufacturing cost, advertising expense, or sales and promotional expenditures. This possibility must be considered before making the calculation as shown here.
- The forecast is for five years only, for simplicity. The price advantage might well go on beyond that, or stop short of that. Each situation should be examined on its own merits. We have previously commented on the possibility of premium price erosion due to the emergence of competition, as an example.

- It is assumed that all of the income attributable to the subject trademark is captured by this technique, though that might not always be the case. The companies that are selling products at the generic price might also have trademarks that are contributing to their earnings and so there might be additional income that could be attributed to the S&R Enterprises mark. We may understate trademark value by this technique.
- The annual present value is calculated at a 14 percent discount rate by the after-tax amount$/(1+0.14)^{0.5}$. The 0.5 time value may seem out of place, but this is a "half-year convention" calculation that assumes all moneys would be received at midyear, yielding a result that more closely approximates the typical constant inflow of economic benefit.

The reader should be sensitive to these assumptions in reviewing the examples that follow. To some extent they are applicable to all.

Valuation Using Gross Profit Advantage

In Exhibit 5.6, we calculated an income stream attributable to S&R's trademark arising from economies of scale that it produced in manufacturing costs. This was reflected in an advantageous gross profit margin for the S&R. In a calculation similar to the one previously mentioned, we can estimate market value in a present value calculation (see Exhibit 7.2).

Here we have subtracted the gross profit of a comparable company group from that of S&R as the basis for the forecasted income attributable to the trademark. Again we assume that all of the difference in gross profit flows to "the bottom line," and so the only other deduction required is for income taxes. The present value of the after tax income attributable to the trademark is $28,298.

The essential caveat in this technique is whether all of the gross profit advantage is in fact attributable to the trademark. There are many elements in the cost of goods sold which is the determinant of gross profit. Is S&R Enterprises really manufacturing its goods or delivering its services in the same way as the comparable companies?

Valuation Using Operating Profit Advantage

This is similar to the preceding example in that we calculate the present value of after-tax net income, under the assumption that all of the advantage is reflected there. This is probably a safer assumption here than in the case of the gross profit advantage because at the operating profit level, nearly all the variables are captured (see Exhibit 7.3).

The present value of the after-tax revenue attributed to the operating profit advantage is $1,881.

Valuation Using Relief from Royalty

In our discussion about Exhibit 5.13, we commented on this common methodology which is based on the concept that if a company owns a trademark, it does not have to "rent" one and, therefore, it is relieved from paying a royalty. The amount of that

EXHIBIT 7.2 Trademark Valuation—Gross Profit Advantage

	1	2	3	4	5	TOTAL
S & R Enterprises						
Unit Sales Forecast (millions)	12,410	12,530	13,454	13,896	14,458	
Price per Unit	2.19	2.19	2.19	2.19	2.19	
Sales Revenue	$ 27,178	$ 27,441	$ 29,464	$ 30,432	$ 31,663	$ 146,178
Cost of Goods Sold PER UNIT	0.73	0.73	0.73	0.73	0.73	
Cost of Goods Sold	9,059	9,147	9,821	10,144	10,554	
Gross Profit	$ 18,119	$ 18,294	$ 19,643	$ 20,288	$ 21,109	$ 97,452
Gross profit margin						66.67%
COMPARABLE COMPANY GROUP						
Unit Sales Forecast	750,000	780,000	811,200	843,648	877,394	
Price per Unit	2.19	2.19	2.19	2.19	2.19	
Sales Revenue	$1,642,500	$1,708,200	$1,776,528	$1,847,589	$1,921,493	$8,896,310
Cost of Goods Sold PER UNIT	0.81	0.81	0.81	0.81	0.81	
Cost of Goods Sold	607,500	631,800	657,072	683,355	710,689	
Gross Profit	$1,035,000	$1,076,400	$1,119,456	$1,164,234	$1,210,804	$5,605,894
Gross profit margin						63.01%
S & R Enterprises						
Sales Revenue	$ 328,500	$ 341,640	$ 355,306	$ 369,518	$ 384,299	$1,779,262
Cost of Goods Sold ADVANTAGE	3.65%	3.65%	3.65%	3.65%	3.65%	
GROSS PROFIT ATTRIBUTABLE TO IP	$ 12,000	$ 12,480	$ 12,979	$ 13,498	$ 14,038	$ 64,996
INCOME ATTRIBUTABLE TO TRADEMARK	$ 12,000	$ 12,480	$ 12,979	$ 13,498	$ 14,038	
Less: Income Taxes	4,800	4,992	5,192	5,399	5,615	
After-tax Income Attributable to Trademark	$ 7,200	$ 7,488	$ 7,788	$ 8,099	$ 8,423	
Present Value of After-Tax Income	$ 6,743	$ 6,152	$ 5,612	$ 5,120	$ 4,671	
Total Present Value	$ 28,298					

EXHIBIT 7.3 Trademark Valuation—Operating Profit Advantage

	1	2	3	4	5	TOTAL
S & R Enterprises						
Unit Sales Forecast (millions)	12,410	12,530	13,454	13,896	14,458	
Price per Unit	2.49	2.49	2.49	2.49	2.49	
Sales Revenue	$ 30,901	$ 31,200	$ 33,500	$ 34,601	$ 36,000	$ 166,203
Cost of Goods Sold PER UNIT	0.73	0.73	0.73	0.73	0.73	
Cost of Goods Sold	9,059	9,147	9,821	10,144	10,554	
Gross Profit	$ 21,842	$ 22,053	$ 23,679	$ 24,457	$ 25,446	
Selling, General & Administrative Expense	11,557	11,669	12,529	12,941	13,464	
Operating Profit	$ 10,285	$ 10,384	$ 11,150	$ 11,516	$ 11,982	$ 55,317
Operating profit margin						33.28%
COMPARABLE COMPANY GROUP						
Unit Sales Forecast	750,000	780,000	811,200	843,648	877,394	
Price per Unit	2.49	2.49	2.49	2.49	2.49	
Sales Revenue	$1,867,500	$1,942,200	$2,019,888	$2,100,684	$2,184,711	$10,114,982
Cost of Goods Sold PER UNIT	0.73	0.73	0.73	0.73	0.73	
Cost of Goods Sold	547,500	569,400	592,176	615,863	640,498	
Gross Profit	$1,320,000	$1,372,800	$1,427,712	$1,484,820	$1,544,213	
Selling, General & Administrative Expense	747,000	776,880	807,955	840,273	873,884	
Operating Profit	$ 573,000	$ 595,920	$ 619,757	$ 644,547	$ 670,329	$ 3,103,553
Operating profit margin						30.68%
S & R Enterprises						
Sales Revenue	$ 30,901	$ 31,200	$ 33,500	$ 34,601	$ 36,000	$ 166,203
Operating Profit ADVANTAGE	2.60%	2.60%	2.60%	2.60%	2.60%	
GROSS PROFIT ATTRIBUTABLE TO IP	$ 803	$ 811	$ 871	$ 900	$ 936	$ 4,321
INCOME ATTRIBUTABLE TO TRADEMARK	$ 803	$ 811	$ 871	$ 900	$ 936	
Less: Income Taxes	321	324	348	360	374	
After-tax Income Attributable to Trademark	$ 482	$ 487	$ 523	$ 540	$ 562	
Present Value of After-Tax Income	$ 451	$ 400	$ 377	$ 341	$ 311	
Total Present Value	$ 1,881					

177

phantom payment is used as a surrogate for income attributable to the trademark, and the calculation of the after-tax present value proceeds accordingly:

EXHIBIT 7.4   Trademark Valuation—Relief from Royalty

	1	2	3	4	5	TOTAL
S & R Enterprises						
Sales Revenue (millions)	30,900	31,200	33,500	34,600	36,000	166,200
Trademark Royalty Rate	8%	8%	8%	8%	8%	
Income Attributable to Trademark	2,472	2,496	2,680	2,768	2,880	13,296
INCOME ATTRIBUTABLE TO TRADEMARK	$ 2,472	$ 2,496	$ 2,680	$ 2,768	$ 2,880	
Less: Income Taxes	989	998	1,072	1,107	1,152	
After-tax Income Attributable to Trademark	$ 1,483	$ 1,498	$ 1,608	$ 1,661	$ 1,728	
Present Value of After-Tax Income	$ 1,389	$ 1,230	$ 1,159	$ 1,050	$ 958	
Total Present Value	$ 5,787					

The royalty used in this type of calculation is best taken from patient analysis of actual transactions from the marketplace relative to comparable trademark assets, though it might be necessary to use rules of thumb in the relevant industry. Again, we point out that our examples use a five-year income forecast when, in most cases, the trademark income might be realized over an extended period. Often the relief from royalty calculation is made by capitalizing the income stream in perpetuity as follows:

$$\frac{\text{Year 1 After-tax income}}{\text{Capitalization rate}} = \frac{\$1,483}{.10} = \$14,830$$

The capitalization rate is equal to the 14 percent discount rate less an anticipated growth rate in the income stream of 4 percent. The substantial difference between the value and that shown in Exhibit 7.4 is due to the fact that the latter is truncated at five years.

Valuation Using Discounted Cash Flow Model

It is our belief that the methodology that captures all of the elements of value utilizes the *discounted cash flow* (DCF) model. Use of this model gives the valuer the tools to reflect all of the financial inputs that affect the value of a trademark. In the examples just presented, we called attention to the fact that a trademark might not be responsible for all of the differences in gross margin or operating income, and that a premium price advantage might not capture all of the trademark value, and we previously discussed the problems with using comparable royalty rates that dim the luster of the relief from royalty approach.

With all of its advantages, however, this model does not relieve the valuer from the tasks of investigation and forecasting. The model's conclusion is only as good as the facts and assumptions that drive it. It does, however, permit the valuer to test the sensitivity of the conclusion to the various inputs. We will be visiting this model again in the next chapter as it relates to a method for estimating royalty rates.

Again, in order to employ a discounted cash flow model we need the amount of future economic benefit, a forecast of how we will receive that economic benefit during the time that it is expected to flow, and an opinion of risk which has been reduced to a percentage rate.

Valuation Precept

The amount of future economic benefit is expressed as the net cash flow that is attributable to brand exploitation.

In the preceding examples, we have made a reasonable assumption that the after-tax income streams were equivalent to net cash flow. When, however, we are employing a full DCF model, we must be attentive to the need to satisfy ourselves that we are in fact discounting net cash flow and not some other form of income.

Net Cash Flow   In Chapter 5, we illustrated the calculation of net cash flow (Exhibit 5.9) for one year's results of operations for S&R. The calculation begins with after-tax net income before extraordinary items. Extraordinary items are eliminated from the net cash flow calculation because by definition they are financial events that are not expected to happen again. Depreciation expense is added back because it is a non-cash expense (no business funds are actually paid to outsiders), and because it represents the "return of" element of investment, and it should therefore be a component of cash flow. Net income plus depreciation is often referred to as *gross cash flow*.

However, if the business is expected to grow, some of the gross cash flow must be reinvested to support that growth. First, if the company's sales are going to grow, inventories and accounts receivable will also grow. Thus, monetary assets will grow, and some of the gross cash flow will need to be invested there. Second, capital investments may be required to replace or add to buildings and equipment or other assets of a capital nature.

Therefore it is necessary to estimate the amount of investment that will be required to meet these needs, and subtract it from gross cash flow. Since we will be

EXHIBIT 7.5 Allocating Income among Assets

ASSET CATEGORY	ASSET VALUE ($ 000's)	RETURNS REQUIRED	AMOUNT OF RETURN ($ 000's)
NET WORKING CAPITAL	3,830	2.7%	103
TANGIBLE ASSETS	13,600	5.7%	775
INTANGIBLE ASSETS	5,000	12.0%	600
INTELLECTUAL PROPERTY	15,080	18.0%	2,714
TOTAL	37,510	11.2%	4,193
TECHNOLOGY IP	5,000	25.0%	1,250
TRADEMARKS	10,080	14.5%	1,462
	15,080	18.0%	2,712

using such a calculation for valuing trademarks, another element should be considered. Advertising expenditures build a trademark just as capital expenditures build a plant. Should we not consider this in the conversion from gross to net cash flow? The answer is yes, and this is probably best done by examining the amount of after-tax net income. Advertising expense has been deducted in arriving at that amount, and is therefore effectively removed from cash flow. If, however, existing advertising expenditures are not sufficient to support the forecasted growth, or if the brand is being "milked" without adequate support, then some downward adjustment should be made to reflect the additional amount of investment that would be required to provide adequate support.

Discount Rate The reader should recall the discussion on allocating income to assets that was presented in the two previous chapters. The essential point is that if we know the value of an entire business and the income that the business can produce, and we know the values and rates of return for some of the assets, we can determine, in an iterative process, the rates of return for the unknown assets.[1]

If we apply this concept to the task at hand, we can utilize the calculations of Exhibit 5.11 in order to estimate the rate of return inputs to a discounted cash flow model (see Exhibit 7.5).

On the top portion of this table, we have calculated the return required (18.0%) for intellectual property, having estimated the value of the business, its income, and the values and returns required for the other assets. On the lower portion, we have estimated the returns for the intellectual property assets, using judgment, but constrained by the bounds of total value and overall return. The return requirement for the trademarks is 14.5 percent.

---

[1] There is a scholarly discussion of the theoretical underpinnings of this in Appendix B, authored by Dr. John A DelRoccili.

With these inputs and a five-year forecast of the entire income statement of the relevant company, division, or product line (in this case Smith & Richey Enterprises), we can calculate a trademark value (see Exhibit 7.6).

Exhibit 7.6 calculates the trademark value into perpetuity. This is accomplished by means of a "reversion" in year 6, or 2018. In this year we capitalize the income into perpetuity and discount it to the current period. This is a difference from previous tables in this chapter. The mathematics is explained in the footnote to Exhibit 7.6. The total present value is shown to be $31,355.

In Exhibit 7.6, we utilized a compound annual growth rate for the sales revenue forecast. Under other circumstances we might well have used one of the growth models of the S-curve type or we might even have been of the opinion that our subject brand was in a decline mode and we might have utilized survivor curve data to assist us with that forecast. Most of the other income statement items were estimated according to their relationship to sales revenue. Estimates of depreciation expense are based upon book values of tangible assets and estimates of future capital requirements must be specifically and individually may.

Because this model contains all of the ingredients to cash flow, we can reflect, as appropriate, changes to any item of income and expense, as well as requirements to add to working capital or to invest in plant in order to support the size of the business we are forecasting. Very importantly, we have included the returns that must be earned on all of the other assets in the enterprise. These returns have been calculated using rates of return representative of current yields. That is, no deduction for a growth component has been made. This is done to avoid making the example unduly complex, recognizing that the indicated trademark value may be understated if, in fact, a growth element is appropriate to recognize.

A trademark does not exist in a financial vacuum. Its earning power is only realized in concert with other assets. Therefore we cannot ascribe more income (and value) to the trademark than is available to it after sharing the income of the enterprise with other assets. This concept is one that we often observe being overlooked in trademark valuations.

The DCF technique has many advantages in addition to its ability to reflect a wide variety of conditions that can affect value. It also enables one to test the sensitivity of a result to changes in the forecast assumptions, such as growth rates, levels of expense (i.e., advertising and promotion) and the need for capital additions.

We also reemphasize the point that this DCF model can be used for a subsidiary, a division, or even a product line within a larger enterprise. We can do this as long as we have access to, or can reasonably estimate, the financial profile of that entity.

Other DCF-based Techniques   It is plain that the DCF model can be used to calculate a value for the entire business enterprise. Using this tool, we can value the business enterprise *with* and *without* a trademark, and the difference indicates the trademark value. See Exhibit 7.7.

The obvious key to this technique is the ability to reflect, in the business enterprise financial performance, the effect of the presence of the subject trademark. This might be reflected as a lessening of growth, increase in expenses, or change in business enterprise risk. If these changes can be discerned, then this method provides a valuation possibility.

EXHIBIT 7.6 Trademark Valuation—Discounted Cash Flow

SMITH & RICHEY ENTERPRISES
Consolidated Statement of Earnings
($ millions)

Year ended December 31,	2012	2013	2014	2015	2016	2017	2018
Net Operating Revenues	$ 30,900	32,136	33,421	34,758	36,149	37,595	39,098
Cost of Goods Sold	14,500	15,104	15,708	16,336	16,990	17,669	18,376
Gross Profit	16,400	17,032	17,713	18,422	19,159	19,925	20,722
Selling, general and administrative expenses	9,000	9,319	9,692	10,080	10,483	10,902	11,339
Other operating charges	275	321	334	348	361	376	391
	9,275						
Operating Income	7,125	7,391	7,687	7,994	8,314	8,647	8,993
Interest income	340	353	368	382	398	414	430
Interest expense	450	418	434	452	470	489	508
Other income — net	80	64	67	70	72	75	78
Income before income taxes	7,095	7,391	7,687	7,994	8,314	8,647	8,993
Income taxes	2,838	2,957	3,075	3,198	3,326	3,459	3,597
Net income	$ 4,257	4,435	4,612	4,797	4,989	5,188	5,396

CALCULATE NET CASH FLOW (1)

Add: Extraordinary items to normalize	0	—	—	—	—	—	—
Add: Depreciation expense	900	925	925	925	925	925	925
Subtract: Additions to Working Capital	180	193	201	209	217	226	235
Subtract: Capital expenditures	600	620	620	620	620	620	620
	$ 4,377	$ 4,547	$ 4,717	$ 4,893	$ 5,077	$ 5,267	$ 5,466

EXHIBIT 7.6 (*Continued*)

Year ended December 31,	2012		2013	2014	2015	2016	2017	2018
ASSETS EMPLOYED (2)								
Net Working Capital	3,830		4,023	4,216	4,416	4,625	4,842	5,067
Tangible Assets	13,600		14,200	14,820	15,440	16,060	16,680	17,300
Intangible Assets	5,000		5,300	5,618	5,955	6,312	6,691	7,093
Technology IP	5,000		5,500	6,000	6,500	7,500	8,500	8,500
LESS RETURNS REQUIRED ON OTHER ASSETS (2)								
Net working capital	103	2.7%	109	114	119	125	131	137
Tangible assets	775	5.7%	809	845	880	915	951	986
Intangible assets	600	12.0%	636	674	715	757	803	851
	1,478		1,554	1,633	1,714	1,798	1,884	1,974
Technology IP	1,250	25.0%	1,375	1,500	1,625	1,875	2,125	2,125
	2,728		2,929	3,133	3,339	3,673	4,009	4,099
NET CASH FLOW ALLOCABLE TO TRADEMARK	$ 1,649		$ 1,618	$ 1,584	$ 1,554	$ 1,404	$ 1,258	$ 1,367
PRESENT VALUE OF NCF ALLOC. TO TRADEMARK		14.5%	1,512	1,293	1,108	874	684	25,884
TOTAL PRESENT VALUE			$ 31,355					

Notes: (1) From Exhibit 5.9
(2) From Exhibit 7.5

Present value in year 2018 includes a reversion calculated by capitalizing year 2018 net cash flow into perpetuity, by dividing it by the discount rate less

2% growth rate, and then calculating the present value of the result. $1,367/(.145 − .02) × (1/(1 − .145)^5.5.

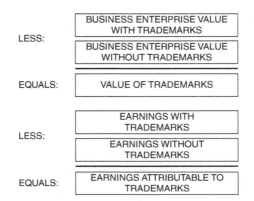

EXHIBIT 7.7 Trademark Value by Subtraction
Source: John Wiley & Sons, Inc. Reprinted with permission.

Some readers may be familiar with the Monte Carlo technique. This is a sophisticated multiple scenario calculation by which, with the aid of a computer, we can perform hundreds or even thousands of DCF calculations. Using it, as an example in Exhibit 7.6, we would have provided this system with an estimate of the upper and lower limits possible of each line item in our income statement along with an estimate of the distribution of values within those limits. The Monte Carlo system would then calculate present values for every one of thousands of combinations and provide a distribution of the result. From a Monte Carlo software system, we can observe the mean, median, average, standard deviation, and distribution in graphic form for each one of the results. It is a useful means of evaluating the sensitivity of various DCF inputs.[2]

MULTIPLE EXPLOITATION SCENARIOS

In Chapter 5, we explored a number of ways in which trademarks are exploited. We also recognized the situation in which a trademark might be exploited in several ways simultaneously, or one in which several possible exploitation scenarios can be seen. How can one reflect this complexity in a valuation?

What is needed is a technique by which the essential differences in the scenarios can be reflected. Typically, the differences are the amount and pattern of potential income, the relative risk, the economic life and the costs to capitalize them. All of these can be inputs to a discounted cash flow model. A complex model can accommodate several scenarios. Another technique is to develop several cash flow models, one for each exploitation scenario, and then combine their results into a single model for present value calculation (see Exhibit 7.8).

In this table, the only variable in the mathematics is the discount rate applied to the net cash flows from the various scenarios. All other variables (net income

---

[2] See Appendix E for a more detailed discussion of the Monte Carlo technique.

EXHIBIT 7.8 Trademark Valuation—Multiple Exploitation Scenarios

		YEAR 1	YEAR 2	YEAR 3	YEAR 4	YEAR 5	REVERSION	TOTAL
PRIMARY EXPLOITATION								
Net Cash Flow		1,200	1,300	1,500	1,600	1,700		
Present Value of Net Cash Flow	16.0%	1,114	1,041	1,035	952	872	5,781	10,794
SECONDARY EXPLOITATIONS								
Similar Product Extensions								
Net Cash Flow		650	700	800	900	950		
Present Value of Net Cash Flow	17.0%	601	553	540	520	469	2,861	5,544
Dissimilar Product Extensions								
Net Cash Flow		150	250	400	450	500		
Present Value of Net Cash Flow	20.0%	137	190	254	238	220	1,079	2,118
Licensing Income								
Net Cash Flow		50	60	70	80	90		
Present Value of Net Cash Flow	20.0%	46	46	44	42	40	194	412
Speculative Extensions								
Net Cash Flow		100	300	500	800	1,200		
Present Value of Net Cash Flow	25.0%	89	215	286	366	440	1,599	2,995
TOTAL PRESENT VALUE								21,862

duration and pattern, capital investment, and the like) are contained in the individual cash flow projections. In this table, the primary exploitation is the core business and it has the lowest discount rate. There are four secondary exploitations forecast. Similar product extensions are anticipated extensions of the core product or service into closely related lines of business. Risk is anticipated to be higher than the core business, but not markedly so. Dissimilar product extensions are just that, and anticipated to be significantly more risky, though growth in cash flow could be significant, if successful. If licensing is anticipated, it might have the same risk as another element, depending on the products or services being licensed and the nature of the license and licensee. Lastly, we might foresee a really speculative extension that, if successful, could be a blockbuster, but that carries considerable risk. The resultant present value of $21,862 represents the aggregate value of these exploitation scenarios.

VALUATION BASED ON INCOME ALLOCATION

In yet another permutation of these investment/rate of return approaches, one can utilize the mathematically closed system of allocating income to estimate trademark value. We have presented these relationships before, as they relate to other elements needed in the valuation process. For this new purpose, they appear in Exhibit 7.9.

The constituents that are known at the start of this calculation are shown in bold type. They are:

- Value of monetary assets
- Value of tangible assets
- Value of the entire enterprise
- Overall rate of return applicable to the entire enterprise
- Rates of return applicable to monetary and tangible assets

EXHIBIT 7.9 Trademark Valuation by Allocation of Income

ASSET CATEGORY	ASSET VALUE ($ 000's)	RETURNS REQUIRED	AMOUNT OF RETURN ($ 000's)
NET WORKING CAPITAL	3,830	2.7%	103
TANGIBLE ASSETS	13,600	5.7%	775
INTANGIBLE ASSETS	5,000	12.0%	600
INTELLECTUAL PROPERTY	15,080	18.0%	2,714
TOTAL	37,510	11.2%	4,193
TECHNOLOGY IP	5,000	25.0%	1,250
TRADEMARKS	10,080	14.5%	1,462
	15,080	18.0%	2,712

■ The income produced by the enterprise

With these boundaries in place, we can input various combinations of value and rates of return for the two unknown assets, that is, other intangibles and trademarks. Those values and rates of return are controlled by the business enterprise value, the overall rate of return, and the amount of enterprise income available. There is a fairly narrow range within which the values can vary, given rates of return that are reasonable and in keeping with the other rates used for monetary and tangible assets.

Using this method, one is assured that all of the pieces fit together in a reasonable way.

Other Income-Related Valuation Approaches

Many grapple with the uncertainties attendant upon the revenue and expense forecasts that are the fundamental building block of an income approach. These are especially troublesome when dealing with new, untested products or services that will be the basis of trademark value. One technique that has been advanced to deal with this type of uncertainty is the use of the Black-Scholes model that investors use to value call options. It is an interesting technique, though it does not eliminate the need for subjective forecasting. We have seen this technique used relative to technology assets, primarily especially those in an embryonic stage. We have not seen it used to value trademarks, most probably because valuations of new trademarks are rarely undertaken.[3]

Other techniques utilize price/earnings multiples or "brand strength" multipliers to convert an income to a value indication. There is nothing wrong with this idea as long as the multipliers come from the investment marketplace and as long as the income stream being capitalized is logically attributable to the trademark being valued. These techniques are becoming more sophisticated (and more correct) as time passes.

SUMMARY

We previously noted that, in a valuation, "the arithmetic is easy, it is the inputs that are difficult". This chapter brings that point into sharp focus. Our lengthy discussions in Chapters 4, 5, and 6 as well as the discussions presented in Appendixes A through E were about techniques for discovering and quantifying the four essential inputs to the Income method. This fairly short chapter presented the mathematics of turning those inputs into an estimate of market value.

All of this is directly indicative of the allocation of time and effort invested in a real-world appraisal.

---

[3] See Appendix E for a more detailed discussion of the Black-Scholes technique.

CHAPTER 8

Trademark Licensing Economics

At the end of the previous chapter, we presented an example of a brand valuation that included brand extensions, a form of secondary internal exploitation. As an alternative, licensing provides an additional method for brand exploitation. Trademark licensing, carried on as a primary business or as an adjunct to a corporation's main product lines, can be a significant business and much has been written about it. Alan Feldman[1] notes that licensing offers corporations a low-cost and rapid way to:

- Expand and reinforce their consumer and retailer awareness
- Strengthen their trademark protection
- Enhance the image of their brands
- Expand their brand beyond its core customers sent
- Introduce new product line extensions or distribution channels
- Build a significant new profit center

From the exploitation perspective, licensing can achieve several objectives:

- It can enhance company value by increasing exposure to important constituencies, and build brand equity by increasing its exposure in the marketplace.
- It can provide a source of otherwise unavailable income.
- It can be a tactical move in an expansion or redirection strategy

Whatever is the reason for a trademark license, it is going to have an economic impact on the licensor's business. The hope is, of course, that a trademark license will produce positive net cash flow for its owner and that this will enhance the value of the owner's enterprise. That is, a license creates an intangible asset in the form of the right to receive this additional income. A license can also be viewed as an enhancement to the earning power of an existing intellectual property, in this case a brand. That new asset or IP enhancement can be valued just like any other right. Our purpose in this chapter is to examine the valuation of such a right and, in doing so, we examine the economics of the licensing process.

LICENSING ECONOMICS

An intellectual property license is a contractual agreement between two parties, one of whom has title to the complete bundle of rights of the property and another who

---

[1] Allan Feldman is President & CEO of Leveraged Marketing Corporation of America, LMCA.

has acquired the use of some of those rights. A license is essentially an agreement by the owner not to prosecute the licensee for what otherwise would be an infringement of his or her rights.

We often compare a license to a hydroelectric dam. A dam impounds a large body of water which is analogous to the total future economic benefit of exploiting the licensed intellectual property. The impoundment is controlled by the dam and released in specific ways (e.g., to generate electricity, to irrigate crops, to control the river below for recreational purposes, etc.). A license also is a means by which we can allocate the total economic benefit to perhaps multiple licensees for perhaps multiple purposes.

Valuation Precept

A license divides the total future economic benefits of intellectual property exploitation between licensor and licensee.

Smith and Parr describe a license in familiar real estate terms:

> *Nearly everyone, at one time or another, has rented real property, even if only a cabin in the mountains or an apartment at the shore for a two-week vacation. When we have found a suitable property and sit down to execute the lease, the landlord or agent pulls out 'Onerous Lease No. 1' from the shelf and pushes it forward for us to sign. If we troubled to read it, as we should, we would find that it puts the entire responsibility of property ownership on us and that the owner is relieved of all obligations, potential liabilities, and possible expenses. We find that we must give one-year's notice before leaving, that we must paint the walls and refinish floors when we vacate, and all of our guests must sign a release absolving the owner of every conceivable liability. Then the negotiation begins. We and the landlord agree to strike out clauses, remove or add a word here and there, perhaps the rent or deposit goes up a bit, but when it is all over, we have an agreement both can live with. This is the licensing process, and no wonder, for what is a license but an agreement to rent property rights in return for some compensation?*[2]

License Clauses

In a trademark license context we can observe typical clauses that the license might contain:

- Royalty payments
- Term
- Termination provisions
- Right to sublicense
- Geographical territory
- Fields of use
- Indemnifications

---

[2] Gordon V. Smith and Russell L. Parr, Intellectual Property: Valuation, Exploitation and Infringement Damages, 4th ed. (Hoboken, NJ: John Wiley & Sons, Inc., 2005) p.427

DUELING VALUES

To the *licensor* the value of a trademark licensing transaction is represented by the present value of the compensation to be received (typically cash payments) less the present value of the costs to be incurred to administer the agreement, cover potential indemnifications, or income foregone by not exploiting the trademark internally.

To the *licensee*, it is the present value of the future economic benefits of exploiting the licensed trademark rights less the present value of the costs of doing so.

- Exclusivity
- Audit and quality control provisions

If we observe these license clauses from the viewpoint of a licensor, it is clear that some represent *cash inflows*, while others represent the potential for *cash outflows*. Royalty payments are obviously a cash inflow to the licensor, and that cash inflow will be influenced by the term, geographical territory, fields of use, right to sublicense, and exclusivity. Audit and quality control provisions will be an ongoing cash outflow while indemnifications represent the possibility of cash outflows at some time in the future.

This looks like what we have been discussing since Chapter 4, does it not? Yes, this is precisely applying the principles of the income method to value the respective rights of licensor and licensee. And, just as in a valuation of a brand in a virtual buy/sell transaction, if the net present value turns out to be negative for one of the parties, a license won't happen.

It is identically based upon the present value of the future economic benefits of ownership, as is the income method. The only difference being that different standards control the pluses and minuses that contribute to the net cash flow. We can develop a DCF model, but instead of using an income statement as the basis, the inputs will be the money effects of various license clauses. As an example, as licensor we might need to calculate the present value of an indemnification that holds the licensee harmless in the case of some infringement action. In order to do that we would need to estimate the potential cost of an infringement defense, estimate when it might occur, and estimate the likelihood of a victory or loss in the proceedings.[3] So again, the arithmetic is not so difficult, but the inputs are. We need to know the amount of future expense, when it will occur, and the risk of it occurring in order to calculate the present value of this potential future cash outflow.

We would then combine this negative present value with other negative and positive present values stemming from other license clauses in order to estimate the net present value of the license transaction from the licensor's viewpoint.

---

[3] See Appendix E for an example of such a calculation.

License Compensation

A trademark license can be in any form that the parties agree upon, and so there are endless variations possible, including the form of compensation to be received by the licensor and paid by the licensee. It has become customary, however, for royalty compensation to be proportional to the usage of the trademark by the licensee.

A so-called running royalty is perhaps the most typical form of compensation. A running royalty is based on some formula which will be the basis for future royalty payments. The most common formula is a *royalty rate* which is to be applied to a *royalty base*. Common forms of a royalty rate are a percentage or a dollar amount per some unit. These relationships could be expressed as

$$Royalty = R_b \times X \, R_r$$

where R_b = the royalty base such as:
　　　　　Net Revenue
　　　　　Net income
　　　　　Expense savings
　　　　　Number of units sold
　　　R_r = the basis of calculation such as a:
　　　　　Percentage
　　　　　　Percentage subject to a minimum
　　　　　　Percentage subject to a maximum
　　　　　Dollar amount per unit sold

There can be a prepayment of royalties, with future royalties credited against the prepayment. There are also many license agreements that call for an initial payment in addition to running royalties. Royalties are often on a sliding scale during the term of the agreement or depending on the volume of goods sold. The royalty base can also change, and it may represent wholesale or retail prices, the price of a specific component, or that of an assembly.

By far the most common trademark royalty arrangements are on the basis of a percentage of net sales, or on dollars per units sold. For the purposes of this discussion, we will use the term to mean a percentage of net revenue. A trademark's *raison d'être* is to enhance sales of a product or service. It makes sense, therefore, to measure its success by relating it to those sales (e.g., net sales revenue).

A NOTE OF CAUTION

The use of net income or expense savings as a royalty base is uncommon, and for a reason. These amounts are clearly under the control of the licensee and can be minimized by management. These amounts can also be difficult to audit.

SOME GENERAL THOUGHTS

The basic economic elements of a licensing transaction are not complex. We have hedged that statement by the use of the word "basic" because under certain circumstances the licensing process can become very complex. One can imagine the complexities introduced in the licensing process if one of the parties is financially unstable, in another country, dealing in foreign currency, or if the license concerns embryonic or fledgling products or services. Absent these sorts of conditions, the economics are straightforward.

The Economics Controlling a Licensing Transaction

The economics controlling a licensing transaction are those of the licensee's business. This fact is often overlooked in the licensing process, even by those experienced in the field. We point it out because it clearly points to the necessity of analyzing the licensee's business or, at the very least, examining the future economic benefit that licensing a trademark can bring. That economic benefit is what must be divided between licensor and licensee—it sets the boundaries of the "playing field."

An Exception   Having stated that, we also observe that in some cases this is a rule that only holds in part. A very strong trademark—one that can command a premium in the marketplace even on goods or services for which it was not originally intended—can break the rules. When the reader is next in an airport, we suggest taking a look at a gift shop. There will be various items carrying an image of the city or state in which the airport is located. Coffee mugs, paperweights, and shot glasses will be decorated with images of Chicago, Texas, or whatever. There will also be the same merchandise carrying the logos of the local professional or college sports teams or well-known local attractions. These are priced significantly higher, in our experience. This is a case in which the economics of the coffee mug business do not control the licensing transaction. The licensor's trademark can drive the price above what would be dictated by the typical merchandise economics. Instead, the price is controlled by the market—what is someone willing to pay for a mug with their alma mater or favorite team's logo on it? With the application of a powerful trademark, the licensee's economics are changed.

The University of Texas (UT) provides an excellent example. A top-ranked NCAA sports team, the UT football team won its most recent national championship game in 2005 and sales of its merchandise bearing the university's trademarks, including the famous Longhorns logo, skyrocketed. From 2005 to 2006, UT earned a record $8.3 million in trademark licensing royalties. With a winning football team fueling the demand for college-related merchandise, UT was able to demand a licensing rate of 8 percent for each licensed item sold and 12 percent for national championship items.[4]

---

[4] "Longhorns Knock Off Tar Heels to Lead Nation in Merchandising Revenue," *USA Today*, Aug. 26, 2006.

Strong Brand *and* Strong Enforcement

Not only strong trademarks but also robust enforcement mechanisms can alter the economics in a trademark license negotiation. The most obvious example arises from the protection afforded the trademarks of the U.S. Olympic Committee (USOC), which include the word "Olympic" and its famous logo consisting of five interlocking rings. The USOC's trademarks are subject to special legislation that protects the marks from unauthorized use on *all* goods and services, without requiring the USOC to prove that the unauthorized use created a likelihood of confusion among consumers—proof usually needed to impose civil or criminal liability in trademark enforcement matters.[5] The lower standard of proof assists the USOC in enforcing its marks by lowering its litigation costs and "warning off" those considering unauthorized use.[6] Congress's primary purpose in passing such legislation "is that of protecting the strength of the Olympic designations so that the licensing of a designation is a commercially attractive proposition."[7] Only official corporate sponsors and licensees of the USOC may associate themselves with the Olympic brand, and that association provides a coveted international marketing platform.[8,9] The success of this approach can be seen in the $94.3 million in royalties received by the USOC for corporate sponsorship and licensing deals in conjunction with the Beijing 2008 Summer Olympic Games.[10]

A Bankruptcy Heads-Up

In a previous section, we discussed license clauses and noted that a termination provision might be one of them. That termination provision might include the possibility of bankruptcy by either licensor or licensee. We point out that, irrespective of what license or and licensee might agree upon, there are legal issues that bear on the handling of a trademark license in a bankruptcy situation. These are discussed more fully in Chapter 10, but we include the first part of that discussion here to alert the reader:

> *Section 365(a) of the U.S. Bankruptcy Code provides, in pertinent part, that "the trustee, subject to the court's approval, may assume or reject any executory contract or unexpired lease of the debtor."*[11] *An executory contract may*

[5] 36 U.S.C. § 220506 (civil liability for unauthorized use of any simulation of an Olympic mark that *tends* to cause confusion); 18 U.S.C. § 2320 (criminal liability for unauthorized and knowing use of a designation identical with or substantially indistinguishable from an Olympic mark).

[6] Steven B. Hay, Guarding the Olympic Gold: Protecting the Marketability of Olympic Trademarks Through Section 110 of the Amateur Sports Act of 1978, 16 SW. U. L. REV. 461, 494-95 (1986).

[7] *Id.* at 469-72.

[8] "What Olympic Sponsorship Means for Stocks," *Forbes*, July 27, 2012, http://www.forbes.com/sites/investopedia/2012/07/27/what-olympic-sponsorship-means-for-stocks/.

[9] "What Olympic Sponsorship Means for Stocks," Forbes, July 27, 2012, available at http://www.forbes.com/sites/investopedia/2012/07/27/what-olympic-sponsorship-means-for-stocks/.

[10] Tripp Mickle, "Beijing Olympics a Financial Boon for USOC," *Sports Business Daily*, June 1, 2009.

[11] 11 U.S.C. § 365(a).

be defined as one in which each party to the contract owes continuing, material obligations to the other so that either party's failure to perform would constitute a breach. Congress specifically exempted copyright and patent licenses from rejection in bankruptcy but did not address licenses for trademarks, service marks, or trade dress.[12] *The legislative history of that section indicates that Congress decided to postpone legislation with regard to the treatment of trademark licenses in bankruptcy and to allow the bankruptcy courts to fashion their own law on this front because the requirement that a trademark licensor exercise quality control over the licensee poses a serious challenge for the bankrupt licensor.*[13]

ROYALTY QUANTIFICATION

The amount of compensation (i.e., rent or royalty) that is positive cash flow to the licensor and negative cash flow to the licensee is not only a critical ingredient in a license negotiation, but is also utilized on its own in valuations and at times in litigation.

Licensing Income Flows

As always, we must be attentive to carefully define the property rights being analyzed. In a license, the owner of intellectual property rents some of the total bundle of rights to another (the licensee). The licensee pays for those rights by means of a royalty. If we add the *value* of the licensor's rights to those of the licensee, we would capture all of the intellectual property value.

If we use an income approach to value intellectual property and wish to use a market royalty rate as a surrogate for the income attributable to the asset we must capitalize both the income realized from the licensor's exploitation of the mark, and the income attributable to the property from the licensee's exploitation. This latter is not necessarily the amount of royalty being paid by the licensee. The essential point is that we need to consider all of the potential income streams that may be associated with licensed intellectual property and understand which streams belong to whom (see Exhibit 8.1).

The value of *all of the rights* in the intellectual property would be obtained by capitalizing the income streams A and B. The income C that is the royalty payment is a portion of income B, and a capitalization of it would be representative of the value of the *license contract* to the licensor. If our task were to value the *licensor's rights* in the intellectual property, we would capitalize income streams A and C. If we were to value the *licensee's rights* in the intellectual property, we would capitalize income stream B less the royalty expense C. It is apparent that there is some overlap here, and one must carefully define the asset to be valued and also carefully define the income associated with that asset before proceeding.

---

[12] 11 U.S.C. § 365(n).

[13] S. REP. NO. 100-505, at 5.

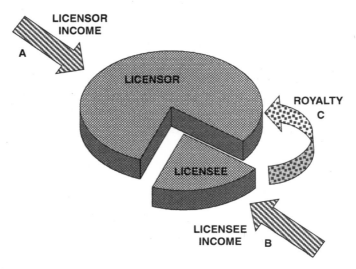

EXHIBIT 8.1   Income Flow in a Licensing Transaction

For those mathematically inclined, the relationships can be expressed as follows:

$$V_t = V_o + V_l$$

where V_t = the total value of all trademark rights.
         V_o = the value of the owner's trademark rights.
         V_l = the value of the licensee's trademark rights.

$$V_o = \frac{I_o + I_r}{C}$$

$$V_l = \frac{I_l + E_r}{C}$$

$$I_r = E_r$$

where I_o = the owner's income attributable to the trademark.
         I_r = the owner's royalty income.
         I_l = the licensee's income attributable to the trademark.
         E_r = the licensee's royalty expense.
         C = a capitalization rate.

If the expressions for V_o and V_l are substituted in the first equation and the result is reduced:

$$V_t = \frac{I_o + I_l}{C}$$

From this we can observe the relationship of the owner's and licensee's income streams that we just noted.

OOPS!

The owner of a commercial building leases the entire structure to another for a period of 75 years at an annual rent of one dollar. What has happened? The owner has essentially sold the property. The bundle of rights to a property can be divided by arrangement or by economics. The owner's rights in this case would be represented by the present value of the land reversion 75 years hence, plus a near- worthless building, and a few dollars in rent. The economic division of the rights bundle can sometimes be inadvertent.

The situation could be even more complicated if the trademark owner did not directly exploit it, but instead licensed it to others, with perhaps even master licensees and sublicensees, as might be the case of a franchise. There would be many income streams to consider, depending on the specific rights being valued.

Royalty rate information can be very useful to the financial analyst and the appraiser. As with any data from "the marketplace" or about "comparable transactions," one must be sensitive to the terms of the transaction and to the nature of the property rights involved.

QUANTIFICATION TECHNIQUES

We suggest that the same cost, market, and income techniques presented previously for valuation purposes are equally applicable tools for quantifying the compensation element in a trademark license. We also observe the advantages, disadvantages, and pitfalls of each.

Cost Technique

The structure of the cost technique is to aggregate the total cost of creating the trademark to be licensed and then estimating the amount of compensation that would be required to provide a return on and a return of that investment during the term of the license.

In Chapter 4, we explored the many shortcomings of this method for valuation purposes. Those same shortcomings appear again if we attempt to use a cost technique to quantify license compensation. The primary and fatal shortcoming is that the cost of trademark creation and development bears no relationship to its market value. An additional shortcoming stems from the fact that that this technique does not consider the future economic benefit that the licensee will garner as a result of the license.

While we have observed attempts to use this method to quantify license compensation (more frequently for technology than for trademarks), we cannot recommend its use.

Market Technique

As previously noted, one technique that can be used to estimate a fair, or arm's length, royalty rate is to observe what others have thought it to be. We use this method to

---

REMEMBER

Be careful of using the price as a benchmark if you don't know much about the deal.

---

put a price on our homes and our automobiles, and to decide what a fair rental rate for property is. It is the essence of the market approach to valuation which we described in Chapter 4. It can be a strong technique as long as we recognize its strengths and weaknesses.

Its strength is that it can provide a direct observation of the marketplace. For an appraiser, the best of all worlds is to discover that an identical (to the subject) home, machine, business, or other property sold yesterday at a known price between unrelated parties. If we are shopping for office space in a building, the fact that the space down the hall rented for $17 a square foot is valuable information indeed. It is valuable provided we can also learn the terms of the lease. Is it three years, five years? Is the first year rent free? Are utilities included, cleaning included; is there allowance for improvements, carpet cleaning, repainting, and the like? Obviously, these terms had an effect on the transaction being concluded at $17. We need to know these things in order to judge whether the $17 rate benchmark is useful to us.

Market Royalty Rates

As a part of a licensing negotiation, a popular royalty rate estimation technique is to look to the market for rates that have been negotiated by others. We have discussed previously the pros and cons of a market approach and the information that is required to execute it successfully. We also need to consider where our "market determined royalty rates" come from:

- The participants in a licensing negotiation may themselves have royalty benchmarks from other deals they have made.
- Valuation professionals and others in the business become aware of licensing transactions through their work. Largely, these cannot be divulged to others because of the confidential nature of the client/consultant relationship. Because of this, these royalty rates usually cannot be used to support conclusions in reports to other clients.
- A variety of public documents such as court records, company annual reports, filings with the Securities and Exchange Commission, articles in the press and professional publications, are sources of royalty information.
- There are commercial databases of licensing transaction data, some of which include royalty rate information.[14]

We have rarely served a client in a trademark valuation, litigation, or royalty rate consultation without being required to sign a confidentiality agreement. This is

---

[14] IPRA, Inc., www.ipresearch.com. CONSOR.com, RoyaltyStat.com, Invotex.com, RoyaltyConnection.com, ktMINE.com, and RoyaltySource.com.

understandable, given the knowledge of sensitive market and strategy information that must accompany such a study.

We would estimate that, if one gathered together all of the trademark royalty rate files in the hands of people other than the owners of the trademarks, the information might cover as much as 20 percent of the trademark licensing transactions made in recent years. If we further eliminate from that information the licensing data relating to cartoon characters, personalities, toy concepts, and trademark licensing by institutions with no profit motive, the amount is probably less than 10 percent. We must therefore be realistic about the magnitude of information available to use in comparable analyses relating to commercial trademarks.

Some Market Data   There are far more licensing transactions for technology-related IP then there are for trademarks. This is especially true for brands that could be called business to business brands or "business-facing" brands. We touched on this in Chapter 5. It is not that these brands have no value, but rather that they do not loom as large in the buying decision and so we must recognize that their importance is less than that of business to consumer brands or "consumer-facing" brands.

We wondered, however, whether there might be some characteristics of the more robust data related to technology licensing that might confirm or cause us to reject some of our brand valuation intuitions. Our research revealed some data regarding a body of nearly 5000 technology licensing transactions that were analyzed and published in *Licensing Economics Review*[15] in December 2012.

In the years that we have observed licensing activities and the royalty rates that result therefrom, we have observed that there is at least a rough correlation between the relative profitability of an industry segment and the royalty rates that emanate from deals within it. The data contained in Exhibit 8.2 suggests that as well. While the Electronics and Semiconductor data might seem to be contrary to that, we have already touched upon the effect of fast-moving technology in the industry, and that causes proprietary technology to be more critical than patented technology in maintaining a competitive edge. In that situation, it is not surprising that industry participants do not rely heavily on licensed technology.

At the other end of the spectrum, pharmaceutical, biotechnology, media and entertainment, software, and Internet licensing activity suggests that profitability influences royalty rate levels. Intuitively, one would also expect stronger consumer influence in licensing decisions in these industries. It would seem that the "patent wars" that we have witnessed recently in the Entertainment, Software, and Internet segments have at least in part been driven by the necessity for the players to have access to content and features that have found popularity in the marketplace. Access requires designing around the IP rights of others or licensing-in.

We are not suggesting that royalty rates in the technology field should be used as market benchmarks for trademark licensing. We do suggest, however, that some of the royalty rate drivers are similar.

In Exhibit 8.3, we have added trademark licensing royalty rates from approximately 600 transactions.[16] These have been divided into two segments: based on

---

[15] *Licensing Economics Review*, published by RoyaltySource, a division of AUS Consultants, Mt. Laurel, NJ royaltysource.com

[16] Provided in an analysis by RoyaltySource.

EXHIBIT 8.2   Technology Licenses - Average Royalty Rates

TECHNOLOGY LICENSES

	Average Royalty Rate (%)
Electrical & Electronics	4.6
Semiconductors	4.6
Chemicals	4.7
Automotive	4.9
Food	5.3
Computers & Office Equipment	5.5
Machines / Tools	5.5
Telecom (excluding media)	5.6
Energy & Environment	5.7
Medical / Health Products	5.8
Consumer Goods, Retail & Liesure	5.9
Pharmaceuticals & Biotechnology	7.9
Media & Entertainment	11.4
Software	12.8
Internet	16.8

whether the licensing parties were business-facing or consumer-facing. Many trademark licensing agreements contain several royalty rates that may apply at different times, or various levels of sales volume, for different territories served, or based on this stage of development of the underlying license property. In the data shown, the "low" royalty is the average of the lowest rate in these multiple-royalty licenses, and the "high" is the average of the highest rate. We have positioned these indicators against those of the technology licenses.

The business-facing segment includes:

■ Service industry
■ Industrial and manufacturing industry

The consumer-facing segment includes:

■ Apparel and apparel extensions
■ Celebrity
■ Character
■ Sporting goods
■ University

This data indicates a clear demarcation between these two types of trademark licensing transactions. Again, these data are averages intended to identify generalities. A more rigorous comparability analysis should be undertaken when market data is used to benchmark a decision about specific trademark property rights.

EXHIBIT 8.3   Comparison of Technology Royalty Rates and Trademark Royalty Rates

TECHNOLOGY LICENSES		TRADEMARK LICENSES		
	Average Royalty Rate (%)	Average Royalty Rate (%)		
		2.7	Low	Business-facing Segments
		3.4	High	
Electrical & Electronics	4.6			
Semiconductors	4.6			
Chemicals	4.7			
Automotive	4.9			
Food	5.3			
Computers & Office Equipment	5.5			
Machines / Tools	5.5			
Telecom (excluding media)	5.6			
Energy & Environment	5.7			
Medical / Health Products	5.8			
Consumer Goods, Retail & Liesure	5.9			
Pharmaceuticals & Biotechnology	7.9	7.6	Low	Consumer-facing Segments
		9.3	High	
Media & Entertainment	11.4			
Software	12.8			
Internet	16.8			

SCORING AND RATING TECHNIQUES

Another royalty rate analysis technique that we often observe is based on the use of scoring or rating criteria that are used to quantify the qualitative difference between the trademark being studied and trademarks that have been licensed, and for which the royalty rate is known. This technique can lend an aura of academic precision to an otherwise subjective process, but we need to understand its limitations.

An example of this method is as follows:

■ Assume that we have made a survey of royalty rates in a business sector similar to our subject, and which are evident in licensing transactions known to us. The range of royalty rates is 4 to 8 percent.

- We then analyze the subject trademark (the one for which we are trying to estimate an appropriate royalty rate), and give it a score for each of its various aspects, using a score from 0 to 100.
- These aspects often include such elements as market share, extension potential, "internationality," stability, strength, "leadership," growth trends, and the size of the market in which the trademarked product or service is present. Those who use this technique seem to have their own unique scoring elements.
- We then compute the average score across all of the criteria, say it is 82.
- Our conclusion is that an appropriate royalty rate is 7.3 percent (falling at the 82 percent mark between 4 and 8 percent. Mathematically, this is expressed as $((8\% - 4\%) \times 0.82) + 4\% = 7.3\%$.

The accuracy of this method is of course dependent upon whether the 4 percent royalty rates known to us were all for trademarks that would score zero on our scale and whether all of the 8 percent trademarks would have received a score of 100 on our scale. This is the "Achilles' heel" of this method. Most of the time, we simply do not know enough about the royalty rates that we extract from exogenous information to know how they might score on a given system. Therefore, we do not know whether they represent a cross-section of deals, or a group of "bad" deals, or a population of "great" deals.

The trademarks licensed in the 4 percent transactions might score very high on our scale, but the low royalty rate might be the result of poor negotiation or a compelling need for cash on the part of the licensor. The 8 percent trademark deals might score poorly on our scale, but may have been made because the licensee was in a high profit business, in heavy competition for the trademark license, and <u>had</u> to pay a high royalty rate to make the deal.

The point is, that for a system such as this to work, we must know whether the high and low royalties from the "marketplace" are driven by the criteria in the scoring system. Or are they driven by completely unrelated factors? It is essential that we know whether the low and high royalty rates we extract from market transactions comport with the low and high scores in our rating system. Only then can we have any confidence that our technique for placing the subject property inside a range of market rates makes any sense.

We might, if we knew all the facts about a group of trademark royalty rates from the marketplace, discover that *all of them* score low (or high) on our scale. If so, the scoring technique we are describing would necessarily place our subject trademark among a skewed population of supposed comparables. Doing so will yield a meaningless answer, and doing so by means of a mathematical score only confuses precision with accuracy.

While we have not observed such a technique in use, perhaps one refinement would be to assign different weightings to each criteria. This might, however, only result in piling subjectivity upon another series of subjective judgments, with no improvement in accuracy.

In our mind, the most glaring deficiency of such a system is that *its conclusion is doomed to be within the range of other transactions that we happen to know about.* The facts of our case should control the conclusion. Our technique should not consign us to a specific and finite range.

Income Technique

In this section, we present some analytical techniques for estimating royalty rates. These methods follow the principles discussed relative to trademark valuation because, indeed, the same principles apply even though the style of transaction is different.

One Analytical Technique

The preceding is an oversimplification, but an appropriate place to start. Assume that we are a marketer of ball-point pens. We designed this pen some time ago, have it manufactured to our specifications and sell it in the northeast U.S. We have a registered trademark, "PEN," and have built a nice business by calling on distributors and retailers in the region. We would like to go national with our product, but lack the capital for the extensive advertising campaign that would be necessary to support such a move.

We are aware of a large, multinational company that manufactures and sells pencils and erasers under its well-known "PENCIL" trademark. They agree to license to us the use of the PENCIL trademark on our pens, which will greatly facilitate our national rollout. They ask for a royalty of 10 percent of net sales. Is that a fair price? We need to analyze the economics of our business before answering.

To illustrate, we will start with PEN's income statement in Exhibit 8.4.

We have added a column to the typical dollar data to show the income statement on a percentage basis. We can observe that our bottom line, or net income is 8.6 percent of net sales. Would a 10 percent royalty wipe out profits? Probably not, because royalty expense is a deduction for income tax purposes but we must reflect the payment of a royalty in the model in order to discern its impact (see Exhibit 8.5).

EXHIBIT 8.4 PEN Income Statement

PEN INCOME STATEMENT FOR FISCAL YEAR ENDING DECEMBER 31, 2013		Percent
Sales, less returns and allowances	373,500	100.0
Less – cost of goods sold	205,000	54.9
Gross margin	168,500	45.1
Less – Selling, general and administrative expenses	74,700	20.0
Net operating income	93,800	25.1
Other income or (expense)	−32,000	−8.6
Net income before income taxes	61,800	16.5
Less – State and federal income taxes	24,720	6.6
Net income before extraordinary items	37,080	9.9
Extraordinary items of income or (expense)	−5,000	−1.3
Net income	32,080	8.6

EXHIBIT 8.5   PEN Income Statement after Payment of Royalty

PEN INCOME STATEMENT
FOR FISCAL YEAR ENDING DECEMBER 31, 2013

		Percent
Sales, less returns and allowances	373,500	100.0
Less – cost of goods sold	205,000	54.9
Gross margin	168,500	45.1
Less – Selling, general and administrative expenses	74,700	20.0
TRADEMARK ROYALTY 10%	37,350	10.0
Net operating income	56,450	15.1
Other income or (expense)	−32,000	−8.6
Net income before income taxes	24,450	6.5
Less – State and federal income taxes	9,780	2.6
Net income before extraordinary items	14,670	3.9
Extraordinary items of income or (expense)	−5,000	−1.3
Net income	9,670	2.6

The model now tells us that net income would be reduced from 8.6 percent to 2.6 percent, or by about 70 percent. This calculation does not provide an easy answer about whether this is a fair deal for us. Dividing the economic benefit of intellectual property between licensor and licensee is one of the knottiest problems there is, but at least now we have some facts on which to base our decision.

This is a very simplified model for analysis and we must consider some of the additional considerations that must be made:

- Becoming a PENCIL licensee and entering the national market ought to bring in many times the sales revenue and net income (in terms of dollars) that we now receive.
- We will, however, need to make an additional investment in our business to maintain a larger inventory, among other things.
- The risk of our business may be increased because we will have to place larger orders with our suppliers that we will be committed to buy even if sales do not materialize as planned.
- The risk of our business may be decreased because we will be selling to a larger base of customers.
- In contrast, we ought to be able to negotiate a lower price for pens and share in the economies of scale enjoyed by our suppliers. This would increase the rate of our profitability.
- Perhaps PENCIL products sell at higher prices than competitors and we could recoup some of the royalty by increasing the price of our product.

In any particular situation, there might be other elements to consider as well, but all of them would be factors affecting the *economics of the licensee's business* (in this case, our business, PEN). There is a range within which negotiations are likely to take place. We have cited the difficulty of dividing the economic benefit between licensor and licensee and that range may define the range of negotiation, but that undertaking cannot begin until the economic benefit is defined.

DISCOUNTED CASH FLOW MODEL

In our opinion, the best analysis model for this purpose is constructed around the discounted cash flow model that was described in Chapter 7, for the valuation of a trademark. The model is used to describe the licensee's business (or the business segment or product line into which the trademark will be licensed) and permits the input of all the economic factors that might affect business for the licensee. We can utilize this discounted cash flow model as a starting point (see Exhibit 8.6).

In this model, we have calculated the value of the licensee's business enterprise, or the value of the licensee's business segment or product line into which the subject trademark will be licensed. In this case, the underlying data is that of *our* PEN business. If we are making these calculations from the licensor's viewpoint, we are not likely to have easy access to the potential licensor's financial data. We might have to make pro forma forecasts on the basis of our own business (in the event that we are in a similar industry) or use surrogate publicly available data.

This Step 1 calculation is the "business as usual" scenario, excluding the potential effect of the trademark on the business. In this model, sales grow at 4 percent annually, and other expenses generally keep pace with sales, and net income remains at about 10 percent during the five-year projection period. We have estimated the amounts of net working capital and tangible assets during the period so that we can calculate the net cash flow that we expect to be produced by the enterprise.

The model calculates the present value of the annual cash flow for 2014 through 2018 (at a discount rate of 10 percent) and adds to that the present value of the value of the business in the year 2019 (a capitalization of that year's income at a discount rate of 10 percent less 4 percent inflation, or 6 percent). The value of the business on this basis is $741,887,000.

In the next step, we reflect in the model the anticipated effect of licensing the trademark (see Exhibit 8.7).

Sales revenues have increased and the cost of goods sold has declined because of economies of scale in manufacture. No other changes have been made in order to clarify the model's use. In fact, any of the effects discussed in the preceding, including changes in working capital or tangible asset requirements, increased risk of the business, or the possibility of premium pricing could be incorporated into the model. With just the elements noted, the value of this business increases to $892,589.

The question we are trying to answer concerns how much royalty the business could pay to achieve these anticipated benefits. We can answer that by inserting a royalty into the model. Adding a royalty expense will reduce the value of the business. If it reduces the value of the business beyond what it was before the

EXHIBIT 8.6 Trademark Royalty Rate Calculation—Step 1

INCOME STATEMENT

($000's)

	2013		2014		2015		2016		2017		2018	
Sales, less returns and allowances	373,500	100.0%	388,440	100.0%	403,978	100.0%	420,137	100.0%	436,942	100.0%	454,420	100.0%
Less – cost of goods sold	205,000	54.9%	213,200	54.9%	221,728	54.9%	230,597	54.9%	239,821	54.9%	249,414	54.9%
Gross margin	168,500	45.1%	175,240	45.1%	182,250	45.1%	189,540	45.1%	197,121	45.1%	205,006	45.1%
Less – Selling, general and administrative expenses	74,700	20.0%	77,688	20.0%	80,796	20.0%	84,027	20.0%	87,388	20.0%	90,884	20.0%
Net operating income	93,800	25.1%	97,552	25.1%	101,454	25.1%	105,513	25.1%	109,733	25.1%	114,122	25.1%
Other income or (expense)	–32,000	–8.6%	–32,640	–8.4%	–33,293	–8.2%	–33,959	–8.1%	–34,638	–7.9%	–35,331	–7.8%
Net income before income taxes	61,800	16.5%	64,912	16.7%	68,161	16.9%	71,554	17.0%	75,095	17.2%	78,791	17.3%
Less – State and federal income taxes	24,720	6.6%	25,965	6.7%	27,264	6.7%	28,622	6.8%	30,038	6.9%	31,517	6.9%
Net income before extraordinary items	37,080	9.9%	38,947	10.0%	40,896	10.1%	42,932	10.2%	45,057	10.3%	47,275	10.4%
Extraordinary items of income or (expense)	–5,000	–1.3%	0	0.0%	0	0.0%	0	0.0%	0	0.0%	0	0.0%
Net income	32,080	8.6%	38,947	10.0%	40,896	10.1%	42,932	10.2%	45,057	10.3%	47,275	10.4%

CALCULATE NET CASH FLOW

	2013	2014	2015	2016	2017	2018
Subtract: Extraordinary items to normalize	–5,000				0	0
Add: Depreciation expense	12,000	12,240	12,485	12,734	12,989	13,249
Subtract: Additions to working capital	2,000	1,800	1,836	1,873	1,910	1,948
Subtract: Capital expenditures	3,000	4,500	4,590	4,682	4,775	4,871
	44,080	44,887	46,955	49,112	51,361	53,704

ASSETS EMPLOYED

	2013	2014	2015	2016	2017	2018
Net Working Capital	90,000	91,800	93,636	95,509	97,419	99,367
Tangible Assets	225,000	229,500	234,090	238,772	243,547	248,418
Intangible Assets	85,000	86,700	88,434	90,203	92,007	93,847
PRESENT VALUE 10.0%		42,798	40,700	38,700	36,792	582,897

TOTAL PRESENT VALUE $741,887

EXHIBIT 8.7 Trademark Royalty Rate Calculation—Step 2

INCOME STATEMENT

($000's)

	2013		2014		2015		2016		2017		2018	
Sales, less returns and allowances	373,500	100.0%	392,175	100.0%	411,784	100.0%	432,373	100.0%	453,992	100.0%	476,691	100.0%
Less – cost of goods sold	205,000	54.9%	195,695	49.9%	205,480	49.9%	215,754	49.9%	226,542	49.9%	237,869	49.9%
Gross margin	168,500	45.1%	196,480	50.1%	206,304	50.1%	216,619	50.1%	227,450	50.1%	238,822	50.1%
Less – Selling, general and administrative expenses	74,700	20.0%	87,104	22.2%	91,459	22.2%	96,032	22.2%	100,834	22.2%	105,876	22.2%
Net operating income	93,800	25.1%	109,376	27.9%	114,845	27.9%	120,587	27.9%	126,616	27.9%	132,946	27.9%
Other income or (expense)	−32,000	−8.6%	−32,640	−8.3%	−33,293	−8.1%	−33,959	−7.9%	−34,638	−7.6%	−35,331	−7.4%
Net income before income taxes	61,800	16.5%	76,736	19.6%	81,552	19.8%	86,628	20.0%	91,978	20.3%	97,616	20.5%
Less – State and federal income taxes	24,720	6.6%	30,694	7.8%	32,621	7.9%	34,651	8.0%	36,791	8.1%	39,046	8.2%
Net income before extraordinary items	37,080	9.9%	46,041	11.7%	48,931	11.9%	51,977	12.0%	55,187	12.2%	58,569	12.3%
Extraordinary items of income or (expense)	−5,000	−1.3%	0	0.0%	0	0.0%	0	0.0%	0	0.0%	0	0.0%
Net income	32,080	8.6%	46,041	11.7%	48,931	11.9%	51,977	12.0%	55,187	12.2%	58,569	12.3%

CALCULATE NET CASH FLOW

	2013	2014	2015	2016	2017	2018
Subtract: Extraordinary items to normalize	−5,000	0	0	0	0	0
Add: Depreciation expense	12,000	12,240	12,485	12,734	12,989	13,249
Subtract: Additions to working capital	2,000	1,800	1,836	1,873	1,910	1,948
Subtract: Capital expenditures	3,000	4,500	4,590	4,682	4,775	4,871
	44,080	51,981	54,990	58,157	61,490	64,999

ASSETS EMPLOYED

	2013	2014	2015	2016	2017	2018
Net Working Capital	90,000	91,800	93,636	95,509	97,419	99,367
Tangible Assets	225,000	229,500	234,090	238,772	243,547	248,418
Intangible Assets	75,000	76,500	78,030	79,591	81,182	82,806
PRESENT VALUE 10.0%		49,562	47,664	45,827	44,049	705,487

TOTAL PRESENT VALUE $892,589

presumed license, it is a royalty that the licensee would not accept. If it reduces the value of the business by only a minor amount, than it is a royalty that the licensor is not likely to accept. We can observe that a 4 percent royalty rate produces royalty expense that reduces the business value to $735,198,000, or about what it was previously (see Exhibit 8.8).

A 4 percent royalty rate therefore represents the highest rate that a licensor could expect to receive or that a licensee would be willing to pay. The concept employed here is one of subtraction that we have discussed in previous sections. We are, in essence, merely adding an additional calculation which relates the income attributable to the trademark to the amount of sales revenue in order to express the income in terms of a percentage royalty on net sales.

The foremost benefit of this cash flow model is that it is based on investment return principles that drive all business decisions and that it facilitates the evaluation of various scenarios. It allows one to change the forecasted economic conditions of the licensee's business and to identify the factors that are influential in the royalty rate decision.

This model is not something new that we are suddenly unveiling for the first time. It simply is a logical extension of the facts and financial relationships that we presented in Chapters 5, 6, and 7.

DIVIDING THE ECONOMIC BENEFIT

We began this chapter by noting that a license is a means of dividing the future economic benefit of brand exploitation between the owner of a mark and the licensee. In the discounted cash flow model presented, we concluded that a 4 percent royalty rate was indicative of the total future economic benefit that we (PEN), as licensee, would gain from licensing the PENCIL trademark. Our DCF calculations also informed us that licensing the PENCIL trademark would make our business more valuable by approximately $150 million.

That is, our business value would increase by $150 million if we could license the PENCIL trademark at no cost. If we had to pay the full 4 percent royalty, our business value would not increase and there would be no economic purpose in pursuing this license. What to do? Should our negotiating target be 1 percent, 2 percent, 3 percent?

That decision will likely be based on our estimate of the cost that we will incur in exploiting the PENCIL trademark and the return we want to achieve on that investment. Since the PENCIL company ought to have modest expenses to administer the license, we (PEN) ought to end up at the low end of this range of royalty rates.

Generally speaking, the party who should get the "lions share" of the future economic benefit in a licensing transaction should be the one who:

- Accepts the most risk that the trademark license will not produce the expected economic benefit.
- Will incur the greatest share of expenses for the exploitation.
- Brings most of the market power to the negotiating table.

EXHIBIT 8.8   Trademark Royalty Rate Calculation—Step 3

INCOME STATEMENT

($000's)

	2013		2014		2015		2016		2017		2018	
Sales, less returns and allowances	373,500	100.0%	392,175	100.0%	411,784	100.0%	432,373	100.0%	453,992	100.0%	476,691	100.0%
Less – cost of goods sold	205,000	54.9%	195,641	49.9%	205,423	49.9%	215,694	49.9%	226,479	49.9%	237,803	49.9%
Gross margin	168,500	45.1%	196,534	50.1%	206,360	50.1%	216,678	50.1%	227,512	50.1%	238,888	50.1%
Less – Selling, general and administrative expenses	74,700	20.0%	87,128	22.2%	91,484	22.2%	96,059	22.2%	100,862	22.2%	105,905	22.2%
Less – Trademark Royalty 4.0%	0		15,687		16,471		17,295		18,160		19,068	
Net operating income	93,800	25.1%	93,719	23.9%	98,405	23.9%	103,325	23.9%	108,491	23.9%	113,916	23.9%
Other income or (expense)	−32,000	−8.6%	−32,640	−8.3%	−33,293	−8.1%	−33,959	−7.9%	−34,638	−7.6%	−35,331	−7.4%
Net income before income taxes	61,800	16.5%	61,079	15.6%	65,112	15.8%	69,366	16.0%	73,853	16.3%	78,585	16.5%
Less – State and federal income taxes	24,720	6.6%	24,431	6.6%	26,045	6.3%	27,746	6.4%	29,541	6.5%	31,434	6.6%
Net income before extraordinary items	37,080	9.9%	36,647	9.9%	39,067	9.5%	41,620	9.6%	44,312	9.8%	47,151	9.9%
Extraordinary items of income or (expense)	−5,000	−1.3%	0	0.0%	0	0.0%	0	0.0%	0	0.0%	0	0.0%
Net income	32,080	8.6%	36,647	9.3%	39,067	9.5%	41,620	9.6%	44,312	9.8%	47,151	9.9%

CALCULATE NET CASH FLOW

	2013	2014	2015	2016	2017	2018
Subtract: Extraordinary items to normalize	−5,000	0	0	0	0	0
Add: Depreciation expense	12,000	12,240	12,485	12,734	12,989	13,249
Subtract: Additions to working capital	2,000	1,800	1,836	1,873	1,910	1,948
Subtract: Capital expenditures	3,000	4,500	4,590	4,682	4,775	4,871
	44,080	42,587	45,126	47,800	50,616	53,581

ASSETS EMPLOYED

	2013	2014	2015	2016	2017	2018
Net Working Capital	90,000	91,800	93,636	95,509	97,419	99,367
Tangible Assets	225,000	229,500	234,090	238,772	243,547	248,418
Intangible Assets	75,000	76,500	78,030	79,591	81,182	82,806
PRESENT VALUE 10.0%		40,605	39,114	37,665	36,258	581,554
TOTAL PRESENT VALUE	$735,198					

209

ANOTHER ANALYTICAL TECHNIQUE

In Chapter 5, we presented a technique for estimating the income allocable to a trademark that involved allocating the income produced by an enterprise among its constituent assets. The summary illustration was contained in Exhibit 5.11, in which we observed that the income allocable to trademarks was $1,462,000. Please note that this data refers to the Smith & Richey company, not the pen and pencil example discussed in the previous section. This information, used in Chapter 5 to develop an estimate of the economic benefit of a trademark, can also be useful in estimating a royalty rate. All that we need to do is relate that income attributable to the subject trademark, to the net sales revenue of the business which produced the income, and we have it (see Exhibit 8.9).

This technique involves balancing some unknowns and the reader should refer again to Chapter 5 to insure that the underlying assumptions are understood. It appears simple, but deceptively so.

Again, this technique reveals the maximum that a licensee would be willing to pay. It assumes that the licensee would be willing to pay over all of the incremental income produced by the trademark to the licensor, which would not be the case in real life. A 7.9 percent royalty (equal to 4.7 percent before 40 percent income tax) would consume all of the income attributable to the subject trademark.

However simple this example may appear, it requires extensive analysis to estimate the inputs and it embodies all of the investment return principles that we have

EXHIBIT 8.9   Allocating Income among Assets to Calculate a Royalty

ASSET CATEGORY	ASSET VALUE ($ 000's)	RETURNS REQUIRED	AMOUNT OF RETURN ($ 000's)
NET WORKING CAPITAL	3,830	2.7%	103
TANGIBLE ASSETS	13,600	5.7%	775
INTANGIBLE ASSETS	5,000	12.0%	600
INTELLECTUAL PROPERTY	15,080	18.0%	2,714
TOTAL	37,510	11.2%	4,193
TECHNOLOGY IP	5,000	25.0%	1,250
TRADEMARK	10,080	14.5%	1,462
	15,080	18.0%	2,712
SALES REVENUE (from Exhibit 7.6)	30,900		
INCOME ALLOCABLE TO TRADEMARK	1,462		
PRETAX INCOME ALLOCATED TO TRADEMARK	2,436		
INDICATED ROYALTY RATE	**7.9%**		

been discussing. This model is a powerful means of calculating both royalty rates and the values of the underlying assets of an enterprise.

RULES OF THUMB

We have also observed the use of rules-of-thumb to derive royalty rates. Some of the most common are:

- "The average of all the royalty rates that we can think of is 5 percent"
- "Whatever rate is customary in our industry"
- "A royalty that will recoup our cost of development"
- The so-called "25 percent rule"

The first two are self-explanatory and their shortcomings are obvious. When a royalty rate opinion is to be used for litigation, deal making, or in a relief from royalty valuation, a high degree of comparability is required.

Basing a royalty on the cost to develop the IP rights being licensed is a method that has some intuitive appeal but also serious flaws. Our discussion of the cost method in Chapter 4 highlights the disconnect between development cost and market value. Remember the example of "Post-it Notes"!

The difficulty with the 25 percent rule is not so obvious. This rule suggests that the licensee should be willing to pay a royalty equivalent to 25 percent of the profit expected from exploitation of the intellectual property rights being licensed. When those royalty dollars are set against the expected sales revenue of the product or service involved, a royalty rate can be calculated.

This method of estimating a royalty rate has been extensively used over the years, especially in deal-making. So it may in some ways take on the aspect of a self-fulfilling prophecy. We would caution against its use, however, in the litigation arena.[17] This technique should be taken for what it is—a generalized assumption whose basis in fact is unclear, as with any rule of thumb.

We suggest that, whenever a royalty rate opinion is needed, whether for deal negotiation, a valuation, or in litigation, the thought process proceed from the assumption that no royalty is warranted. That is, a "null hypothesis" in more scientific terminology. From that point, one can build up a royalty rate by examining all of the pros and cons, recognizing some and discarding others. We feel that this logic will produce a more supportable opinion.

---

[17] In January 2011, the United States Court of Appeals for the Federal Circuit (CAFC) rendered its decision in *Uniloc U.S.A., Inc. v. Microsoft Corp*. The issue before the Court was the quantification of patent infringement damages. In its decision, the Court emphatically rejected the use of the 25 percent rule that was used by one of the expert witnesses as a tool to quantify damages.

SUMMARY

The highlights of this chapter include:

- A license divides the future economic benefit of exploitation between licensor and licensee.
- Almost every license clause has some economic effect.
- The economics of the licensee's business is often what controls the deal.
- We need to clearly understand the money flows that result from a licensing transaction.
- A cost approach to royalty quantification is not recommended.
- A market approach to royalty quantification can be a strong indicator as long as there is good transaction comparability.
- An income approach to royalty quantification can yield a solid result, albeit the input data is more difficult to develop.

CHAPTER 9

Quantification of Harm in Trademark Enforcement Cases

One might wonder why we introduce this discussion of enforcement issues related to trademark rights. The traditional method for measuring damages is to subtract the value of property *after* some damaging event from the value of that property *prior to* the event. This has not come to be, in the statutes or in the courts, a method for measuring damages to trademark rights and so trademark market values are typically not an issue. Monetary recovery in civil litigation, while not a direct measure of diminishment in trademark value, acts as a surrogate for that measure if the recovery is compensatory in nature.[1] In criminal proceedings, criminal fines are the only monetary penalty in issue and, while fines are not tied to the value of a trademark, criminal sentences for federal trademark counterfeiting are governed by the retail value of the counterfeits in issue, which may be measured by the retail value of the genuine items.

While specific valuations are not present, monetary issues are important in enforcement actions and there are additional reasons why we feel that this subject of damage enforcement is useful to understand:

- Throughout our previous discussions of trademark valuation, the element of risk was identified as a primary driver. One element of risk in creating and exploiting a brand is the possibility that trademark rights come into question or that financial penalties may erode the mark holder's economic benefit forecast. An understanding of the potential legal issues is therefore essential to a full understanding of that risk.

---

[1] *See* Michael J. Freno, *Trademark Valuation: Preserving Brand Equity*, 97 Trademark Rep. 1055 (2007), in which the author discusses the relationship between monetary recovery in civil trademark enforcement actions and valuation of a trademark. Mr. Freno points out that trademarks are one of several factors that contribute to a sale, including for example, manufacturing efficiencies, trade secrets, and good management, so that a loss of sales and, hence, a loss of revenue due to a defendant's wrongdoing, reflects a loss attributable to all the foregoing factors. He suggests that a reasonable royalty award more closely approximates loss in the value of a trademark because a royalty focuses on the value attributable to the trademark alone. Of course, when the award is directed at deterrence or some other equitable objective not directly related to compensating the mark holder, little connection exists between the value of the trademark and monetary recovery.

- We feel that there is a greater array of potential legal (and economic) pitfalls with respect to trademarks in contrast with other types of intellectual property. There is a wide river of subjectivity with respect to trademark infringement, as an example. Even the basic tenet of likely confusion is difficult to define and quantify.
- It is also essential to understand the international nature of these legal issues. While it is true that brands cross international borders fluidly, it is also true that legal frameworks for trademark rights are not homogeneous from country to country. This introduces another element of risk.
- All of the ingredients of trademark valuation that we have covered in previous chapters are also elements useful in quantification of damages in an enforcement action, such as the importance of financial statement analysis, the methods for extracting the economic benefits of a brand from that of the entire enterprise, and all of the underlying financial principles that support the quantification of market value.

Within the United States, the 1946 federal Lanham Act provides a useful model for monetary awards in civil trademark enforcement actions because the Act establishes liability for conduct that is generally actionable under state trademark enforcement schemes as well, and for such violations, the Act authorizes types of monetary recovery that accord with recovery available under most state statutes and the common law. Due to international efforts to harmonize intellectual property law in order to stimulate trade between nations, most national schemes direct trademark enforcement toward the same or similar types of misconduct as the Lanham Act, although principles governing monetary recovery vary more widely from country to country. This discussion should be considered a starting point for exploring monetary recovery under other national trademark enforcement schemes. Again, as a result of harmonization, most nations address the scourge of trademark counterfeiting by prosecuting such behavior criminally.

CIVIL TRADEMARK ENFORCEMENT ACTIONS

The following pages discuss various civil trademark enforcement actions including infringement, counterfeiting, dilution, cybersquatting, and deceptive advertising.[2]

Infringement

The most common trademark enforcement action is a claim for trademark infringement, which may be used to enforce registered and non-registered marks. Resolution

---

[2] Throughout this discussion the terms "mark holder" and "plaintiff" are used interchangeably because the mark holder normally initiates legal proceedings in a civil enforcement action and the terms "wrongdoer" and "defendant" are used interchangeably because the party accused of wrongdoing with regard to a trademark normally defends the action, unless that party initiates an action for a declaration that there has been no wrongdoing or an action asserting a claim of wrongdoing against the mark holder who then counterclaims with a trademark enforcement theory.

of trademark infringement claims hinges on a showing of likelihood of confusion. That standard may be stated generally as the likelihood that consumers will misidentify the commercial source of the infringer's products or services, in most cases, concluding that they originate with the mark holder, or that consumers will be under the mistaken impression that the mark holder is affiliated with or has endorsed the infringer's products or services in some manner.[3] An obvious example is use of the word "Windy's" to offer fast food services, thereby infringing the well-known "Wendy's" fast-food service mark. To choose a less obvious example, consider the infringement probability created by appropriating the "Green Giant" trademark, made famous with respect to canned and frozen vegetables, to sell a line of vegetable juicers.

In order to assess likelihood of confusion, courts analyze a set of factors that vary slightly from court to court but generally amount to the same considerations. These factors include the inherent distinctiveness and commercial strength of the plaintiff's mark; the visual and phonetic similarity of the parties' respective marks, as well as similarity in their meaning; the similarity between the parties' respective goods and services and the marketing channels each is using; the sophistication of the purchasers of the product or service in question; the defendant's intent in adopting its mark, specifically the presence or absence of deceptive intent; the presence or absence of actual consumer confusion; and, if the parties are not in direct competition, the likelihood of plaintiff's expansion into defendant's market. No one factor is controlling; instead, the court may accord some factors more or less weight given the facts and context of the case in determining whether infringement has occurred.

Counterfeiting

Trademark counterfeiting is a subset of infringement and has been singled out by Congress for special treatment as the "most egregious form" of infringing conduct.[4] Like infringement, counterfeiting must result in a likelihood of confusion to be actionable but, unlike simple infringement, direct consumers often harbor no confusion over the non-genuine nature of their purchase, particularly if it falls into the category of luxury goods. Knock-offs of famous brands are a favorite with purchasers who seek the status of owning the brand but want to do so at a discount price. Consider, for example, the prevalence of knock-offs of such status goods as "Rolex" watches, "Prada" handbags, and "Dolce & Gabbana" sunglasses. In such cases, counterfeiting may be established if nonpurchasers are likely to see the counterfeit and to be confused as to its source. In order to rise to the level of counterfeiting, the defendant must use a mark that is identical to or substantially indistinguishable from a federally registered mark, and the use must be in conjunction with goods or services explicitly listed in the registration or on items such as patches, stickers, labels, and the like, intended for use with the listed

---

[3] A less common type of likely confusion is reverse confusion occurring when the infringer creates an impression of role reversal in the marketplace. Specifically, reverse confusion arises when the infringer extensively promotes its infringing goods or services to the point that consumers are likely to misidentify the infringer as the mark holder and the mark holder as the infringer. For an example of reverse confusion, refer to the "Bigfoot" tire case discussed later in this chapter under corrective advertising campaigns.
[4] See 130 Cong. Rec. 31,675 (1984) (Joint Legislative Explanatory Statement). "[A] counterfeit mark is the most egregious example of a mark that is 'likely to cause confusion.'".

goods or services. If these elements are proven, Congress has authorized harsh remedies not otherwise available to mark holders that are discussed later in this chapter.

Dilution

Dilution is a civil wrong that does not require a showing that consumers may be harmed through likely confusion. Instead, dilution requires a showing that a well-known or famous trademark is likely to suffer from blurring, defined as harm to the distinctive value of the mark, or from tarnishment, defined as harm to the reputation of the mark, caused by the defendant's conduct. In this way, dilution extends protection of the mark beyond the goods and services with which it is in use in commerce and may be used to challenge conduct on the part of a defendant that has no relationship to competition. An example of blurring would be adopting the "Xerox" trademark, made famous through its use to sell photocopiers and photocopying products and services, to market skateboards. The mark holder might argue that its famous "signal" is being blurred by the defendant's unauthorized use of the mark, despite the fact that consumers are not likely to believe that the Xerox Corporation has decided to start a skateboard line or to license its mark to a skateboard seller. Similarly, the Mattel Corporation might argue that the unwholesome association created by an adult escort service's use of the "Barbie" trademark is likely to tarnish a mark made famous by marketing fashion dolls to children.

Cybersquatting

Cybersquatting relates to domain names on the internet and denotes liability for registration, sale or offer to sell, or use of a domain name with a bad faith intent to profit from the goodwill of another's trademark, generally illustrated by incorporating the trademark into the domain name. This conduct rises to the level of wrongdoing when the domain name is identical or confusingly similar to another's trademark, whether the mark holder has a registration for the mark or not, or when the domain name is identical or confusingly similar or dilutive of another's famous trademark. In this manner, cybersquatting incorporates aspects of infringement and dilution but is distinguished by its dependence on a showing of bad faith. An example of cybersquatting would be registration of the domain name, "steinway.com," by an entity that posts pictures of a beer stein collection on the website and immediately thereafter contacts Steinway, Inc., world famous manufacturer of pianos, and offers the domain name for sale for a healthy sum. Note that the defendant need not be a competitor but the illustration would hold if a competitor in the sale of pianos purchased the domain name, posting the same collections of photos, in an effort to frustrate the efforts of Steinway, Inc., in developing a web presence.

Deceptive Advertising and Unfair Competition

Finally, deceptive advertising is a cause of action under the Lanham Act and is often encompassed in state unfair competition schemes as well; it involves false claims or misleading statements that are material to the purchasing decision and likely to result in harm to consumers. A state or common law cause of action for unfair competition generally establishes liability for a wide variety of dishonest acts in trade or business that have the effect of unduly hindering commercial activity. While deceptive advertising may or may not affect the value of a brand, depending upon whether the advertising claim in issue disparages the plaintiff's products or services, this cause of action does not normally involve diminution in the value of a trademark itself. However, a charge of unfair competition based upon a defendant's passing off his goods or services as those of another is a version of trademark infringement with the attendant potential for harm to the value of the mark. *Reverse passing off*, or removing the mark holder's mark from his goods or services and distributing or selling them under the defendant's mark, would also constitute unfair competition. State and common law unfair competition schemes may also extend to misappropriation of another's creations, for example, trade secrets, not otherwise the subject of intellectual property protection. At bottom, state or common law unfair competition covers a broader range of misconduct than that encompassed in the trademark enforcement provisions of the Lanham Act, unfair competition typically requires some showing of bad faith intent in regard to the defendant's conduct.

MONETARY RECOVERY IN CIVIL ACTIONS

The Lanham Act authorizes monetary recovery in the form of the defendant's profits or the plaintiff's damages, or both if the two types of recovery do not duplicate one another, as well as enhancement of the base award up to three times. These types of recovery are available to compensate trademark holders pursuing any of the causes of action available under the Act, including infringement, dilution, and cybersquatting, although infringement is the primary enforcement action to yield such recovery. This is so because harm is extremely difficult to quantify in dilution cases and requires a showing of willful misconduct while plaintiffs in cybersquatting cases generally follow the route of recovery that is easiest to prove, specifically statutory damages. Statutory damages constitute monetary recovery quantified by statute as opposed to resulting from a calculation of harm to the trademark holder. Under the Lanham Act, statutory damages are available as an alternative to other types of monetary recovery only for the most egregious form of infringement, that is, counterfeiting, and for cybersquatting. Finally, in exceptional cases, the Act allows the trial court to award reasonable attorney's fees for any of the causes of action for enforcement of a trademark. Although the Act does not explicitly address prejudgment interest, courts exercise their discretion in making or declining to make such awards.

This discussion of monetary relief should not obscure the fact that most trademark enforcement actions hang on the award of injunctive relief and monetary recovery is generally a secondary concern, with cases often settling once a preliminary injunction hearing has been held. The primary reason injunctive relief reigns supreme in trademark enforcement cases is the difficulty of calculating the amount of harm that has been done to the trademark holder. The principal harm to a trademark holder is a loss of control over how the mark is being used. The trademark holder has not lost the use of the mark himself, just the *exclusive* use of the mark, and that is a harm often best remedied by ordering the defendant to "cease and desist," or stop the conduct in the complaint. When the court rules on the trademark holder's request for a preliminary injunction, that is, an order prohibiting the conduct during the course of the case, litigants usually discern which way the court is leaning and may be encouraged to settle the dispute.

EXHIBIT 9.1   Sample Income Statement

Gross Sales	$10,000,000
Less: Returns	50,000
Net Sales	9,950,000
Cost of Goods Sold	6,500,000
Gross Profit	3,450,000
Selling, General, and Administrative Expense	1,250,000
Net Operating Income	2,200,000
Interest Expense	400,000
Other Income (Expense)	(250,000)
Pre-Tax Net Income	1,500,000
Income Taxes	620,000
Net Income	$880,000

Source: John Wiley & Sons, Inc. Reprinted with permission.

Defendant's Profits: Profit Measuring Complexities

While it may seem straightforward, the quantification of a defendant's profits may prove to be quite difficult. To put this task in perspective, let us examine the sample income statement shown in Exhibit 9.1.

For purposes of this task, we will assume that the income statement reports only the financial results relating to the infringing product or service. Beginning at the bottom of the income statement, let us evaluate the various possible measures of the defendant's profit.

Net Income   While this might be presented by the defendant as a proper measure of profits, is it appropriate when the defendant has violated the plaintiff's trademark rights? This is open to question, because expenses of running the defendant's business, such as income taxes, may or may not be judged deductible from a profits measure.

Pretax Net Income   Using this level of income removes the tax issue, but we can observe that this measure of profits is reduced by the amount of interest expense of the defendant as well as by other expenses, which may not be specifically related to the infringing product. One must deal with the question of whether profits associated with the alleged infringement should be influenced by the manner in which the defendant has chosen to capitalize its business, or by unrelated income or expenses.

Net Operating Income   This measure eliminates some issues, but even this level of income is affected by the magnitude of selling, general, and administrative expenses. These are highly variable and could, for example, be quite high if the alleged infringer was breaking into a new market with the infringing mark. That would, at the least, reduce this measure of damages and could even eliminate it. It is not unusual to have no, or negative net operating income in the circumstance of market penetration activities. Should a profits calculation result in "zero" in that case?

Gross Profit   From an accounting and economic perspective, measuring profits at this level perhaps makes the most sense. It is unlikely that someone would enter into a business in which the gross profit was marginal or negative. That could be the case with a new product if there was a very steep learning curve associated with its production, or if there were great economies of scale in the production process that had to be achieved over time, but it would not be very common. In addition, if the alleged wrongdoer was enjoying greater than normal profits by selling a common product at a price made premium by the use of a purloined trademark, the gross profit would capture this benefit.

Keep in mind that the discussion of profit measuring complexities so far has involved consideration of an income statement based on the sales of *only* the goods or services that violate the mark holder's rights. This is unlikely to be available in real life, so we may be faced with the task of creating such an income statement (or at least parts of it that we deem relevant) from the information that is available.

Isolating the Relevant Income Streams   The example in Exhibit 9.1 represents a stand-alone income statement for the offending product or service. That is not typical. A small company is not likely to have accounting systems in place to permit such segregation. A large company is likely to have financials by product line, but these will contain many allocations of expense that cloud the determination of profits by product or service.

Even if a product income statement is available, the infringing item may have had only limited geographical or retailer distribution. This requires further subdivision of the data. The process is one of defining the relevant markets.

Expense Allocations   In a multiproduct business, many expenses such as those associated with treasury, legal, accounting, research, or corporate advertising functions are not reported on a product line basis and must be allocated to each product according to some formula. Such a formula may be based on elements such as sales revenue, number of employees, square footage of production facilities, capital employed, accounts receivable, or any combination of these. Expense allocations in a large organization may be made more complex by being multilevel. Some expenses may be allocated among several products within a product line. At the same time other expenses are allocated to a product based on its place in a division, subsidiary, or business segment. Expenses may be allocated based on legal entities that are quite different than operating groups.

Our approach is generally to reduce these allocations to their "lowest common denominator" so that we can reassemble them selectively, using those we find appropriate, and discarding the others.

One-Time or Out-of-Period Events   We must also be aware of the presence of costs resulting from one-time or unusual events. As an example, if a manufacturing plant is closed, the costs of closing as well as ongoing expenses associated with the discontinued operation (such as rent payments until a lease expires) may be allocated to the surviving operations. Obviously, these would not be appropriate expenses to reflect in a determination of a defendant's profits. A casualty loss and accounting adjustment are other examples. We must also be sensitive to adjustments made for events that took place before the period of wrongdoing.

Accounting Issues   Another conceptual issue that must be addressed is whether expenses should be based on *incremental* or *fully absorbed costs*. Financial statements are typically expressed on the basis of fully absorbed costs. Simply stated, this means that each accounting entity, whether a product, product line, division, or segment, must bear its share of allocable resources.

For example, assume an infringement situation involving a manufacturing plant designed to make chocolate chip cookies. These cookies are a distinctive brand—the plant is operating at 75 percent capacity and the brand is profitable. Management decides to introduce a line of cookies with nuts instead of chocolate chips under a different trademark and the new product infringes an established product. The nut cookie brand uses the remaining 25 percent plant capacity. On a fully absorbed accounting basis, the nut cookie brand must bear 25 percent of the plant costs, even though no additional employees were hired and no new machinery was installed. The chocolate chip cookie brand that formerly bore all of the plant costs becomes even more profitable because the nut cookies are absorbing some costs.

The essential question is whether the profits of the infringing nut cookies should be calculated as if there were only minimal manufacturing costs (because it was an incremental product), or whether they should be assumed to bear their share of total manufacturing costs. The difference could be substantial. The nut cookies, accounted for on an incremental basis, would get a free ride on the plant costs and might appear to be extremely profitable. Courts take varying approaches to measurement of the wrongdoer's profits as discussed below.[5]

Defendant's Profits: Principles Governing Awards

An award of the wrongdoer's profits may rest on one, or any combination, of the following—proof of sales diverted from a plaintiff-competitor, a concern that the defendant has been unjustly enriched in some other fashion, or a desire to deter future misbehavior by the defendant. Importantly, a plaintiff may obtain an accounting of defendant's profits on the latter two bases without proof of any actual damage to the mark holder.[6] Larry Marshak learned this lesson when he continued to promote a doo-wop singing group using a name incorporating the mark, "The Drifters," despite

---

[5] For a description of three different profits calculation methodologies in trademark enforcement actions, see James M. Koelemay, *A Practical Guide to Monetary Relief in Trademark Infringement Cases*, 85 Trademark Rep. 288 (1995). The author describes the differential or marginal cost rule that allows deductions for expenses that would not have been incurred but for sales of the offending product. Noting that application of this rule garners the largest recovery for the mark holder, the author points out that the approach has been used to calculate plaintiff's lost profits on lost sales. Additionally, he outlines the direct assistance rule, which allows deductions of expenses, including some overhead costs, directly assisting in manufacture and sale of the offending product. Finally, he describes the fully allocated cost rule, which allows all deductions that can be allocated to the offending product under generally accepted accounting principles.

[6] This rule renders an award of defendant's profits a particularly useful remedy when the wrongdoer and the mark holder are not in direct competition with one another, a situation in which diversion of sales may be difficult, if not impossible, to prove. Although a plaintiff's inability to prove lost profits or other damages will not alone preclude recovery of the wrongdoer's profits, the lack of actual damages is relevant to the court for purposes of fashioning an equitable remedy. For example, in *Menendez v. Faber, Coe & Gregg, Inc.*, 345 F. Supp. 527, 560 (S.D.N.Y. 1972) an accounting of infringer's profits was denied for equitable reasons because the record revealed no damage to the mark holder or to the public by virtue of the complained-of infringement.

a prior court order establishing ownership of the mark in Faye Treadwell, widow of the original manager of The Drifters. Citing Marshak for contempt because he had continued to infringe the mark, the court noted the absence of any evidence of actual damage resulting from Marshak's behavior but held such evidence to be unnecessary when an award of the infringer's profits is directed at deterrence.[7] Similarly, a discount cigarette retailer suffered an award of its profits in a trademark dilution action brought by R. J. Reynolds Tobacco Company, despite no evidence of actual damage to the latter, because the court found that the discounter's actions had unjustly enriched him. The trial court took the view that the discounter had diluted the distinctiveness of the "Camel," "Winston," and "Salem" trademarks by introducing R. J. Reynolds products, intended for sales overseas and in other parallel markets, into the domestic market, thereby affording the dilutor profits that he should never have been able to realize.[8]

META-INFRINGEMENT

A manufacturer of these items, Venture Tape Corporation, charged McGillis Glass Warehouse, an Internet-based retailer of stained glass supplies, with infringing the mark "Venture" by embedding it in the metadata of the McGillis website and imprinting it invisibly on the white wallpaper of the site in white letters. McGillis admitted that it had followed this course of action to attract Internet users who had typed "Venture" into their search engines. The trial court found McGillis liable for infringement and awarded Venture $230,339.17 of the infringer's $1.9 million in gross sales over a three-year infringement period. McGillis objected to the award on appeal, arguing that it vastly overstated both the actual harm to Venture and McGillis's actual profits. On the latter point, McGillis pointed out that the Venture had been given access to the company's records during the litigation and, so, should have informed the trial court that McGillis's net profits were closer to 1 percent of gross sales or approximately, $19,000. The appellate court dismissed McGillis's arguments by noting: first, that a mark holder's inability to prove specific instances of lost sales does not preclude recovery based upon "a rough measure" of the mark holder's harm; and, second, that the law only requires the mark-holder to prove gross sales which Venture had done by introducing copies of McGillis's tax returns for the relevant time period, and Venture had not countered that proof with evidence of any allowable deductions.[9]

---

[7] *Marshak v. Treadwell*, 595 F.3d 478, 495 (3d Cir. 2009).

[8] *R. J. Reynolds Tobacco Co. v. Premium Tobacco Stores, Inc., et al.*, 71 U.S.P.Q.2d 1670 (N.D. Ill. 2004).

[9] *Venture Tape Corp. v. McGillis Glass Warehouse*, 540 F.3d 56, 63–64 (1st Cir. 2008). If the mark holder is unable to obtain records of defendant's gross profits through the litigation discovery process, either because the records do not exist or because the defendant does not cooperate in discovery, courts will allow the mark holder to rely upon any reasonable source of evidence. For example, *Louis Vuitton, S.A. v. Spencer Handbags Corp.*, 765 F.2d 966, (2d Cir. 1985), in which the appellate court upheld an award of infringer's gross profits, calculated on the basis of a handbag counterfeiter's statements about its profits per bag made in an undercover investigator's videotape, where the defendant refused to produce financial records during discovery.

When a court makes an award of the wrongdoer's profits on the first basis mentioned, the diversion of sales, the court often notes that the award is "a rough measure" of the harm done to the competitor-mark holder. This is so because such an award implicitly assumes that the plaintiff would otherwise have made all the defendant's sales subject to complaint and that the profit margins of both parties are identical. In most instances, these assumptions will be off the mark and, if so, it is up to the wrongdoer to submit proof to that effect and the mark holder bears no obligation to help him out in that regard.

This rule is illustrated in a case involving specialty adhesive tapes and foils used in the stained glass industry.

Note, however, that a wrongdoer who sells multiple product lines or the same product in multiple markets, only one of which results in infringement, will only be liable for infringing product sales or infringing market sales, and it is incumbent upon the mark holder to establish gross sales within that limitation. Failure to carry its burden to isolate profits based on infringement resulted in denial of the Lindy Pen Co.'s request for Bic Pen Corp.'s profits on the sale of its "Auditor's" fine point pen. Although Lindy asserted infringement of its "Auditor's" trademark by Bic without market limitation, the Ninth Circuit affirmed a likelihood of confusion only in the telephone order submarket of the telephone sales market, and excluded sales made either in the telephone solicitation submarket of that market or in the mail order market, from liability. The appellate court remanded the case for a determination of the proper monetary recovery but the lower court refused Lindy's request for Bic's profits because Lindy failed to delineate the amount of gross profits attributable to the relevant submarket of the telephone sales market.[10]

Once the mark holder establishes the wrongdoer's relevant gross profits, the wrongdoer may reduce that number by bringing forward proof of such deductible items as overhead and operating costs. Overhead costs represent a particularly troublesome area from a legal and an accounting standpoint as explained at the beginning of this section. If the wrongdoer makes and sells different products, or utilizes more than one trademark, only one of which is improper, on the same product, and only one trademark use violates the mark holder's rights, then the court must decide whether, and how, to apportion overhead costs, to arrive at an appropriate award. At this point, it suffices to note that the courts take one of two principal approaches to this problem, with some courts endorsing the incremental approach in that exercise and others favoring the full absorption method. Where the courts entertain the full absorption method, they may require the defendant to establish some connection between a general overhead expense and the use under complaint.[11] As a

---

[10] *Lindy Pen Co. v. Bic Pen Corp.*, 14 U.S.P.Q.2d 1528, 1534 (C.D. Cal. 1989), supplemental op., 1989 U.S. Dist. LEXIS 17449 (C.D. Cal. Dec. 15, 1989), *aff'd*, 982 F.2d 1400 (9th Cir. 1993).

[11] See, for example, *Louis Vuitton Malletier v. Dooney & Bourke, Inc.*, 525 F.Supp.2d 525, 578 (S.D.N.Y. 2007), adopting recommendation of special masters that mark holder's damages expert be allowed to testify to incremental approach conditional upon infringer being unable to establish connection between overhead expenses and infringing conduct, *sum. j'ment granted*, 2008 U.S. Dist. LEXIS 42787 (S.D.N.Y. May 28, 2008).

rule of thumb, however, the wrongdoer whose financial records unduly complicate apportionment is unlikely to benefit from its poor recordkeeping.[12]

In accord with the discussion of deductible costs, the wrongdoer bears the burden of proving a reasonable and equitable basis for apportionment and, where that proof cannot be made, the wrongdoer is generally held liable for all of the profits it earned while misusing the subject mark. For an example of a successful proof of profits apportionment, consider the case of the former franchisee of the Holiday Inn motel chain that continued to display the franchisor's sign outside its establishment for several years after termination of the franchise agreement. The infringer obtained apportionment of its profits or the holdover period by proving that 70 percent of its business during that period had been weekly trade obtained through the manager's personal outreach and only 30 percent represented transient trade likely to have been attracted by the infringing sign.[13]

If the wrongdoer produces proof that indicates a failure to realize any profit by virtue of its misconduct, the court may nevertheless award the defendant's gross revenue in order to remove any incentive to misuse another's trademark. For example, a counterfeiter who sold a number of nongenuine Polo shirts to a fellow counterfeiter at cost once the mark holder filed suit suffered an award of the revenue from those sales on appeal because the appellate court found that the lower court's failure to make the award "did not remove all of . . . [the counterfeiter's] economic incentive to buy and sell counterfeit Polo shirts." The appellate court pointed out that the award of gross revenue put the counterfeiter in the same position that he would have been in had he destroyed the counterfeit merchandise instead of passing it to another counterfeiter.[14] A similar result is likely if the wrongdoer simply proves to be unable to generate a profit, in order to avoid prejudicing the mark holder for the wrongdoer's lack of business acumen.

As we see from the previous discussion, concerns of fairness and equity underlie an award of the wrongdoer's profits. For that reason, these awards are never automatic and courts have discretion to refuse to make them in the interests of achieving a just result. Although it has not always been the case, most courts today require some proof of a willful violation of the mark holder's rights before they will order an accounting.[15] Willfulness may be defined as some knowledge of the mark holder's rights plus intentional action taken in derogation of those rights. In the absence of such proof, the courts almost always decline the requested accounting. For example, a decades-long dispute between two German business entities regarding ownership

---

[12] For example, *Manhattan Indus., Inc. v. Sweater Bee by Banff, Ltd.*, 885 F.2d 1, 21–23 (2d Cir. 1989), in which a party sanctioned for contempt for failing to observe a court order regarding trademark usage on its "Kimberly" line of women's apparel could not allocate a portion of fixed selling expenses to the offending product line by estimation because the onus of producing satisfactory records to demonstrate "a sufficient nexus" between each expense claimed and the Kimberly line falls on the defendant.

[13] *Holiday Inns, Inc. v. Airport Holiday Corp.*, 493 F.Supp. 1025, 1027–28 (N.D. Tex. 1980), aff'd, 683 F.2d 931 (5th Cir. 1982).

[14] *Polo Fashions, Inc. v. Dick Bruhn, Inc.*, 793 F.2d 1132, 1135 (9th Cir. 1986).

[15] For a survey of modern cases under the Lanham Act discussing the willful intent requirement, see 5 McCarthy on Trademarks § 30:62, at 30–149–157.

of the trademark "Zeiss," a mark that each was using to sell optical equipment in the United States, was resolved in one party's favor only after a long and complex fact-finding process that involved consideration of the effect of Soviet occupation of East Germany after World War II, on German law. Although the trial court ordered an accounting of the infringer's profits, that award was overturned on appeal because the record showed a legitimate difference of opinion over ownership of the mark, a less than clear-cut question.[16] Generally, relying in good faith upon the advice of legal counsel, however erroneous that advice might be, yields the same result.[17]

Plaintiff's Damages: Principles Governing Awards

Monetary recovery in the form of plaintiff's damages rests on the notion that the mark holder should be compensated for any actual loss or harm it experiences as a result of the wrongdoer's conduct and attempts to achieve a balance between granting the wronged party an undeserved windfall and undercompensating a party that has experienced economic harm. Plaintiff's damages and the defendant's profits may both be awarded to a mark holder seeking to enforce its trademark rights but the combination may not result in a double recovery for the same loss. An obvious illustration of an impermissible double recovery arises if a mark holder garners a wrongdoer's profits in addition to his own lost profits for the same diverted sales. In addition to out-of-pocket costs incurred as a result of the wrongful behavior, courts recognize a variety of theories of damage that may inure to a mark holder as a result of the defendant's unauthorized use of the mark. Whatever theory the plaintiff invokes in an infringement action, however, courts generally require the plaintiff to prove that some consumers were actually confused or deceived by the conduct under complaint.

The rule normally cited for calculation of plaintiff's damages is that such damages may not be remote or speculative. This rule refers to the first step in a court's analysis of the proper compensation, that is, a determination that some damages are the "certain result" of the conduct subject to the complaint. Once a mark holder proves the *fact* of damage with reasonable certainty, the mark holder is held to a lower burden of proof in quantifying the *amount* of damage. Specifically, the mark holder discharges his obligation by introducing enough data and factual information to allow the court to draw reasonable inferences as to the amount of probable loss. As stated by the U.S. Supreme Court, the rationale for the lesser burden of proof to support the second step of the court's analysis is that "the most elementary conceptions of justice and public policy require that the wrongdoer shall bear the risk of the uncertainty which his own wrong has created."[18]

---

[16] *Carl Zeiss Stiftung v. VEB Carl Zeiss Jena*, 433 F.2d 686, 707 (2d Cir. 1970).

[17] For example, *Robert Bruce, Inc. v. Sears, Roebuck & Co.*, 343 F.Supp. 1333, 1349 (E.D. Pa. 1972), in which a requested accounting of defendant-retailer's profits for sales of "Neets N Grubs" jeans was denied because, although the defendant had notice of the plaintiff's claim to the mark "Grubbs" for well-tailored boy's and men's wearing apparel, the defendant marketed the jeans in reliance upon its attorney's erroneous advice that a descriptive term, even when applied ironically, was incapable of trademark protection.

[18] *Bigelow v. RKO Radio Pictures, Inc.*, 327 U.S. 251, 265 (1946).

Plaintiff's Damages: Various Theories

Courts are generally willing to entertain innovative theories with regard to damages incurred by the defendant's misuse of a mark holder's trademark. The following pages give various examples.

Present Lost Profits   Zebco, a division of the Brunswick Corporation, relied upon this theory to seek compensation for infringement of its uniquely shaped, closed face spin cast fishing reel by the Spinit Reel Company. The two parties were the only suppliers of spin cast reels in the unique shape pioneered by Zebco, leading Zebco to assert that every sale of the subject reel by Spinit was a lost sale to Zebco. The trial court denied recovery, stating that, although Brunswick had proven its entitlement to damages, it failed to produce clear proof of the quantification of those damages, suggesting that other brands of reels on the market may have accounted for some of Zebco's lost sales. The appellate court overturned the denial of a damage award, opining that the plaintiff's theory of lost profits stated the "upper range" of damages. The appellate court pointed to evidence in the record that, although Zebco had suffered a 5 percent decline in sales over all its models of spin cast reels during the infringement period, comparable to the 6 percent industry-wide decline due to a recession at the time, sales of Zebco's closed face spin reels during the same period declined by 16 percent. Highlighting this disparity and the direct competition of the parties with regard to the subject reel, the appellate court remanded the case, noting that the evidence of record gave the trial court "a broad basis from which it may arrive at a fair, if not precise, amount" to compensate Zebco.[19]

Future Lost Profits   Broan Manufacturing, a supplier of bathroom fans and other home ventilation equipment, asserted a claim for future lost profits against Associated Distributors with whom it had enjoyed a successful business relationship prior to the distributor's importation of "knock-off" copies of Broan's "Nautilus" line of bathroom fans. After two years of distributing "Nautilus" fans to West's building supplies stores, Associated arranged to have infringing versions of the fans manufactured in Taiwan and imported into the United States for distribution to West's stores in place of the genuine product. Despite Broan's argument that it had expected to have a long-term relationship with Associated, which Associated's misconduct disrupted, the trial court denied the claim for future lost profits as too speculative, accepting Associated's argument that it would have terminated its relationship with Broan when it started importing the infringing items in any event. The appellate court disagreed noting that a plaintiff need only establish the fact of damage with reasonable, not absolute, certainty. The appellate court found that Broan's evidence regarding its prior successful relationships with Associated and its other customers, in conjunction with Associated's infringing importation scheme, met the requisite level of proof that damage had occurred, and the court remanded the case for the jury's quantification of future lost profits.[20]

---

[19] *Brunswick Corp. v. Spinit Reel Co.*, 832 F.2d 513, 525–26 (10th Cir. 1987).
[20] *Broan Mfg. Co. v. Associated Distributors, Inc.* 923 F.2d 1232, 1236-38 (6th Cir. 1991).

Head-Start Advantage   Taco Cabana International, Inc., an operator of six Mexican fast-food restaurants in San Antonio, Texas, prevailed in an infringement action against Two Pesos, Inc., a restaurant operator that copied the plaintiff's Mexican-themed trade dress for its competing restaurants in the Houston area. Taco Cabana made an innovative argument that Two Pesos had foreclosed the Houston market to Taco Cabana by wrongfully seizing a head-start advantage through trade dress infringement and that the plaintiff had suffered lost profits as a result. The jury awarded Taco Cabana lost profits, apparently by applying a 6 percent profit margin to sales of $1.7 million per foreclosed store, assuming five such stores.[21]

Royalties for Sales of Unlicensed Product   Like many educational institutions, Texas Tech University (TTU) in Lubbock, Texas, was faced with a local merchant selling unlicensed apparel, banners, signs, and other items bearing university trademarks and sports team logos. The merchant was a former licensee of the TTU whose license had been terminated for failure to pay royalties on sales of licensed merchandise. The terminated agreement called for a royalty of 8 percent on all items sold with TTU marks. Taking its lead from the terminated agreement, the court awarded damages of 8 percent of gross profits on all unlicensed items sold during the infringement/ dilution period, no deductible costs having been shown by the merchant.

If no prior licensing arrangement exists between the mark holder and the wrong-doer, the court may award damages in the form of a reasonable royalty, arrived at by positing a hypothetical license negotiation between the parties. One court's calculation of this form of relief is illustrated in the successful infringement action brought by A&H Sportswear, Inc., a manufacturer and distributor of women's swimwear, against Victoria's Secrets Stores, Inc., a lingerie retailer, for its infringing use of the former's "Miraclesuit" trademark on its "The Miracle Bra" line of swimwear. Noting that A&H Sportswear would never have agreed to a license agreement with Victoria's Secrets due primarily to competition concerns, the court gave particular consideration to defendant's concession that its "The Miracle Bra" swimsuit is the key to its success in the swimwear industry and the fact that a license between the parties would have had special value to Victoria's Secret because it would have allowed the retailer to extend the success of its own "The Miracle Bra" mark without infringing the "Miraclesuit" mark. The plaintiff's expert offered its opinion that a reasonable royalty would amount to 6 percent of the defendant's offending sales, and the defendant's expert countered that the 6 percent should be multiplied by the ratio of "The Miracle Bra" swimwear sales over "The Miracle Bra" sales of all products, arriving at a 1.7 percent reasonable royalty, due to defendant's established and legitimate use of "The Miracle Bra" on other products. The court arrived at a reasonable royalty of 4 percent, disregarding the defendant's expert opinion because it did not confine the reasonable royalty to swimwear sales and endorsing a modification of the plaintiff's expert opinion to account for the indirect nature of Victoria's Secret's infringement.[22]

---

[21] *Taco Cabana Int'l, Inc. v. Two Pesos, Inc.*, 932 F.2d 1113, 1126-27 (5ᵗʰ Cir. 1991), *aff'd*, 505 U.S. 763 (1992).

[22] *A&H Sportswear, Inc. v. Victoria's Secrets Stores, Inc.*, 967 F.Supp. 1457, 1479-80 (E.D. Pa. 1997).

Corrective Advertising Campaign Monetary compensation to fund an advertising campaign designed to "undo" the damaging effects of the wrongdoer's conduct is a relatively common remedy for unauthorized use of a trademark, whether the mark holder has already issued corrective advertising and seeks to be compensated for it or the mark holder has been financially unable to run such a campaign. This relief originated with a modified jury award against Goodyear Tire & Rubber Company for infringement in an action involving the mark "Bigfoot" for tires. Goodyear adopted a mark that it knew to be owned by a 14-state consortium of independent tire dealers in the Southwestern United States and proceeded to promote the mark for its own tires to the point that it created the likely impression among the consuming public that Goodyear was the mark holder and the plaintiff-consortium was the infringer. The jury award of $2.8 million seems to represent 28 percent of the $10 million that Goodyear spent to advertise the infringing product, with 28 percent reflecting the consortium's portion of the national market by state presence (50 divided by 14). The appellate court reduced the award to approximately $700,000 to approximate sanctions typically issued by the Federal Trade Commission (FTC) for deceptive advertising; the FTC normally requires advertisers who have engaged in such practices to spend 25 percent of their advertising budget in corrective advertising.[23]

Future Mistaken Product Liability Claims In addition to lost profits in the case involving bathroom fans described above, Broan was allowed to collect damages for investigative and defense costs that it expected to incur in handling and settling product liability claims likely to be pressed by confused consumers who had purchased infringing versions of the plaintiff's Nautilus line of bathroom fans. The manufacturer presented proof that consumers routinely misidentify the infringing products as originating with Broan and, because the infringing items are vastly inferior in quality and are likely to start fires, Broan could reasonably anticipate future mistaken product liability claims.[24]

ENHANCEMENT OF MONETARY RECOVERY

The Lanham Act authorizes courts to modify a monetary award in trademark enforcement actions by increasing plaintiff's damages up to three times the base amount and/or by increasing or decreasing an award of the wrongdoer's profits by any amount if the court finds the profit award to be either inadequate or excessive. Generally, courts have wide discretion to modify monetary awards but the Act cautions that increasing an award "shall constitute compensation and not a penalty." Courts have struggled to justify enhancement of monetary recovery for reasons other than those related to punishment and have generally opted to enhance awards when damage calculations prove particularly difficult and likely to undercompensate mark holders. The clearest example of this situation arises when the damage award is in the form of a reasonable royalty, in effect, a mandatory license thrust upon the mark holder by the circumstances of defendant's wrongdoing. Two rationales underlie enhancement of a reasonable royalty award, that is, to prevent potential defendants

---

[23] *Big O Tire Dealers, Inc. v. Goodyear Tire & Rubber Co.*, 408 F.Supp. 1219, 1233 (D. Colo. 1976), modified, 561 F.2d 1365 (10th Cir. 1977).
[24] *Broan Mfg. Co. v. Associated Distributors, Inc.*, 923 F.2d 1232, 1238–39 (6th Cir. 1991).

from viewing a reasonable royalty as simply an acceptable cost of doing business and to place the burden of uncertainty that accompanies calculation of a hypothetical license negotiation squarely on the shoulders of the wrongdoer.[25] Where a defendant has engaged in willful misconduct, the court generally bases enhancement of the monetary award on deterrence of future misconduct as opposed to punishment for past wrongdoing in order to avoid imposing a penalty. An exception arises if the defendant is found to have engaged in counterfeiting, an egregious type of infringement that triggers mandatory trebling of monetary damages, purely as a penalty.

Many state trademark enforcement schemes authorize punitive damages, usually where the conduct subject to a complaint is viewed as egregious, outrageous, oppressive, or otherwise deserving of a harsh response from the courts. The general rule is that punitive damages will not be awarded unless an underlying award of monetary damages has been made, even if that award is minimal, and the multiplier applied to achieve punitive damages will virtually never exceed nine times the base award, a substantive limit that assures the award will not be so grossly excessive as to violate constitutional guarantees of due process.[26]

Statutory Damages in Counterfeiting and Cybersquatting Cases

Under the Lanham Act, statutory damages provide an alternative to an award of the plaintiff's actual damages or the wrongdoer's profits, in a counterfeiting case or in a cybersquatting case. In either case, the mark holder must choose the alternative of statutory damages before the trial court enters final judgment. Although the Act establishes a range of such damages, it does not otherwise guide the court's discretion in making such an award.

The range of statutory damages in counterfeiting cases was increased two-fold by amendment of the Lanham Act to read as follows:

1. Not less than $1,000 or more than $200,000 per counterfeit mark per type of goods or services sold, offered for sale, or distributed, as the court considers just; or
2. If the court finds that the use of the counterfeit mark was willful, not more than $2,000,000 per counterfeit mark per type of goods or services sold, offered for sale, or distributed, as the court considers just.

The rationales for statutory damages in counterfeiting cases are deterrence of particularly objectionable behavior and assistance in obtaining recovery where quantification of harm would otherwise be difficult given the tendency of counterfeiters to keep few or incomplete financial records of their dealings.[27] Not surprisingly,

---

[25] See *Sands, Taylor & Wood v. Quaker Oats Co.*, 34 F.3d 1340, 1351 (7th Cir. 1994), corrected, substituted op., in part, 44 F.3d 579 (7th Cir. 1995), on remand 1995 WL 221871 (N.D. Ill. Apr. 11, 1995), in which an appellate court upheld the lower court's doubling of a reasonable royalty award computed as 1 percent of the wrongdoer's sales of an isotonic beverage for the first year of infringement and 0.5 percent for subsequent years where the wrongdoer engaged in an aggressive advertising campaign using the mark holder's trademark and no license agreement was ever contemplated between the two parties).

[26] *State Farm Mut. Auto. Inc. Co. v. Campbell*, 538 U.S. 408 (2003).

[27] For example, *Louis Vuitton Malletier & Oakley, Inc. v. Veit*, 211 F. Supp. 2d 567, 583 (E.D. Pa. 2002).

COWBOY COUNTERFEITER

Note the example of the counterfeiter who knowingly imported 8 million cigarettes bearing unauthorized versions of the famous "Marlboro" and "Marlboro Red Label" trademarks and having a street value of millions of dollars. The defendant declined to appear and defend himself in the action against him for counterfeiting, and the court had no hesitancy in entering a default judgment for the mark holder, Phillip Morris U.S.A., Inc., in the amount of $2 million in statutory damages, the maximum amount allowable under the Act prior to the 2008 amendment previously recited.[28]

---

courts assign statutory damages within the authorized range by reference to the nature of the defendant's conduct, with innocent wrongdoing at the bottom of the range and particularly willful conduct at the top of the range.

Cybersquatting cases rarely involve an award of damages or profits because the best resolution from the standpoint of the mark holder is often the quickest and least expensive one, that is, forfeiture or cancellation of the disputed domain name or transfer of the domain name to the mark holder.[29] Statutory damages promote this resolution by encouraging a wrongdoer to settle and agree to such a transfer in order to avoid the risk of a substantial monetary penalty assessed against him.[30] Statutory damages may also provide an effective deterrent in cases involving domain tasting, that is, situations where cybersquatters own or use domain names for only a short time, perhaps to monetize the domain names with click-through advertising for just a few days or to attempt to sell the domain names for a tidy profit.[31] In cybersquatting cases, statutory damages range from "not less than $1,000 and not more than $100,000 per domain name, as the court considers just."

Prejudgment Interest and Reasonable Attorneys' Fees

Although prejudgment interest and attorneys' fees involve monetary recovery unrelated to trademark value, a brief discussion is included here in the interest of completeness. Prejudgment interest on a monetary award of plaintiff's damages and/or infringer's profits is not explicitly mentioned in the Lanham Act but some courts take

---

[28] *Philip Morris U.S.A. Inc. v. Castworld Prods.*, 219 F.R.D. 494 (C.D. Cal. 2003).

[29] This desired result likely accounts for the popular alternative to litigation provided under the Uniform Dispute Resolution Procedure, arbitration rules promulgated by ICANN, for which only disposition of the domain name and no monetary remedies are available. *See* http://www.icann.org/en/help/dndr/udrp.

[30] See Gideon Parchomovsky, *On Trademarks, Domain Names, and Internal Auctions*, 2001 U. ILL. L. REV. 211, 225 n.70, noting the goal of statutory damage awards in cybersquatting cases.

[31] For example, *Shields v. Zuccarini*, 254 F.3d 476, 487 (3d Cir. 2001). An award of statutory damages upheld despite the fact that cybersquatting, after passage of the Lanham Act's anti-cybersquatting provisions, continued for only 60 days.

the view that such recovery should be de rigeur for victims of federal law violations, especially trademark infringement.[32] Other courts exercise their discretion, reserving prejudgment interest for exceptional cases.[33] The Act does provide for the discretionary award of attorneys' fees in exceptional cases and for a mandatory award of attorneys' fees if counterfeiting is proven. When the mark holder prevails in a trademark enforcement action, courts generally consider a case to be exceptional in the face of a defendant's intentional, willful misconduct. When the accused prevails, courts take a variety of approaches but generally consider the case to be exceptional if it lacks all merit or if it was brought in bad faith to harass the defendant or for other improper motive.[34]

Procedure for Establishing Monetary Recovery

A trial court enjoys broad discretion in the procedures that it may follow to make determinations regarding monetary recovery in a trademark enforcement action. One case management tool used more and more often by courts is the appointment of a special master to address complicated issues, including accounting of a wrongdoer's profits and the mark holder's damages.[35] As discussed below, the trial court may also use a special master to determine reliability and admissibility of expert testimony.

Financial experts frequently offer testimony at trial with regard to the proper measure of monetary recovery for the parties in a civil trademark enforcement action. The trial court must act as a "gatekeeper" to ensure that any testimony with regard to scientific or technical matters or testimony based upon other specialized knowledge is not only relevant but reliable, largely to prevent the jury from giving such testimony undue weight simply because it comes from an expert. The Federal Rules of Evidence govern the trial court's determination as to whether to admit or exclude expert testimony, but trial courts are accorded broad discretion within the Rules. Rule 702 permits a qualified expert to testify as to matters that will assist the trier of fact in understanding the evidence or in determining a factual issue if: "the testimony is based upon sufficient facts or data; ... the testimony is the product of reliable principles and methods; and ... the expert has applied the principles and methods reliably to the facts of the case." Even if a trial court deems expert

---

[32] For example, *United Phosphorous, Ltd., v. Midland Fumigant, Inc.*, 205 F.3d 1219 (10th Cir. 2000), stating, "[I]n the federal context, this Court has adopted a preference, if not a presumption, for prejudgment interest."); *R. J. Reynolds Tobacco Co. v. Premium Tobacco Stores, Inc.*, 75 U.S.P.Q.2d 1206 (N.D. Ill. 2005). Applying the prime rate to award $1.3 million in prejudgment interest on $3.5 million award of infringer's profits in order to fully compensate the mark holder for the time value of money.

[33] For example, *American Honda Motor Co. v. Two Wheel Corp.*, 918 F.2d 1060, 1064 (2d Cir. 1990), which denied an award of prejudgment interest on infringer's profits because damage to the mark holder was minimal in that the infringer, no longer an authorized Honda motorcycle dealer, was selling genuine Honda products.

[34] For a full discussion of reasonable attorneys' fees in trademark enforcement cases, see 5 McCarthy on Trademarks § 30:98-104.

[35] For example, Rule 53(a)(1)(B)(ii), Federal Rules of Civil Procedure, authorizes a trial court to appoint a special master "to perform an accounting or resolve a difficult computation of damages."

testimony reliable under Rule 702, it may exclude the testimony under Rule 403 if the probative value of the testimony is substantially outweighed by the risk of unfair prejudice, confusing the issues, or misleading the jury.

In order to make the determinations required by Rule 702, the trial court may hold a pretrial *Daubert* hearing, named after the first of several U.S. Supreme Court decisions establishing the guidelines codified in the Rule.[36] During the hearing, the trial court may look at evidence of the following factors to determine reliability of an expert opinion on monetary recovery, but is not confined to them:

1. Whether the expert's technique or theory can be and has been tested—that is whether the expert's theory can be challenged in some objective sense, or whether it is instead simply a subjective, conclusory approach that cannot reasonably be assessed for reliability;
2. Whether the technique or theory has been subject to peer review and publication;
3. The known or potential rate of error of the technique or theory when applied and the existence and maintenance of standards and controls that govern the application of the expert's process; and
4. Whether the technique or theory has been generally accepted in the relevant community of experts.[37]

An example of testimony from financial experts not deemed reliable can be found in the special masters' report in a trademark dispute between two handbag manufacturers, Louis Vuitton Malletier and Dooney & Bourke, over a repeating multicolor monogram pattern. In an attempt to prove dilution caused by Dooney & Bourke's marketing of handbags bearing a multicolor monogram, plaintiff Louis Vuitton offered expert testimony in the form of a regression analysis conducted on the basis of only one factor, that is, a proportionate downturn in United States sales of the plaintiff's multicolor monogram handbags as compared to its sales of the handbags outside of the United States during the time period under complaint. Apart from other problems with the expert's testimony, including his lack of qualifications in the field of statistical analysis, the special masters pointed out that a single factor regression analysis does not conform to standard methodology which requires that other factors, that is, obvious alternative explanations such as disproportionate counterfeiting, be considered, analyzed, and ruled out. In the same case, Dooney & Bourke's financial expert offered testimony intended to support the contention that the plaintiff had not suffered lost profits as a result of infringing sales of the defendant's handbags. Plaintiff challenged the testimony as unreliable, arguing that the expert focused solely on cash flow analysis and ignored the effect of infringement on

---

[36] *Daubert v. Merrell Dow Pharmaceuticals*, 509 U.S. 579 (1993). Note that a trial court need not hold a *Daubert* hearing when the evidentiary record pertinent to the expert opinion is extensive and well-developed. See, for example, *Louis Vuitton Malletier v. Dooney & Bourke, Inc.*, 525 F.Supp.2d 576, 14 (S.D.N.Y. 2007). Finding by special masters that a *Daubert* hearing is unnecessary in a trademark enforcement dispute because each challenged expert had been deposed, their positions had been extensively briefed by the parties, and their reports had been submitted to the trial court.

[37] *Louis Vuitton Malletier v. Dooney & Bourke, Inc.*, 525 F.Supp.2d 576, 12 (S.D.N.Y. 2007), excerpted from the Special Masters' Report.

the goodwill of the plaintiff's subject mark. Because the expert's analysis considered future cash flows as well, the special masters found that the expert took the monetary value of goodwill into account and, therefore, was reliable under *Daubert*.

VALUING COUNTERFEITS FOR PURPOSES OF CRIMINAL SENTENCING

Trademark counterfeiting, acknowledged to be a worldwide concern for trademark owners and law enforcement alike, poses unique problems on the valuation front. Once, largely an issue for those involved in the luxury or status goods market, counterfeit merchandise has expanded across multiple product sectors, leading one prominent U.S. lawmaker, the late Senator Arlen Specter, to declare: "[F]or almost every legitimate product manufactured and sold within the United States, there is a parallel counterfeit product being sold for no more than half the price."[38] The import of this product expansion for purposes of determining sentences in criminal convictions, is layered.

For example, counterfeiting of status goods—handbags, shoes, watches, and the like—is often an activity in which consumers are complicit. In other words, the purchaser of such items generally knows, by virtue of an inexpensive purchase price, a discount vendor, or possible shoddy workmanship, that she is not acquiring the genuine item. At the other end of the spectrum, counterfeiting of products such as pharmaceuticals, baby formula, medical devices, and airplane and automobile parts, most often threatens the safety and well-being of unsuspecting consumers. The degree of deception is relevant because it provides some indication of whether the sale of a counterfeit item is likely to have displaced a sale of the genuine item, a factor that affects the court's valuation decision.

A concern that the counterfeiter has diverted sales from the brand owner, or has otherwise unjustly profited, underlies federal law governing criminal sentences in the United States. The offense level for purposes of sentencing an individual convicted of trademark counterfeiting under 18 U.S.C. § 2320, is determined by the infringement amount and that amount is calculated in accordance with § 2B5.3 of the Federal Sentencing Guidelines Manual. The calculation is based on the retail value of the counterfeit or infringing item, unless certain factors are present that counsel utilizing the retail value of the genuine or infringed item, multiplied by the number of infringing items.[39] The commentary to § 2B5.3 defines retail value of either the counterfeit or genuine item as "the retail price of that item in the market in which it is sold" and allows a court to utilize the retail value of the genuine item when, among things:

- The infringing item . . . is, or appears to a reasonably informed purchaser to be, identical or substantially equivalent to the infringed item.

---

[38] 152 Cong. Rec. S1367, S1368 (2006).

[39] Valuation of counterfeits using retail value has been criticized as overvaluing the trademark holder's asset for sentencing purposes because criminal infringement involves only interference with the rights holder's exclusive use of the asset and not dispossession of it, in contrast to theft of a tangible asset. See Brian M. Hoffstadt, *Dispossession, Intellectual Property, and the Sin of Theoretical Homogeneity*, 80 S. Cal. L. Rev. 909, 952-66 (2007), suggesting that sentencing guidelines be revised to require valuation of counterfeits by resort to the cost of a license to use the trademark.

BEANIE BABIES FAKES

Beanie Babies stuffed animals, manufactured by Ty, Inc., and subject to widespread counterfeiting during the late 1990s, illustrate the proposition that a reasonable estimate is sufficient in the criminal context. In 1999, Perry DeFreitas was tried and found guilty of one count of conspiracy to traffic in counterfeit goods and one count of trafficking in counterfeit goods, based upon his sale of Beanie Babies toys bearing counterfeit trademarks. The court noted that the genuine toys sold at retail for a uniform price of $5 apiece but that an active secondary market existed for "retired" versions of the toys leading to retail prices for the genuine item as high as $75 in some cases. Although not clear in the amended presentence report, the government apparently urged the court to adopt a retail value for at least some of the counterfeits based on the inflated price obtainable for the genuine items in the aftermarket. The court declined to accept the value proposed by the government, noting trial testimony that the inferior quality of the counterfeits caused many dissatisfied customers to seek a refund and pointing out that such items would never command aftermarket prices. Because the court found the retail value of the counterfeits impossible to ascertain, the court calculated the infringement amount using the retail value of the genuine item or $5, as an estimated "ceiling" for the retail value of the counterfeits, and multiplying that figure by the number of infringing items.

- The retail price of the infringing item is not less than 75 percent of the retail price of the infringed item.
- The retail value of the infringing item is difficult or impossible to determine without unduly complicating or prolonging the sentencing proceeding.
- The retail value of the infringed item provides a more accurate assessment of the pecuniary harm to the . . . trademark owner than does the retail value of the infringing item.[40]

Because counterfeiting is an activity that is rarely well documented, valuing counterfeits can be an imprecise process. The Federal Sentencing Guidelines specifically provide that a reasonable estimate will suffice. In the civil context, a plaintiff may elect statutory damages, which renders proof of actual damages unnecessary, a remedy added to the Lanham Act precisely because revenue from a counterfeiting operation is often difficult, if not impossible, to prove.[41] In both criminal and civil proceedings, a counterfeiter who fails to maintain sales records, or who fails to cooperate in producing those records, will not be allowed to object to a lack of specificity in the court's valuation calculation.

---

[40] U.S. Sentencing Guideline Manual, § 2B5.3 cmt. 2(A) (2012)

[41] Congress added statutory damages to counterfeiting remedies authorized by the Lanham Act in 1995 "because counterfeiters' records are frequently nonexistent, inadequate, or deceptively kept . . ., making proving actual damages in these cases extremely difficult if not impossible." S. Rep. No. 104-177, at 10 (1995).

The sentencing guidelines emphasize the quality of the counterfeit goods in determining which retail value the court should use. A level of quality that renders the counterfeit items indistinguishable from the genuine goods suggests that the counterfeit sales will displace sales of the genuine item, although query whether that holds true if the counterfeit is of a luxury item and is sold under circumstances that telegraph its lack of authenticity, such as in a flea market or for prices too good to be true.[42] For example, recent advances in manufacturing technologies accessible to counterfeiters, result in a brisk trade in well-made but nongenuine handbags and shoes and other luxury goods that are knowingly purchased by consumers seeking "a deal." When an individual is convicted of trafficking, or attempting to traffic, in counterfeit labels, patches, tags, and so on, intended for use with counterfeit goods, the relevance of quality to diversion of sales becomes even more attenuated. If the label or other identifying material, had it been affixed to the counterfeit item, "would appear to a reasonably informed purchaser to be affixed to, enclosing or accompanying an identifiable, genuine good," the court may use the retail value of the genuine item to calculate the infringement amount. In other words, if the label and any other identifying features look genuine enough, the court assumes that the product would as well.

SUMMARY

The purpose of this chapter is to provide a comprehensive view of the legal environment as it relates to trademark protection. We have noted throughout this book the fact that, while brands can be extremely powerful in economic terms, they are also vulnerable to a myriad of conditions that can seriously impair that strength. This in spite of a well-developed legal system that provides avenues for redress.

We feel that it is essential to have some understanding of the legal environment because this relates strongly to the element of risk discussed in Chapter 6.

---

[42] This rule can create an interesting "Catch 22" for a criminal defendant. For example, after his conviction for trademark counterfeiting (*United States v. Alim*, 256 Fed. Appx. 236 (11th Cir. 2007)), Husain Alim objected to the sentencing court's use of the retail value of genuine goods to establish the infringement amount, but the reviewing court pointed out that Alim's stepson had testified at trial, apparently on the defendant's behalf, that he worked at the business and was unable to discern that the merchandise confiscated by the authorities was counterfeit. That testimony, together with other evidence in the case, justified the court's use of the higher retail value of genuine items to calculate the infringement amount.

CHAPTER 10

Special Trademark Valuation Situations

Up to this point, our discussions about brand value assumed that trademarks and brand attributes are in continued use. That is, the subject brands would continue to be used without interruption as part of the total portfolio of assets of the business that owns them.

In this chapter, we examine what happens to trademark value when marks are separated from their business and their complementary assets or, in other cases, when the virtual valuation transaction is not on a "willing buyer—willing seller" basis.

TRADEMARKS IN FINANCE

Monetization is an increasingly popular subject today, especially as it relates to intellectual property rights. In the current economic climate, businesses worldwide are seeking to enhance returns on their investments and, increasingly, those investments are in the form of building intellectual property rights, such as trademarks. A dictionary would tell us that to monetize something is to "convert it into or express it in the form of currency." Monetization can take a number of different forms, each with its own characteristics, advantages and disadvantages, and likelihood of success. Different terms are used to describe the process, such as "pledging," "securitization," "collateralization," and "sale-and-leaseback."

Collateral

Probably the oldest method to extract value from an illiquid asset is the use of loans, the repayment of which is secured by the underlying asset itself. Hernando de Soto, the noted Peruvian economist, argues that the reason most of the world's poor remain mired in poverty is not that they do not have assets of value, but instead that they are unable to use the legal and financial mechanisms that can tap the wealth of their assets. As more and more of the world moves into the information age economy, a similar problem is hindering the creation of wealth, and that is the ability to tap into the value of intangible assets. Valuable assets such as trademarks possess what can be referred to as potential value. Potential value is untapped capital generation potential that exists within a given asset and that can be separated from the asset without giving up the asset itself.

Secured financing provides one of the most common examples of the potential value in assets. Asset owners are able to leverage the value of their assets by using them as collateral to obtain loans on terms that are much more favorable than could be obtained without collateral. Land, buildings, and machinery have long been used as loan collateral and have helped to increase debt-market efficiency and dramatically expand investment capital availability. One would think that possession of valuable assets such as trademarks would be useful as collateral in obtaining financing. Unfortunately, the opposite has often been the case and traditional financing can be difficult to obtain when using intellectual property such as trademarks as collateral.

Given the characteristics of brands and intellectual property trademark rights that we discussed in previous chapters, one might assume that the use of trademark rights as collateral is a classic oxymoron. In the past, it was just that because lenders in secured financing transactions looked exclusively to tangible assets as collateral. Intellectual property rights were just too risky for them to consider. The primary reason for this being that in the case of default and foreclosure, the lender would be taking possession of an asset that it had no ability to exploit commercially, and whose market was likely quite limited and, therefore, disposal of the asset could be a lengthy and costly process.

Using trademarks as collateral has increased in popularity because there are more corporations, and some very large ones, that are not rich in tangible assets because of the nature of the enterprise. They simply don't have enough bricks and mortar to pledge. As an example many large and well-known apparel companies rely on contract manufacturers to supply their products. The company itself may have little in the way of tangible assets, but its brands are the key to its profitability and its market value.

Securitization

Transforming intellectual property into a financial asset requires a number of carefully executed steps that usually result in the creation of *special purpose vehicle* (SPV) to hold and service the rights to collect the cash flow associated with the intellectual property. These are sometimes commonly referred to as *IP holding companies* although perhaps the more accurate name should be *IP management companies*.

There are two paths to transforming intellectual property into a financial asset suitable for securitization. One would involve a loan to the intellectual property owner with the IP serving as collateral. This method brings up the complications previously discussed. The attraction of securitization is that the investor (or more accurately, the SPV set up by the investor) does not have to hold, and manage, the intellectual property asset, but instead merely holds and manages the rights to collect the cash flow. Another option would involve the transfer of the intellectual property to the SPV, but this too has potential complications, particularly for trademark assets where such a transfer might be considered an assignment in gross.[1]

Trademarks are increasingly being used for asset securitization. Fashion designer BCBG Max Azria raised $53 million in a complex transaction in 2004 that was claimed as the first major apparel brand securitization that was structured to include a retail component to complement the intellectual property component.[2] The

---

[1] This is discussed in Chapter 1.
[2] "Money Men," *Vogue*, December 14, 2004, http://www.vogue.co.uk/news/2004/12/14/money-men.

BCBG Max Azria asset securitization was subsequently named "Deal of the Year" by Securitization News.[3]

Other companies in the fashion and apparel business have followed. Athlete's Foot, a privately owned international footwear retailer, raised $34.5 million from asset-backed securities sold by an SPV it created and to which it sold its trademark and more than 550 franchise fee contracts. In 2003, well-known fashion apparel company Guess Inc. completed a $75 million securitization of licensing revenue deriving from fifteen different accessory manufacturing agreements. The company transferred the Guess trademark to a shell company called IP Holder LP, which then issued bonds backed by the royalty license fees. Oscar de la Renta raised $5 million in a similar fashion in 2004.

In mid-2004 Wise Foods, Inc., the maker of "Wise" brand potato chips and "Cheez Doodles" brand snacks used its trademarks as collateral to obtain $43 million in financing. It is instructive that one of the financial institutions involved in this transaction has noted that IP asset securitization deals typically have loan to value ratios of 10 percent to 40 percent, in contrast to expected loan to value ratios of 65 percent to 75 percent when inventory is the asset or 80 percent to 85 percent when a company's receivables are the asset.[4] This probably reflects the increased uncertainty and risk currently associated with IP asset securitization arrangements when compared to situations involving more conventional assets.

In Chapter 4, we cited the example of Calvin Klein Inc. and musician David Bowie securitizing loans with royalty streams from existing licenses. Other examples include companies such as Bill Blass (apparel), Triarc (Arby's restaurants), Dream Works SKG, and Vivendi Universal (motion pictures) that have securitized financing supported by trademarks and film catalogs.

In 2006, facing substantial operating losses, Ford Motor Company pledged all of its assets to secure a $23.5 billion loan. Among those assets was its iconic "Blue Oval" trademark, along with other marks such as "Mustang" and "F-150." When the company paid off the loan and regained its investment grade debt rating in 2012, all of the assets were released back to Ford.

Cautions

As attractive as these arrangements might be from a financial point of view, there are some unique pitfalls with respect to using trademarks as collateral. This book is not intended to be a source of legal advice, but by now the reader understands that ownership and risk are important ingredients of market value. Trademarks are unique intellectual property rights in that their ownership carries with it some obligations. To ignore these obligations can jeopardize the intellectual property protection of a mark. Renewal fees must be paid, infringers must be detected and chased away, trademark usage that might lead to genericide needs to be policed, and, importantly, brand quality and characteristics must be maintained in the marketplace. One of the tenets of trademark law in the United States is that the public must not be confused as to the

---

[3] *Securitization News*, February 8, 2005.
[4] Keith Bergelt and Edward Meintzer, "IP Collateralization in Perspective, *IAM*, October 2005, http://www.iam-magazine.com/issues/article.ashx?g=d5cba63d-411b-4873-a680-d00a11592f76.

source of goods and services that are identified with the trademark. This is why, when the trademark changes hands (is "assigned"), the goodwill connected with the mark must be part of the transfer. In this context, goodwill has been taken to mean that the buyer of the trademark receives everything that is needed to provide goods and services with the same quality and characteristics that the public has come to expect from the previous owner.

In any sort of monetization scheme, these factors introduce risks for both parties to the transaction.

A lender who might not understand these unique trademark characteristics might feel that the most convenient deal would be to take ownership of the trademark rights and license them back to the former owner. Such an arrangement would simplify foreclosure in the case of a default on the lease payments. To the contrary, this sort of an arrangement very likely increases the risk to the lender rather than reducing it. Depending on the specifics of the arrangement, the lender might be taking on the responsibility for renewal fees, monitoring infringement, and verifying quality and the licensee's use of the mark. More importantly, a lender needs to have ownership of whatever else it would need to produce the trademarked product or services (even including tangible assets), otherwise the lender, faced with a default, might not be able to carry on a proper business support of the trademark in order to keep it from being considered as abandoned. In addition, the lender would have an incomplete property in the event that a foreclosure sale took place.

There are many ways to accomplish monetization of a trademark. However, a trademark owner must recognize the additional risks if a monetization involves an effective change of ownership (whether it was intended or not). The loss of the control that is needed in order to maintain the viability of trademark rights greatly increases the risk of future exploitations if the transaction is not carefully done. Errors or mismanagement on the part of the lender (now owner) can put the trademark rights in jeopardy for both parties. Giving a lender a security interest, as in a typical collateralization, would seem to be a preferable course from a trademark owner's standpoint.

TRADEMARKS IN BANKRUPTCY

After winding down its operations in November 2012, Hostess Brands Inc. began arranging for the sale of its assets which include a family of well-known trademarks for bakery products. These famous brands include snack cakes such as "Hostess," "Ho Hos," "Drakes," "Dolly Madison," "Twinkies," and "Ding Dongs" and "Wonder" bread. In March 2013, Hostess sought bankruptcy court permission to conclude the first of several auctions and sell the Twinkies, Dolly Madison, Ho Hos, and Ding Dongs brands as well as five bakeries and equipment for $410 million. A new company, Hostess Brands, LLC, was formed around these assets and the snack cake brands headed by "Twinkies" began to appear on store shelves in July, 2013. More auctions will follow.

Hostess was forced into bankruptcy by a nationwide strike of some of its unionized employees that overwhelmed its financial resources.

This is a large scale bankruptcy and it involves some well-known brands that were extremely important to the Hostess enterprise. It appears that so far the auctions have included brands as well as associated tangible assets. Subsequent auctions may be instructive about values and circumstances when brands are separated from the business that created them. There are a number of reasons why a valuation may be necessary for trademarks that are a part of a business enterprise that is insolvent. This includes providing input to recovery planning, assisting a trustee, or to clarify the economic position of a lender or stockholder. If the insolvency results in bankruptcy, the value of trademarks may become a subject in litigation.

Because increasing numbers of business enterprises rely on intellectual property such as trademarks for their earnings base, trademarks are frequently involved and are presenting new and unique problems in the liquidation circumstance. Business people, attorneys, lenders, and other professionals must often estimate the value of assets in liquidation in advance of the event, in order to develop a strategy to minimize loss.

Obviously, business enterprise insolvency affects the market value of all of a company's asset portfolio. To understand how the situation affects brand market value, it is helpful to observe the entire asset spectrum.

This discussion amplifies the discussion in Chapter 2 under the heading "Alternative Exchange Conditions," in which we present the several definitions of fair market value which are used in order to differentiate the various motivations of buyer and seller. We discuss market value in continued use as the value of business assets that are a part of an economically viable enterprise and as if they were to exchange between willing buyers and sellers.

When business assets are valued under some form of liquidation premise, it is usually the result of the business losing its economic viability and it is assumed that the seller is compelled for some reason to consummate a relatively rapid sale. Its assets have become part of a distressed sale because they are disposed of in order to pay creditors or to enable the owners to redeploy the proceeds. This is still market value, but under a specific premise.

There is also the assumption that the assets will be sold to meet whatever use to which they might be put, which might be quite different from their use within the original enterprise. The forced nature of the transaction mandates a sale into whatever market exists at the time (and sometimes the place). Thus we find a multilevel parking garage in Cambridge, Massachusetts, turned into a "street of shops" or a ship sold for scrap. Even if there is a buyer who could utilize the special nature of an asset (i.e., employ it to its "highest and best use"), if he or she is the only such buyer and knows that alternate users represent the only other market, the price will be driven down to the "alternate user" level.

Exhibit 10.1 illustrates the difference between "value in use" and "value in liquidation" on the classifications of business assets.

For the purpose of this illustration, we contrast value in use, referring to the standard market value premise, with value in liquidation, which presumes some compulsion on the part of the seller. The vertical distance between the heavy lines represents the difference between the values estimated under these premises as they are applied to various forms of property.

We include in our discussion the characteristics of monetary and tangible assets, even though they are not the focus of this book. Examining their values under a liquidation premise will help in understanding the value impact on trademarks as well.

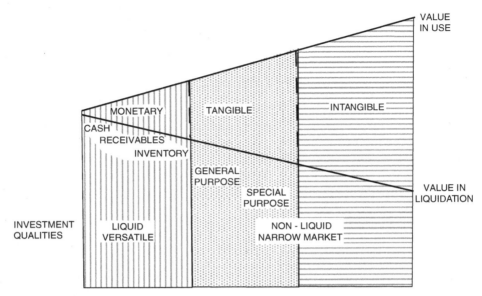

EXHIBIT 10.1   Asset Characteristics

Monetary Assets

On the left side of the exhibit, where the lines meet, there is no difference in value under either premise for cash assets. Cash is completely liquid and extremely versatile. There is an increasing difference, even for other forms of monetary assets, as one moves toward the right of the exhibit. Receivables are "cash like," but time is required for collection in order to realize the liquidity of cash. One could convert receivables into cash more rapidly by selling them to a factor, for instance, but the amount realized would be less than the amount recorded as receivable. In either case, there is some degradation in value in the liquidation situation, hence the difference in value as measured by the two premises.

Inventory assets have the same characteristics but they are more accentuated. An example would be a stock of various types of animal hair for use in manufacturing artists' paintbrushes. Such an inventory might be very valuable within the going business, but if it became necessary to liquidate it, the proceeds would be expected to be quite low. Within the inventory category, raw materials would tend to have less of a value difference than finished goods. There may be a ready market for sheet steel, but once it is cut, bent, and painted (work in process) or made into washing machines (finished goods), its value is much more subject to the vagaries of the marketplace. These are broad examples and care must be exercised if one is attempting to judge likely markets before testing them. Even the sheet steel example just given is subject to refinement. Steel is manufactured to a myriad of exacting specifications. The sheet steel stock for washing machine manufacture may have special characteristics for strength, malleability, or coating that may well narrow its attractiveness for other uses in a liquidation situation.

Tangible Assets

An inventory of finished goods, from the standpoint of *in use* versus *liquidation* value, is very much the same as tangible assets. Some tangible assets such as land, buildings, general-purpose machinery, or vehicles can serve many business functions and are relatively liquid. Other tangible assets, designed for narrow purpose, can have a very low liquidation value in a distressed sale situation. One reason for this may be that the distressed sale itself may be the result of the disappearance of the narrow market for which the property was designed.

High-technology tangible assets usually display this marked difference even though they may not be designed for special purpose. The reason is the rapidity with which they become functionally obsolete and lose their attractiveness in the market. Computers are an example. Here again, however, general rules are just that and the observer must be aware of the exceptions. A computer can be technically obsolete and have little or no value in the marketplace, but can be providing quite useful service within a business. If the function that it serves does not require the enhanced speed and features of the superior computer, and if there is no economic penalty suffered by the enterprise, then there can still be a substantial difference between the values as measured by these two premises.

Intangible Assets

As shown in Exhibit 10.1 (right side), intangible assets and intellectual property display the most dramatic differences in value by these two premises. This is because intangible assets and intellectual property are usually created within the enterprise and are so intertwined with it that they may have little value outside of it. The degree to which this is true depends on the versatility of the asset. A versatile asset should have a wide range of potential buyers. For example, one would expect to have a number of potential buyers for a contract to receive coffee at a better than market price because there is an almost universal, active market for this commodity.

Debt and Equity Financing

An additional characteristic centers around risk.[5] The risk of investing in monetary, tangible, or intangible assets is quite different. Because of this, monetary and tangible assets can usually be financed with debt because their ownership is perceived to be lower on the spectrum of risk. This lower risk results from the smaller difference between their values in use and in liquidation. When collateral is liquid and marketable, the risk of ownership is reduced and debt financing is more readily available and at a lower cost. An example of this would be a loan secured by cash in the bank—a so-called "passbook loan."

A possible exception to this would be a large electric generating facility of an operating utility. This highly specialized property would normally be perceived to be a risky investment because of the enormous difference between its value in use

---

[5] These characteristics are illustrated in Chapter 2 as Exhibit 2.2.

and its value in liquidation. The essential point is that regulatory and governmental constraints and protection can have considerable bearing on the difference between value in use and liquidation value, as we have recently observed in government bailouts.

A lender always considers liquidation value because that is what he is likely to receive if the loan becomes nonperforming. A lender, therefore, looks to lower risk assets (as they are defined) as collateral. The business owner, in turn, focuses on these assets because a greater percentage of their cost can be financed with debt capital. A lender might, as an example, be willing to lend 90 percent of the cost of raw materials purchased for inventory but only 50 percent or less of the cost of a custom designed machine. While the economic value of the machine to the business may be greater than the raw material, its value in liquidation is proportionately so much lower that an investor (creditor) is uncomfortable. The lender has the ability to reduce the risk by reducing the loan to value ratio. In that way he is more assured of recouping the amount of the loan from the liquidation proceeds, if that action becomes necessary. There are many other techniques used by lenders to accomplish a desired level of comfort relative to financing various types of assets, such as cross-collateralization, coverage tests, dividend restrictions, and the like. We are using the "loan to value" ratio to illustrate this point. We also must consider that lenders (those providing debt financing to the business) are not the only investors who recognize differences in the risk of the portfolio of assets that comprise a business.

Equity investors (buyers of the company's common stock) and trade creditors are also concerned, and suit their market actions so as to ameliorate risk. Their actions must be less direct because they, unlike the debt holder, usually have no immediate claim on the assets of the business in a liquidation situation. Therefore, they are less focused on the differences between value in use and liquidation value, but this difference is factored into their investment decision-making.

As one moves toward the right in Exhibit 10.1, toward the intangible asset category, there is an increase in perceived investment risk. When liquidity of the underlying assets is low, then capital becomes much more difficult to obtain or is available only at very high cost. The development of assets such as that must be financed with equity.

This would be especially true for the expenses of brand building. These statements, as with all generalizations, do not always hold true, however. Would the Coca-Cola trademark be more risky than other assets of its business? No. Would it be far less valuable in liquidation? No (depending on what caused the liquidation). We once appraised the "Ringling Bros. and Barnum & Bailey Circus" trademark. In our report, we stated that if one were given that trademark, its power could fill a coliseum the day after. Of course, the risk would be whether we could stage a quality show. If not, even that powerful mark would begin to deteriorate, as would the Coca-Cola mark if our beverage products did not meet standards.

Some Case Examples

From the previous discussion, we can observe that:

- Trademarks are less versatile than many other business assets.
- Trademarks may be more risky than many other business assets.

- Trademarks are created by equity investment.
- The value of trademarks in liquidation would be expected to be substantially lower than their value in use.

We have already cited some instances in which trademarks have been sold out of a bankruptcy situation. Certainly many have been sold as insolvency loomed. They are sold to:

- Competitors who wish to increase market share by keeping the brand alive
- Competitors who wish to increase market share by killing the brand
- Market entrants who wish to smooth their entry and reduce advertising expenses
- Market participants who wish to launch a new line

In the bankruptcy of Washington Mutual, Inc., the court concluded in 2011 that the trademarks of this largest savings and loan association in the United States did not have significant value due to a damaged reputation:

> *The intellectual property consists largely of trademarks including the names "WaMu" and "Washington Mutual." . . . The Debtors respond that an appraisal would merely establish that the trademarks are virtually worthless because they are associated with the largest bank failure in the country's history. . . . Further, the fact that WMI has virtually no remaining business operations convinces the Court that the marks, if owned by WMI, have insignificant value.* [6]

In the 2008, bankruptcy proceedings of 3dfx Interactive, Inc., the court was persuaded to accept an income approach and assigned a fair market value of $11.31 million to the 3dfx trademark portfolio. There was expert testimony that the value of the trademarks was immaterial due to the type of business and due to the lack of profitability:

> *First, in his view, brand names and brand recognition do not sustain product loyalty in the relevant 3D graphics market. Instead, state-of-the-art designs, performance and timely product launch are more important. Second, 3dfx's Trademark value was diminished when 3dfx changed to add-in board sales in mid-1999 because in that market a developed brand name is not as important as product cost and performance. Third, nVidia did not use the Tradenames in any products and there was no apparent market interest in licensing the Tradenames to third parties. In addition, the fact that 3dfx had not generated a positive operating margin for approximately two years indicated that the branded products were not generating any excess profit for 3dfx.* [7]

---

[6] *In re Washington Mutual, Inc.*, 442 BR 314 (Bankr. Court, D. Delaware 2011).
[7] *In re 3dfx Interactive, Inc.*, 389 B.R. 842, 874 (Bankr. N.D. Cal. 2008).

But the court concluded that a previous allocation of purchase price which assigned a fair value of $11.31 million to the trademarks was a stronger indication of value:

> *The Court finds the D&T valuation convincing because it was performed in advance of any litigation and was based on facts known or knowable at the time of the Transaction. At the time, nVidia had indicated it planned to exploit these Trademarks.*[8]

Pan American World Airways went into bankruptcy in 1991, and its "Pan Am" trademark and other assets were sold in 1993 for $1.3 million. About six years later, Pan Am came alive again as a low-fare carrier based at New York's Kennedy Airport. In its most recent incarnation, the Pan Am brand, America's first international airline, will be the flag of Pan American Airways flying cargo out of Brownsville, Texas. This is the fifth attempt to revitalize this once famous brand. As resilient as this brand has been, it has little versatility and its strong identification with the airline industry keeps it anchored there.

The trademarks of the Jenkins Valve Company were auctioned in Philadelphia (along with, but separately from other assets). These marks, associated with a product line that had little market share in the U.S. were bought by Crane Company (a competitor), for a bid of $1,050,000.

In 1992, He-Ro Group Ltd. paid $7.9 million ($4.5 million over a seven-year period) for the "Russ Togs," "Crazy Horse," "Villager," and "Red Horse" apparel trademarks and other assets and inventory from the bankruptcy estate.

The "After Six" apparel trademark sold in early 1993 for approximately $7 million in a bankruptcy auction. A small amount of machinery and inventory was included in the sale.

In the unpublished case of Steve Zimmer Paige, the court considered an extensive effort to market the domain name "FreeCreditScore.com." It found that the negotiated sale price of the domain name ($1.9 million), which roughly mirrored that of a previous auction that fell through, was the market value "as a result of these marketing efforts and because of the special nature of the property at issue, the proposed value is, ipso facto, the market value of the property."[9]

VALUATION DIRECTIONS

We believe that the manner in which a business becomes insolvent is a critical consideration in the market value of a trademark under the ensuing circumstances. Insolvency can result from what we have termed internal and external events. Internal events include:

- Financing decisions (such as a leveraged buy-out, a "poison pill," or other takeover deterrents) resulting in an overburden of debt

---

[8] Id.
[9] *In re Paige*, 05-34474, 2006 WL 4846378 (Bankr. D. Utah Dec. 8, 2006).

- The loss of key management
- An uninsured loss of plant, property, or equipment
- An acquisition that turned out to be a cash drain
- Illegal activities
- An imprudent expansion or a new product line that failed
- Lack of capital
- Expensive correction of an environmental or safety problem
- Expensive litigation
- Labor strife.

External events that can result in insolvency for an enterprise include:

- Depressed general economic conditions
- Technological obsolescence of major product line(s)
- Overwhelming competition
- Product "disaster" such as contamination, or discovery of a health hazard or side effect
- Changing tastes (as for a consumer or recreation product)
- An advertising program that goes awry
- Customer perception of declining quality or performance.

In general, internally caused insolvency will have minimal effect on the liquidation value of trademarks. If, as an example, the management takes on an overlarge amount of debt in order to finance a buy-out and a moderate downturn in business results in inadequate cash flow to service the debt, insolvency may result. It is possible that the customers of that business may be completely unaware of the situation and that the company's products or services can maintain their market acceptance unimpaired. The trademarks of the business ought to retain their value even though the business may be insolvent because of an imprudent financing scheme that is not really associated with the earning power of the assets in the enterprise.

The most recent news about the former Hostess Brands Inc. indicates that the new owner of the Twinkies, Ho Hos, and Ding Dongs brands, Hostess Brands LLC, enjoyed a bubble of pent-up demand for these snack cake brands when they appeared on store shelves. If the enthusiasm continues, this relatively rapid restructuring should bring these brands back unscathed.

Timing is also important. If the cash flow problems existed over a long time and management applied stringent cost-cutting measures that gradually degraded product quality or service, then there would be some impairment of trademark value in liquidation. In this case, an internal problem (imprudent financing) would have become an external one (market rejection of a brand).

It is therefore necessary to examine the nature of the insolvency, gain some knowledge of the events leading up to it, and understand how it has affected the enterprise and its perception by outsiders. Only with this knowledge can one make a reasonable estimate of market value of trademarks in a potential liquidation situation.

Going back to Exhibit 10.1, we should also consider the versatility of the mark, its facility for brand extensions, its age, and its acceptance in the market.

Income Approach

Using this approach in the case of insolvency employs the same tools presented in Chapter 7. The underlying assumptions would almost surely differ, however. In a DCF calculation, one might well reflect a period of low or no cash flow and higher than usual expenses during the time that the trademark is being "rescued." A relief from royalty calculation might reflect a rate at the very bottom of the market range. Gross profit margins might deteriorate because of the necessity of using outside manufacturing.

All of this is dependent on what caused the demise of the business, how long it took, and what steps are possible to rehabilitate it. The models we have presented are capable of accommodating these and other assumptions.

Cost Approach

This approach can be applicable by estimating the value of the trademark on an in-use basis, and subtracting from that the cost to cure the damage caused by the business disaster. An example might be the case of a product contamination:

- *Recall expense*. Includes the cost of temporary employees, rental equipment, public safety messages, special testing, handling, disposal and crises management, and PR consulting fees
- *Replacement cost*. All of the costs associated with replacing the product previously delivered
- *Lost profits*. This can include profits lost on withdrawn products as well as future profits lost due to sales decline caused by the incident
- *Brand rehabilitation expense*. Including extra advertising, incremental expenses associated with rushing new product to market, and special promotions to rebuild public trust in the manufacturer and its products
- *Principle of substitution*. A classic measure of asset value is the cost to acquire a substitute asset, or one that can perform the same function. This measure becomes important in the liquidation situation. A trademark does not really have an alternate use in the same sense that a parking garage can be converted to a retail center. It can be used for different, but logically related goods or services, but it will remain a trademark.

    Therefore, we need to think in terms of a substitute trademark. The Pan Am situation is a good example. If we wanted to start up a new, low-fare airline with a limited number of destinations, we would make financial forecasts of the start-up business. Included would be the necessary advertising and promotion costs of a new entrant in the market. Those costs would inevitably be lower if we could acquire a trademark such as Pan Am that might be able to help us get over the hurdle of "who we are" and we might only have to tell the world where we fly and for how much. That reduction in cost, as well as perhaps some acceleration in revenue inflows, would be a measure of how much we would be willing to pay for the rights to use such a trademark.

    Again we are back to investment principles. What is the financial difference between building a new trademark and buying an existing one? What investment would it require to get additional market share as opposed to buying the trademark of a troubled competitor?

Market Approach

We noted some evidence of market transactions in the previous discussion, but we must ask ourselves whether it is much help. The same difficulties arise in using the market approach in an unusual business situation as they do in a "business as usual" case. Comparability is a large obstacle to overcome.

When U.S. Bankruptcy Law Changes the Playing Field   The valuation of a brand in the bankruptcy situation must consider a unique situation that exists relative to trademark rights that have been licensed to others by the debtor.

Section 365(a) of the U.S. Bankruptcy Code provides, in pertinent part, that "the trustee, subject to the court's approval, may assume or reject any executory contract or unexpired lease of the debtor."[10] An *executory contract* may be defined as one in which each party to the contract owes continuing, material obligations to the other so that either party's failure to perform would constitute a breach. Congress specifically exempted copyright and patent licenses from rejection in bankruptcy but did not address licenses for trademarks, service marks, or trade dress.[11] The legislative history of that section indicates that Congress decided to postpone legislation with regard to the treatment of trademark licenses in bankruptcy and to allow the bankruptcy courts to fashion their own law on this front because the requirement that a trademark licensor exercise quality control over the licensee poses a serious challenge for the bankrupt licensor.[12]

Currently, uncertainty exists regarding the effect of rejection of trademark licenses in bankruptcy.[13] Courts seem to agree that a bankrupt licensor may reject a trademark license that is executory in nature, but they appear to disagree as to the effect of such rejection on the licensee's rights to use the trademark. The uncertainty in the law, and the potential that the law could be resolved in favor of termination of the licensee's rights, forces potential licensees to address the matter in the trademark license negotiation process. In one recent case, a fan manufacturer contracted to supply a specific number of trademarked boxed fans to the licensor/distributor and, because it knew the licensor/distributor was financially unstable, the manufacturer negotiated for the right to sell the fans in the event of the other party's default. Three months into the contract, the licensor/distributor declared bankruptcy and sought to reject the contract under § 365(a). While agreeing that the distributor could reject the contract, the U.S. Court of Appeals for the Eighth Circuit held that, although rejection constituted breach of the contract, it did not alter the general rule that an intellectual property licensee's rights survive a licensor's breach.[14] This case stands in conflict with prior case law upholding a bankrupt's decision to reject a trademark license in order to terminate the licensee's

---

[10] 11 U.S.C. § 365(a).
[11] 11 U.S.C. § 365(n).
[12] S. REP. NO. 100-505, at 5.
[13] *Lewis Bros. Bakeries Inc. v. Interstate Brands Corp.*, 690 F.3d 1069 (8th Cir. 2012); *Sunbeam Prods., Inc. v. Chicago American Manufacturing, LLC*, 686 F.3d 372 (7th Cir. 2012).
[14] *Sunbeam Prods.*, 686 F.3d at 376-77.

rights and pursue a more advantageous business arrangement.[15] Additionally, the case raises the specter of a naked license, that is, a license not subject to quality control by the licensor.

In response to the current conflict in the law, the International Trademark Association (INTA) passed a recent resolution calling for legislative exemption of trademark licenses from the rejection provisions of the Bankruptcy Code and imposition of quality control obligations on any trustee appointed in bankruptcy. INTA endorses this approach to protect the interests of consumers in greater competition and choice from the detrimental effects of commercial uncertainty and to protect the licensee's business from disruption caused by the licensor's financial instability.[16]

TRADEMARKS AND AD VALOREM TAXES

What we know as property taxes are based on the value of property, hence are known as *ad valorem taxes*. Taxable property typically comprises real property (land, land improvements, and buildings) and personal property (movable machinery and equipment, household furnishings, and the like). The laws governing ad valorem taxes are written at the state or local level, and so differ greatly from place to place in the United States. Generally speaking, intangible assets and intellectual property are excluded from taxation or, in some cases, separately taxed.

We are witness to the explosion in the value and importance of intangible assets and intellectual property in U.S. business. This has not gone unnoticed by the tax collectors, hard pressed to increase tax revenues for their local governments in the face of federal support reductions. Combine this situation with the fact that most of the relevant laws were written at a time when these assets were largely poorly defined because there was no particular concern about them. The result is significant litigation among taxpayers and tax collectors. In some cases, this litigation involves the value of intangible assets and intellectual property, and, in others, it concerns to what extent different type of intangible property are taxable.

Controversy does not arise with respect to residential properties, because a local assessor can delineate the tangible assets present and there are good tools to measure value, such as an active real estate market and cost of replacement data. Intangible asset questions arise with industrial properties, especially those with unique assets or those which extend over several tax jurisdictions.

In these cases, the usual tools are not applicable, and the assessor must start with a capitalization of income or market approach that produces the value of the entire enterprise. As the reader now recognizes, that is just a starting point in the task of estimating the value of the constituent parts of the enterprise portfolio. The assessor may stop with the enterprise value, however, or make adjustments to remove nontaxable assets in a way that the taxpayer disputes.

---

[15] *Lewis Bros.*, 690 F.3d at 1074-75, following *Lubrizol Enters., Inc. v. Richmond Metal Finishers, Inc.*, 756 F.2d 1043 (4th Cir. 1985).

[16] International Trademark Association, "Board Resolutions, Trademark Licenses under the U.S. Federal Bankruptcy Code," November 7, 2012.

Obviously, in a jurisdiction in which intangible assets are not taxed, the value of a trademark (along with the values of other intangible assets) should be removed from the enterprise value in a calculation of taxable property.

SUMMARY

There are a number of special circumstances in which the market value of the brand may become an issue. We emphasize, however, that these conditions do not give rise to new or different valuation methodologies. Instead, these special circumstances may change our ways of developing the critical valuation inputs, not the application of the cost, market, and income methods.

CHAPTER 11

Global Trademark Issues

Property valuation technology first developed in areas of the world where views on private property and its rights—and perhaps its use as a basis for taxation—provided impetus. Valuation skills are spreading worldwide and have become an object of intense interest in many countries where state-owned property is being privatized or in developing countries in which the business communities are seeking international commercial relationships. In both of these situations, there is a great need to attract capital in order to establish and maintain a high level of innovation. This greatly increases the need to perform credible property valuations.

Trademarks are increasingly important in international commerce. The typical path of intellectual property development that we have observed in emerging economies often has the following structure:

- Commercial enterprises are small and intellectual property may exist, but largely unrecognized. Counterfeiting may be a significant activity.
- Enterprises begin to consolidate and become absorbed in contract manufacturing of low-tech components for others. Little or no intellectual property is involved.
- As skills improve, contract manufactured products become more complex. Intellectual property may be licensed-in as part of the manufacturing contract.
- Original know-how begins to emerge as a result of the more complex manufacturing experience which may now be for finished goods and which may also include some design work.
- Original intellectual property begins to surface if the legal environment is in place to protect it.
- Manufacturing moves toward finished goods for in-country consumption. The role of contract manufacturing diminishes.
- Entry into world markets takes place with innovative, branded goods or branded components.

Trademark development tends to come at the end of this progression, but it is essential for developing enterprises to make the leap into world markets. Once this is accomplished, the new brands provide an umbrella for growth.

In Chapter 3, we discussed the international harmonization of financial reporting as well as some tax issues which are very international in scope. Our Chapter 9 discussion on the legal protection of trademarks touched on international differences as well. In this chapter, we present several specific topics with international implications.

TRADEMARK HOLDING COMPANIES[1]

Tax-planning strategies can provide firms with a significant competitive advantage. Cost-effectively reducing a firm's tax liabilities increases its profitability and thereby provides the firm with greater net resources to pursue its business strategies or reward its owners. Intellectual property assets, including trademarks, have become an increasingly popular focus for tax-reduction strategies. When developing these strategies, trademarks provide key advantages. Unlike the relocation of the factory or the movement of large supplies of tangible goods, trademark transfers can be accomplished with little more than the signing of a contract.

As extremely mobile assets that can be moved inexpensively from one jurisdiction to another, trademarks provide an excellent asset for strategic structuring for tax reduction both internationally and domestically. Furthermore, this ease of relocations means that if another taxation regime location offers a more attractive tax treatment for income generated from a firm's trademark assets, it is a simple matter to move the assets to that more favorable location.

Not unexpectedly, the growth of intellectual property–based tax-reduction strategies has not escaped notice at the IRS. In 2006, then IRS commissioner Mark Everson remarked, "Tax issues associated with the transfer of intangibles outside the United States have been a high risk compliance concern for us and have seen a significant increase in recent years. Taxpayers, especially in the high technology and pharmaceutical industries, are shifting profits offshore."[2,3]

As an example, Google was reportedly able to reduce its U.S. federal tax liability by $3.1 million for the three years from 2007 to 2010. It first moved certain intellectual property assets to Ireland and Holland, and then it moved profits from worldwide operations first through an Irish company (Google Ireland Holdings) and then through a Dutch entity, eventually ending up in a holding company in tax-friendly Bermuda.

One thing that all these tax saving structures and transactions have in common is that they involve transfer pricing. As the economy becomes increasingly global in scope and companies and individuals carry on trade that spans various taxation borders, the potential effect of transfer pricing to the various participants grows. According to a group of experts assembled by the United Nations, transfer pricing "is probably the most important tax issue in the world."[4]

Transfer pricing, as the name suggests, refers to the price at which an asset or service is transferred within an organization or between related organizations or individuals. It differs from true market pricing because transfer pricing, by definition, does not involve independent participants in an arm's length transaction. As such,

---

[1] Our colleague, William Murphy is a primary contributor to this section.

[2] Mark Everson, Written Testimony before Senate Committee on Finance on Compliance Concerns Relative to Large and Mid-Size Businesses, June 13, 2006.

[3] See also the discussion of transfer pricing tax issues in Chapter 3.

[4] Ad Hoc Group of Experts on International Cooperation in Tax Matters, "Transfer Pricing: History, State of the Art, Perspectives," United Nations Document 2 (June 26, 2001), ST/SG/AC.8/2001/CRP.6.

transfer pricing is ripe for manipulation by the buyer and seller. Developing a justifiable transfer price therefore tends to be one of the most significant determinants in the overall success of a trademark–based tax-reduction strategy. A transfer price valuation that is properly conducted can yield an effective and legal arrangement, whereas an improper or overly aggressive valuation can lead to costly challenges from taxation authorities.

Intellectual property assets, such as trademarks, are particularly well suited for transfer-pricing structures. The idea is to transfer the bulk of the business organization's valuable intellectual property assets to a subsidiary (an intellectual property holding company) located in a lower-tax jurisdiction. The intellectual property holding company will then license the intellectual property assets to the organization's operating subsidiaries and thereby transfer a portion of the operating subsidiaries' taxable income to the intellectual property holding company.

Once the basic intellectual property–based transfer-pricing structure is established, its tax-reduction role is not limited solely to transfer pricing. The intellectual property holding company can also be used to license the organization's intellectual property to third-party customers outside the parent company's home jurisdiction and allow the organization to earn that taxable income in a lower-tax jurisdiction. In addition, the holding company can be used as part of an asset securitization structure.

Actual structures frequently involve multiple subsidiaries performing the basic function of the intellectual property holding company, and such subsidiaries may be located in multiple jurisdictions around the world. The Google structure cited earlier is a prime example. Loan and dividend payments are then layered over the basic structure to transfer funds throughout the business organization. Much of this added complexity is motivated by a desire to repatriate the after-tax profits to an entity in the organization that can best use the extra funds, but without triggering substantial new tax obligations.

There is nothing illegal about shifting income to a lower-tax jurisdiction via a transfer-pricing structure as long as the transfer prices reflect the true economic realities of the transaction. Of course, what the structuring party may believe to be fair can be disputed by taxing authorities.

THE SCOURGE OF TRADEMARK TROLLS

Trademark trolling is a relatively new type of misconduct in the intellectual property arena. Several definitions of the activity abound, but, in the words of one commentator: "If one thing defines all trademark trolling, it is the attempted enforcement of rights by an individual who—allegedly—has no business owning them."[5] The activity runs the gamut from outright fraud to unduly aggressive enforcement of questionable rights. However defined, the activity drains the financial resources of legitimate trademark owners, through litigation costs or through the extortion of licensing or assignment fees, and provides an unwelcome distraction from running their businesses.

---

[5] Simon Crompton, "Who Are You Calling A Troll?" *Managing Intellectual Property*, May 7, 2012, http://www.managingip.com/Article/3023944/Who-are-you-calling-a-troll.html.

In the United States, the activity tends to take the form of the acquisition of weak trademark rights or the establishment of a quasi-legitimate claim, followed by aggressive enforcement for purposes of financial remuneration. The following case illustrates trademark trolling.

In *Premier Pool Management Corp. v. Lusk*, the plaintiff applied to the USPTO to register the mark "Premier Pools & Spas," which it was using through a licensee, to offer swimming pool and spa construction services.[6] The application was rejected as conflicting with a prior registration for "Premier Pools Construction, Inc.," for swimming pool construction services. Subsequently, the plaintiff and the registrant agreed upon a $5,000 purchase price for the registration with the relatively modest price reflecting doubt as to whether or not the mark had ever been used in interstate commerce. The plaintiff's attempt to purchase proved unsuccessful because an unidentified higher bidder intervened and gained the registration. The bidder was later disclosed to be a *search engine optimization* (SEO) consultant that had been hired by the plaintiff to assist it in other business enterprises. The SEO consultant's business plan was to extract exorbitant royalties from the plaintiff and other pool construction companies for use of the Premium brand. The relationship between the plaintiff and the SEO consultant deteriorated and resulted in litigation that was resolved by a default judgment against the latter, and the registration was canceled for failure to show use in interstate commerce.

Although the trademark troll in the foregoing case defaulted when forced to prove use of the mark in commerce, some trademark trolls resort repeatedly to the courts in an attempt to intimidate their targets into a licensing fee or an agreement to cease use of the subject "mark" altogether. Leo Stoller is perhaps the most notorious trademark troll to pursue this strategy. He filed so many actions in the U.S. District Court for the Northern District of Illinois that the Executive Committee of that court sanctioned him and entered an injunction precluding him from filing any further lawsuits without first obtaining leave of court.[7] Although Stoller did not win any of the numerous suits that he instituted, he caused numerous litigants to expend money and time in defending them.

On the international stage, China has been highlighted as a haven for trademark trolling. Under current Chinese law, the first entity to register a trademark is its lawful owner, even if the mark has been used previously in China but not registered by the prior user. Only one exception to this rule pertains, that is, when an unregistered mark has been used so intensively and extensively that it has acquired nationwide fame or renown among the relevant public, prior to a third party's attempt at registration. The first-to-file situation in China has been exploited by trademark trolls—Chinese companies and individuals—who identify, apply for, and register trademarks belonging to competitors who, for whatever reason, have failed to pursue registration. Noting the commercial uncertainty created for foreign investors in China, a commentator remarks on the additional concern that litigation may resolve in favor of the troll:

> [I]n some cases the IP rights can be enforced against the foreign investor for opportunistic and unfair motives as was the case this year when a European

---

[6] 2012 U.S. Dist. LEXIS 63350 (E.D. Cal. 2012).

[7] *In re Leo Stoller* (No. 07-cv-01435 (N.D. Ill. Mar. 8, 2007).

wine manufacturer, Castel Freres SAS, was ambushed by a Chinese com-
petitor over a "stolen" trademark with catastrophic consequences. In April
2012, Castel was ordered to pay more than $5 million in compensation, one
of the largest ever sums of damages in an IP infringement case in China.[8]

The foregoing case illustrates a distinct trademark trolling strategy, for example, to block a competitor from access to a burgeoning market.

INTERNATIONAL VALUATION STANDARDS

The appraisal standards and best practices that we have described in the previous chapters are primarily those in use in the Americas, as is the terminology we have used. They are standards that have been promulgated by organizations such as the Appraisal Foundation, the Appraisal Institute, the American Institute of CPAs (AICPA), and the American Society of Appraisers.[9] Appraisal standards in the Americas tend to be nationally sourced, but there is very little, if any, substantive differences in principle though there may be minor differences in terminology. This is true not only for ethical and reporting standards but also for valuation methodologies.

These statements also hold true internationally. In our view, basic valuation principles remain quite consistent throughout the world though there may be terminology differences and nuances of technique.

International Organization for Standardization

The International Organization for Standardization (ISO) has published an International Standard on "Brand Valuation—Requirements for Monetary Brand Valuation" (ISO 10668:2010(E)).[10] It provides terms and definitions related to trademark valuation, as well as discussing general valuation requirements, specific requirements as they relate to brands, valuation approaches and methods, necessary valuation inputs, and standards for reporting a valuation result.

Its description of brands and trademarks is quite similar to our discussion in Chapter 1. Valuation methods cited are the cost, market, and income approaches. Within the income approach, ISO 10668 discusses a price premium method, a volume premium method, an income-split method (present value of the economic profits attributable to the brand), a multiperiod excess earnings method (present value remaining after subtracting returns of other assets), an incremental cash flow

---

[8] "$5M Case Highlights Risk from Chinese Trademark Trolls," *Law 360*, October 17, 2012, available at http://www.law360.com/articles/386205/5m-case-highlights-risk-from-chinese-trademark-trolls.

[9] The Appraisal Foundation, 1155 15th Street, NW, Suite 1111, Washington, DC 20005 (www.appraisalfoundation.org); Appraisal Institute, 200 W. Madison, Suite 1500, Chicago, IL 60606 (www.appraisalinstitute.org); American Institute of CPAs, 1455 Pennsylvania Ave., NW, Washington, DC 20004-1081 (www.aicpa.org); American Society of Appraisers, 11107 Sunset Hills Rd, Suite 310, Reston, VA 20190 (www.appraisers.org).

[10] International Organization for Standardization, ISO Central Secretariat, 1, ch. de la Voie-Creuse CP 56, CH-1211 Geneva 20, Switzerland (www.iso.org).

method, and royalty relief method. These were covered in our Chapter 5 as techniques for estimating the amount of economic benefit.

ISO 10668 becomes a bit misty in its discussion of the "behavioral aspects" of a brand, and the necessity to consider them as part of the application of the cost, market, or income approaches. This section highlights a need to analyze a brand's situation, strength, and relevance as evidenced by stakeholders' perceptions. There are some useful thoughts here, but few specifics.

International Valuation Standards Council

The International Valuation Standards Council (IVSC) is an independent not for profit organization with headquarters in London.[11] It is funded by membership descriptions and sponsorship by valuation professional groups, valuation providers, and valuation users. It is currently supported by 74 member groups from 54 countries.

The IVSC publishes Valuation Standards applicable for all categories of property. Those relating to intangible assets are set out in Standard 301.02. This standard characterizes intangible assets within the four groups: marketing related intangible assets, customer or supplier related intangibles, technology related intangibles, and artistic related intangible assets. Trademarks fall into the category of marketing related intangible assets that include:

- Trademarks, trade names, service marks, collective marks, and certification marks
- Trade dress, such as unique color shape or package design
- Internet domain names
- Noncompete agreements

As to valuation methods, the ID ASC standards include:

- Direct market comparison approach
- Cost approach
- Income approach

Within the income approach, the IVSC Standards recommend three principal valuation methods: the relief-from-royalty method, the premium profits method, and the excess earnings method.

Conclusions

There are no material differences about the basic valuation methodologies or the financial principles that underlie them. If there are any differences at all, they are within some of the techniques used to obtain the necessary inputs to the basic methodologies. The emergence of the International Financial Reporting Standards (IFRs)

---

[11] International Valuation Standards Board, 41 Moorgate, London EC2R 6PP, United Kingdom. (www.ivsc.org).

that we described in Chapter 3 has further brought valuation standards together, even in terminology.

We are confident that the use of the valuation methods and techniques presented in this book will be understood anywhere in the world.

COUNTERFEITING: A WORLDWIDE CONTAGION

Trademark counterfeiting is broadly defined as willful trademark infringement and results in the illegal trafficking of simulations or copies of branded goods. Once focused mainly on the luxury or status goods market, counterfeiting has expanded into virtually every market segment. Commenting on the need for heightened protections against counterfeiting, the late Senator Arlen Specter observed: "[F]or every legitimate product manufactured and sold within the United States, there is a parallel counterfeit product being sold for no more than half the price."[12]

Widespread counterfeiting poses serious risks to consumer health and safety and undermines the viability and stability of economic markets. These dangers coupled with the development of low-cost manufacturing technologies that produce high-quality copies, the ease and speed with which goods and their component parts move across borders, and the highly lucrative nature of counterfeiting combine to create a contagion that has aroused the concern of governments around the globe. The World Intellectual Property Organization (WIPO) effectively summarizes the resultant economic and social concerns on its website, and that summary is reproduced here:

> *Piracy and counterfeiting activities not only affect the (private) rights of intellectual property right holders and their concomitant economic and moral interests, but also harm national economies and social structures. Exact figures of the impact on a worldwide scale are difficult to measure; however certain trends and consequences can be assessed.*
>
> *Economic consequences of piracy and counterfeiting to the right holders are obvious. However, the economic consequences of a widespread piracy and counterfeiting business in a country may go much further. Manufacturers of affected products have a direct loss in sale revenues; this is often directly related to losses in tax revenues, and may also result in job losses. In social terms, the illegal business of counterfeiting and piracy brings with it all the negative side effects of clandestine labor.*
>
> *In addition, a certain market destabilization can be seen in areas heavily affected by counterfeiting and piracy. Manufacturers, both local and from abroad, loose trust in the market place if they realize that their IP rights are not respected and cannot effectively be enforced. This has been demonstrated to lead to a decline in investment. In a classic study (Mansfield 1995), a large percentage of chemical, drug, machinery and electrical equipment firms surveyed reported that the strength or weakness of intellectual property protection in any given country was an important aspect of their decision to make direct investments there.*

---

[12] 152 Cong. Rec. 1367, 1368 (2006).

Additionally, an unsound environment for invention and cultural creativity as such can be a disincentive to engaging in creative work and research. This in turn will affect the cultural, economic vitality and development of a country.

Another negative impact is the illegal and often criminal environment in which the illicit piracy and counterfeiting activities take place and the resulting negative impact on the public order. Because of the high profit and the relatively low risk, counterfeit and piracy activities are in many cases related to organized crime. Profits made from illicit activities can be employed to fund other criminal activities. This interrelation between IP rights infringements undertaken on a commercial scale on the one hand, and criminal infrastructures on the other, has heightened awareness among policy makers and law enforcement agencies around the world.

Finally, the aspect of a concrete risk for security and health of consumers is becoming an ever greater threat. The highly dangerous effects on consumers of fake medicines, cosmetics, surgical equipment, food, cigarettes, alcoholic drinks, vehicle and aircraft parts, etc. receives increasingly attention among policy makers in the past years. The World Health Organization maintains a list of various cases of counterfeit medicines, some of which are less efficacious or even contain no active ingredients. In the worst cases, such medicines even contained poisonous elements, and led to disastrous effects among consumers.[13]

Governments have responded with a flurry of enforcement legislation, ranging from increased civil liability for egregious trademark infringement, administrative measures often aimed at seizure of counterfeit goods at the border, and enhanced criminal penalties for counterfeiting. The governments of Italy and France, countries with economies centered on the design and manufacture of luxury items, have taken the unprecedented step of imposing criminal penalties on the ultimate consumers of counterfeit goods.[14] Despite these legislative reactions, the problem continues and has generated a multinational effort to develop a coordinated response to counterfeiting.

Most recently, international coordination has resulted in the Anti-Counterfeiting Trade Agreement (ACTA), a plurilateral trade agreement designed to implement an international legal framework for intellectual property rights enforcement.[15] In particular, ACTA establishes general standards for civil enforcement, border measures, criminal enforcement, and enforcement in the digital environment. ACTA requires that its signatories conform their domestic laws and policies to the agreement's provisions. The agreement has been widely criticized for its semisecret negotiation

---

[13] World Intellectual Property Organization, "Enforcement of IP Rights—Frequently Asked Questions," *WIPO Program Activities*, http://www.wipo.int/enforcement/en/faq/.

[14] Lisa Lynn Cunningham, "Trademark Counterfeiting and Individual Purchaser Liability," *National Law Review* (2011), http://www.natlawreview.com/print/article/trademark-counterfeiting-and-individual-purchaser-liability.

[15] Ministry of Foreign Affairs of Japan, Anti-Counterfeiting Trade Agreement, May 2011, http://www.mofa.go.jp/policy/economy/i_property/pdfs/acta1105_en.pdf.

among a limited number of nations.[16] Most of the 11 signatories have yet to ratify ACTA so it is too early to assess what its effect will be in addressing the counterfeiting problem.

POLITICAL/INVESTMENT RISK

In Chapter 1, we touched upon brands in a global setting and, in Chapter 3, we noted some of the complexities of international taxation. MNEs are acclimated to doing business across national borders. Today, however, every business must think in international terms and be ready to take advantage of international opportunities. When we focus on brands, we must think in terms of how well a brand will travel and we must consider the risks involved in exposing a brand to a new national environment. Exhibit 7.7 presents a valuation model that aggregates several valuations of disparate brand extensions. This could just as well be a model for valuing a brand resident in different nations or regions of the globe. The reader will recall that, in Exhibit 7.7, we made several forecasts of net cash flow for different potential brand exploitations and we reflected our opinion of the relative risks of those brand extensions by means of different discount rates.

As a real-world example, we are witnessing a commercial battleground in the market for smartphones between Samsung and Apple. Even though the largest field of battle may be in the United States, it is a worldwide conflict. It is obvious that, taken on a country by country or region by region basis the relative position of these two companies and their financial profiles will be quite different. Should we not then try to reflect these regional or national differences in a valuation of the Apple or Samsung brand?

Think back to the ingredients needed for the income method—the *amount* of future economic benefit, the *economic life* of the future economic benefit, the *pattern* by which we will receive it, and the *risk* of receiving it as planned. And then consider all of the inputs that are needed to estimate these four essential ingredients, such as size of market, market share, price, culture, availability of infrastructure, and local and regional economy to name just a few. Are those elements the same in the United States and Vietnam and Portugal and Korea?

If we were appraising the Samsung brand, presumably Samsung is doing business in each of these countries. So we would expect that there is some amount of net cash flow attributable to the Samsung brand in each country. But is it proportional to Samsung's sales revenue there? We think not, but even if the income attributable to the Samsung brand was proportional to the level of business in each country, would the brand's market value also be proportional? Again, we think not because the national environments are not the same. The economic life, pattern of growth (or decline), and risks are sure to be unique in each nation. So the worldwide market

---

[16] See, for example, comments by the Electronic Frontier Foundation (EFF): Carolina Rossini, Maria Sutton, and Gwen Hinze. "Anti-Counterfeiting Trade Agreement," *EFF*, https://www.eff.org/issues/acta; and Maria Sutton, "US Trade Office Calls ACTA Back From the Dead and Canada Complies," *EFF*, March 1, 2013, https://www.eff.org/deeplinks/2013/03/us-trade-office-calls-acta-back-dead-and-canada-complies.

value of the Samsung brand is an aggregation of national or, perhaps, a regional, market values, each of which reflects the effect of localized cultural, political, and economic differences.

Some have attempted to encapsulate the wide spectrum of country or regional differences in terms of a country risk measure. There are country risk measures being published (see the following pages). We discuss these considerations in terms of political and investment risk.

Political Risk

Political risk is often defined by the difficulties that can arise for a business enterprise resulting from political decisions. It typically focuses on actions or conditions by governments that affect all foreign businesses in a country or region. An example of political risk would be policies that might restrain the free movement of employees into and out of the country, or affect hiring practices, salaries, or benefits. Restrictions on trade, types of investment, or restrictions on moving currency in and out of the country are examples, as well as governmental instability that could lead to terrorism, riots, or insurrection. Some would argue that it is less important what the regulations and policies are, than the fact that they remain stable. Perhaps a stable but unfriendly regime is preferable to a friendly but unstable one. It would seem logical that this also applies to the makeup of the government itself.

Political risk can also be focused on an individual company, a specific type of product, or perhaps a number of enterprises within the same industry. These conditions might result in favoritism to local business, a threat of nationalization, or the effects of entrenched corruption.

There are a large number of firms and research sources that analyze various forms of country and regional risks.[17] Some even publish risk ratings or risk indexes.

Investment Risk

In Chapter 7, we presented a discussion of risk as it applies to a brand and we referred the reader to Appendix C and its discussion about estimating an appropriate discount rate for a DCF calculation. One of the estimation methods noted in Appendix C was the so-called "built-up method," whereby we start with a risk-free rate of return and, add to that, premiums to reflect market history, specific company or industry risk or, perhaps, a special risk premium due to the type of property that is producing the net cash flow in a DCF model. Adding these building blocks together results in an estimate of an appropriate rate of return.

As this is written, we can observe some financial information about government bond rates of return in various countries, as reported daily in the financial media. For example in the *Wall Street Journal* in late April 2013, the yield on two year government bonds ranged from 0.023 percent (Germany) to 1.953 percent (Spain).

---

[17] See, for example, Fitch Ratings (http://www.fitchratings.com/), Moody's (http://www.moodys.com/cust/default.asp), *Euromoney* magazine (http://www.euromoney.com/), Standard & Poor's (http://www.standardandpoors.com/), Economist Intelligence Unit (http://store.eiu.com/), and Eurasia Group (http://www.eurasiagroup.net/).

For 10-year bonds the range was 1.235 percent to 4.501 percent, again for Germany and Spain.[18] Obviously, there are significant differences in national financial markets.

Aswath Damodaran, Professor of Finance at the Stern School of Business of New York University regularly publishes his estimate of equity risk premia for 118 nations.[19] His list is accompanied by a schedule of local currency ratings by Moody's. As of January 2013, the lowest premium was 5.80 percent, shared by Australia, the United States, Singapore, and several northern European nations. The highest was Belize at 20.80 percent with a number of less developed countries in the teens, and the rest somewhere in between.

SUMMARY

Our conclusion is that when developing a weighted average cost of capital or an equity rate of return, one should give consideration to investment premiums such as this to reflect what are obviously—and significantly—the different national costs of capital.

---

[18] See *Wall Street Journal*, April 23, 2013, C7
[19] See http://pages.stern.nyu.edu/~adamodr/New_Home-Page/datafile/ctryprem.html

Basic Investment Principles

This appendix is intended to be a primer on basic investment principles that are at the heart of the valuation process by an income method. Why *investment* principles? Because when our willing buyer agrees to exchange dollars for some property rights, he or she is making an investment with the hope of financial gain.

It is a widely accepted principle that investors seek both a return *on* and a return *of* their investment. This is illustrated in Exhibit A.1. Note that we specify that the investor is seeking an *opportunity* for a return of and a return on. Nothing is certain in this world, least of all an investment in business assets, be they tangible or intangible, so lurking somewhere inside investment theories is the concept of risk (see Exhibit A.1).

One of our definitions of market value is that it is equal to "*the present value* of the future economic benefits of ownership." To fully understand market value and the methods for estimating it, we must understand the underpinnings of the concept of present value.

A CERTIFICATE OF DEPOSIT EXAMPLE

To illustrate this concept, we will use the example of a *certificate of deposit* (CD). CDs are very common in the United States, but perhaps less common or simply known by other names elsewhere. The principle is not complicated. A CD is a contract between an individual investor and a bank. The investor purchases a CD from the bank, handing over cash to make the purchase. There exists a contract between the investor and the bank by which the bank agrees, after some specified period of time (e.g., one year, two years, five years) to return the investor's original amount plus interest at a compound rate agreed upon in the contract. Investors view this as a fairly low-risk investment, given the expected stability of the bank and its financial ability to fulfill the contract. As a result, interest rates for CDs tend to be at the low end of the range of possible investments, reflecting this low-risk perception.

In Exhibit A.2, we illustrate this transaction with the purchase of a $1,000 CD by an individual investor. In our example, the investor will receive the $1,000 back at the end of five years. According to the terms of the contract, the bank has agreed to pay compound interest at the rate of 4 percent, which amounts to $216.65 so, therefore, the investor will receive $1,216.65 in five years.

This example also illustrates two terminologies that the reader will encounter elsewhere in our valuation discussion. Note that the amount of interest, $216.65, is at the

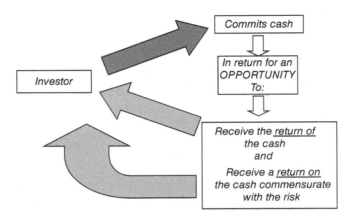

EXHIBIT A.1   The Investment Transaction

same time the cost of capital to the bank and the return on the investment for the investor. That is, the bank's purpose of entering into this transaction is to obtain the $1,000,
which becomes part of its capital that it can lend to others for other purposes at a higher
rate of interest than it is paying our investor. The spread represents revenue to the bank.
In that situation, then, we can term that interest amount as the cost of capital for the
bank. For the investor, the $216.65 represents his return on investment, or the amount
that he is compensated for giving up control of his $1,000 of capital for five years.

   The compound interest in this example is computed as follows in Exhibit A.3.

   In a *simple interest* calculation, the investor would receive $40 interest each and
every year. With *compound interest*, each year's interest is based on the previous
years' accumulated interest.

   We now introduce a complexity to our basic example. Suppose that our original
investor decides after a month or two that he has need for the $1,000 that he gave
to the bank and would like to get his money back. Assume also that the CD contract
with the bank precludes that, or at least imposes a monetary penalty for doing so.
An alternative for our investor might be to sell his CD contract with the bank. He
has a friend who is interested in making such a CD investment and so he and she
discuss that possibility.

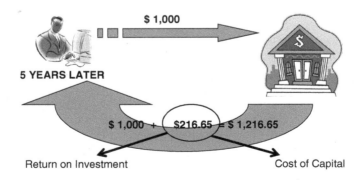

EXHIBIT A.2   Certificate of Deposit Example

Certificate of Deposit Compound Interest		
Interest rate = 4%		
Principle		$1,000.00
Interest @ 4.00%	Year 1	40.00
		$1,040.00
Principle		$1,040.00
Interest @ 4.00%	Year 2	41.60
		$1,081.60
Principle		$1,081.60
Interest @ 4.00%	Year 3	43.26
		$1,124.86
Principle		$1,124.86
Interest @ 4.00%	Year 4	44.99
		$1,169.86
Principle		$1,169.86
Interest @ 4.00%	Year 5	46.79
		$1,216.65

EXHIBIT A.3 Calculation of Compound Interest

She, as a potential buyer, views the situation as follows: In return for a payment of some amount, she will receive the contract amount of $1,216.65 at the end of the five-year period originally contracted for. Those contract terms cannot be changed. But, the amount she is willing to pay for that right is now up to her. This is illustrated in Exhibit A.4.

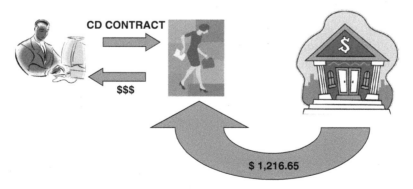

EXHIBIT A.4 Sale of CD Contract

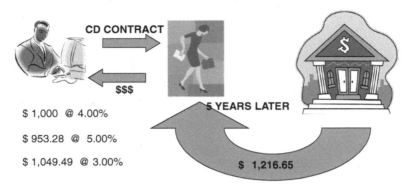

$ 1,000 @ 4.00%

$ 953.28 @ 5.00%

$ 1,049.49 @ 3.00%

EXHIBIT A.5   Repricing the Contract

The rate of interest that the bank agreed to was 4 percent. That interest rate will yield the $1,216.65 that she, as the prospective buyer, would receive. The only way that she can control the terms of this situation is in the amount that she is willing to pay for this contractual right. If she pays less than $1,000, she will in essence receive a higher percentage interest rate than the contract calls for. If she were to pay more than $1,000, she would be agreeing to receive an interest rate less than that contained in the contract. Let's assume for a moment that she is of the opinion that interest rates in general, as well as for CDs, will rise. This would make her somewhat unwilling to enter into an investment contract that yields 4 percent when she expects the interest rate environment to rise. She would, therefore, be expected to offer our original investor something less than $1,000. If, as an example, our investor would be willing to accept $953.28, then then she would receive a return on her investment of 5 percent rather than the contractual 4 percent (see Exhibit A.5).

We can see by even this very simple example that the essential ingredients are:

- The amount of delay before an investment will be returned
- The amount of return on the investment and when it will be received
- The amount of risk that this transaction will ultimately be consummated at the expected terms and that economic conditions remain stable during the contract

In our example, the buyer opined that economic conditions would not be the same, and that they would make the contract interest at the rate of 4 percent unattractive. So she adjusted her risk assessment upward and offered a price that would reflect her 5 percent forecast.

THE ARITHMETICAL FOUNDATION

The following pages discuss both simple and compound interest.

Simple Interest

The following calculations have been excerpted from a text published 66 years ago titled *Mathematics of Investment*. In Chapter 1, we find the following discussion about the calculation of interest on principle (P). We include this little mathematical exercise to show that the underpinnings of the income method are not some newly invented concept and that we are simply applying tried-and-true principles to a new situation.

Suppose that P is invested at simple interest for t years at the rate r. Let I be the interest and F be the final amount at the end of t years. Then the interest for one year is P_r and, by definition, the simple interest for t years is $t(P_r)$ or P_{rt}. That is

$$I = P_{rt} \tag{1}$$

Since the amount equals the principle plus the interest,

$$F = P + I \tag{2}$$

From equation (1), $P + I = P + P_{rt} = P(1 + rt)$, and, therefore,

$$F = P(1 + rt)$$

We can then take this very basic and accepted financial discussion one step further. Assume that we know F, the final amount to be received at the end of t years, and we know the interest rate r, we can then calculate P, or the amount that needs to be invested in order to receive it:

$$P = F/(1 + rt)^{[1]}$$

This easily understandable mathematics is at the heart of the income method. The difficulty lies in estimating F, r, and t. F is the amount of future economic benefit that the subject intellectual property can reasonably be expected to produce—how much will that be? How long (t) will it be before F appears? And what is the risk (r) that F won't appear at all, or in the amount that we expect?

Compound Interest

The financial world lives by compound interest principles rather than the preceding simple interest calculations. Without going into the basic mathematics again, the preceding formula on a compound interest basis is

$$F = P(1 + i)^n$$

where i = the interest rate per future period.
n = the number of periods.

Converting to the present value form:

$$P = F/(1 + i)^n$$

---

[1] William R. Hart, *The Mathematics of Investment* (Boston: D. C. Heath and Company, 1934).

Expressing i and n on a per period basis enables us to make the present value calculation on a monthly, quarterly, or annual basis as long as the interest (risk) rate is kept consistent with the time periods to which it applies.

Present Value Formulas

Exhibit A.6, A.7, and A.8 present the present value formulas that we use, as appropriate in all discussions and illustrations of the income method.

$$PV = \frac{\text{AMOUNT (\$)}}{\text{RATE (\%)}}$$

EXHIBIT A.6   Direct Capitalization

Used when investor receives an unchanging amount in each period into perpetuity.

$$PV = \frac{\text{AMOUNT} \times (1 + \text{Growth Rate})}{(\text{Rate} - \text{Growth Rate})}$$

EXHIBIT A.7   Direct Capitalization with Growth

Used when investor receives a constantly growing amount each year into perpetuity.

$$PV = \frac{\text{AMOUNT 1}}{(1 + \text{Rate})} + \frac{\text{AMOUNT 2}}{(1 + \text{Rate})^2} + \frac{\text{AMOUNT 3}}{(1 + \text{Rate})^3} + \cdots$$

EXHIBIT A.8   Discounting

Used when investor receives varying amounts in each period for a finite number of periods.

Theoretical Foundations for the Determination of a Fair Rate of Return on Intellectual Property

Dr. John A. Del Roccili

The basis for the determination of a fair royalty rate for a specific asset can be derived from the business enterprise valuation equation discussed in Chapter 1. This states that every business enterprise comprises a portfolio of assets that includes monetary assets, tangible assets, intangible assets, and intellectual property. This implies the market value of the business equals the sum of the assets that constitute the business. That is:

$$BEV = MA + TA + IA + IP$$

where: BEV = Business Enterprise Value
 MA = Monetary Assets
 TA = Tangible Assets
 IA = Intangible Assets
 IP = Intellectual Property

This portfolio of assets is expected to generate an overall rate of return, r_{bev}, which is simply the weighted average expected return of the individual assets in the company with the weights being the fraction of the business enterprise value invested in the asset.

$$r_{bev} = w_{wc}r_{wc} + w_{ta}r_{ta} + w_{ia}r_{ia} + w_{ip}r_{ip}$$

Here the r_is (where $I = bev, ma, ta, ia,$ and ip) are the expected returns on the individual assets, and the w_is are the weights. Note that w_i is the proportion of the portfolio's dollar value invested in that asset and that the w_is must sum to 1.0.

Multiplying through by BEV and assuming that a company will invest in an asset up until the point where the expected return is equal to the marginal product of the asset yields the following expected profit equation:

$$\pi = \partial\pi / \partial ma MA + \partial\pi / \partial ta TA + \partial\pi / \partial ia IA + \partial ip / \partial ip IP$$

This suggests the expected profit function is homogeneous of degree 1 because by Euler's theorem we know that the value of a linearly homogeneous function can always be expressed as the sum of terms, each of which is the product of one of the independent variables and the first-order partial derivative with respect to that variable.[1] This property means that if each asset is paid the amount of its marginal product, the total profit will be exactly exhausted by the distributive shares for all the assets constituting the enterprise.

This implies that a fair rate of return on intellectual property can be estimated through an allocation of the expected return or weighted average cost of capital among the business enterprise assets of the company. This approach is described in Chapter 5. The value of intellectual property and intangible assets is commonly established by first determining the value of the entire business enterprise, via the market or income approach, and then allocating this value to all the other asset categories. This leaves a residual amount that can be ascribed to intellectual property. If the individual asset categories are first valued, then their aggregated values must comport with the value of the entire business enterprise.

The importance of Euler's theorem relates to the fact that the values one can attribute to a particular asset are tied to its marginal contribution to profit, which in turn is reflective of its relative riskiness. Further, it states that the sum of the marginal products of each factor times the level of use of that factor exactly and identically adds up to total profit. This suggests that the value that can be placed on an individual asset is *bounded* by the enterprise relationship and the rates of return attributable to the other assets employed by the enterprise.

Thus, while the relationship does not provide you with an exact formula for determining the fair rate of return for intellectual property, it does provide a method with reasonable bounds for establishing fair value. First, we have to make the implicit assumption that businesses tend to employ their assets efficiently and that the marginal product of the asset is equal to its expected return. Second, we assume that the business enterprise can be expected to earn a fair rate of return equal to its weighted average cost of capital. Then, we have to estimate both the business enterprise value and the value of the assets composing the enterprise using the methods described in Chapters 4, 5, and 6. Since we know how to determine the weighted average cost of capital as well as the appropriate rates of return for different types of assets, using Euler's theorem, we can solve for the fair rate of return on intellectual property. This is accomplished by determining the expected profit of the enterprise and substituting the appropriate rates of return for each asset except intellectual property, along with the estimated values for each of the assets. The rate of return on intellectual property can then be obtained by solving the following equation:

$$\partial\pi \,/\, \partial ip = (\pi - (\partial\pi \,/\, \partial ma MA + \partial\pi \,/\, \partial ta TA + \partial\pi \,/\, \partial ia IA) \,/\, IP)$$

---

[1] For a discussion of Euler's theorem see Eugene Silberberg, *The Structure of Economics: A Mathematical Analysis* (New York: McGraw-Hill Book Company, 1978) pp. 90–91.

Investment Rate of Return Requirements

Trademarks are a form of investment that should be judged using the same framework that incorporates the dynamics of risk and investment rate of return into valuation decisions. This appendix provides an overview of some of the ways that appropriate investment rates of return can be derived and applied in the valuation of trademarks.

The foundation of value is the present value of the expected stream of economic benefits over the remaining economic life of the asset or investment that is under analysis. In order to derive value, we must first, then, forecast a stream of economic returns and determine the required rate of return that should be associated with the specific asset being valued. This holds true for the valuation of common stocks, real estate, and investments in intellectual property such as trademarks. The economic benefits must be determined with consideration for the following:

- The amount of the benefits
- The form in which they will be provided
- The timing of the benefits
- The trend expected in the amount of benefits
- The duration of the economic benefits

A comprehensive discussion of modern investment theory goes beyond the scope of this book. Complete books and careers are dedicated to the study of the relationship between risk and return. Indeed, significant differences of academic opinion exist as to the proper measure of risk as well as the proper measure of return. We have included this appendix to acquaint the reader with the basic concepts of risk and return and the references at the end of this appendix provide a collection of books and articles that should be studied to further appreciate the relationship between risk and return.

The goal is to assure that when trademarks are being valued, proper consideration is given to the risks associated with their exploitation. Those risks should be translated into an appropriate rate of return. The rate of return consideration introduces the uncertainty associated with actually receiving the stream of economic benefits. The required rate of return is that amount that is necessary to compensate investors for accepting various levels of risk. Equally important is the proper determination of risk and return for use in establishing royalties. The royalties that are associated with a trademark must be at a level to assure that a fair rate of return is being earned on its value.

INVESTMENT RISK

Trademarks should be viewed as investment assets and valued in accordance with prevailing theories of investment risk and return. Investment risk, whether that of a stock portfolio or an investment in intellectual property, is comprised of four broad components:

- Purchasing power risk
- Business risk
- Interest rate risk
- Market risk

Investors expect a return on all investments and require compensation for the various components of risk.

Purchasing Power Risk

Even if the expected stream of economic benefits from an investment could be determined with absolute certainty, risk still exists with regard to the purchasing power of the future dollars that are expected to be received. There always exists the risk that inflation will intensify and consume any gains that may be realized from investment performance. The Consumers Price Index (CPI) shows that between 1946 and 1986 inflation averaged 4.4 percent. If this rate could be expected to continue in the future at this same level, then investment planning could include an element in the rate of return requirements to assure that this amount of inflation were incorporated into the contemplated investment returns. In a sense, the purchasing power risk would be eliminated. Unfortunately, there are periods within the 40-year span between 1946 and 1986 with wide and unanticipated swings of inflation. It is the unanticipated changes that introduce investment risk. The following provides a sample of the level of inflation during selected time periods.

Period	Inflation Rate
1980–1986	6.1 percent
1987–1993	4.0 percent
1994–2000	2.6 percent
2001–2007	2.7 percent
2008–2012	2.1 percent

Unanticipated events such as inflation greatly affect the amount of investment returns that are actually achieved. This represents risk, and a portion of investment rates of return on all types of investment properties must include an element that compensates for this risk component.

Interest Rate Risk

This risk element presents uncertainty similar to purchasing power risk. Alternate forms of investment such as corporate bonds, treasury securities, and municipal debt provide another investment opportunity with which an intellectual property investment must compete. If the future brings with it higher returns that are available from investments of lesser risk, then the value of the intellectual property investment may be diminished.

Business Risk

This element of risk is very specific to the company or trademark that is being studied. It involves the ability of the company to maintain customer loyalty, to achieve enough earnings to meet operating and debt expenses, to meet competitor challenges, and ultimately the risk associated with achieving a return for the equity investors. Incorporated into this element of risk are the business-cycle risks associated with specific industries, product liability obligations, and workforce harmony.

This risk can be thought of as the determinant of earnings volatility from all factors other than inflation. Of all the risk elements, business risk is the only element to which an investor (through the choice of management personnel) can actively respond. Actions can be taken to prevent and limit exposure to many types of business risk, but it still exists. Compensation for its acceptance must be part of the overall return. Almost all investments have a finite remaining life after which economic benefits will cease to be enjoyed: bonds, apartment buildings, and machinery. Most of these lives are well-defined. In the case of trademarks, there are a myriad of factors affecting economic life. There are discussed in Chapter 6.

Market Risk

A unique and often unkind element of risk is, in large part, associated with market psychology. Irrespective of any fundamental changes in the expected performance of an investment, market risk reflects the fluctuation in the demand for a specific type of investment. On April 14, 2000, the stock market plunged in value by over 600 points as measured by the Dow Jones Industrial Average (DJIA). There was no fundamental change in economic outlooks, nor was there the declaration of a world war. Yet the value of all investments plunged. This is indeed an example of market risk.

An additional component of market risk is the risk associated with investment marketability. An investment for which an active market exists is more valuable, all else being equal, than an investment for which no active market exists. While the purchasing power, interest rate, and business risk elements are easy to conceptualize, the marketability risk is a little less obvious. Market risk is therefore comprised of market psychology risk and the risk of illiquidity; the ability to convert the investment into cash.

REQUIRED RATE OF RETURN COMPONENTS

There are three primary components integrated within the required rate of return:

- Risk-free rate
- Expected rate of inflation
- Risk premium

The risk-free rate is the basic value of money, assuming that there is no risk of default on the principal and that the expected earnings stream is guaranteed. Under this scenario, the investor has only sacrificed the use of the money for a period of time. Typically, the rate on long-term treasury securities serves as a benchmark for the risk-free rate.

Because investors are interested in a real rate of return, a portion of the required rate of return must include an amount that is sufficient to offset the effects of inflation. Therefore, the rate of return at which long-term treasury securities have been traded to yield represents two components of the required rate of return: the real risk-free rate and the expected inflation rate. At March 28, 2013, the Federal Reserve Statistical Release reported that the average rate provided by long-term treasuries was 3.10 percent. Assuming that the long-term outlook for inflation is expected to be 2.25 percent, then the real risk-free rate of return that is demanded by investors is presently about 0.85 percent.

Most investments are, however, not risk-free and must provide additional return to compensate for the risks that are associated with businesses. This is typically referred to as the *risk premium*. It represents compensation for the possibility that actual returns will deviate from those that are expected. Evidence can be easily found that higher rates of return are required by investors where higher levels of risk are present. By focusing on the yield that is provided by different fixed income securities, this principle can be demonstrated. The following table compares the yield on selected security investments as reported by The Federal Reserve Bank Statistical Release on March 28, 2013.

Investment	Yield
Treasury bill (6 month)	0.11
Treasury bill (1 year)	0.14
Certificates of Deposit (90 days)	0.21
Long-term treasury securities	3.10
Corporate bonds, rated Aaa	3.90
Corporate bonds, rated Baa	4.83

The yield differential between the six-month and one-year Treasury bills represents the risk associated with purchasing power losses because the safety of principal and interest in both cases is guaranteed by the U.S. government. The 90-day certificates of deposit cover a shorter period and represent less exposure to unanticipated changes in inflation, but they are not as secure with regard to principal and interest as are the government securities. The long-term fixed income securities are represented by Treasury securities and two corporate issues with different ratings. While they are all subject, for the most part, to the same purchasing power risks, the safety of principal and interest are different. The higher the risk, the higher the rate of return that investors expect.

RATE OF RETURN MODELS

We will briefly describe five different approaches that are commonly used as a means to develop a required rate of return. They are:

- Dividend growth model
- Buildup method

- Capital asset-pricing model
- Arbitrage pricing theory
- Venture capital

Dividend Growth Model

The formula for valuing a share of preferred stock presents a simple version of the dividend growth model:

$$\text{Value} = \frac{\text{Dividend}}{\text{Required rate of return}}$$

The dividend stream is known with certainty because it has been contractually set. It is promised to continue into perpetuity at the established level. This eliminates the complex assignment of trying to determine the rate at which the dividend will grow. The growth rate is zero.

If the value of the preferred share of stock is known, possibly because it has traded in the public market, and the dividend is known, then the equation is easily solved for the unknown value and provides an indication of the required rate of return.

$$\text{Required rate of return} = \frac{\text{Dividend}}{\text{Value}}$$

The resulting rate is the rate of return that investors are requiring for investments that provide a fixed dividend into perpetuity, possessing characteristics of risk similar to the specific issue being valued.

Preferred stock is not riskless. The dividends are paid only after debt obligations are satisfied. The indicated rate could be used as a benchmark for any investment that promises a fixed cash flow stream into perpetuity, possessing the same characteristics of risk and to the same degree (this model also assumes that the risk that the preferred shares will be called by the issuing corporation does not exist.)

Application of the dividend growth model to common stock is more complex but, if properly applied, can provide a meaningful indication of the required rate of return for equity investments with certain characteristics of risk.

In the case of common stock, the future level of the cash streams and the rate at which they might grow is not known with certainty. Expansion of the model used to value preferred stock is presented as

$$V = \frac{D_1}{(1+i)} + \frac{D_2}{(1+i)^2} + \frac{D_2}{(1+i)^3} + \cdots$$

where V = the value of the common stock.
        D = the amount of dividend during each successive time period.
        i = the required rate of return on the stock.

The value of the stock is presented as the discounting of all future dividends. Rather than attempt to determine the amount of dividends that will be paid in each future year, an assumption is generally made regarding the rate at which the current dividend will grow. Introduction of this factor into the model along with algebraic manipulation provides a useful form for the dividend growth model:

$$V = \frac{D_o(I + g)}{i - g}$$

The value of the stock is related to the growth of the current dividend, D_o, at the growth rate, g, capitalized at the required rate of return, i. If the value of V, D_o, and g can be determined, then the required rate of return for an equity investment possessing comparable characteristics of risk can be derived.

An important assumption is that the growth rate selected will be constant into the future. Also, the growth rate must be a value that is less than the required rate of return. This last requirement may seem to be too restrictive.

What about a company that is growing at a fantastic pace? If the growth rate is indeed going to continue at the fantastic rate indefinitely, then the dividend growth model is not useful. It is important, however, to consider the realistic likelihood of being able to sustain an abnormally high growth rate forever. In many cases, where reasonable estimates can be made for the value of the investment and the growth rate of the cash flow, an indication of the required rate of return can be calculated.

The dividend growth model is most useful for defining appropriate rates of return for intellectual properties that are close to the mature portion of their economic lives and already proven as commercially viable. At this point of the life cycle, future growth rates are more predictable, and the overall market for the product or service with which the property is associated is well defined. One of the other rate of return models may turn out to be more appropriate for fast-emerging intellectual property.

Buildup Method

This method is very subjective, but it can be used to directly reflect the amount of risk that is associated with the major risk factors that have been discussed. This method lists each of the components of risk and assigns an amount of return to compensate for each risk component. A hypothetical estimate of the cost of equity for a company operating in the electronics industry with a market capitalization of $275 million would be as follows.

Risk Component	Required Return
Risk-free rate of return	2.4 percent
Equity Risk Premium	6.7 percent
Industry Risk Premium	1.8 percent
Small Size Premium	3.8 percent
Total required rate of return	14.7 percent

Source: From 2013 Ibbotson® SBBI® Valuation Yearbook

This method is quite attractive because it addresses each of the risk components individually and can reflect an individual investor's own perceptions of the relative degree of risk presented by each of the components. Unfortunately, specific quantification of the exact amount of return that is necessary to compensate for each risk component is not easily quantifiable. Too much conservatism in setting the rates can make an otherwise viable investment appear too risky. A rosy outlook can encourage investment in a project for a rate of return that is too low in relation to the risk that was accepted. The buildup method is rarely used because of the unreliability associated with setting of the specific rates.

Capital Asset-Pricing Model

The *capital asset-pricing model* (CAPM) is one of several factor models. These models associate the proper rate of return to various investment factors. In the case of CAPM, the appropriate rate of return is considered to be determined by one factor: the volatility of returns relative to the returns that can be achieved by a broad market portfolio. Presented here is one form of the equation that describes the model:

$$R_e = R_f + B(R_m - R_f)$$

where R_e = the equity rate of return.
  R_f = the risk-free rate of return.
  R_m = the rate of return provided by the overall market portfolio of investments.
  B = beta, a measure of the volatility for a specific investment relative to the market portfolio.

Application of CAPM is traditionally associated with assessing the risk and return for specific stock positions taken by investors. The risks and return of a particular stock are related to its asset base, industry position, and competitor attacks, as well as to changes in inflation and other economic forces.

CAPM can be used to estimate the required rate of return for specific intellectual property such as a trademark by analyzing the required rates demanded by investors on specific stocks that operate in the same industry as that in which the intellectual property plays. Analysis of stocks of companies that are dominated by the type of intellectual property being studied will more directly reflect required rates of return for intellectual property in specific industries.

CAPM and Beta

Beta is a measure that indicates a company's susceptibility to changing conditions. These changes include inflation rate trends, monetary policy, world oil prices, and other factors that affect the rates of return on the entire market. Beta is a broad measure of the amount of risk possessed by a specific investment when compared to the diversified risk of a broad market portfolio.

If the stock of a company fluctuates more than the price of the broad market portfolio, then the stock and the underlying business assets are more susceptible to macroeconomic shifts than a broad market portfolio. If the stock's price over the past is more stable than the broad market, then the stock is considered less risky. A common stock that has a beta of 1.0 moves in perfect unison with the overall broad market. If the market rises by 10 percent, then the specific stock with beta equal to 1.0 will also rise 10 percent. This stock is no more or less volatile than the broad market. When beta is less than 1.0, the underlying stock moves in the same direction as the market, but to a smaller degree, and it is less volatile and less risky than the overall market. When beta is greater than 1.0, the underlying stock moves in the same direction as the market, but to a larger degree, and it is riskier and more volatile than the overall market. Beta values are calculated for specific stocks by many investment advisory services and brokerage houses, such as Merrill Lynch, Value Line, Standard & Poors, and Zack's Investment Service.

A risk measure for valuing intellectual property such as a trademark can be determined by studying the betas of publicly traded companies that are highly dependent upon the same type of trademark for which a value is desired. If the risk of comparable and public companies in the same industry is the same as those affecting the subject intellectual property, then a study of their betas can serve as a risk benchmark.

CAPM and Ibbotson Associates, Inc.

The studies conducted annually by this company have examined total long-term returns as comprised of dividends, interest payments, and capital appreciation. The investments studied include all New York Stock Exchange (NYSE) stocks, corporate bonds, and U.S. Treasury securities, such as bonds, bills, and notes. Using these studies, the return from investment in a broad market portfolio, R_m, can be determined for insertion into the CAPM model. Controversy abounds regarding the period over which returns are analyzed and the appropriate method for translating the data into a useful basis for future expectations.

Critics of CAPM point to several assumptions that must be accepted for the model to be useful:

- The rate of return for the broad market, R_m, must be established in an efficient market where all available information is properly reflected in the price of financial securities.
- The broad market portfolio can be defined and measured accurately.
- All elements of systematic risk can be captured by the beta factor.

ARBITRAGE PRICING THEORY

This theory asserts that an asset's risk is related to more than type of investment risk. APT attributes total return to the sensitivity of investment returns to *unanticipated* changes in five factors:

- Default risk
- The term structure of interest rates
- Inflation
- The long-run expected growth rate of profits for the economy
- Residual market risk

The arbitrage pricing theory can be expressed by the equation:

$$R = E + (B_1)(F_1) + (B_2)(F_2) + (B_3)(F_3) + (B_4)(F_4) + e$$

where R = the actual return on an asset.
   E = the expected return on an asset.
   B_n = the asset's sensitivity to a change in F_n.
   F_n = a specific-economic factor
   e = the return attributed to idiosyncratic factors specific to the asset.

Determination of the sensitivity of asset returns to each economic factor is not an easy task. Stock price movements are not easily traced to a given factor because so many different economic and idiosyncratic forces affect the stock price movement. CAPM is appealing because the sensitivity factor, beta, can be readily determined. Yet, this model denies the sensitivity of returns to specific factors for specific investments.

Presently, implementation of the inferences of APT theory can be accomplished by requiring premium rates of return on investments where the expected returns can be significantly affected by unanticipated changes in the identified economic factors. The important lessons of the APT studies that support this model is realization that certain investments are more sensitive than others to unanticipated changes in specific economic factors.

Unexpected inflation might have only a minor effect on the profits of certain consumer product industries where it is relatively easy to pass along the inflationary costs in the form of higher product pricing. Other industries, in which product pricing is very inelastic, could be significantly affected by inflation. Investments in firms and industries that use a high degree of leverage are very sensitive to unanticipated interest changes and are therefore sensitive to default risk: the risk of principle or interest expense default.

Many industries are nondiversified and are very sensitive to unanticipated changes in the general prosperity of the overall economy. As valuation and royalty rate decisions are contemplated, the sensitivity of the intellectual property investments to unanticipated changes in many of these factors is an important consideration.

VENTURE CAPITAL

So far, we have discussed how to determine appropriate rates of return for an equity investment where risk quantification is possible by comparative analysis. CAPM and APT are typically used when commercial viability of the investment is either already proven or highly likely. Rates of return for-investments possessing similar risk characteristics serve as the basis for development of an appropriate rate.

Investments in emerging technology carry much higher risks with considerable potential for complete loss of the initial investment. In addition to the risks previously discussed, such as inflation, competition, changing economic climates, and so on, emerging technology carries additional risks.

Additional risks include the possibility that laboratory scale success may not survive the transition to pilot plant production or that pilot plant scale successes may not be economically successful at full-scale levels of commercial production. Embryonic technology investments may not even be defined past the pencil and paper stage of development when laboratory experimental success is not even assured.

These types of intellectual property investments involve substantial risks, and investors expect substantial "pay days" if the commercial viability ever materializes. Seed money for such risky investments is provided more and more by venture capitalists. Sometimes the word "venture" is replaced with "vulture" because of the seemingly extraordinary rate of returns that these investors require. But, considering the high potential in these cases for complete loss of millions of dollars of seed money, the required investment returns are not really out-of-line.

At various stages of development, the venture capital required rate of return changes with the amount of risk that is perceived at each stage. Presented here is an estimate of the amount of return required at different development stages:

Stage of Development	Required Rate of Return
Start-up	50 percent
First stage	40 percent
Second stage	30 percent
Third stage	25 percent

The various levels of venture financing can be expressed as follows:

- *Start-up* is a company with an idea and not much else. This is the riskiest level of embryonic intellectual property investment and requires the largest amount of return. The funds are used for basic research and possibly development of a prototype. Revenues at this stage are not even part of management goals.
- *First stage* companies may have a prototype that has proven its capabilities, but further development is required before commercial scales of production can be achieved. Positive net cash flows may still be several years away.
- *Second stage* companies may have experienced success in the commercial production of the product or service, but expansion of market penetration requires substantial amounts that a bank may be unwilling to provide. At this point, the ability to make a profit may be already proven, but rapid expansion requires more than present operations can provide.
- *Third stage* financings begin to blur with fast-growth companies that can get limited bank loans or additional funds from a public offering. Strong profit levels may be consistently achieved, but more funds are needed for national or global expansion.

Venture capital companies are not long-term investors. They typically try to get out of the investment in five to seven years with a three- to tenfold increase in the original investment. This is usually accomplished by selling the interest in the developed company to a larger corporation or taking the developed company public.

WEIGHTED AVERAGE COST OF CAPITAL

The discussion thus far has presented various concepts and methods that help define the rate of return on equity investments. However, investments are usually financed by a combination of equity and borrowed funds.

Corporate investments typically must pass hurdle rates in order to be considered as viable opportunities. Since debt and equity funds are used to finance these investments, the return that is provided must be sufficient to satisfy the interest due on the debt and also to provide a fair rate of return on the equity funds. The hurdle rate must be this weighted average cost of capital, at a minimum. In a complex financial structure, the hurdle rate must consider the cost common, preferred equity, secured long-term debt, unsecured notes payable, convertible debt and other financing instruments.

A corporation that is financed with both debt and equity might have a capitalization structure that is comprised of 25 percent debt and 75 percent equity. A good bond rating might allow the corporation to finance debt at 4.5 percent. An appropriate equity rate, as determined from one of the preceding models, might be 14.0 percent.

Exhibit C.1 shows a simple example of a weighted average cost of capital calculation. The tax deductibility of interest expense makes the after tax cost of debt only 60 percent of the stated interest rate for corporations that pay a combined state and federal income tax of 40 percent. Equity returns are in no way tax deductible. When the cost of these capital components are weighted by their percentage of the total capital structure, a weighted average cost of capital of 11.2 percent is the result. This is the amount of return that the company must earn on its investment, at a minimum, in fixed equipment purchases, acquisitions of competitors, or intellectual property.

A multinational corporation, for which an 11.2 percent weighted average cost of capital is appropriate, is likely to be a well-diversified "basket" of assets. Some of the assets are more risky than others. Overall, the rate of return that these assets must earn is 11.2 percent. If we apply this concept to a small company, or an isolated subsidiary of a multinational company, the weighted average rate of return requirement can also be allocated among the assets that are employed within the defined business enterprise. The allocation is conducted with respect to the amount of investment risk that each component represents to the business enterprise.

The weighted average cost of capital for a small company, or subsidiary, would comprise an equity and debt rate which reflect the risk and return dynamics that are unique to the industry of the defined business enterprise. As discussed in previous chapters, the business enterprise is the sum of the fair market value of the invested capital (debt and equity). This is also represented by the sum of net working capital (monetary

EXHIBIT C.1 Business Enterprise Weighted Average Cost of Capital

INVESTED CAPITAL COMPONENT	AMOUNT ($ MILLIONS)	PERCENT OF INVESTED CAPITAL	COST OF CAPITAL	AFTER TAX COST OF CAPITAL	WEIGHTED AVERAGE COST OF CAPITAL
EQUITY	75.0	75.0%	14.0%	14.0%	10.5%
DEBT	25.0	25.0%	4.5%	2.7%	0.7%
TOTAL	100.0	100.0%			11.2%

EXHIBIT C.2   Required Rate of Return among Assets

ASSET CATEGORY	AMOUNT ($ MILLIONS)	PERCENT OF INVESTED CAPITAL	RETURN REQUIRED	WEIGHTED RETURN REQUIRED	PERCENT OF TOTAL RETURN
NET WORKING CAPITAL	20.0	20.0%	2.5%	0.5%	4.5%
TANGIBLE ASSETS	30.0	30.0%	4.5%	1.4%	12.1%
INTANGIBLE ASSETS	50.0	50.0%	18.6%	9.3%	83.4%
TOTAL	100.0	100.0%		11.2%	100.0%

assets), tangible assets, and the intangible assets. Just as the *weighted average cost of capital* (WACC) is allocated among the debt and equity components of the invested capital it is also possible to allocate a portion of the WACC to the asset components.

Exhibit C.2 shows an allocation of the weighted average cost of capital for a business enterprise allocated among the business assets. The various rates of return assigned to each of the assets reflect their relative risk. The relative returns provided by each asset category is also indicated.

Appropriate Return on Monetary Assets

The monetary assets of the business are its net working capital. This is the total of current assets minus current liabilities. Current assets are comprised of accounts receivable, inventories, cash, and short-term security investments. Offsetting this total are the current liabilities of the business such as accounts payable, accrued salaries, and accrued expenses.

Working capital is considered to be the most liquid asset of a business. Receivables are usually collected within 60 days and inventories are usually turned over in 90 days. The cash component is immediately available and security holdings can be converted to cash with a telephone call to the firm's broker. Further evidence of liquidity is the use of accounts receivable and/or inventories as collateral for loans. In addition, accounts receivable can be sold for immediate cash to factoring companies at a discount of the book value. Given the relative liquidity of working capital the amount of investment risk is inherently low. An appropriate rate of return to associate with the working capital component of the business enterprise is that which is available from investment in short-term securities of low risk levels. The rate available on 90-day certificates of deposit or money market funds serves as an appropriate benchmark.

Appropriate Return on Tangible Assets

The tangible or fixed assets of the business are comprised of production machinery, warehouse equipment, transportation fleet, office buildings, office equipment, leasehold improvements, office equipment and manufacturing plants. An indication of the rate of return that is contributed by these assets can be pegged at about the interest rate at which commercial banks make loans, using the fixed assets as collateral.

While these assets are not as liquid as working capital they can often be sold to other companies. This marketability allows a partial return of the investment in fixed assets should the business fail. Another aspect of relative risk reduction relates to the strategic redeployment of fixed assets. Assets that can be redirected for use elsewhere in a corporation have a degree of versatility which can still allow an economic contribution to be derived from their employment even if it isn't from the originally intended purpose.

While these assets are more risky than working capital investments they possess favorable characteristics that must be considered in the weighted average cost of capital allocation. Fixed assets that are very specialized in nature must reflect higher levels of risk which of course demands a higher rate of return. Specialized assets are those which are not easily redeployed for other commercial exploitation or liquidated to other businesses for other uses.

Appropriate Return on Intangible Assets and Intellectual Property

Intangible assets are considered to be the most risky asset components of the overall business enterprise. These assets may have little, if any, liquidity and poor versatility for redeployment elsewhere in the business. This enhances their risk. Please keep in mind that this typical case does not always apply to brands. Brands can be at either end of the versatility spectrum. Generally speaking, a higher rate of return on these assets is appropriate.

Since the overall return on the business is established as the weighted average cost of capital and since reasonable returns for the monetary and tangible assets can be estimated, we are then in a position to derive an appropriate rate of return to be earned from the intangible assets.

The following equation presents the means by which the 18.6 percent rate was derived for the intangible assets in our example:

$$WACC = \frac{V_m}{V_{bev}}(R_m) + \frac{V_t}{V_{bev}}(R_t) + \frac{V_i}{V_{bev}}(R_i)$$

where $WACC$ = the weighted average cost of capital for the overall business enterprise.

V_m, V_t, V_i = the fair market values of the monetary, tangible, and intangible assets, respectively.

R_m, R_t, R_i = the relative rates of return associated with the business enterprise asset components.

V_{bev} = the fair market value of the business enterprise, which is the total of V_m, V_t, and V_i.

A little algebraic manipulation and we can solve this equation for the appropriate rate of return on the intangible assets:

$$R_i = \frac{WACC(V_{bev}) - R_m(V_m) - V_t(R_t)}{V_{bev}}$$

If the WACC developed is for a diversified multinational corporation, the proper rate to use in conjunction with a specific intellectual property investment could be far greater. The WACC represents an overall return from the diversified investments or asset base of the business. The rate attributed to a specific intellectual property must reflect the various risks associated with the division in which the specific property is used.

The process of quantifying intellectual property investment risk may first require determination of an appropriate WACC for the whole business. Followed by a determination of a WACC for each operating division, working toward the business segment in which a specific intellectual property resides.

The example that was presented yielded an 11.2 percent WACC. This was based on use of an equity rate of return of 14 percent. Such a rate would imply that the business is commercially viable and that the associated intellectual property has also been proven. Embryonic and emerging intellectual property possesses more risks and as such would most likely be analyzed using a venture capital rate of return.

Overall, the business enterprise is comprised of various types of assets each possessing different degrees of investment risk that correlates with the weighted average cost of capital. Risk quantification for intellectual property and intangible assets can be accomplished by looking at relative investment risks for business enterprise asset components.

REFERENCES

Berry, Michael A., Edwin Burmeister and Marjorie B. McElroy. 1988. "Sorting Out Risks Using Known Apt Factors." *Financial Analysts Journal* 44 (March–April): 29.

Cohen, Jerome B., Edward D. Zinbarg, and Arthur Zeikel. 1982. *Investment Analysis and Portfolio Management,* 4th ed. Homewood, IL: Richard D, Irwin, Inc.

Copeland, Tom, Tim Koller, and Jack Murrin of McKinsey & Company, Inc. 1990. *Valuation—Measuring and Managing the Value of Companies.* New York: John Wiley & Sons.

Gray, William S. III. 1985. *The Historical Record—Insights for Forecasting Expected Return and Risk.* Homewood, IL: The Institute of Chartered Financial Analysts/Dow Jones-Irwin.

Harrington, Diana R. 1983. "Stock Prices, Beta, and Strategic Planning." *Harvard Business Review* 61, no 3 (May–June): 157.

Jereski, Laura. 1988. "Too Much Money, Too Few Deals." *Forbes,* March 7, 144.

Levine, Sumner N., ed. 1975. *Financial Analyst's Handbook, Portfolio Management.* Homewood, IL: Dow Jones-Irwin.

Maginn, John L., and Donald L. Tuttle, eds. 1983. *Managing Investment Portfolios, A Dynamic Process.* Boston: Warren, Gorham and Lamont.

Morningstar, Inc. 2013. *Ibbotson® SBBI® 2013 Valuation Yearbook, Market Results For Stocks, Bonds, Bills, And Inflation 1926–2012.* Chicago.

Parr, Russell L.1991. *Investing in Intangible Assets—Finding and Profiting from Hidden Corporate Value.* New York: John Wiley & Sons, New York.

Reilly, Frank K. 1985. *Investment Analysis and Portfolio Management,* 2nd ed. Chicago: The Dryden Press.

Roll, Richard, and Stephen A. Ross. 1984. "The Arbitrage Pricing Theory Approach to Strategic Portfolio Planning." *Financial Analysts Journal* 40. (May–June): 14–26.

Smith, Gordon V., and Russell L. Parr. 2005. *Intellectual Property Valuation, Exploitation and Infringement Damages.* Hoboken, NJ: John Wiley & Sons, Inc.

Predicting Sales and Revenues for New Ventures with Diffusion Models

Richard A. Michelfelder, Ph.D., Rutgers University,
School of Business–Camden

Maureen Morrin, Ph.D., Temple University,
Fox School of Business–Philadelphia

New product revenue and sales forecasting approaches can be as simple as "guess-timating" the first year sales of a given product and escalating it for future year forecasts by an annual growth rate until a specific level of saturation is reached. This simple approach assumes that sales will continually grow throughout the product's lifecycle. Is there justification for assuming that sales will grow in such a pattern other than it is the result of an inexpensive and easy-to-apply forecasting tool? Although there are a myriad of both qualitative and quantitative methods for new product sales forecasting from simple growth escalation to forecasting with econometrically estimated demand functions, a question arises as to whether there is a causal theory of new product sales in the market research academic literature that lends guidance to the type of forecasting method chosen. This matter is of practical importance when doing the "road show" for raising venture capital and for convincing oneself of the credibility of your forecasts. We discuss an intuitive, common sense method for predicting sales and revenues backed by a hundreds of academic and industry articles. Use of such methods show potential investors as well as the entrepreneurs that the prediction embodies a general pattern of new product sales and revenue growth founded by academic marketing professionals and reinforced by applications in many different industries and markets.

The purpose of this paper is to provide a brief summary of market research literature regarding the forecasting of sales of new products with guidance that goes beyond an ad hoc choice of a forecasting tool. The guidance provided by years of market research will lead to the recommendation of a forecasting model that has been developed from product adoption theory and rigorously tested in its ability to perform. Thereby, the justification and documentation for the choice of such a model structure in a business plan is one that is based on market research theory and robust empirical testing.

NEW PRODUCT SALES FORECASTING MODELS: PRODUCT DIFFUSION

Much literature in marketing research strongly demonstrates that product sales life cycles follow a *sales curve* (S-curve) pattern. An S-curve pattern implies that new product sales initially grow at a rapid rate, then the rate of growth tapers off, and finally declines with time. Historical analysis of new product sales curves indicates this is one of the most common, if not the most common pattern of new product sales over time.

The new product sales model we will recommend explains this S-curve shape based on diffusion theory. Diffusion theory is actually a theory of communication regarding how information is dispersed within a social system over time. Because people place different emphases on how much they rely on media and interpersonal communication for new ideas and information, they "adopt" new products either earlier or later in a product's lifecycle. The consumer product adoption process based on relative adoption time categorizes individuals as innovators, early adopters, early majority, late majority, and laggards. Exhibit D.1 shows the cumulative percentage of the potential market (i.e., total number of adopters) that has made an initial purchase of a new product. As you move up and to the right of the S-curve in Exhibit D.1, that is, as you look at the rate of adoption of a new product over time by first time purchasers, you initially have the innovators buying the product, then early adopters, and so on as you move up the S-curve, until you get to the point of market saturation, where the last set of first-time buyers are known as the *laggards*.

Exhibit D.2 shows the time of adoption of buyers for the product. If the buyer is to the left of the vertical line in their time of adoption they are innovators, early adopters or part of the early majority, if to the right they are the late majority or the laggards.

Exhibit D.3 displays different types of S-curves developed from alternative types of product sales forecasting models. They will be discussed in detail in a later section of this appendix.

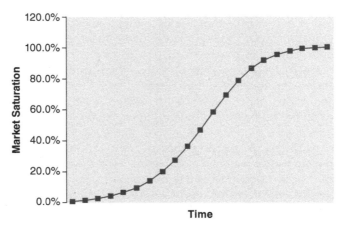

EXHIBIT D.1 S-Curve Example

Source: John Wiley & Sons, Inc. Reprinted with permission.

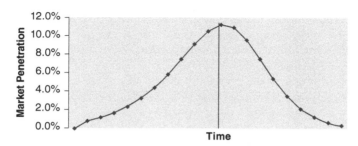

EXHIBIT D.2 Time of Adoption of Innovation
Source: John Wiley & Sons, Inc. Reprinted with permission.

The S-curve model is what is known as a *single-purchase model* in that it forecasts sales of products that are typically bought just once, or infrequently, such as consumer durables or industrial products such as mainframe computers. In addition, the model can be used to forecast trial or first time purchases for repeat purchase goods such as snack foods and detergents, but it does not provide a forecast of repeat purchase levels. In order to estimate repeat purchase sales and differentiate them from trial sales, businesses would typically need to carry out test markets or simulated test markets and apply different forecasting methods that would provide a steady-state market share estimate rather than a time-based adoption curve as is provided by diffusion models. However, all products, regardless of how often they are purchased, have a first-purchase sales volume curve (Mahajan and Wind 1986).

Diffusion models are dependent on a number of assumptions, each of which should be considered prior to implementing such models. The assumptions include:

1. *The product whose sales are being forecast by the model is a product that is destined to be a successful new product introduction.* Estimates of new product failure rates vary from 33 percent (Booz, Allen & Hamilton, Inc. 1982) to 60 percent (Silk and Urban 1978) or higher. The present model is appropriate only for successful new product entries. The present model cannot predict which new

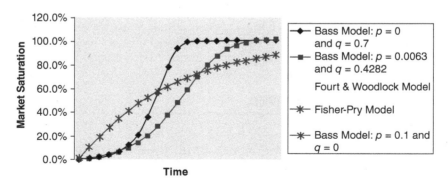

EXHIBIT D.3 S-Curves for the Diffusion of Innovations
Source: John Wiley & Sons, Inc. Reprinted with permission.

product launch will be successful; it is instead designed to project sales volume over time for those product launches that are successful.

2. *Potential market size.* The model requires that the user input an estimate for the total market size for the particular brand within the product category (i.e., total number of adopters of the branded product). To the extent that this estimate is inaccurate, the new sales forecasts will also be inaccurate. The user firm may choose to use historic sales data, however it needs to produce an estimate of potential market size, and then estimate the brand's share within the market.

3. *The nature of the competition.* When the user estimates their brand's market share within the product category, a number of underlying assumptions about competitive response underlie such an estimate. It is possible that competitive response, such as imitative competitive alternatives, or heavier promotional responses, will adversely affect the share of the new product's sales. Again, to the extent that the market share estimate is inaccurate, the new product sales estimates will also be inaccurate.

The model recommended here has been developed from theoretical work in the area of diffusion processes and the customer new product adoption process. Diffusion process models attempt to forecast the market penetration rates of innovative products (air conditioners, cell phones, the Internet, hybrid gas/electric cars, a new brand of coffee, etc.) over time. The customer adoption process refers to differences among customers in the degree to which they are innovative, and thus willing to try a new product. Some customers are very innovative and are the first to try new products, whereas others are less so, and typically wait until many of their neighbors, and the like have already bought the new product before they do the same. The speed of adoption of a new product has been shown to be a function of several factors including (Rogers 1983, 2003):

- The product's relative advantage over existing products
- The degree to which the new product is compatible with existing operations and attitudes
- The degree to which the new product is simple (rather than complex)
- The degree to which the new product can be tried on a limited basis
- The degree to which the product is observable.

To the extent that a new product possesses each of these characteristics, its likelihood of success in the market is improved. The first two factors, relative advantage and compatibility are particularly critical (Rogers 2003). However, models that have attempted to use managers' input regarding these factors have not fared particularly well.

TYPES OF PRODUCT DIFFUSION MODELS

There are at least three major types of models that have been proposed for forecasting new product first purchase sales (models are discussed later on in this appendix):

1. Pure innovative models (e.g., Fourt and Woodlock 1960)
2. Pure imitative models (e.g., Fisher and Pry 1971, Mansfield 1961)
3. Combination models (e.g., Bass 1969)

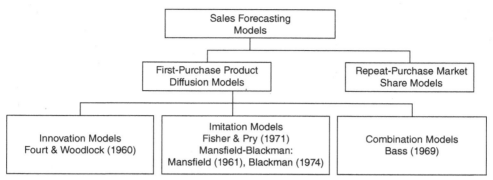

EXHIBIT D.4 Product Sales Forecasting Diffusion Models

Source: John Wiley & Sons, Inc. Reprinted with permission.

The investigation in this appendix focuses on first purchase product models for application in forecasting initial product sales of a newly introduced product. Exhibit D.4 displays the types of diffusion models, including the highly adopted Bass (1969) model that combines the innovation and imitation properties into one increasingly generalized model.

The *innovation* model of Fourt and Woodlock (1960) is a market penetration curve that was developed retrospectively after analyzing the market penetration curves of a number of new products. Pure innovative models assume that cumulative sales exhibit an exponential curve shape and that adoptions are based on individuals' exposure to external information sources such as marketing expenditures in mass media, rather than on word-of-mouth or other imitative effects. The equation that they found to be a reasonable approximation of these product curves is (see Exhibit D.3):

$$f_t = rM(1 - r)^{t-1}$$

where f_t = (change in cumulative sales at time t)/(potential sales).

$\quad\quad r$ = rate of penetration of potential sales.

$\quad\quad M$ = (total potential sales)/(all buyers), or market saturation percentage.

All of these variables are assumed to remain constant throughout the product sales life cycle, except for time, t and f_t. As an example, assume that the market saturation for a new luxury durable good was 50 percent of all households and that r = 10 percent, therefore the annual rates of new buyer penetration are:

1st year: $f_t = rM (1 - r)^{1-1} = 0.2 (0.1) = 0.02$ or 2 percent

2nd year: $f_t = rM (1 - r)^{2-1} = 0.2 (0.1) (0.8) = 0.016$ or 1.6 percent

3rd year: $f_t = rM (1 - r)^{3-1} = 0.2 (0.1) (0.8)^2 = 0.0128$ or 1.28 percent

20th year: $f_t = rM (1 - r)^{20-1} = 0.2 (0.1) (0.8)^{19} \approx 0$

Note that the incremental cumulative sales as a fraction of potential sales, exponentially declines in every time period from the initial product introduction year and that the curve flattens out at the time that the market saturation level of 50 percent is reached.

The *imitative* model of Fisher and Pry (1971) contains the notion that a new product replaces an older type of product, and that the rate of adoption of the new product is dependent on the percentage of the old product still in use. The Fisher and Pry (1971) model is the classic logistic S-shaped curve:

$$f = \frac{1}{1 + e^{-b(t-t_0)}}$$

where f = percentage of market that adopted new product.
b = growth to potential constant.
t = time since introduction.

The preceding equation can be rewritten in log-linear form as

$$\left(\frac{f}{1-f}\right) = e^{b_0 + bt}$$

The Mansfield-Blackman model (Blackman, Seligman, and Solgliero 1973, Blackman 1974, Manfield 1961, 1968) adapts the Fisher and Pry (1971) model to include the upper limit in market share or saturation level of the newer product:

$$\left(\frac{f}{L-f}\right) = e^{b_0 + bt}$$

where L = market saturation percentage.

This adaptation provides a constraint on the maximum level of market share that the newer product can attain.

THE BASS MODEL

These two basic types of models described, the pure *innovation* model and pure *imitation* model, have been combined into one more generalized model, the Bass model, to capture both the innovative and imitative aspects of product adoption. The Bass model captures the innovative characteristic with its coefficient, p, and the imitative characteristic with its coefficient, q (described in more detail to follow). In the Bass model, when $p = 0$, the model defaults to the Mansfield (1961) model, and when $q = 0$, the model defaults to the Fourt and Woodlock (1960) model.

The Bass model is an aggregate demand model that represents an empirical generalization or "a pattern or regularity that repeats over different circumstances and that can be described simply by mathematical, graphic, or symbolic methods" (Bass 1993, 1995). It is designed to be used as a pre-launch forecasting model that is estimated prior to the introduction of a new product, that is, before preliminary sales figures have been obtained. Formulations of the Bass model have been used by corporations such as Kodak, IBM, RCA, Sears, and AT&T (Rogers 1983, 2003).

The Bass model is similar in some respects to models of infectious diseases or contagion models, in that it attempts to estimate how many customers will buy a new product as the new product gains more acceptance over time. The model represents not the spread of a disease, but the impact of communication efforts about a new product, whether those efforts are external in nature, such as mass advertising, or more informal in nature, such as via word-of-mouth communication or observation and imitation. The model assumes that there are differences among customers in terms of how innovative they are in their tendencies to adopt new products, and which types of information about a new product are most persuasive prior to adoption. When a new product is introduced, there exists uncertainty in the minds of potential adopters regarding how superior the new product is versus existing alternatives. Individuals attempt to reduce this uncertainty by acquiring information about the new product. More innovative customers tend to acquire such information via mass media and other external outlets. More imitative customers tend to acquire such information from interpersonal channels such as word-of-mouth communication and observation. The relative influence of these two basic types of customers is captured in the Bass model.

The Bass model thus assumes that new product adopters are influenced by two types of communication: mass media and interpersonal communication, and that the mass media effects, which have a greater impact on innovative customers, will be greater at the outset of the product launch, whereas the interpersonal communication effects, which have a greater impact on the much larger number of imitative customers, will be greater during the later periods of the diffusion process (Rogers 2003).

A review conducted in 1990 (Mahajan et al. 1990) found that there were over 150 published extensions of this model. A recent search of online databases suggests that since 1990 at least 30 additional papers have been published using some form of the Bass model. The recent applications cover areas as varied as internet broadband use (Konstantinos and Vasilios 2011), public policy innovations (Boushey 2012), doctors' adoption of new medicines (Dunn, Braithwaite, Gallego, Day, Runciman, and Coiera 2012), Web-based instructional techniques (Soffer, Nachmias, and Ram 2010), wind power (Usha Rao and Kishore 2008), and the spread of social media (Hu and Wang 2009). One or more variables in these model extensions are typically altered or added, but the basic S-shaped Bass model continues to prove to be a robust method for forecasting new product sales among real world applications (Mahajan, Sharma, and Bettes 1988). Jeuland (1994), for example, fit the basic model to 35 different datasets for varying time periods and across different countries and typically found R-squared values greater than .9, suggesting very good fits (The R-squared statistic measures the degree of fit of a regression model to the data. An R-squared of 1.0 is a perfect fit.).

Considerable research across many disciplines including marketing, agriculture, sociology, and anthropology, suggests that most successful innovations have an S-shaped rate of adoption, although the slope of the curve varies (Rogers 2003). The Bass model adjusts the slope of the S-shaped curve according to two main parameters: p and q, the coefficient of innovation and the coefficient of imitation. Since most innovation diffusion processes tend to be very social in nature, typically the coefficient of imitation is considerably more important in determining the rate of adoption. Some innovations, such as VCRs and cell phones, have required only a few years to reach their maximum or near-maximum penetration levels, exhibiting a relatively steep S-curve, whereas others can require decades, such as use of the metric system in the United States (Rogers 2003).

The formula for the Bass model requires that a business manager or group of business managers provide a single estimate for first-year sales and total product lifetime sales (i.e., year one adopters and total adopters). Since few new products enjoy monopoly status or enjoy it for long, managers need to estimate total product category adopters in light of competitive alternatives and responses. Parameter estimates of p and q are then estimated to produce the following equation:

$$Q_t = p(M - A) + q\left(\frac{A}{M}\right)(M - A)$$

The preceding can be simplified to

$$Q_t = \left[p + q\left(\frac{A}{M}\right)\right](M - A)$$

where Q_t = number of adopters or unit sales at time t.

       p = coefficient of innovation, or "the likelihood that somebody who is not yet using the product will start using it because of mass media coverage or other external factors" [Van den Bulte (2002)].

       q = coefficient of imitation, or "the likelihood that somebody who is not yet using the product will start using it because of "word-of-mouth" or other influence from those already using the product" (Van den Bulte 2002).

       M = market size, or ultimate number of adopters or unit sales.

       A = cumulative number of adopters or unit sales to date.

The coefficient of innovation (i.e., p) captures the relative importance of innovative customers in generating sales for the new product. The coefficient of imitation (i.e., q) captures the relative importance of imitative customers in generating sales for the new product. The model operates such that, regardless of the values of p and q, as more and more customers adopt or buy the new product, the relative impact of imitative customer purchases takes on greater importance in determining the *sales curve* (S-curve). The S-curve that is then produced represents cumulative sales to date. A metaanalytic-based algorithm can be used to provide both a point or exact numerical estimate for sales in each time period, as well as an error band[1], within which sales are expected to fall. Thus, a "feasibility space" can be provided (Mahajan, Muller, and Bass 1995) for managers to forecast new product sales. For more rigorous risk analysis of market projections, Monte Carlo analysis can be used by including differing estimates of $p, q, A,$ and M combined with their probabilities of

---

[1] The error band can be obtained in alternative manners. For example, they may be developed from the use of differing assumptions of the size of the market and first year sales in the Bass model, Monte Carlo simulation, or inference from regression estimations of the Bass model. The availability of a specific method depends upon data availability.

occurrence can provide scenario analysis of sales and different states of the market environment. Historical analogies are often a more accurate method for estimating the necessary parameters, because prior efforts to fit curves based on just a few periods of early sales (e.g., three to four periods) have enjoyed limited success and accuracy (Pae and Lehmann 2003) and usually there are not enough data points for statistical significance of the p and q estimates. Studies also suggest that the coefficients p and q are relatively constant over time, within a given industry (Norton and Bass 1987, Pae and Lehmann 2003). The p and q coefficients from academic publications are typically estimated post hoc, that is, after a particular product innovation has been fully or nearly fully adopted throughout a market.

Two other key estimates that can be made with estimated parameters include the following. These expressions have been obtained by taking the first derivatives of the Bass model and solving for the optimal time to peak sales and size of peak sales:

$$\text{Time to peak sales: } t^* = \frac{1}{(p+q)}\left[\ln\left(\frac{q}{p}\right)\right]$$

$$\text{Size of peak sales: } s^* = M\left[\frac{(p+q)^2}{4q}\right]$$

The Bass model with the mean values of $p = 0.0063$ and $q = 0.4282$ from Pae and Lehmann (2003) result in the Bass curve that is shown on Exhibit D.3. Note that when $q = 0$, that is, there is no imitation, the diffusion curve defaults to the pure innovation curve of Fourt and Woodlock (1960), which is the declining growth exponential model. The Bass curves in Exhibit D.3 are shown with differing values of p and q. Note that relatively higher values of q will result in an accelerated Bass curve where market saturation is reached faster. As the sales process continues over time, imitators increase over time relative to innovators whose numbers decrease over time.

Also, the model defaults to a pure imitative one when $p = 0$. Exhibit D.3 demonstrates that in this case, the Bass curve has a similar shape as the Fisher-Pry imitative model. Note that the Bass curve with innovative and imitative properties embodied in the curve, that is, when neither p nor q equal 0 reflects both forces affecting market sales projections.

The investigation in this appendix finds that the Bass model is the model of choice based on its theoretical characteristics, its widespread use by business sales forecasters, and the exhaustive academic literature that addresses many tests, applications, validity of its theoretical foundations, and its forecast performance. Finally, the main caveats are discussed then the conclusions follow.

CAVEATS OF THE BASS MODEL

There are a number of assumptions underlying use of the Bass model, which should be considered prior to and during its application. These include (Mahajan and Wind 1986):

- The size of the potential market of total number of adopters remains constant over time. This may not be true if the new product gains in popularity either by spawning more competitors than anticipated, for example.

- There is only one product bought per new adopter. This is clearly not true for frequently repeated purchase products, or those that may break down or need replacement before the end of the product's lifecycle.
- The coefficients of innovation and imitation remain constant over time. This may not be true if, for example, need or desire for the product suddenly increases midway through the product lifecycle.
- The new product innovation itself does not change over its life cycle. This would not be the case if the firm introducing the new product updated or improved the product during early stages of its life.
- The innovation's sales are confined to a single geographic area. This would not be true if, for example, due to the product's success, the firm decided to launch the same product overseas.
- The impact of marketing strategies by the innovator is adequately captured by the model's parameters. Historical analogies, on which the model's forecasts are based, may not be applicable if, for example, the firm launching the new product supported it with atypically large promotional support or if an aggressive pricing strategy is being deployed.
- There is no seasonality in sales of the new product.
- The application of the model presumes that the statistically estimated parameters of the model used to develop p and q (involves the estimation of three regression coefficients) are statistically significant. Otherwise the p and q may not be representative of the true model and may lead to larger sales forecast errors. The Phase II of the project will discuss the statistical estimation of the Bass curve when historic sales data are available.

SUMMARY

The investigation in this appendix has involved the analysis and research of the major S-curve models, sometimes known as diffusion curves, to make a recommendation on which model or models to use for product sales and revenue forecasting. Each and every S-curve or logistical model type has not been reviewed as there are many models that have been proliferated in the sales forecasting literature, all addressing (or claiming to address) some unique property of a product sales forecast. The investigation in this appendix searched for the model that has received the most attention in terms of research, testing, application, and ability to understand and apply. The choice of the "best" model depends on many characteristics, many of which have not been discussed in this report. Although the focus is narrowed to the Bass curve, there are many dimensions for choosing the most appropriate values of p and q. One example that can impact p and q is what type of countries the firm is targeting its product. These will certainly be different for emerging economies v. mature economies. The market size and first year sales must also be estimated as model inputs in the absence of sales data. The purpose of the focus on S-curves is to obtain a systematic sales forecasting methodology based on marketing, economic, and statistical theory, analysis, research, and practice. There are many simple and complex forecasting methods that are ad hoc and are not based on any systematic approach to understanding and modeling the structure of a market. Although the diffusion curve literature is no panacea for sales and revenue forecasting issues, it is based on sound marketing, mathematics, economics, and statistical principles. Additionally, it has stood the test of time and application as it has performed well in predicting the pattern of new product sales for many products going back to the 1960s. It is always better to have more information and well-developed, systematic methods for obtaining the most accurate forecast possible.

REFERENCES

Bass, Frank M. 1969. "A New Product Growth Model for Consumer Durables." *Management Science* 15 (January): 215–227.

Bass, Frank M. 1993. "The Future of Research in Marketing: Marketing Science." *Journal of Marketing Research* 30 (February): 1–6.

Bass, Frank M. 1995. "Empirical Generalizations and Marketing Science: A Personal View." *Marketing Science* 14 (3): G6–G19.

Blackman, A. Wade Jr. 1974. "The Market Dynamics of Technological Substitutions." *Technological Forecasting and Social Change* 6 (1): 41–63.

Blackman, A. Wade, Jr., E. J. Seligman, and G. C. Solgliero. 1973. "An Innovation Index Based Upon Factor Analysis." *Technological Forecasting and Social Change* 4: 301–316.

Booz, Allen & Hamilton, Inc. 1982. *New Products Management for the 1980s.* New York: Booz, Allen & Hamilton, Inc.

Boushey, Graeme. 2012. "Punctuated Equilibrium Theory and the Diffusion of Innovations." *Policy Studies Journal* 40 (1): 127–146.

Dunn, Adam G., Jeffrey Braithwaite, Bianca Gallego, Richard O. Day, William Runciman, and Enrico Colera. 2012. "Nation-scale Adoption of New Medicines by Doctors: An Application of the Bass Diffusion Model." *BMC Health Services Research* 12 (1): 248–256.

Fisher, J. C., and R. H. Pry. 1971. "A Simple Substitution Model for Technological Change.," *Technological Forecasting and Social Change* 2: 75–88.

Fourt, Louis A., and Josepd W. Woodlock. 1960. "Early Prediction of Market Success for New Grocery Products." *Journal of Marketing* 25 (October): 31–38.

Hu, Haibo, and Xiaofan Wang. 2009. "Evolution of a Large Online Social Network." *Physics Letters A* 373 (12/13): 1105–1110.

Konstantinos, Salpasaranis, and Stylianakis Vasilios. 2011. "A New Empirical Model for Short-Term Forecasting of the Broadband Penetration: A Short Research in Greece." *Modelling & Simulation in Engineering* 2011: 1–10.

Mahajan, Vijay, Eitan Muller, and Frank M. Bass. 1990. "New Product Diffusion Models in Marketing: A Review and Directions for Research." *Journal of Marketing* 54 (January): 1–26.

———. 1995. "Diffusion of New Products: Empirical Generalizations and Managerial Uses." *Marketing Science* 14 (3): G79–G88.

Mahajan, Vijay, and Yoram Wind. 1986. *Innovation Diffusion Models of New Product Acceptance.* Cambridge, MA: Ballinger Publishing Company.

Mansfield, E. 1961. "Technical Change and the Rate of Imitation." *Econometrica* 29 (October): 741–766.

———. 1968. *The Economics of Technological Change,* New York: W. W. Norton & Company.

Norton, John A., and Frank Bass. 1987. "A Diffusion Theory Model of Adoption and Substitution for Successive Generations of High-Technology Products." *Management Science* 33 (September): 1069–1086.

Pae, Jae H., and Donald R. Lehmann. 2003. "Multigeneration Innovation Diffusion: The Impact of Intergeneration Time." *Journal of the Academy of Marketing Science* 31 (1): 36–45.

Rogers, Everett M. 1983. *Diffusion of Innovations,* 3rd ed. New York: Free Press.

————. 2003. *Diffusion of Innovations*, 5th ed. New York: Free Press.

Silk, A. J., and G. L. Urban. 1978. "Pre-Test Market Evaluation of New Packaged Goods: A Model and Measurement Methodology." *Journal of Marketing Research* 15: 171–191.

Soffer, Tal, Rafi Nachmias, and Judith Ram. 2010. "Diffusion of Web Supported Instruction in Higher Education – The Case of Tel-Aviv University." *Journal of Educational Technology & Society* 13 (3): 212–223.

Sultan, Fareena, J. U. Farley, and D. Lehmann. 1990. "A Meta-Analysis of Applications of Diffusion Models," *Journal of Marketing Research*, 27(Feb): 70–77.

Usha Rao, K. and V.V.N. Kishore. 2009. Wind Power Technology Diffusion Analysis in Selected States of India," *Renewable Energy: An International Journal*, 34(4): 983–988.

Van den Bulte, Christophe. 2002. "Want to Know How Diffusion Speed Varies Across Countries and Products? Try Using a Bass Model," *PDMA*

Dealing with Uncertainty and Immeasurables in Trademark Asset Valuation

William J. Murphy

If there were no uncertainties and if all the important factors associated with a particular trademark were easily measurable, the valuation exercise would be a trivial undertaking. It would yield a specific result in which one would have a high degree of confidence. If an evaluator had such perfect information, the valuation analysis would generate few challenges. The perfect information would be plugged into a reasonable valuation method that would generate an easy-to-interpret valuation result. Not surprisingly, in the real world, perfect information is either a white tiger (a very, very rare creature) or a unicorn (a nonexistent mythical beast).

Even if one had a trademark with a definite and guaranteed stream of future royalty payments that could be plugged into an appropriate income method of valuation, there always exists a variety of events, some probable but not certain and others less so, that could bring significant upside or downside effects. A trademark might suffer from a disastrous association with a defective or deadly product or with a disreputable celebrity. On the other hand, in this modern world of instant communication and social media, a trademark might suddenly "catch-on" in the common culture and "go viral" with substantial positive results. How can one consider such possibilities when evaluating a trademark? What methods exist to help us capture these possibilities, these information imperfections, in a logical way that does not overwhelm or distort our evaluation task?

In this appendix, we examine two related aspects of the valuation exercise: (1) dealing with uncertainties regarding the future that may have an impact on the trademark value, and (2) how to measure elements that are either difficult or impossible to measure directly but whose measurement is called for by a particular valuation technique.

ELEMENTS OF VALUATION ANALYSIS

Any valuation analysis has three elements:

1. Information inputs
2. Valuation techniques that translate the information inputs into value results
3. Interpretation of the value results.

Much of the academic literature seeking to improve valuation analysis focuses on the second element—improving valuation techniques. This is not surprising since developing more quantitative models that apply sophisticated mathematical methodologies can give an appearance of rigorous analysis and numerical certainty.

In reality, a valuation technique's benefit (no matter how sophisticated the technique) remains heavily dependent on the quality of the other two elements, particularly the first—the information inputs. For example, a discounted future economic benefits income method valuation is often seen as the best way to ascertain the value of an economic asset such as a trademark. The calculations associated with this method are not overly challenging or controversial. What is challenging is developing sufficiently accurate inputs to make the discounted future economic benefits calculation meaningful, and where the information inputs are less reliable or certain, making sure that the interpretation of the value results takes these factors into consideration.

Assessment of the information inputs associated with the all-important first element can be viewed through two lenses—one to determine how certain are we regarding a particular input and the other to determine whether we can measure the desired input directly or must we use some substitute or surrogate measure?

Determining Future Benefits

While essential to the income approach, determining the future benefits of ownership is at the heart of all three methods of valuation—the cost method,[1] the market method[2], and the income method.[3] As the reader can easily imagine, the valuation problem under each method becomes one of looking into the future to determine what those future benefits might be. Since no one has a crystal ball of sufficient clarity to precisely calculate this benefit stream, the search for methods that can assist in the forecasting process has drawn widespread attention.

The standard method for incorporating future risks into income valuation calculations is through the discount rate.[4] The main shortcoming is the loss of information because the discount rate is an accumulation of future risk and uncertainty estimates

---

[1] See Chapter 4.
[2] See Chapter 4.
[3] See Chapters 5, 6, 7.
[4] See Chapter 6.

and predictions rolled into a single number.[5] As a consequence of this aggregation, important distinctions can be lost and insights can be occluded by generalization.

The pervasive availability of computers and, more particularly, specialized software to aid in the forecasting process, coupled with procedures grounded in statistics and probabilities, have added a number of sophisticated techniques to the trademark valuation process that can take us beyond the discount rate. This appendix addresses a specific collection of popular modern methods that can be extremely useful in helping one incorporate uncertainty and risk into the valuation process.

It is first useful to explore the concepts of uncertainty, probability, and risk as they pertain to the valuation of trademark assets. These were introduced in Chapter 6 and play a significant role in valuation. This is especially true for trademark assets where future events or developments might have a significant effect on the value of the assets and those future events or developments have a high degree of uncertainty surrounding them.

Risk vs. Uncertainty

Over the past eighty-six years a debate has smoldered over what exactly is meant by risk and uncertainty.[6] For some, the two are separate and distinct concepts. For others, the two are interchangeable. While a definitive answer is not critical to the techniques put forward in this appendix, an appreciation of the debate can provide useful insights.

For those who argue that an important distinction exists, the term *risk* refers to situations where the outcomes and relative probabilities associated with those outcomes are known, but exactly which one of the possible outcomes will occur is not known.[7] Selecting a random card from a shuffled deck would be an example. The risk of selecting the ace of hearts is known (1 in 52), but whether or not the ace of hearts will be selected next is not. In the intellectual property valuation context one could say that there is a risk that a specific trademark application will be granted or not, since the outcomes are known (yes or no) and furthermore, by examining past examples and patent office practices it should be possible to assign relative probabilities to each of those outcomes.

---

[5] The discount rate has five component parts, each representing a different element that needs to be considered: (1) enjoyment deferral, (2) opportunity costs, (3) inflation rate during the future period, (4) uncertainty (or risk), and (5) illiquidity adjustment. The preferred method for determining an appropriate discount rate is to assess each of the five components separately and then later recombine these five assessments to derive the rate but this is not often done. For most valuation exercises, the fourth element—uncertainty—accounts for the largest portion. For more on this topic see, William J. Murphy, John L. Orcutt, and Paul C. Remus, *Patent Valuation: Improving Decision Making through Analysis* (Hoboken, NJ: John Wiley & Sons, 2012), 151–159.

[6] The debate can be traced to University of Chicago economist Frank H. Knight, who argued in his now famous 1921 paper entitled "Risk, Uncertainty and Profit" that there was a distinction between risk (randomness with knowable probabilities) and uncertainty (randomness with unknowable probabilities).

[7] Although in common usage, the term *risk* generally is used to express a positive probability of something bad happening, a negative result is not a requirement.

Correspondingly, those adhering to this precision in terminology would limit the application of the term uncertainty to situations where the outcomes and relative occurrences are not known; where they cannot be expressed in terms of specific mathematical probabilities.[8] In contrast to risk, for those who observe the distinction, the use of the term *uncertainty* would be limited to circumstances in which there is no basis on which to form any calculable probability. For example, the likelihood that any specific trademark will be instrumental in the commercialization of a product or will suffer harm through unfortunate association with a fallen celebrity would be characterized as uncertain since any probability assessment would be more conjecture than not.

The difference between the two concepts is starkly illustrated by the incredible six-year history of Long-Term Capital Management, a hedge fund founded by an elite collection of financial experts, including Nobel Prize-winning economists Myron Scholes and Robert C. Merton, the former vice chairman of Salomon Brothers John Meriwether, and former vice chairman of the Board of Governors of the Federal Reserve System David Mullins, among others. Long-Term Capital Management created immense wealth for a period of time by controlling and managing investment risk, but eventually succumbed to a series of political uncertainties that were not in their sophisticated investment models.

No matter where the reader comes out on this debate, there are important insights to be gleaned from recognition of the subtle distinction between the concepts.[9] Because the decision analysis method discussed in this appendix is founded on the ability to decompose a situation into various decisions, chance occurrences and outcomes, and then using mathematical techniques to logically frame and recompose the inputs to derive a result, the need to deal with probabilities is required.[10] However, it may be that the probabilities used are merely subjectively assigned expressions of beliefs representing uncertainty, rather than known real-world probabilities as in the more precise conceptualization of risk. In this appendix, the terms will be used interchangeably, but the reader is advised to remain aware that sometimes a probability is used in a technique that is little more than a best guess.

Objective vs. Subjective Probabilities

Rather than focus on the terms risk and uncertainty in this appendix, the terms *objective* and *subjective* probability are used where appropriate to help highlight

---

[8] John Maynard Keyes endorsed the distinction between risk and uncertainty as can be seen in this quote from his 1937 article "The General Theory of Employment," published in the *Quarterly Journal of Economics* 51:

[9] By "uncertain" knowledge, let me explain, I do not mean merely to distinguish what is known for certain from what is only probable. The game of roulette is not subject, in this sense, to uncertainty.... The sense in which I am using the term is that in which the prospect of a European war is uncertain, or the price of copper and the rate of interest twenty years hence.... About these matters there is no scientific basis on which to form any calculable probability whatever. We simply do not know. (213–214)

[10] The reader may recognize a resemblance to the notion of *expected utility*, first propounded by famous mathematician Daniel Bernoulli, in *Exposition of a New Theory on the Measurement of Risk* (1738), argued that the valuation of a risky venture could be thought of as the sum of utilities from the possible expected outcomes weighted by the probabilities of those outcomes.

differences in probabilities used in the techniques and to assist in the interpretation of the value results. *Objective probability*, as the name suggests, refers to probability assessments that are based on observations in the real world. Much like the definition of risk, objective probability is grounded upon witnessed facts. The roll of an honest six-sided die has a one-sixth chance of delivering any particular number (one to six) as the die comes to rest. The uncertainty that a particular roll of the die will result in a five is quantifiable as a one-in-six chance or a probability of 16.<u>66</u> percent. This is an objective probability.

Subjective probability, as its name suggests, is a subjective assessment of the probability associated with an event occurring where there is no observational or logically deduced basis for making an exact assessment of the probability. Most of the assessments we make every day regarding risks to undertake (e.g., "Should I seek shelter during a thunderstorm?") are based more on subjective than objective probability calculations. I know that there is some risk of injury from being struck by lightning during a thunderstorm, but I have no real or precise probability assessment of the likelihood of that happening.[11] Similarly, many of the probability assessments one might make regarding the uncertainties associated with valuing a particular trademark will be more subjective than objective.

While this inability to derive exact objective probabilities is often raised as a fatal flaw argument against the decision analysis techniques that require probability inputs, this is not the case. By using the best probability estimate in these techniques, even if it is a best guess or even a mere guess, means that the best available information is incorporated, even if imperfect. This imperfection can be considered and appraised in evaluation of the result but at least it is included. And, as additional information is obtained that reflect on the original probability estimate that original probability estimate can also be systematically considered and incorporated into the valuation by means of Bayes theorem, as will be discuss later in the chapter. The normal progression in such a valuation exercise is to make an initial probability assessment and then adjust it as new information is obtained.

DECISION ANALYSIS AND DECISION TREES

Valuation and decision analysis are inevitably intertwined. A valuation exercise, either explicitly or implicitly, is at the heart of every decision and every decision involves a value determination. When one alternative is chosen over another, the decision maker has, either consciously or subconsciously, valued the chosen decision higher than the competing choices.[12] If a company decides to acquire asset A rather than asset B, the firm has determined that the net benefits that will come from owning asset A are greater than if the company acquired asset B.

---

[11] And even when the probabilities of such occurrences in the everyday world are known, interpreting them and making rational decisions regarding them often elude us. According to the National Weather Service, the probability of being struck by lightning in the United States in a given year for the period 2001–2010 (based of reported deaths and injuries) was 1 in 1,000,000 or 0.000001. It is unlikely that many of us could make useful sense of a probability of this small size.

[12] See Murphy, Orcutt, and Remus, 43.

Decisions, and their imbedded valuation exercises, can be significantly improved by recognizing that they can be quantified, compared, and evaluated.[13] If done with care and foresight the decision maker can determine the value of the decision in terms of a quantifiable, common measurement—usually money—and then make an apples-to-apples comparison to alternatives based on the common measurement.

There are a number of methods that can be used to make a decision, some rational and some not. In ancient times, an important decision might rest on the interpretation of an omen.[14] Even today, many make important personal decisions based on the advice of horoscopes, the flip of a coin, or the message on a plastic icosahedron floating inside a "Magic 8-Ball."[15] While it may sometimes appear that the modern business world is little more than an elaborate casino in which the fortunes, or misfortunes, of companies and individuals are left to the vagaries of luck or fate, much of modern decision making is grounded in processes that follow a logic of consequences and preferences. Decision analysis is a way to make sure the consequences are logical and explicitly considered, and that preferences are rationally understood and incorporated.[16] Another benefit is the verifiable decision making record that it leaves behind. This increased decision making clarity and transparency can then provide useful knowledge to subsequent decision makers and allows for easier modifications and adjustments when new information develops.

The essence of decision analysis techniques is decomposition, whereby a complicated situation is broken down (*decomposed*) into its constituent parts for easier understanding and assessment. Separation of any inquiry into its critical elements, which are then individually assessed and subsequently reassembled in a logical and consistent manner, is a well-recognized and powerful valuation technique.

One of the most powerful tools for disassembling, analyzing, and reassembling trademark valuation problems is a decision tree. Decision trees, which get their name from the graphic representation of the technique that resembles a tree on its side, use diagrams to force the valuator to disassemble the item (or decision) being valued and to analyze each component part carefully.

Once the separate components have been assessed they need to be reconstituted into a coherent solution that is applicable to the original decision under scrutiny. Decision analysis provides us with the tools to accomplish the decomposition and reconstitution processes through the use of decision trees.

It should be remembered that using numbers in a valuation exercise is, in itself, a simplification process. Numbers are used to distill a complex reality into a more manageable form and to provide a convenient method to represent and manipulate inputs and evaluate resulting outputs. It should also be remembered that in any simplification process some information is lost. The objective is to employ simplification methods

---

[13] Ibid., ix.

[14] In classical Greece what self-respecting leader would make an important decision without consulting the Oracle at Delphi?

[15] The classic Magic 8-Ball toy has been popular since it was invented in 1946. The trademark is currently owned by Mattel Inc.

[16] This even includes methods to deal with preferences that might be "irrational" as is discussed in a subsequent section of this chapter on the effects of perception and bias on decision making.

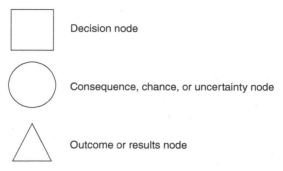

EXHIBIT E.1   Standard Graphical Conventions for Decision Trees

Source: William J. Murphy.

that retain as much critical information as possible without having the burden of superfluous or distracting information. Because there is always a nontrivial chance that some significant information is lost in the process, an understanding of the various simplification methods available in the decision analysis process will greatly assist in the selection of the best method and the ultimate interpretation of results.

Decision Tree Components and Conventions

The key tool in decision analysis is the decision tree, generally depicted with a single trunk on the left and branches growing off to the right. The modern decision tree technique was first formally introduced by mathematician John von Neumann and economist Oskar Morgenstern in their famous treatise on game theory, which was developed while both were at Princeton University during World War II.[17] Over the years the technique has spread to become a staple of business school curriculum worldwide.[18]

In constructing a decision tree, there are three basic components or nodes: decisions (under the decision maker's control), chance occurrences (not under the decision maker's control), and outcomes (what happens when certain decisions are made in light of the elaborated chance occurrences). While various authors or software packages might give different labels to these components, such as choice or selection for decisions, uncertainty or consequence for chance, and terminal or results for outcomes nodes, there is a common convention to the graphic representation. Decision nodes are represented as squares. Consequence, chance, or uncertainty nodes are represented by circles. And, outcome or results nodes are represented by triangles (see Exhibit E.1).[19]

---

[17] John von Neumann and Oskar Morgenstern, *Theory of Games and Economic Behavior* (Princeton, NJ: Princeton University Press, 1944).

[18] Increasingly, the technique has found it way into the curriculum of government and public policy programs, medical schools, particularly when assessing alternative treatment regimens, and even law schools.

[19] Of course, some software programs or published materials might not be capable of producing these exact shapes, and substitutions may occur.

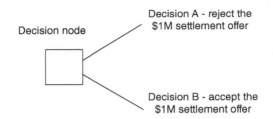

EXHIBIT E.2   Mapping out the Decision Alternatives

Source: William J. Murphy.

To construct a decision tree, the decision maker mentally walks through the sequence of events involved. Usually the process starts with a decision to be made. For example, a company has been offered a sum of money to license the use of a trademark it owns. Should the company accept the offer? Fundamentally, this is a valuation problem. Is the offer worth more than what is believed to be the value of not accepting the offer?

As the name implies, decision analysis focuses on making a rational decision among possible alternatives. Therefore, the first step in constructing a decision tree is to specify all the decision alternatives. To help clarify the process, let us assume that a decision has to be made on whether or not to accept an offered $1 million settlement payment in a trademark infringement lawsuit. In this simple example, there are two alternatives to the decision, accept the settlement or reject the settlement and continue with the lawsuit. In the common graphical decision representation, this decision would appear as in Exhibit E.2. There are three basic types of "nodes" in decision trees: decision nodes, consequence or uncertainty nodes, and outcome nodes. Decisions nodes are generally represented as squares in decision trees.

The next step is to predict all the possible consequence for which decision alternative. In our example, if the offered settlement is accepted there is no further uncertainty or risk involved and that ends that branch of the decision tree. For the other branch, where the settlement is rejected, there is an uncertain consequence. The lawsuit would continue to trial with a possibility of winning or losing. Since we have identified two possible consequences in our simplified example, winning at trial or losing at trial, the decision analysis technique now requires us to assign a probability estimate to each of these two consequences. Let us assume that we assess our chances of winning at the trial at 75 percent.[20] Since both consequence branches must add up to 100 percent, that leaves a probability of losing at trial at 25 percent. Adding these consequences to our example gives us the decision tree shown in Exhibit E.3. The common convention is to depict consequence or uncertainty nodes as circles in decision trees.

---

[20] There are a number of ways to assess this probability. Some may have a measurable basis, such as looking at past cases with similar circumstances and then determining their win/lose ratio (objective probability). And sometimes it could be estimated on no more than a gut feel (subjective probability). Examination of the source of these estimates is important to understand how robust the resulting calculation might be. Conducting a sensitivity analysis of an estimate that one is not sure about is one method to help the decision maker assess the result that is derived from the decision tree.

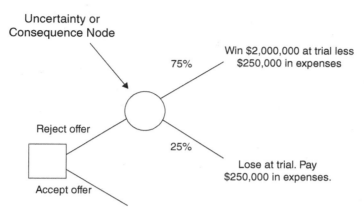

Uncertainty or
Consequence Node

75%   Win $2,000,000 at trial less
$250,000 in expenses

Reject offer

25%

Lose at trial. Pay
$250,000 in expenses.

Accept offer

EXHIBIT E.3   Adding the Uncertainty or Consequence Node
Source: William J. Murphy.

Of course a decision tree modeling an actual sue or settle decision would be much more complex, with multiple decisions and a large number of consequences to include but the basic elements would be the same.[21] Again, it is the function of the decision tree process to decompose a complex situation into smaller, more manageable parts that can later be recombined in a logical manner. That is its strength.

The next step in our simple sue-or-settle example is to determine the outcomes associated with each branch of the tree. Our example tree only has three branches, but the technique would be the same if the tree had three or three hundred branches.[22] For the one branch associated with the decision to accept the settlement the outcome is known, namely the $1 million offered settlement. We now have to assess the outcomes for the two branches associated with going to trial. For purposes of the example, let us assume that if we win the lawsuit we will receive $2 million less costs of $250,000. If we lose we will only have the $250,000 in costs. These outcomes are shown on our growing tree in Exhibit E.4. Outcomes are often depicted as triangles, but since many decision analysis computer programs have difficulty in producing triangles (particularly the early ones) this graphical convention is less followed that the use of the square and circle for decision and uncertainty nodes.

---

[21] For more detailed examples of decision tree use in this context the reader is invited to explore the publications of Marc B. Victor, one of the early proponents of using decision analysis techniques to aid decision making in the litigation environment. For those with a particular interest in intellectual property, see Marc B. Victor, Chapter 50, "Risk Evaluation in Intellectual Property Litigation," in *Intellectual Property Counseling And Litigation* (New York: Matthew Bender & Company, 2002). For two interactive demonstrations (one involving a personal injury and products liability lawsuit and the other medical malpractice case) the reader is directed to "For Evaluating Frequently Arising Claims," *Litigation Risk Analysis Software Models*, 2010, http://www.litigationrisk.com/frame-sw-models.htm.

[22] This, of course, is where the widespread availability of computers and applicable software has made what would have been an impossibly tedious and time consuming chore into an accessible and relatively friendly valuation tool.

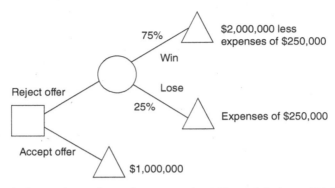

EXHIBIT E.4 Calculating the "Value" of Rejecting the Offer and Going to Trial
Source: William J. Murphy.

The final step is to perform the necessary calculations in order to make original decision. In decision tree parlance, this is referred to as "rolling back the tree." What occurs is that the program (or individual with pen and paper if unassisted by technology) starts with the outcomes and continues back to original decision (usually right to left), assessing each consequence or uncertainty node according to the desired criteria (which, in our example, could be to maximize or minimize the expected outcomes, depending on whether one is the plaintiff or the defendant). The mathematical method is to combine the assessed probability assigned to each uncertainty branch with the numerical value coming into that branch.[23] Application of this technique to our example tree appears in Exhibit E.5.

The decision maker now only needs to compare the probability-weighted value of the reject offer branch ($1,250,000) to the accept offer branch ($1,000,000) to

$$(.75)(2,000,000 - 250,000) + (.25)(-250,000) = \$1,250,000$$

Probability weighted value of this uncertainty node

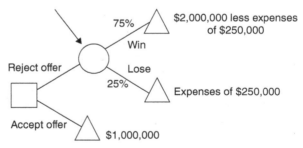

EXHIBIT E.5 Calculating the Value of the Uncertainty Node—Rolling Back the Tree
Source: William J. Murphy.

---

[23] In our example, the outcomes are expressed in dollars, but anything that can be expressed as a numerical value can be used—such as years in prison in a criminal case, or years of life when comparing one medical treatment regimen to another.

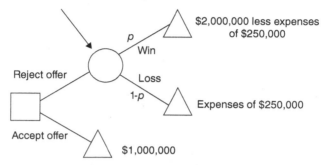

$(p)(2,000,000 - 250,000) + (1-p)(-250,000)$
Probability weighted value of this uncertainty node

EXHIBIT E.6 Performing a Sensitivity Analysis on Our Probability Estimate
Source: William J. Murphy.

determine which decision to make. In this case, rejecting the offer is expected to be worth $250,000 more than the offer on the table.

The decision tree process also makes it relatively easy to perform sensitivity analysis on the assessed probabilities assigned to any particular uncertainty node. For example, let us say that we are concerned about our estimate that we have a 75 percent chance of winning the lawsuit. We can test how sensitive our decision is to our probability estimate by inserting a variable (p) for the probability that we will win the lawsuit, and $(1-p)$ for the probability that we will lose.[24] Substituting these variables into our example tree yields the tree in Exhibit E.6.

Now we need to solve for p. To do this we set the probability-weighted value of the uncertainty node equal to the settlement offer of $1,000,000. This will give us a value for p where we are indifferent to the two decision options. In other words, at this calculated value of p both decisions will be equal. Completing this step is shown in Exhibit E.7.

What this tells us is that if our estimate of the probability of winning at trial falls below 62.5 percent we should change our decision and accept the $1,000,000 settlement offer. Performing sensitivity analysis helps identify those probability assessments where additional scrutiny and examination are most useful.[25]

By using these basic building blocks, decision trees of great complexity, which include numerous decision, uncertainty and outcome nodes, can be constructed.[26] The strength of the analysis is that what might be an impossibly complex problem

---

[24] Assuming we have articulated all possible outcomes, the branches of the uncertainty node must equal 100 percent. Therefore, if the upper branch is defined as p then the law then the lower branch is 100 percent less p, or in other words $1 - p$.

[25] Many decision tree software programs have built-in sensitivity analysis capabilities. Some, such as *TreeAge Pro*, permit the simultaneous examination of two or three variables in this manner.

[26] Some excellent examples of more complex decision trees can found at "Resources," *Tree Age Software*, http://treeage.com/resources/example.html.

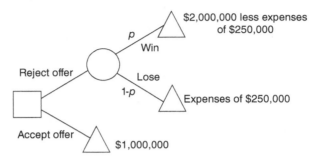

Set the reject offer branch equal to the accept offer branch
$(p) (2,000,000 - 250,000) + (1-p)(-250,000) = \$1,000,000$
then solve for p
$p = 1,250,000 / 2,000,000$ or 62.5%

EXHIBIT E.7   Sensitivity Analysis—Solving for p

Source: William J. Murphy.

can, through careful consideration of the various subelements and the proper linking of these subelements into the complete decision tree, yield insights not otherwise obtainable or obvious. It is through this software-aided process of disaggregation and subsequent reaggregation that decision analysis has become an increasingly useful tool for dealing with uncertainty and risk, or at least explicitly including uncertainty and risk into the decision-making or valuation activity.

Even if you can account for a significant amount of risk through the use of multiple scenarios with assigned probabilities, you may still need to factor in some additional uncertainty. Have all the scenarios been anticipated? Are the assigned probabilities correct? With trademark assets it is usually impossible to anticipate all possible future occurrences. The goal with decision analysis techniques in a valuation exercise is to logically account for as much future uncertainty as possible. One benefit of the techniques is that by collecting more information or by conducting extra scrutiny one may be able to transform ambiguous uncertainty into quantifiable risk.[27]

There is a significant limitation to standard decision tree analysis and that is that it requires the articulation of discrete possible outcomes and the assignment of probabilities to each of the resulting branches. Sometimes, as a practical matter, the outcomes are overlapping.[28] In other situations enumerating the sheer number of possible outcomes can overwhelm even the most determined analyst and severely tax the most robust computer driving the software programs. In these latter situations, the technique of Monte Carlo simulation can be most helpful.

---

[27] The subsequent section on Bayesian analysis discusses a method to accommodate subsequently acquired probability information into the decision making process.

[28] In these overlapping outcome situations the use of fuzzy logic has been advocated, and one might expect to see its incorporation in future decision tree software programs. For further information see, C. Z. Janikow, "Fuzzy Decision Trees: Issues and Methods," IEEE Transactions on Systems, Man, and Cybernetics, Part B, *Cybernetics* 28, issue 1 (February 1998): 1–14.

MONTE CARLO TECHNIQUES[29]

Where the future has a large number of random configurations, developing decision tree models can be unwieldy and unduly complex. Here the Monte Carlo technique can be effective.[30] The Monte Carlo method uses random numbers and probability statistics to investigate complex systems. Basically the technique uses statistical sampling to calculate approximate solutions to quantitative problems.[31]

Again, an illustrative example might be helpful. Suppose a company has developed a trademark for a line of pharmaceutical products. In modeling the future to determine the value of the trademark, assume for illustration purposes that four sequential variables have been identified that are relevant to the trademark's value:

1. The legal strength of the trademark
2. The effectiveness of the pharmaceutical products in the market
3. The size of the market for the trademark products
4. The regulatory approval of the pharmaceutical products by the appropriate governmental bodies permitting entry and continued access to customers

The sequence of variables is depicted in Exhibit E.8.

One could represent the variables in a decision tree analysis with discrete branches representing various possible outcomes for each variable. Let us just have two discrete branches for each of the four variables. The decision tree depicting this situation is shown in Exhibit E.9.

As you can see, even with only four variables and each with only two possible discrete outcomes, the decision tree already has 16 branches to evaluate. It is easy to see how a more robust decision tree could quickly develop so many branches as to be effectively useless. By using a Monte Carlo simulation technique an outcome for each of the four variables would be selected on a probability-weighted basis. This would constitute one "run" of the simulation. Thousands of runs would be

EXHIBIT E.8   Examples Variables

Source: William J. Murphy.

---

[29] Monte Carlo techniques were briefly mentioned in Chapter 12.2(e) page 251.

[30] Stanislaw Ulam, a Polish-born mathematician—who worked with John von Neumann on the Manhattan Project in 1944 and Edward Teller on the hydrogen bomb in 1951—is credited with inventing the modern Monte Carlo technique in 1946. The first paper published using the term is by Nicolas Metropolis and Stanislaw Ulam, "The Monte Carlo Method," *Journal of the American Statistical Association* 44, no. 247 (1949): 335–341. Nicholas Metropolis is reported to have coined the term "Monte Carlo" for the method.

[31] Ulam was not the first person to recognize that statistical sampling could assist in solving quantitative problems, but he did recognize that the development of computers during World War II could make the process less difficult. To this end, he developed the statistical sampling computer algorithms.

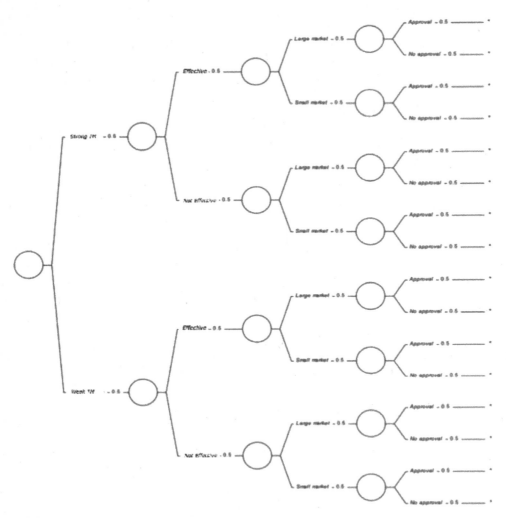

EXHIBIT E.9   Decision Tree with Only Two Outcomes for Each of the Four Variables
Source: William J. Murphy.

calculated in this manner, each selecting an individual potential future scenario with differing assumptions regarding the outcomes of uncertain events. These runs are subsequently combined, and usually presented in the form of a frequency distribution, to paint a more complete picture of the future than would be possible if a single, even if most likely, future was used.

   Without the aid of computers, the use of the Monte Carlo technique would be impractical. But, low-cost computing power and relatively easy to use software programs have made this a widely available tool to assist decision makers.[32] Once again,

---

[32] Sometimes Monte Carlo simulation software is part of a decision tree program, and sometimes it is offered as a stand-alone product (such as @Risk from Palisade Corporation (http://www.palisade.com/), which is an add-in for Microsoft Excel spreadsheets).

the accuracy of Monte Carlo technique is limited by the probabilities assigned and any estimate of the distribution of the potential scenarios.[33]

Bayesian Analysis

There are many situations were new information or evidence is obtained and has to be combined with existing knowledge or beliefs. When this new data involves probabilities that have to be combined with existing probability knowledge or beliefs, the average human mind is notoriously poor at performing the task correctly.[34] In these circumstances, a 300-year-old formula known as *Bayes' theorem*, or *Bayes' revision*, can make the difference between reasonable judgment and costly error.[35]

Bayes' theorem is a widely used mathematical formula that makes use of prior estimates of probability to revise assessments that an uncertain event will happen based on information obtained after the original probability estimates are made.[36] Named after the eighteenth-century amateur mathematician Reverend Thomas Bayes, the technique has found its way into a variety of modern decision-making situations from the algorithms in spam filters, which determine if a particular e-mail is legitimate or not, to the interpretation of medical testing information.[37,38] It can also be used in decision trees to help the decision maker properly incorporate new information that might be obtained, and as a consequence this powerful analytical technique is often included in commercially available decision analysis software.[39]

The classic decision used to illustrate Bayes' revision is derived from the once popular television game show *Let's Make A Deal*. The contestant is shown three

---

[33] While many distributions would be expected to be normal, there are situations where a log-normal or triangular distribution might be more accurate.

[34] As an example, the reader is invited to consider the Monty Hall problem discussed later in this section.

[35] Bayes' theorem is a method to logically update our beliefs as new information is obtained. The Bayesian view of probability is as statements about our beliefs or confidence and it provides a measure of the strength of our beliefs in a quantitative way. Contrast this with the Frequentist view of probability, where probabilities are derived from observations about the relative frequency of occurrences. Where probabilities in decision analysis are based on beliefs rather than the observed frequency of occurrence, the resulting analysis is obviously dependent on the validity of those beliefs.

[36] Mathematically Bayes' theorem is $P[B] \times P[A|B] = P[A] \times P[B|A]$, which means that the probability of B times the probability of A given B is equal to the probability of A times the Probability of B given A.

[37] An example is the *SpamBayes* program, based on the work of software programmer Paul Graham, developer of the ARC dialect of the Lisp computer language and author of *Hackers and Painters: Big Ideas from the Computer Age* (Sebastopol, CA: O'Reilly Media, 2004).

[38] See, for example, David B. Matchar, David L. Simel, John F. Geweke, and John R. Feussner, "A Bayesian Method for Evaluating Medical Test operating Characteristics When Some Patients' Conditions Fail to Be Diagnosed by the Reference Standard," *Medical Decision Making* 10, no. 2 (1990): 102–111.

[39] An example would be Tree Age Pro, a popular decision tree software program that includes Bayes' revision. TreeAge Pro is a product of TreeAge Software, Inc., 1075 Main Street, Williamstown, MA 01267.

doors on stage and hidden behind one is a fabulous prize. The other two hide objects of much lesser value. The contestant selects one of the doors, but rather than opening the selected door Monty Hall, the emcee, opens one of the two doors not selected to reveal one of the lesser objects. Monty then asks the contestant if he or she would like to change their original selection to the other remaining door. Should the contestant make the switch? In other words, is the decision to switch to the other door more valuable (a choice with a higher chance of exposing the sought-after prize) than a decision to stay with the original door choice?

Bayes' theorem tells us, counterintuitively, that the chances of winning the fabulous prize that is behind one of the two remaining unopened doors is improved if the contestant makes the switch. The normal intuition is that the choice between the two unopened doors is equal; namely, that there is a 50:50 chance that the prize is behind either door. Bayes' theorem is powerful precisely because our normal intuition about these probabilities is incorrect.[40] Again, modern software and ready access to computers makes inclusion of Bayes' revision a relatively painless task that can provide better assessments of the risks and uncertainties involved in a valuation and lead to improved decision making.

Consider another example of how Bayes' theorem can be used to revise probability beliefs based on subsequently obtained new information.[41] You go to the family doctor complaining about some pains. Based on this initial consultation and examination, your doctor estimates that you have a 50 percent chance of condition A, 40 percent chance of condition B, and a 10 percent chance of having condition A. Each of the conditions requires different treatment regimens and these are exclusive, meaning that your doctor cannot treat you for more than one of the conditions without serious drug interactions. Your doctor is worried because conditions B and

---

[40] At the beginning of the game, the probability that the prize will be behind any given door is 1/3. Assume that you choose door A, and that the host opens door B.

The probability that the host opens B if the prize were behind A is 50:50 or 1 in 2. This can be expressed as $P(\text{host opens } B|A) = 1/2$. The probability that the host opens B if the prize were behind B is zero (since the host always opens a losing door and never the one with the prize). This can be expressed as $P(\text{host opens } B|B) = 0$.

The probability that the host opens B if the prize were behind C is 100 percent (since, once again, the host always opens a losing door and never the one with the prize). This can be expressed as $P(\text{host opens } B|C) = 1$.

Combining these we find that the probability the host opens door B is then $P(\text{host opens } B) = P(A) \times P(\text{host opens } B|A) + P(B) \times P(\text{host opens } B|B) + P(C) \times P(\text{host open } B|C)$, which is 1/6 + 0 + 1/3 or 1/2.

Using Bayes' theorem, $P(A|\text{host opens } B) = P(A) \times P(\text{host opens } B|A)/P(\text{host opens } B)$, which is $(1/6) \times (1/2)$ or 1/3, so in other words the probability of the prize being behind your original choice of door A is 1/3, just as it was at the start of the game. $P(C|\text{host opens } B) = P(C) \times P(\text{host opens } B|C)/P(\text{host opens } B)$, which is $(1/3) \times (1/2)$ or 2/3. In other words, the probability that the prize is behind door C given that the host has open door B is 2/3. It is to your advantage to switch from door A to door C.

[41] This example and the chart are based on the lectures of Professor Michael Starbird, University of Texas at Austin, as captured in his excellent series *What Are the Chances? Probability Made Clear* (The Teaching Company, 2006).

EXHIBIT E.10 Using Bayes' Theorem to Update Our Hypothesis

Condition under Investigation	Initial Probability Assessment after Doctor Visit	Probability from Test Alone	Updated Probability Using Bayes' Theorem
A	50 percent	10 percent	20 percent
B	40 percent	30 percent	48 percent
C	10 percent	80 percent	32 percent

Source: William J. Murphy.

C are both very serious and often fatal if not treated quickly, so she gives you a test for condition C that is described as "80 percent accurate."

A few days later you return to your doctor's office and discover that the test for condition C has come back positive. It is known from a long history of the condition C test being given to thousands of patients over the years that the following probabilities are associated with a positive test result: If the test is positive you have only a 10 percent probability of having condition A, a 30 percent probability of having condition B, and an 80 percent probability of having condition C. This information is the source of the "80 percent accurate" description. The question now is what is the probability, after you receive this positive test result, that you actually have condition C, and that starting the treatment regimen for condition C is the correct decision?

At first blush, the response might be that the test indicates that you have an 80 percent chance of having condition C and treatment for it is the right approach, but using Bayes' theorem to revise our prior beliefs yields a somewhat surprising probability that you have only a 32 percent chance of having condition C, a 20 percent chance of having condition B, and a 48 percent chance of having condition B. In other words, the best treatment regimen based on all the information is that you should begin the treatment regimen for condition B instead. Exhibit E.10 shows the situation.

The use of Bayes' theorem to adjust probabilities is sometimes criticized because it requires an initial probability assessment. In situations where this initial assessment can be readily made or discovered, the application of Bayes' theorem is a powerful and relatively uncontroversial tool. But even if the initial probabilities are largely speculative or tentative, the results from application of the theorem should provide better results than those that ignore the new information, even though one must be careful to note that the updated assessment may inherit some the shortcomings of this prior estimate of probabilities and is no magic bullet that instantly transform subjective probabilities into objective probabilities.

Markov Chains

While the use of decision trees to assist in a complex assessment of value might be attractive in the abstract, the practical limitations of determining all the various decision points and outcomes in order to construct the tree can be overwhelming.

In situations where event timing is important, where critical events may happen more than once, or where risk is continuous over time, the use of techniques based on Markov chains may be helpful in making an otherwise immense assessment task more manageable.

In 1909, the Russian mathematician Andrei A Markov disclosed a theory of stochastic processes, processes involving the operation of chance, now commonly known as *Markov chains*. Technically, a Markov chain consists of a sequence of chance events that are independent of each other, but where information regarding the probabilities of a particular event in the sequence depends on the value of a prior event in the sequence.

In a process that can be described by a Markov chain, there are various states and the process evolves from state to state at random. The evolution is said to be "memory-less" because the probability of moving from one state in the process to another is determined solely by the current state. In a Markov chain, the future is conditionally independent of the past.

An example would be the famous "random walk theory" for stock prices from financial research. This theory, made popular by Princeton University economist Burton G. Malkiel in his 1973 book *A Random Walk down Wall Street,* claims that stock prices are not predictable but fluctuate randomly.[42] This means that past movements or trends in the price of a stock cannot be used to predict its future movement. But even if the particular direction a stock price might take the next day is unpredictably random, the price, whether up, down or unchanged, is more likely to be in the vicinity of the current price then some distant point, and this relationship can be expressed as a probability. Just as a wandering drunk might randomly stagger down the sidewalk, the location of the drunk's next step (although random) is related to the drunk's current position. In other words, it is more likely that the drunk's next location will be in the vicinity of the drunk's current position than some other random location on the sidewalk.

Another example involving trademarks might be useful in demonstrating how this type of analysis can help determine future benefit streams that affect valuation. Markov chains have long been effective in marketing research for examining and forecasting the brand loyalty of customers (which has obvious utility in helping estimate the value of a trademark).[43]

Consider a market with three brands of a particular product, A, B, and C. Brand A has the strongest consumer loyalty, with Brand B and Brand C following in that order. As with many markets the most robust predictor of what brand a consumer will purchase next is the brand the consumer last purchased. But, also assume that in this market there are a certain number of consumers who will switch brands on their next purchase. Exhibit E.11 graphically depicts the situation with percentages shown for those consumers who will switch to another brand on their next purchase.

---

[42] Burton G. Malkiel, *A Random Walk Down Wall Street*, rev. ed. (New York: W. W. Norton, 2003).

[43] Robert J. Thierauf, *An Introductory Approach to Operations Research* (Santa Barbara, CA: John Wiley & Sons, 1978), 269.

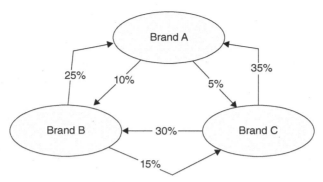

EXHIBIT E.11 Three Brand Market with Percentage of Switching Customers Shown
Source: William J. Murphy.

The three-brand market depicted in Exhibit E.11 can be also expressed as a matrix as shown in Exhibit E.12. In Exhibit E.12 the relative brand loyalties generated by each brand are shown. As the reader can appreciate from examining the matrix, the probability of the brand that the consumer will purchase next is dependent on the current brand of the customer. The matrix shows that while 85 percent of Brand A current customers will again select Brand A as their next purchase, 10 percent will switch to Brand B, and 5 percent will switch to Brand C. In a Markov chain, these conditional probabilities are known as transition probabilities, and it is these probabilities that make Markov chains such powerful tools to help deal with uncertainty.

This Markov chain that we have developed for a simple three-brand market can be extremely informative when combined with current market share data, to chart possible market share change and evolution. In this regard, one should remember that current high brand loyalty may not be correlated with current high market share, and often is not. For example, while Brand A generates the highest brand loyalty, it might not be the brand with the largest current market share. One only has to think of car buyer loyalty to appreciate how universal this assumption might be in the marketplace. Certain luxury automobiles with relatively low market shares, such as Mercedes Benz or Rolls-Royce, generate very high brand loyalty, whereas certain car brands with much larger market shares might have relatively low brand loyalty.

EXHIBIT E.12 Brand Loyalty in the Three Brand Market

Current Brand	Brand Next Purchased		
	A	B	C
Brand A	.85	.10	.05
Brand B	.25	.60	.15
Brand C	.35	.30	.45

Source: William J. Murphy.

EXHIBIT E.13   Matrix from the Seafarer's Aphorism

Time of Day	Sky	Future Weather
Morning	RED	NOT GOOD
	Not Red	—
Nightfall	RED	GOOD
	Not Red	—

Source: William J. Murphy.

When trying to predict the uncertain future of our three-brand market as part of a valuation exercise, the Markov chain regarding brand loyalty developed in Exhibit E.14 can be used to predict how market share outcomes, consistent with our loyalty assumptions, may develop over time. This utility of Markov chains to help understand and model an uncertain future has not escaped the attention of decision tree software providers, who routinely include Markov chain capabilities in their products. Without the Markov chain and Markov matrix, a decision tree that attempted to model our simple three-brand market in the conventional way would generate nine branches for the first time period and then nine branches for each of the original nine branches in the second period, and so on. It is easy to see that using the conventional decision tree approach without Markov chains would quickly become too complex to use and too computation resource intensive to be practical.[44]

Markov chains are also useful in situations where there is a readily observable or measurable status that might help predict a hidden or future status of interest. For example, it would be desirable in predicting a future event (hidden or immeasurable) if there is some known relationship to a measurable or observable phenomenon in the present or past. Perhaps the classic example is the seafarer's aphorism, "Red sky at night, sailors delight. Red sky at morn, sailors be warned." A matrix of this aphorism is shown in Exhibit E.13, and since the aphorism is silent on what is the meaning of a sky that is not red, those parts of the matrix are left blank.

One would expect that the color of the sky and the future weather is not a perfect correlation, but that the observed sky color is related to the future weather in a manner that can be expressed as a probability relationship. Assume that this relationship is measured for a period of time and that the resulting probabilities are determined. With the probability relationship between the current sky color and a future weather condition now known, a Markov chain for this aphorism can be developed. (This is shown in Exhibit E.14.) In this example it is assumed that when the sky is not red, there is an equal chance (50:50) of good or not good weather.

Being able to predict the future weather, from the color of today's sunset, or sunrise is extremely useful. If we can determine a probabilistic relationship between an observable state that we can measure and a hidden or future state that we really

---

[44] Computer programs that evaluate models containing Markov chains often use Monte Carlo simulation methods to perform the analysis.

EXHIBIT E.14   Markov Chain from the Seafarer's Aphorism

Time of Day	(Observed State) Sky Color	Future Weather GOOD	NOT GOOD
Morning	RED	.35	.65
	Not Red	.5	.5
Nightfall	RED	.80	.20
	Not Red	.5	.5

Source: William J. Murphy.

want to determine, then we may be able to use the measurable state to form a better prediction of the immeasurable state. Markov chains are a method to connect, through probabilities, an observable state to a hidden state that is of interest.

OBTAINING INFORMATION FROM INDIRECT OBSERVATION

Standard economic theory explains that the collective actions of buyers and sellers will cause a market price to develop for a traded item. The market price, which is the point at which supply and demand converge, will represent the best estimate for the value of the traded item if the market is sufficiently competitive.[45] Unfortunately, for many items there might not be an organized marketplace with readily observable market prices. This is particularly true for trademark assets.

Often in a valuation exercise it is not just ambiguity regarding the probabilities associated with a particular version of the future that is of concern but the inability to directly measure one or more of the required inputs. Examining the various possibilities associated with market methods might help illustrate.[46] Exhibit E.15 sets forth the various types of market methods divided into two main groups: revealed preference methods and stated preference methods. The former encompasses those methods where the inputs to the methodology are revealed in the market (although sometimes indirectly). The latter involves inputs that are purposefully extracted through alternative devices. Stated preference methods ask the decision makers involved in the valuation event, and possibly other relevant individuals, to state their preferences in such a way that an implied value can be extracted from the stated preferences.

Stated preference methods are frequently used for difficult valuation problems such as the value of life or the effect of environmental degradation. It is also possible, however, to devise a stated preference methodology for use in trademark valuation, particularly within an organization that has expertise in making decisions regarding the relevant trademarks and the markets where the trademarks may be commercially

---

[45] For more on market methods see Chapter 4.
[46] Market methods were discussed in Chapter 4.

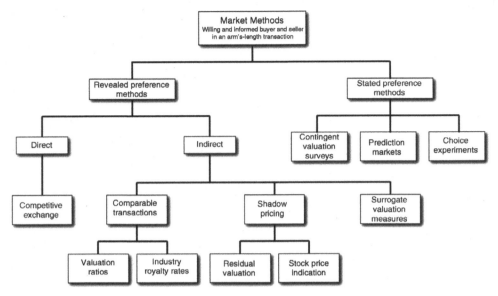

EXHIBIT E.15 Diagram of Various Market Methods

Source: William J. Murphy.

useful. The way stated preference methods work is as the name suggests. Interested parties are asked to state their preferences regarding the relevant valuation data. There are a variety of methods for making the ask. Choice experiments,[47] contingent valuation surveys,[48] and prediction markets[49] are all commonly employed techniques for teasing out stated preference data.

---

[47] See, for example, Francisco Alpizar, Fredrik Carlsson, and Peter Martinsson, "Using Choice Experiments for Non-Market Valuation," *Working Papers in Economics* 52 (2001).

[48] See, for example, Peter Diamond and Jerry Hausman, "Contingent Valuation: Is Some Number Better than No Number?" *Journal of Economic Perspectives* 8 (1994): 45.

[49] The utility of prediction (or information) markets has been championed as a method to extract useful information regarding an uncertain future event. Employing a betting type of system, participants place wagers on various future outcomes. The participant whose wager prediction comes closest to the actual outcome is rewarded. In the standard information market, the participant buys a type of futures contract on the outcome of a specified event or result. If that event or result comes to pass, the holder of that contract will be rewarded with either real or artificial currency. In certain circumstances, these markets can outperform both experts and opinion polls. This insight was popularized by James Surowiecki in his 2005 book *The Wisdom of Crowds.* The outcome of political elections and sporting events have long been the subject of public wagering with websites such as the Iowa Electronic Markets, InTrade, and Paddy Power providing opportunities to the general public to make predictions with the incentive of a reward for predictions that turn out to be correct. See also Bo Cowgill, Justin Wolfers, and Eric Zitzewitz, "Using Prediction Markets to Track Information Flows: Evidence from Google," January 2009, http://www. bocowgill.com/GooglePredictionMarketPaper.pdf; Robert Hahn, "Using Information Markets to Improve Policy," AEI-Brookings Joint Center for Regulatory Studies, Working Paper 04-18 (2004); Justin Wolfers and Eric Zitzewitz, "Prediction Markets," *Journal of Economic Perspectives* 18 (2004): 107; and Robin Hanson, "Shall We Vote on Values, but Bet on Beliefs?" October 2007, http:// hanson.gmu.edu/futarchy.pdf.

Revealed preference methods are more closely aligned with what one normally views as a market method. For example, if the trademark being assessed had recently been subject to an arm's length market transaction involving a willing, independent, and knowledgeable buyer and a similarly situated seller then that market price would be an excellent indication of the trademark's value, assuming that the context of that market transaction was similar to that currently under consideration. This would be a direct revealed preference involving a competitive exchange.

Because of the unlikelihood of finding such a situation we often resort to using inputs that are stand ins for those that are difficult or impossible to measure directly. In Exhibit E.15, these are referred to as indirect revealed preference methods and there are three main types: comparable transactions, shadow pricing, and surrogate measures.

Comparable Transactions

In this method, the value of an asset is determined by looking at the range of prices paid in past or current transactions for similar assets. The value stems from the premise that a reasonable buyer would not pay more for property than it would cost to purchase a comparable substitute. Furthermore, if the comparable transaction took place in the past, it is assumed that the information derived from that past transaction remains relevant for the transaction under review.

One of the most common methods for using comparable transactions involves ratio analysis. Mechanically, ratio analysis involves identifying valuation ratios from the prices at which similar assets were sold in the past and then applying that valuation ratio to the asset being valued. Valuation ratios are multiples that are calculated by dividing the price at which the similar asset sold by a relevant economic variable of the asset. In the financial marketplace the PE or Price Earnings ratio is widely used in this manner. In a similar manner ratio analysis can be used in trademark valuation.[50]

The difficulty in applying ratio analysis to trademark transactions is not the calculation; rather, it is coming up with the comparable data that is needed to feed the calculation. The general dearth of publicly available data about individual trademark transactions and the comparability problems that accompany data that are available limits the applicability of ratio analysis for trademark valuation analysis in many situations.

Sometimes in an attempt to compensate for the lack of available individual transaction data, parties may employ industry or aggregate royalty rates. The parties to a license transaction, for example, may use industry royalty rates to help to determine the appropriate royalty rate for their specific transaction. Using aggregate industry royalty rates is also fraught with difficulties and should be used with care. Even when data on potentially comparable transactions is available, the unique nature of individual trademarks can make using such data particularly challenging to employ in a valuation analysis.

---

[50] See discussion of ratio analysis in Chapter 3.

Shadow Pricing

In the prior section on Markov chains, we discussed how it can be helpful to use a readily observable or measurable status to help predict a hidden or uncertain status of interest. Another method used to extract information about the item of interest that might not be directly measurable is to derive the information by logically linking value judgments made for related activities or decisions that might be observable or measurable. This method is referred to as shadow pricing. As the name implies, it involves looking for indirect information (the shadow) of the pricing information that is of interest. The method uses a chain of value judgments that logically links the monetized value of any element in the chain to the value to be determined. For example, if one claims that X is better than Y and Y has a value of $1,000, then one can logically say that X has a value of more than $1,000 (the value of Y).

Probably the best example of shadow pricing is in putting a value on life. We often claim a life is priceless or beyond any measure of value, but in reality every day we are forced to put a value on life, and other supposedly priceless items, by the decisions that confront us. A decision to drive or take an airplane to a distant location, a decision to purchase a certain safety option in the new car, or the decision to select one medical treatment versus another all contain information about the decision maker's valuation of life.

Government regulation that implies a certain balance of values is often a fertile source for shadow prices.[51] For example, when a governmental body decides to enact a regulation that will have a predicted impact of a certain number of lives saved, and the cost of the regulation to save those lives is known or can be estimated, an implied value of life can be extracted. For example, suppose the government proposes a regulation that will cost $100 million to implement that will reduce a cancer-causing chemical in the workplace, and it is known that the reduction will save 100 lives. From these facts we can show that the shadow price of life implicit in this regulation is $1 million.[52] This means that the value of a life, based on this regulatory decision, is worth at least $1 million. To put it another way, the value of a life implicit in this regulatory example is not less than $1 million.[53]

One form of shadow pricing that has received a fair amount attention in the intellectual property valuation literature and is discussed in detail in Chapter 3 is the

---

[51] Professor W. Kip Viscusi, John F. Cogan, Jr. Professor of Law and Economics and currently Director of the Program on Empirical Legal Studies at Harvard Law School is probably the leading researcher in this area. His research discloses a wide range of implied values of life in various regulatory actions. The values vary widely but seem to cluster in the $3 million to $7 million range. W. Kip Viscusi, *Rational Risk Policy: The 1996 Arne Ryde Memorial Lectures* (Oxford: Oxford University, 1998)

[52] The calculation is as follows: the total cost of the regulation ($100 million) divided by the number of lives saved (100) equals the minimum value of a life ($1 million) implied by the regulatory action.

[53] Of course, it may be worth much more. The logic only tells us that $1 million is the minimum implied value of a life based on the facts in this regulatory example.

residual valuation method.[54] This method can be employed to determine the market value of an intellectual property right that is held by a publicly traded firm that has one dominant intellectual property right in its intellectual property portfolio, such as a pharmaceutical company that sells a single drug for which it holds the patent rights. In such a case, the patent right can be valued by calculating the firm's residual value after subtracting the value of all the other assets from the firm's market value.

Similar to the residual valuation method is what we refer to as the stock price indication method. This method is based on the premise that the stock market may have something to say about the value of a publicly traded company's intellectual property. The simplest example of the stock price indication method is when a company's stock price reacts to major news about one of the company's trademarks. For example, if a company's stock price drops on the release of news that one of the company's trademarks has been invalidated—and assuming no other major news releases by the company and a relatively calm day in the stock markets—the company's drop in market valuation (which could be measured over multiple days to reduce the risk that investors had an immediate overreaction to the news) could be inferred to be the market's valuation of that trademark right.

Absent news events about a particular trademark, stock prices can still provide information about trademark values. Stock prices can provide a crude and indirect indication of the value of a company's overall trademark portfolio. Assuming the company trades on a liquid and relatively efficient stock market, a company's financial ratios can provide insights as to how the market values its trademark portfolio. When a company has a significant trademark portfolio and better-than-average financial ratios (the company's stock is trading at a price that is higher than its financial performance would normally justify), the market could be indicating its estimate that the trademark portfolio has significant value. A number of empirical studies have shown that corporations' market value correlates with their intellectual property assets.[55]

Surrogate Measures

In many valuation contexts, it can be convenient to use something that is readily observable or measurable to help estimate something that is difficult to observe or measure. Shadow pricing does this by linking the asset that is the focus of the valuation exercise to a revealed market price for another item. It is also possible to extract useful information from observable non-price data that are revealed by decisions

---

[54] See, for example, Gordon V. Smith and Russell L. Parr, *Valuation of Intellectual Property and Intangible Assets* (New York: John Wiley & Sons, 1989), 204–206; Robert Pitkethly, "The Valuation of Patents: A Review of Patent Valuation Methods with Consideration of Option Based Methods and the Potential for Further Research," Judge Institute Working Paper WP 21/97 (1997), 7–8; F. Russell Denton and Paul Heald, "Random Walks, Non-Cooperative Games, and the Complex Mathematics of Patent Pricing," *Rutgers Law Review* 55 (2003): 1175, 1185–1186; and Anne Layne-Farrar and Josh Lerner, "Valuing Patents for Licensing: A Practical Survey of the Literature," March 2006, 8–9, http://papers.ssrn.com/sol3/papers.cfm?abstract_id=1440292.

[55] United Nations Economic Commission for Europe, *Intellectual Assets: Valuation and Capitalization* (2003), 67.

made in the marketplace. We refer to this useful nonprice data as *surrogate valuation measures*.

One of the most interesting examples of a surrogate valuation measure dates back to eighteenth-century Great Britain. In 1784, William Pitt the Younger, then head of the British government, needed to raise taxes to reduce the national debt. An income tax was rejected as requiring too great an intrusion into private affairs, so a property tax increase was proposed. A property tax solution, however, created its own problem. How could the government quickly and inexpensively value all the property that would need to be taxed? The solution that Pitt employed was one that had a long history in England.[56]

Pitt's solution was to employ a "window tax" and use windows as a surrogate measure for property value. The window tax was based on the number of windows that a building had. Windows at the time were very expensive. As a result, it was reasoned that more valuable buildings would have more windows than less valuable structures. The number of windows and the building's value were roughly correlated. The advantage of the window tax to the tax collector was that windows were easy to count. Not surprisingly, taxed citizens responded to Pitt's increased tax by filling in windows with solid walls to reduce their tax burden. Examples of these blind windows (called "Billy Pitt's Pictures") can still be found in Scotland.

In patent valuation, the use of more easily obtained surrogate valuation measures has been suggested as a possible technique to overcome the dearth of readily accessible market price information for patents. A number of academics have noted that surrogate measures derived from publicly available patent data sources (such as the U.S. Patent and Trademark Office and the European Patent Office) can provide useful insights into patent valuations.[57]

Unfortunately, equally robust efforts to develop surrogate measures applicable to trademarks have yet to emerge but there has been some limited examination in the academic literature of surrogate measures involving trademarks.[58] In this age of big data, there is no reason to believe that efforts to uncover surrogate measures in the trademark area would not yield fruitful results.[59]

---

[56] The original window tax was introduced in 1696 with amendments and modifications made throughout the next century and a half. Andrew Glantz, "A Tax on Light and Air: Impact of the Window Duty on Tax Administration and Architecture, 1696–1851," Pennsylvania History Review 15 (2008): 18.

[57] Nils Omland, "Economic Approaches to Patent Damages Analysis." In *The Economic Valuation of Patents: Methods and Applications,* ed. Federico Munari and Raffaele Oriani (Cheltenham, UK: Edward Elgar Publishing Ltd, 2011), 171–182.

[58] For a critical analysis of using the infringer's profits are a surrogate measure of the trademark holder's own lost profits in a trademark infringement action see Dennis S. Corgill, "Measuring the Gains of Trademark Infringement," *Fordham Law Review* 65, no. 5 (1997): 1910.

[59] For a discussion of how marketing metrics can serve as surrogate measures for firm value see Shigufta Hena Uzma, "Marketing Metrics: A Surrogate of Firm Valuation," http://dspace .nitrkl.ac.in/dspace/bitstream/2080/1841/3/Marketing+Metrics_Abstract+Uzma.pdf. See also Ankur Singla, "Valuation of Intellectual Property," http://bus6900.alliant.wikispaces.net/file/ view/article233.pdf, citing the use of market surrogates in Gordon V Smith, Russel L Parr, *Intellectual Property: Valuation, Exploitation and Infringement Damages* (Hoboken, NJ: John Wiley & Sons, 2005), 164.

OPTION PRICING MODELS

One of the limitations of traditional *net present value* (NPV) calculations using the *discounted cash flow* (DCF) method is that they fail to capture future flexibility and choices.[60] To better understand how this inability to adequately address flexibility effects valuation consider the following example.

A company has a promising project underway that may result in a collection of trademarks for an emerging commercial market. There are a number of uncertainties facing the decision makers, but they can be divided into two major categories; uncertainties about the acceptance and consumer impact of the trademarks, and uncertainties about the emerging commercial market for the associated products. Both will have significant impact on the valuation of the potential trademarks under development.

Using the DCF method to determine a value for the potential trademark requires the determination and application of a suitably large discount rate to be applied to the expected cash flows to address these uncertainties. What is missing from this type of valuation analysis is the important fact that there are a series of decisions that stretch into the future, and that some of these decisions will depend on facts that are not yet known, but will be known at the time the decision will need to be made. For example, the decision to continue investing in advertising and promotion a year or two from now may depend on how attractive the commercial market has become; something that might not be readily known at the time of the valuation exercise. If the market is hot, a decision to increase investment at that time can be made. If the market has failed to develop, a decision to scale back or abandon the trademark can be made at that later date, and substantial costs can be saved. How to incorporate this information into the valuation exercise can be difficult, if not impossible, using a traditional NPV methodology.

This is precisely the situation facing investment decision makers involving options in the financial marketplace. An option is a contract that gives the owner the right, but not the obligation, to buy or sell a specific asset at a specific price and a specific time in the future. If the contract is to sell it is referred to as a *put*, and if it is to buy, it is called a *call*.

In order to better explore how an option contract can provide a useful level of flexibility, consider the following situation involving a call option. An investor purchases an option to buy an asset three months from now for a specified price. If the asset has a value at that future point that exceeds the price specified in the contract, the contract can be exercised and the asset purchased at a profit. On the other hand, if the value of the asset at that future time is below the exercise price the holder of the contract can choose not to purchase.

How to properly value these option contracts confounded analysts until 1972 when Fischer Black and Myron Scholes published a paper describing a method that would become one of the most important concepts in modern financial theory and

---

[60] For a discussion of net present value and the discounted cash flow method see Chapters 4, 5 and 6.

today is widely known as the *Black-Scholes option pricing model*.[61] The brilliance of the Black Scholes option pricing model was that it was able to remove the difficult-to-measure risk element from the valuation calculation through the use of dynamic hedging.[62] With risk removed from the calculation, the remaining five components to the formula were readily observable or able to be estimated. One of the key remaining determinants in the Black Scholes option pricing model is future volatility.[63] Since future volatility is, by definition, unknown, historical volatility is often used as an estimate or substitute measure. Again, we see the use of something that can be more readily observed or estimated to help clarify a future uncertainty.

The potential application of option models to intellectual property assets such as trademarks has drawn the attention of a number of authors and scholars, but obstacles remain to its practical use.[64] The main attraction of option models is the inclusion of decision flexibility into the model. To better illustrate this, consider a valuation exercise involving a patent. In many ways a patent is like an option. By investing in the getting the patent (the price of the option), the owner has the right, but not the obligation, to exploit the patented technology and to exclude others from using the technology without permission during a 20-year period. In other words, if the marketplace for the patented technology becomes sufficiently attractive during the twenty year patent term, the patent owner will "exercise their option" to use or license the technology. If the market is not sufficiently attractive, the patent holder is not obligated to invest further.

---

[61] Fischer Black and Myron S. Scholes, "The Valuation of Option Contracts and a Test of Market Efficiency," *Journal of Finance* 27, no. 2 (1972): 399–418. Although the 1972 paper in the *Journal of Finance* was the first published discussion of their theory, a paper that was subsequently published in 1973 (but was referenced in the 1972 paper that beat it into print) in the *Journal of Political Economy* is considered the landmark work. Fischer Black and Myron S. Scholes, "The Pricing of Options and Corporate Liabilities," *Journal of Political Economy* 81, no. 3 (1973): 637–654.

[62] Dynamic hedging to remove the risk component was a major contribution to the concept made by Robert Merton. See Robert C. Merton, "Theory Of Rational Option Pricing," *Bell Journal of Economics and Management Science* 4, no. 1 (1973): 141–183.

[63] The five inputs used in the Black-Scholes algorithm to produce an estimate the value of a call on a stock are (1) an estimate of the risk-free interest rate now and in the near future, (2) current price of the stock, (3) exercise price of the option, commonly referred to as the strike price, (4) expiration date of the option, and (5) an estimate of the volatility of the stock's price. One of the key insights of the Black Scholes option pricing model is that increased volatility in the value of the underlying asset increases the value of the option. In hindsight this may appear obvious, but its implications for patents is profound, since if a patent can be properly characterized as a type of option to participate in a market, then the patent's value is increased as the volatility in the underlying market increases.

[64] For a summary of various valuation methods and an exploration of the potential utility of option pricing models to intellectual property rights, the reader is invited to examine Robert Pitkethly, "The Valuation of Patents: A Review of Patent Valuation Methods with Consideration of Option Based Methods and the Potential for Further Research," Judge Institute Working Paper WP 21/97, The Judge Institute of Management Studies (1997), http://www.oiprc.ox.ac.uk/RPWP0599.pdf.

While there may be some agreement that certain types of intellectual property function in a manner similar to options, there is considerable difficulty in trying to apply the valuation tools from the financial option marketplace to the intellectual property realm. For example, as mentioned earlier the Black Scholes option pricing model uses dynamic hedging to eliminate the risk component in the calculations. Whether or not there are comparable techniques applicable to intellectual property assets is not clear. Even if that hurdle is surmounted, a measurement of the volatility component applicable to intellectual property assets, as would be required in the Black Scholes option pricing model, is currently problematic.

Perhaps the best method to include the flexibility inherent in a delayed decision associated with intellectual property development would be to model that future decision into a decision tree and use that technique to derive a valuation. Using option pricing models to help value intellectual property is a promising line of thought that requires much greater analysis before it can be truly useful.

GOOD ENOUGH DECISION MAKING

Few disagree with the principle that trademark decision making would benefit from valuation analysis. Resistance is usually not with the concept of valuation, but instead with its practical application. There are two primary reasons valuation analysis may appear too onerous for general use in broader decision making:

1. Belief that valuation analysis is extremely complicated and expensive to perform and requires valuation experts to do it properly
2. Recognition that valuation analyses are likely to be inexact and flawed

The first concern, while widely held and appropriate is some limited situations (such as a financial audit or infringement litigation), is generally incorrect. While expert guidance and assistance can be beneficial, most valuation techniques are within the understanding of anyone. The second concern tends to be the more problematic one. Because valuation is an inherently inexact undertaking—valuation analyses never lead to a single, absolutely correct determination of an asset's value—many will ask what is the point of spending resources to obtain a valuation determination that is almost certainly wrong. The problem with the second concern is that it fails to appreciate the breadth of strategies that can be employed for making decisions and thereby fails to appreciate the decision-making improvements that can come from inexact, but still useful, valuation analyses.

In this regard we can consider three general strategies:

1. Maximizing strategies where the decision maker or evaluator will not be concerned with information-gathering costs and will obtain as much information as possible so as to make the best possible decision
2. Optimizing strategies where the decision maker continues to seek the best possible option, but understands that there may be a need to rely on a more restricted amount of information and that closer attention need to be paid to cost-benefit analysis when determining whether to extend the valuation analysis

3. Satisficing strategies where the decision maker does not try to find the best possible option, but instead sets a search limit that causes her to settle for the first option that is satisfactory

Matching up the importance of the trademark valuation or decision making exercise with the appropriate level of inquiry can yield extraordinary benefits and save significant time and money. While a maximizing strategy may be appropriate in some circumstances (such as valuing trademark rights for a major trademark-infringement litigation), maximizing strategies are appropriate for only a tiny minority of trademark decisions. The vast majority of trademark decisions are best served by a satisficing strategy. Namely, the decision can be improved by conducting minimal, but thoughtful, valuation analysis.

Managing Portfolios by Combining Knowledge: Relative Value Technique

Complex decisions with multiple dimensions of analysis are difficult to assess without a proper structuring of the process to guard against over-simplification or a limited focus that overlooks important elements. The best method to guard against such shortcomings is to dissemble the problem into component elements, analyze those components in a clear and consistent way, and then to logically recombine or reassemble the components into a final result that can be readily understood. The first step, the process of disassembling a valuation task into its component parts, helps the evaluators identify the various key aspects to be considered. Undertaking this task alone can yield important insights or at least trigger useful debate. Once the problem has been disassembled it remains to select a useful reassembly and interpretation process.

The problem is how to consider and incorporate an assessment of all these factors into a simple and relatively inexpensive valuation exercise. This is particularly true when the valuation exercise involves a portfolio of trademarks assets. Many of the most fundamental trademark decisions for firms or organizations with substantial trademark portfolios involve prioritizing individual trademark within the portfolio so that those with the greatest potential value receive the appropriate level of organizational resources and management attention. A firm's trademark portfolio can generate significant value for the firm, but it almost certainly requires managing the portfolio so as to achieve that positive result.

Conducting a complete valuation of each trademark in an extensive portfolio is likely to be too onerous, too time consuming, and too expensive for most firms to consider. Complete valuations may be possible for a few trademarks, but to deal with the overall portfolio a cheaper method will almost certainly be required (a satisficing strategy).

Conducting a portfolio valuation audit using the relative value technique uses the visual power of a cluster map to accomplish this objective. In the example that follows the relative value technique reduces a trademark's various economic and legal dimensions to x and y coordinates that can be plotted on a two-axis chart. When repeated for various trademarks in the portfolio the relative value technique allows the valuator to place each individual trademark on the chart and then easily compare the various trademarks across all the two selected dimensions.

This audit is not meant to establish definitive values for the various trademarks, but instead to identify inexpensively three broad categories for trademark management within the portfolio based on an assessment along two separate dimensions:

1. The strategic or economic importance of the trademark
2. The strength of the legal relationship to the trademark

The value of a trademark is a function of both its commercial qualities and its legal qualities and requires an analysis of both to develop a reasonable estimate. Unfortunately, most firms use either an attorney or a businessperson to manage their trademark portfolios, which can result in biased analysis. If the portfolio is managed by an attorney, there is a significant risk that any portfolio analysis will overemphasize the legal aspects of the issue. Specifically, the attorney will be most concerned with inadequately protected or legally weak trademarks, even if those trademarks are not very strategically important to the firm. If the portfolio is managed by a businessperson, the opposite bias is likely. The businessperson is likely to be most concerned with the strategically important trademarks without appreciating potential legal dangers. The portfolio audit using the relative value technique makes it easy for the firm's legal and business agents to both contribute to the analysis and to combine their collective wisdom.

The portfolio audit using the relative value technique reduces the various business and legal dimensions associated with a particular trademark to x and y coordinates that can then be plotted on a two-axis chart (see Exhibit E.16). This technique allows the valuator to plot a point (or bubble, if another measured dimension is added) for each identified trademark asset.[65]

The audit can be reduced to a four-step process. First, identify the trademarks and develop a clear picture of the firm's portfolio. Second, determine the strategic or economic importance of each trademark. Third, determine the firm's legal relationship with the trademark asset. And fourth, plot the calculated results from steps 2 and 3 on a chart and evaluate the findings.

Steps 2 and 3 involve a similar method but are usually conducted by separate evaluators. The method is to develop a uniform score sheet that applies to each trademark asset and then to score each trademark in accordance with that uniform score sheet.

For step 2 the first task is to identify the factors that make trademarks strategically or economically important for that particular firm. Exhibit E.16 provides an example. The factors listed in Exhibit E.16 are illustrative and will not apply to every firm. To obtain more information from the exercise, we recommend weighting the importance of the factors rather than treating all factors as equal. The combined weights of all the factors must add up to 1 (or 100 percent). The uniform score sheet will be used for all the firm's trademarks so that apples-to-apples comparisons can be made among trademark assets in the portfolio.

---

[65] For example, the radius of the bubble centered on the plotted point could be an estimate of the cash flow associated with the particular trademark. This visually displays the importance of each plotted trademark in cash flow terms on the chart.

Strategic Importance Factor	Weight (0–1)	X	Score (0–5)	=	Calculated Factor Value
Enhances competitive position	.4	X	3	=	1.2
Lowers Costs	.2	X	4	=	0.8
Raises entry barriers	.1	X	4	=	0.4
Provides marketing advantage	.2	X	5	=	1.0
Compliments other products	.1	X	2	=	0.2

Total of weights must add up to 1.0

Add all calculated factor values and plot on x-axis ⟶ 3.6

EXHIBIT E.16   Example of Completed Strategic or Economic Importance Score Sheet
Source: William J. Murphy.

The next task is to score each trademark asset on a 0–5 scale for each strategic importance factor (see Exhibit E.16). Each factor score is multiplied by that factor's weight to yield a factor value. All the factor values are added up to yield a single strategic or economic importance value for the trademark asset being examined. This value will be the x value on the trademark portfolio audit chart.

The process of discussing and determining the weights and scores for a firm's trademark assets is, in and of itself, a highly useful endeavor and maintaining an active involvement in the process can lead to a deeper understanding and appreciation on the part of the firm's decision makers about the relevant factors that affect value. Such understanding and appreciation is not captured as effectively if the task is performed by someone removed from the ultimate decision-making activities or by outside experts (although their assistance may be helpful).

For step 3, the tasks involved are similar. A uniform score sheet that applies to all the trademark assets is developed (generally with the help of legal counsel). This score sheet includes the legal relationship factors that affect the certainty of control the firm possesses over each trademark (see Exhibit E.17). As with the strategic or economic importance score sheet, the legal relationship factors are weighted, with the combined weights adding up to 1 (or 100 percent). Once this is done each trademark is scored on a 0–5 scale for each identified factor (see Exhibit E.17). Each factor score is then multiplied by that factor's weight to yield a factor value. All the factor values are added up to yield a single legal relationship value for the trademark asset being examined that will be the y value on the portfolio audit chart.

Exhibit E.18 shows how the score sheet values for the illustration trademark (Exhibit E.16 and Exhibit E.17) are combined into the x and y coordinates on the portfolio audit chart.

Once the portfolio of trademark assets is plotted on the valuation chart, guidance for action and decision making is made clearer. For example, using the chart in Exhibit E.19 it is apparent that trademark asset 7 requires attention (legal or

Legal Relationship Factor	Weight (0–1)	X	Score (0–5)	=	Calculated Factor Value
Strong mark	.4	X	2	=	0.8
Prior sucessful defense of mark	.2	X	4	=	0.8
Federal registration	.1	X	2	=	0.2
Distinctive elements	.2	X	3	=	0.6
Extensive foreign registrations	.1	X	4	=	0.4

Total of weights must add up to 1.0

Add all calculated factor values and plot on x-axis ⟶ | 2.8 |

EXHIBIT E.17   Example of Completed Legal Relationship Score Sheet
Source: William J. Murphy.

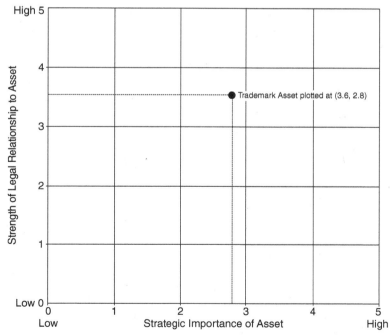

EXHIBIT E.18   Plotting of the x and y Coordinates for the Example Trademark Asset
Source: William J. Murphy.

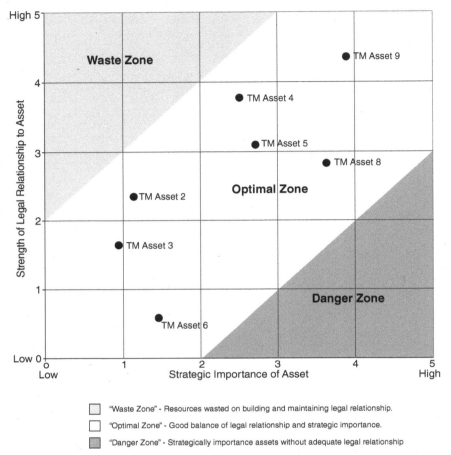

EXHIBIT E.19   Example of Portfolio Audit Chart
Source: William J. Murphy.

otherwise) to strengthen the company's relationship to the asset. In contrast, trade-mark asset 1 is overprotected relative to its strategic value, indicating that valuable resources have been wasted on it. Using this chart, management can quickly identify strategically important trademark assets to which the company has an inadequate legal relationship as well as trademark assets that are legally overprotected given their importance.

The portfolio audit chart in Exhibit E.19 contains two shaded areas that can be useful indicators for management action. The shaded zone in the lower right of the chart represents what we call the danger zone. Any trademark asset that is determined by the portfolio audit exercise to reside in this zone requires immediate management attention; the chart tells us that the trademark asset in question has a strategic importance that is not commensurate with its legal relationship. The port-folio audit chart identifies which trademarks to focus on and what needs to be done: strengthen the legal relationship.

On the other hand, the shaded zone in the upper left of the chart represents what we call the waste zone. Trademark assets that fall in this area have legal relationships that exceed their strategic importance, indicating that resources were spent on securing or protecting the legal relationship in excess of the economic benefits expected from the asset. This situation presents the trademark manager with a more complicated future course of action. Some trademark assets in the waste zone should receive a lower priority and should not receive additional resources. For others in the waste zone, the best course of action may be to invest resources to improve the assessed strategic importance of the asset. The factor and score sheets developed for the technique give the trademark manager a list of factors on which to concentrate. If there is little prospect that the trademark asset will ever develop as an important strategic asset for internal use, there may be an outside licensing market for the trademark that might provide a significant cash flow.

One of the more powerful benefits from this type of approach is the ease with which it can be updated or modified. Because each of the evaluated factors and final score is represented as a numerical projection, the decision makers can go back later and measure the accuracy of the projections. Furthermore, they can improve their performance over time by reevaluating the accuracy of their past decisions on a regular basis.

Limitations on Rationality in Decision Making: The Effects of Perception and Biases on Decision Making

In the past few decades there has been a revolution in cognitive science that has changed our perceptions of how people act in economic circumstances. Described under various titles such as behavioral economics, neuroeconomics, or cognitive economics, the new thinking on thinking recognizes that people are often not the rational, utility maximizing economic decision makers that classic economics had once postulated.[66]

Most of the models discussed in this appendix assume a rational decision maker, and that rationality becomes part of the model. Recent research into real world decision makers and the human mind reveals that humans are often not rational, but are subject to a variety of biases that arise from perception or context.[67] One of the best known biases that affects valuation decisions is *risk aversion*.[68]

---

[66] The beginning of the revolution perhaps can be traced to Herbert Simon's 1955 groundbreaking paper (for which he won the 1978 Nobel Prize in economics) that introduced the concepts of bounded rationality and satisficing as an alternative to maximizing. Herbert A. Simon, "A Behavioral Model of Rational Choice," *Quarterly Journal of Economics* 69 (February 1955): 99–118.

[67] For an entertaining (and growing) list of cognitive biases the reader is invited to examine (and perhaps contribute) to the *Wikipedia* article "List of Cognitive Biases," http://en.wikipedia.org/wiki/List_of_cognitive_biases.

[68] Paradoxically, research indicates that while people may tend to avoid risks, once they have experienced a loss they may adopt risk seeking behavior in order to eliminate the loss. A. Tversky and D. Kahneman, "The Framing of Decisions and Psychology of Choice," *Science* 211 (1981): 453–458.

Risk aversion is a well-recognized trait in humans that demonstrates a systematic preference to avoid the uncertainty of a potentially larger reward in favor of a more certain one. When asked whether they would prefer $1 million guaranteed or a 75 percent chance to win $1.4 million, the preferred choice of most people is for the former even though the probability-weighted value of the latter is greater. Fortunately, a person's degree of risk aversion can be included into the decision analysis, and most decision tree software programs have this capability.

As if risk aversion were not enough of a complication for rational decision making, research has shown that people systematically overestimate small risks with significant or "noticeable" outcomes (such as death) and underestimate larger risks with less significant outcomes (such as minor injury). There is also the phenomenon that is known as risk dread that emerges in situations where there is lack of control but risk of serious injury.[69] Attempts to bring these cognition insights from the real world decision-making process into decision analysis models and techniques continues.

SUMMARY

Virginia Postrel, author of *The Future and Its Enemies*, has argued that both uncertainty and surprise are essential for progress.[70] She points out that when electricity was discovered, there were predictions of electric lighting, but not electric guitars. When the laser was discovered, there were predictions of laser weapons, but none of lasers in every home as integral components of CD and DVD players. Her point is that our human infatuation with predictability can impede progress because innovation depends on the unpredictable, that is, on surprise. This was the critical fallacy of centralized planning—no one is smart enough to eliminate all risks, no one has a crystal ball that sees the future with perfect certainty. It is the ability of sophisticated computer-assisted methods to address uncertainty in valuation with enhanced predictability that is both their allure and their danger.[71]

While these techniques are based in mathematical logic and can provide extremely useful knowledge, they are not a substitute for what is ultimately the art of valuation. In fact, there is the danger that because the techniques are mathematical in nature, and are generally performed by a complex computer program, that we will believe that the ultimate truth is the inevitable result. In reality, these techniques are just one part of an increasing arsenal of tools available to the trademark valuation practitioner. In the right hands, with the proper understanding of their strengths and limitations, they can provide otherwise unattainable insights. Misused or misunderstood, they can mislead or do worse.

---

[69] Probably the most common form of risk dread is fear of flying.

[70] Virginia Postrel, *The Future and Its Enemies: The Growing Conflict Over Creativity, Enterprise, and Progress* (New York: Free Press 1998).

[71] An example of the allure and the danger can be found in the success and then subsequent meltdown of the Long-Term Capital Corporation discussed earlier in this appendix. It used sophisticated modeling techniques in an attempt to remove risk from their portfolio of investments. However, when a series of unforeseen events occurred, the company found itself on the wrong side of over $1 trillion worth of investment wagers.

About the Authors

GORDON **V.** SMITH is Chairman Emeritus of AUS Inc., a multidiscipline consulting and market research firm, a member of the Board of Trustees of the University of New Hampshire School of Law, and Distinguished Professor of IP Management at the law school's Franklin Pierce Center for Intellectual Property. During his long consulting career, he has advised clients on the value of intellectual property and closely held stock and has consulted in support of transactions, litigation, and tax-related matters. He is the author and coauthor of several books on IP valuation and exploitation strategies. An active international lecturer, Smith is Chair of the Advisory Board of the Licensing Economics Review, as well as an Adjunct Professor at the National University of Singapore (Division of Engineering & Technology Management). Mr. Smith earned an A.B. degree from Harvard University in 1959.

SUSAN **M.** RICHEY is a Professor of Law at The University of New Hampshire School of Law (formerly the Franklin Pierce Law Center) and a former Associate Dean of the law school. She recently completed an appointment as Visiting Distinguished Scholar with the International Economic and Commercial Law Group at the University of Limerick in Ireland. Richey has been involved in numerous programs teaching intellectual property concepts to nonlawyers, including workshops sponsored by the World Intellectual Property Organization and UNITRAD, the training arm of the United Nations. Active in the International Trademark Association (INTA), she served a three-year appointment as an editor of The Trademark Reporter, a scholarly publication of INTA, a two-year appointment as Chair of INTA's Panel of Neutrals, and she currently serves on INTA's Academic Committee.

A

Aaker, David, 13

Accept offer branch, probability weighted value (comparison), 306–307

Accounting
  depreciation
    appraisal depreciation, difference, 56
    explanation, 68
    issues, 219–220
    principle, 141–142

Accounting Standards Codification (ASC)
  805/350, 55
  reference, 66

Acquiring secondary meaning, 9

Active property market, 96

Ad valorem taxes, trademarks (relationship), 248–249

Advertising
  campaign, 227
    development, 91
  costs, reduction, 116
  deception, 216–217
    FTC sanctions, 227

Aesthetic design feature, 11

African Intellectual Property Organization (OAPI), 19

African Regional Industrial Property Organization (ARIPO) filing, 19

After Size apparel trademark sale, 244

After-tax revenue, present value, 175

Aggregate demand model, 290–291

Aggregated unit costs, 87, 89–90
  method, 89e
  usage, 92

Agreements, 35

American Institute of Certified Public Accountants (AICPA), 255

American Machine & Foundry Co. (AMF), founding, 149

American Society of Appraisers, 255

Amortization, 140–141

Analytical technique, 203–205, 210–211

Annual growth rate. *See* Compound annual growth rate
  change, 158

Annual present value, calculation, 175

Anti-Counterfeiting Trade Agreement (ACTA), international coordination, 258–259

Apple Corporation, economic impact, 2

Appraisal
  depreciation, accounting depreciation (differences), 56
  literature, 52
  recipient, 52

Appraisal Foundation, 255

Arbitrage pricing theory (APT), 278–279
  expression/equation, 279
  inferences, implementation, 279

Arbitrary marks, 9

Arm & Hammer brand
  primary exploitation, 110–111
  secondary exploitation, 113

Arm's length standard, 78

Arm's length transaction, 58

As-is, where-is basis, 54

Assembled workforce, 37
  goodwill, combination, 37

Asset-backed securities, SPV sale, 237

Assets
  age, knowledge, 153
  aggregate value, 32
  bounding, 270
  characteristics, 240e
  classifications, 127
  disaggregation, 65–76
  earning power, scenarios, 147
  economic life patterns, 154
  enterprise asset characteristics, 46e
  income allocation, 180e
  intangible assets, 33–34
  monetary assets, 32–33
  portfolio, 165
    groupings, 32
    rate of return, generation, 269
  problems, 147
  profitability, 95
  required rate of return, 282e
  returns, sensitivity (determination), 279
  rights, 35–36
  service life, 140
  tangible assets, 33
  tax-reduction strategies, 252
  technique, comparable return, 124–130
  types, 32–36
  valuation, cash flow (importance), 124

Assumption, 59

Athlete's Foot, trademark sale, 237
Attorneys, fees, 229–230
Auction, 54
    prices, 99–100
Audit chart, example. *See* Portfolios
Audit provisions, 191
Aunt Jemima icon, brand extension, 113–114

B
Babcock, Henry, 51
Balance sheet, 54, 61
    consolidated balance sheet, 64e
    intangible assets, listing, 70e
    obligations, 67
    sections, 63, 65
Bank of America, purchase, 98
Bankruptcy, 194–195
    U.S. bankruptcy law, impact, 247–248
Bankruptcy Code, 248
Bankruptcy trademarks, 238–244
    case examples, 242–244
    debt/equity financing, 241–242
    intangible assets, 241
    monetary assets, 240
    tangible assets, 241
Bass model, 163–164, 290–293
    aggregate demand model, 290–291
    caveats, 293–294
    example, 164e
    innovation model, imitation model
        (combination), 163
Bayesian analysis, 311–313
Bayes' theorem, usage (example), 313e
Bayes, Thomas, 311
BCBG Max Azria, transaction, 236–237
Beanie babies, fakes, 233
Benelux Office for Intellectual Property
        (BOIP), 19
Berghoff beer brand, purchase, 98
Beta, 277–278
Betty Crocker
    brand, marketing, 146
    icon, brand extension, 113–114
Biases, effects, 331–332
Bill Blass, trademarks, 237
Billy Pitt's Pictures, 322
Bingo.com domain name, purchase, 98
Black, Fischer, 323–324
Black-Scholes model, usage, 187
Black-Scholes option pricing model, 324
Blass, Bill, 100
Blue sky, references, 16
B&M bake bean brand, sale, 98
Book assets, rate of return (net cash flow), 126e
Book cost, 56–57
Book value, 57
Brainstorming, 91
Brand-based gTLDs, 8

benefits, 8
Brand extension
    analysis, 91
    economic benefit, 114
    economic underpinnings, 115
    examples, 113–114
Branding policy, development, 91
Brands
    assets, liquidation, 15
    attributes, 12–13, 100
        economic benefit, trademarks (impact), 14
    building, 13
    buyer perspective, 12–14
    characteristics, 236
    defining attribute, 13
    definition, disagreement, 11–12
    discount rate, opinion, 169
    distinguishing name/symbol, 13
    enforcement, 194
    equity, 11
    example, 74–75
    exploitation, 108–110
    knock-offs, 215–216, 225
    leveraging, importance, 8
    loyalty, 315e
    market
        forces, impact, 139
        switching customers, 315e
        value, impact, 146–147
    owner perspective, 12
    products/services, 20–28
    promise, comparison, 13–14
    rehabilitation expense, 246
    scoring, 57
    strength multipliers, 187
    strong brands, 194
    survivor curves, relationship, 157
    trademarks, relationship, 11–15
    valuation, subjective scoring system, 101
Brand values, consolidation, 112e
Brokerage houses, 278
Brunswick Corporation, 225
Buick brand, valuation, 111
Built-up method, 260–261, 274, 276–277
Business.com domain name, purchase, 98
Business enterprises, 31–46
    assets, 32–36
        principles, application, 65–66
    disaggregation, 75e
    equation
        enterprise value, 72e
        intangible asset value, 73e
    equation, expansion, 70–71
        formula, 71e
    financial reporting, 61–62
    insolvency, 239
    intellectual property, 41–46
        ownership, 41

relationships, 37–38
rights acquisition, 35
undefined intangibles, 38–41
weighted average cost of capital (WACC), 281e
Business enterprise value (BEV), 72e, 186
calculation, 269
consolidation, 112e
elements, 32e
sum, 111
Businesses
business-cycle risks, 273
customer relationships, 37–38
fixed assets, 282–283
growth, 179
liquid asset, working capital, 282
owners, example, 147
purposes, 80
risk, 272, 273
decrease, 204
tangible assets, 282–283
transactions, 96
valuation, cash flow (importance), 124
value, increase, 208
Business-facing brands, 199
Business to business brands, 199
But for logic, 120–121
Buyer penetration, annual rates (calculation), 289

C
Call, 323
Capital
absence, 245
allocation, weighted average cost, 283
Capital asset-pricing model (CAPM), 274, 277
application, 277
beta, relationship, 277–278
criticism, 278
Capitalization rate, equivalence, 178
Capital recovery, 57
depreciation, calculation, 140
Case studies, usefulness, 48
Cash flow
gross cash flow, 124
importance, 124
model, benefit, 208
net cash flow, 124
Cash inflows, 191
Cash outflows, 191
Casualty loss, 40
Caterpillar brand cachet, 114–115
Cease and desist, 217
Certificate of deposit (CD), 263–266
contract
repricing, 266e
sale, 265e
example, 264e
Certification mark, 5
Certified public accountant (CPA), 27

Chance nodes, 303
China, trademark trolling, 254
Choice experiments, 318
Civil trademark enforcement actions, 214–217
advertising, deception, 216–217
competition, unfairness, 216–217
counterfeiting, 215–216
cybersquatting, 216
dilution, 216
infringement, 214–215
monetary recovery, 217–227
Clauses, 190–191. *See* Licenses
Closely held company, shares (private holding), 73
Coca-Cola
awareness, 139
Company 10-K report, 62
iconic shape, 10–11
report, 61–62
stock, common share (purchase), 101
trademark, 242
Coefficient of imitation, 291
Coefficient of innovation, 291
Coined marks, 9
Collateral, 235–236
trademark usage, 236
Collateralization, 235
Collective mark, 5–6
variant, 6
Collective membership mark, 6
Combination models, 288
Commercial enterprises, impact, 251
Commercial magnetism, 16
Commercial planning/scripting/recording, 91
Commercial real estate, appraisers, 169–170
Commodities, 24
Community Trade Mark (CTM), trademark
protection, 19
Company management, narrative, 62
Company-relationship relationship, importance,
38
Comparability
analysis, 128
federal tax regulations, 129
Comparability, prevention, 95
Comparable companies
analysis, 128
data, 129
economic conditions, 130
property/services, 130
risks, 130
Comparable group (CG), 124
Comparable property, 95–96
Comparable transactions, 319
Competition. *See* Unfair competition
characteristic, 288
impact, 141
unfairness, 216–217
Complete valuations, 326

Compound annual growth rate (CAGR), 157–158, 160
  example, 158e
    variation, 158e
  usage, 181
Compound interest, 266, 267–268
  calculation, 265e
  formula, 267
Computer software, 45–46
  operational software, 45
  product software, 45
Concept development, 91
Consequence node, addition, 305e
Consolidated balance sheet, 64e
Consolidated statement of earnings, 63e
Consulting expenses, 91
Consumer-facing brands, 199
Consumer loan contract, economic life, 144
Consumer products
  adoption process, 286
  trademark, 28
    categories, 22
Consumer services trademarks, 27–28
  categories, 22
Contemporaneous transactions, 96
Contingent valuation surveys, 318
Contracts, types, 35–36
Contractual life, 143
Contractual rights, value, 35
Contractual terms, 129
Copyright Office, copyright protection, 44
Copyrights, 31, 44–45
  protection, 44
  U.S. Code definition, 44–45
Corporate character, 27
Corporate financial statements, intangible assets, 54
Correlation, 83
Cosmopolitan, 115
Cost of capital, 167
Cost of replacement new (CRN), 86
Cost reduction, 114
Cost savings, 121–124
  benefits, 122
Cost technique (quantification techniques), 197
Cost valuation method (cost method), 58, 84–87
  flowchart, 90e
  schema, 85e
  summary, 94
  usage, 90–94
Cost, value (difference), 65–66
  understanding, 66
Counterfeiting, 215–216
  cases, statutory damages, 228–229
  impact, 257–258
Counterfeits, valuation, 232–234
Covenants, 35
Cowles, Harold A., 155

Criminal sentencing, counterfeits (valuation), 232–234
Crowell, Henry Parsons, 108
Cultural obsolescence, 152
Current assets
  current liabilities, subtraction, 32
  elements, 33
  monetary assets, 66–67
Current liabilities
  elements, 33
  monetary assets, 67
Customer relationships, 37–38
Cybersquatting, 216, 217
  cases
    damages award/profits, 229
    statutory damages, 228–229

D
Daubert hearing, 231
Debt
  financing, 241–242
  overburden, 244
Decision alternatives
  consequences, 304
  mapping, 304e
Decision analysis, 301–308
Decision analysis techniques, 302
Decision making. *See* Good enough decision making
  perception/biases, effects, 331–332
  rationality, limitations, 331–332
Decision trees, 301–308
  complexity, 307–308
  components/conventions, 303–308
  construction, 303–304
  graphical conventions, 303e
  modeling, 305
  outcomes/variables, 310e
  process, 307
Decomposition, 302
Deductible costs, discussion, 223
Default risk, 278
Defendant profits
  accounting issues, 219–220
  awards, principles, 220–224
  expense allocations, 219
  gross profit, 219
  income streams, isolation, 219
  net income, 218
  net operating income, 218
  one-time events, 219
  out-of-period events, 219
  pretax net income, 218
  profit measuring complexities, 218–220
Demand, impact, 141
Depreciation
  accounting depreciation, 56, 68

appraisal depreciation, 56
  calculation, 140
  physical depreciation, 85
Descriptive marks, 9
de Soto, Hernando, 235
Dexatrim brand, sale, 98
DHL trademark, U.S. rights (purchase), 98
Diffusion
  combination models, 288
  models, 289e
    types, 288–290
    usage, 285
  process models, 288
  pure imitative models, 288
  pure innovative models, 288
  S-curves, usage, 287e
Dilution, 216, 217
Direct capitalization, 103e
  formula, 268e
  growth, inclusion, 103e
    formula, 268e
Direct estimates, 157–158
Disaggregation, monetary assets, 73–75
Discounted cash flow (DCF)
  calculation, 104, 208
  DCF-based techniques, 181, 184
  example, 182e–183e
  method, usage, 323
  model, 205–208
    development, 191
    inputs, 184
    usage, 178–184
  technique, 132–133
    example, 132e–133e
  usage, 179
Discounting, 103–105
  example, 104e
  formula, 268e
Discount rate, 105
  usage, 180–181
Discrete period present value calculations,
  103–104
Distribution contracts, 143
Distribution functions, 129
Distributor relationships, 37, 38
Dividend growth model, 274, 275–276
  form, 276
Dividend stream, knowledge, 275
Domain name, registration, 216
Domain name sales, transactions
  (sample), 98–99
Dooney & Bourke, dilution, 231
Dow Chemical, 24–25
Dow Jones Industrial Average (DJIA), 273
Dream Works SKG, 100
  trademarks, 237
Duesenberg (automobile brand), 93

E
Earnings, variability, 165
Economic benefit
  amount, quantification, 144
  calculation, 122
  determination, 271
  division, 208
  duration, 144
    example, 153e
  legal rights, symbiotic relationship, 14
  pattern, example, 153e
  quantification, 116–117
  realization, risks, 165
Economic benefits, expected stream (present
  value), 271
Economic factors, impact, 141
Economic importance score sheet,
    example, 328e
Economic life, 139, 170
  defining, 140–144
  estimation, 155
  indefinite economic life, 143–144
  patterns, 154e
    summary, 164
Economic obsolescence (EO), 86–87,
    146–148
    Kodachrome example, 147–148
  usage, 93–94
Economic risk, 139
Economic substance, 80
Economies of scale, provision, 116
Edery, David, 7
Edsel, trademark problem, 14
End-users, attention, 145
Enterprise assets
  characteristics, 46e
  financial characteristics, relationship, 46
Enterprises, consolidation, 251
Entertainment trademarks, 28
  categories, 22
Equity financing, 241–242
Equity investors, impact, 242
Euler's theorem, 269–270
  importance, 270
Event obsolescence, 148–150
Everson, Mark, 252
Excess earnings
  presence, 40
  undefined intangible, 39–40
Exchange value, 52
Exclusivity, 191
Executory contract, definition, 247
Expected profit, equation, 269
Expenses
  allocations, 219
  escalation, 40
  reducers, 116–117

Exploitation
  primary exploitation, 110–112
  reasonableness, 109–110
  scenarios, 184–186
    example, 185e
  secondary exploitation, 112–115
  term, usage, 108
Extractive/commodity trademarks, 23–24
  categories, 20–21

F
Fair market value, 52, 54
Fair value, 52, 54–57
  book cost, 56–57
  concept, 55
  original cost, 56
  replacement, cost, 56
    depreciation, impact, 56
  reproduction, cost, 56
    depreciation, impact, 56
  standard, requirement, 56
  tax basis, 57
Fanciful marks, 9
Faust v. Rohr, 39
Federal Reserve Bank Statistical Release (2013),
    274
Federal Rules of Evidence, Rule 702, 230–231
Federal Sentencing Guidelines Manual (2B5.3),
    232–233
Federal Trade Commission (FTC) sanctions, 227
Feldman, Alan, 189
Finance, trademarks, 235–238
  collateral, 235–236
  securitization, 236–237
Financial Accounting Standards Board (FASB)
  Accounting Standards Codification (ASC), 66
  intangible assets definition, 33
Financial experts, testimony, 230–231
Financial information, 61
Financial performance, usage, 128
Financial reporting
  international harmonization, 251
  standards, 52, 141–143
    compliance, 142
Financial statements
  capital recovery, 57
  notes, 68e
  value, 65–76
Finished goods trademark categories, 21
Firefly Digital Inc. v. Google Inc., 149
First-order partial derivative, impact, 270
First stage companies, 280
Fisher, John, 162
Fisher-Pry imitative model, 290
Fisher-Pry model, 162
  example, 162e
Florsheim trademark, sale, 98

Follow the dollars, 75–76
Forced liquidation, 54
Forecasting, 152–154
Form 10-K (SEC), 62
Franchises, 36
  agreements, 143
  relationship, creation, 36
  strong franchises, 36
  weak franchises, 36
Free cash flow (net cash flow), 124
Fully absorbed costs, 219–220
Functional obsolescence (FO), 85–86, 145–146
  usage, 92–93
Future benefits, determination, 298–299
Future decline, straight-line path, 153–154
Future dollar benefits, expectation, 102
Future economic benefits, 107–116
  amount, 259
  description, 139
  estimates, 107
  receiving, pattern, 105
Future lost profits, 225
Future market value, 101
Future risks, incorporation, 298–299

G
Galle, Johann, 76–77
Game theory, 303
Generally accepted accounting principles
    (GAAP), 27
General Mills Company, 114
General Motors (GM) brand, 110–111
Genericness, 149–150
Generic terms, 9–11
Generic top level domain (gTLD), 8. *See also*
    Brand-based gTLDs
Global brands, 12
Global trademarks, 251
  political/investment risk, 259–261
Gloria Vanderbilt trademark, sale, 98
Going concern value, undefined intangible, 40–41
Going to trial, value (calculation), 306e
Gompertz, Benjamin, 161
Gompertz curve, lateral position (adjustment),
    161
Gompertz model, 161–162
  example, 162e
Good enough decision making, 325–332
Goods (selection), trademarks (impact), 2
Goodwill, 3
  absence, 40
  assembled workforce, combination, 37
  concept, problem, 16–17
  examination (Accounting Research Study
    No. 10), 39
  FASB definition, 34
  IVSC definition, 34

patronage, 39
representation, 40
symbols, 15–16
trademarks, relationship, 15–17
    U.S. Supreme Court, 16
    undefined intangible, 38–39
Goodyear Tire & Rubber Company, infringement
    action, 227
Google, U.S. federal tax liability reduction, 252
Gore-Tex, 151
Gore, Wilbur Lee, 151
Governmental/institutional trademarks, 23
    categories, 20
Great Seal of the United States, 23
Gross cash flow, 124, 179
Gross margins, difference, 179
    calculation, 121
Gross profit, 219
    advantage
        example, 176e
        usage, 175
    determinant, 175
    establishment, 222–223
    margins, 246
Groups, comparability, 128–130
Growth
    forecast, 157–160
    model growth patterns, 160
    patterns, example, 160e
    prospects, value (relationship), 96
    rate, increase, 116
    steady growth, 103

H
Harley-Davidson, basis, 149
Head-start advantage, 226
Heinz brand, awareness, 139
He-Ro Group Ltd., trademarks asset, 244
Hershey Co. v. Promotion in Motion, Inc., 150
Heterogeneous products, 28
High-technology tangible assets, 241
Historical analogies, accuracy, 293
Historical costs, 91
Historical data
    availability, 159
    extrapolation, 158–159
        example, linear regression (usage), 159e
Historical development costs, 87e
    segregation, 91
Historical life, studies, 154–157
Hoelter, Timothy K., 149
Holmes, Oliver Wendell, 51
Home ownership, benefits (present value), 101
Homogeneous products, 28
Hostess Brands, Inc. assets, 245
    liquidation, 15
    sale, 238–239

I
Ibbotson Associates, Inc., 278
IBM trademark, success, 150
IKEA names, pronunciation problems, 152
Imitative model, 290
Implied guaranteed attribute, 26
Impulse products, 28
Income
    allocation, 180e
        basis, 186–187
        example, 186e
        royalty, calculation, 210e
    calculated amount, present value calculation,
        102, 103e
    calculation, 132
    flow, 196e
    income-producing capability, analysis, 111
    income-related valuation approaches, 187
    licensing flows, 195–197
    method, elements, 259
    statement, 61
        example, 203e, 218e
        information, 72
        royalty payment, impact, 204e
    stream, capitalization, 178
    tax rates, variation, 78
Income method, 163
    valuation
        gross profit advantage, usage, 175
        operating profit advantage, usage, 175
        premium price, usage, 173–175
        royalty, relief, 175, 178, 178e
Income-split method, 255
Income stream
    amount, forecast, 59
    duration/pattern, 59
    isolation, 219
    licensing, 135e
Income valuation method (income method),
        58, 59
    components, 59
    economic life, 139
        basis, 140
    economic risk, 139
    mathematics, 102–105
    summary, 105
    usage, 101–106
Incremental cash flow method, 255–256
Incremental costs, 219–220
Indefinite economic life, 143–144
Indemnifications, 190
Indirect techniques, 133–137
Industrial/commercial services trademarks, 27
    categories, 22
Inertia, 37–38
Inflation, 278
    expected rate, 273

Inflation (*continued*)
  unanticipated events, 272
  unexpected inflation, impact, 279
Information
  availability, 37
  inputs, 298
    assessment, 298
  obtaining, indirect observation (usage),
      317–322
Information-gathering costs, 325
Infringement, 214–215, 217. *See also* Meta-
      infringement
  action, 226, 227
  damages, calculation, 136–137
  defense, cost (estimation), 191
  item, retail price, 233
Innovation
  adoption, time, 287e
  Bass model, 290–293
  diffusion, S-curves (example), 287e
  model, imitation model (combination), 163,
      289
Inputs, extraction, 50
Insolvency
  external events, 245
  mergers, relationship, 148–149
Intangible assets, 31, 33–34
  accounting theory definition, 33
  amortization, 141
  categorization, 34
  cost method, 91
  creation, 241
  FASB definition, 33
  impact, 241
  International Financial Reporting Standards
      definition, 34
  monetary assets, 69–73
  ownership risk, 166
  problems, 147
  rate, derivation, 283
  return, 283–284
    rates, 167
  valuation, 57
  value, 70e
    basis, 56
    example, 74e
Intellectual property (IP), 34, 41–46
  assets
    involvement, 100
    suitability, 253
    tax-reduction strategies, 252
    valuation, 101–102
  assets, cash allocation, 132
  commercial databases, 80
  computer software, 45–46
  copyrights, 44–45
  creation, 241

development path, 251
differences, 31
enhancement, 189
focal point, 136
holding companies, 236
income, calculation, 132
investments, 280
  risk, quantification process, 284
IP-based transfer-pricing structure,
    establishment, 253
management companies, 236
market-dominating intellectual property, 122
ownership, 41
patents, 43–44
problems, 147
proprietary technology, 41–42
rate of return
  determination, theoretical foundations, 269
  equation, 270
reliance, 239
return, 283–284
  calculation, 180
rights
  enforcement, ACTA framework, 258–259
  value, 135, 195
  change, 157
risk quantification, 284
trademark rights, characteristics, 236
transformation, 236
valuation
  income approach, usage, 135
  practice, 104
Interest rate risk, 272–273
Interest rates, term structure, 278
Intermediate goods/services trademarks, 25–26
  categories, 21
Internal Revenue Code, modification, 140–141
International Accounting Standards (IAS) 38,
    intangible assets, 55
International Accounting Standards Board (IASB),
    reorganization, 55
International arm's-length standards, OECD
    Guidelines, 78
International Financial Reporting Standards
    (IFRS), 55
  emergence, 256–257
  intangible assets definition, 34
International Organization for Standardization
    (ISO), 255–256
  10668, 255–256
International Trademark Association (INTA)
  registration mechanisms, 19
  resolution, 248
International valuation standards, 255–257
International Valuation Standards Council
    (IVSC), 256
  goodwill definition, 34

Valuation Standards, 256
Internet Corporation for Assigned Names and
    Numbers, gTLD voting, 8
Intracompany transfer pricing, 128–129
In use value, 241
Inventory
    assets, 240
    valuation, 166
Investment
    function, 3
    principles, 263
    rate of return
        requirements, 271
        technique, 130–132
    risk, 260–261, 272–273
    transaction, 264e
iPhone 5 smartphone, purchase/popularity, 1
ITU registration, renewal, 99

J
Jenkins Valve Company, trademarks (auction),
    244
Jorda, Karl F., 41
Jordan, Michael, 152

K
Kane, Siegrun, 15–16
Kapferer, Jean-Noel, 113
Know-how, 31. *See also* Original know-how
Kodak, color film (Kodachrome)
    economic obsolescence, 147–148
Kodak, color film (Kodachrome), introduction,
    145–146

L
Laggards, 286
Land improvements, 33
Lanham Act (U.S. Trademark Act of 1946), 2, 214
    amendment, 17
    remedy, 233
Leased property, improvements, 33
Leases, 143
Legal lives, 140–141, 143
Legal relationship score sheet, completion
    (example), 329e
Legal rights, economic benefit (symbiotic
    relationship), 14
Legal trademark rights, maintenance, 144
Legislated lives, 140–141
Lenovo Group Limited, founding, 12
Let's Make A Deal (Bayes revision), 311–312
Leveraged buy-out, 244
Leveraging, importance, 8
Le Verrier, Urbain, 76–77
Licensed vehicles, 33
Licensee
    present value, 191

rights, valuation, 195
Licenses
    agreements, 143
    clauses, 190–191
    comparison, 190
    compensation, 192
    contracts, 35
    granting, 36
    impact, 100
    value, 226
Licensing
    activities, observation, 199
    advantages, 189
    economics, 189–192. *See also* Trademarks.
    income, 120
        flows, 195–197
    negotiation, royalty benchmarks, 198
    transaction
        control, economics (impact), 193
        data, commercial databases, 198
        income flow, 196e
Licensor
    quality control, 247
    rights, valuation, 195
    royalty rate, 208
    value, 191
Linear regression, usage, 159e
Lipitor, patent (loss), 93, 150
Liquidation
    forced liquidation, 54
    orderly liquidation, 53–54
    term, usage, 53
    trademarks, value, 243
    value, 241
        consideration, 242
Liquor trademarks, purchase, 98
Loan agreements, 35, 143
Location dependent, 37
Long-Term Capital Management, history, 300
Lost profits, 246
Louis Vuitton Malletier, dilution, 231
Low-inertia customer relationships, 38

M
Machinery/equipment, 33
Madrid Agreement, 19
Madrid Protocol, 19
Malkiel, Burton G., 314
Mansfield-Blackman model, 290
Manufacturing efficiencies, 122
Marketable securities, 66
Market capitalization, 276
Market data, 199–200
Market destabliization, 257
Market determined royalty rates, 198
Market-dominating intellectual property, 122
Marketing functions, 129

Marketing intangibles, value, 79
Market methods, diagram, 318e
Market participants, 55
Market penetration, ease, 116
Market portfolio, risk diversification, 277
Market research, 91
Market risk, 272, 273
Market royalty rates, 198–200
Market share
   increase, 116
   profitability, association, 95
Market size, potential, 288
Market technique (quantification techniques),
      197–198
Market transactions, usage, 95
Market valuation method (market method),
      58, 94–97
   basis, 95
   summary, 97
   usage, 98–101
   variant, 100–101
Market value (MV), 52–54, 86
   auction prices, 99–100
   bottom line, 94–95
   definitions, 53
   economic criteria, 54
   estimation, 68
   exchange, conditions, 53
      alternatives, 53–54
   flowchart, 97e
Mark holder
   mandatory license, 227–228
   term, usage, 214
Markov, Andrei A., 314
Markov chains, 313–317
   development, 315
   example, 317e
   usefulness, 316
Marquette, Arthur F., 108
Marshak, Larry, 220
Mathematical complexity, impact, 48
Mattel Corporation, arguments, 216
McDonald's brand, analysis, 117
Merger and acquisitions (M&As), 142
Mergers
   insolvency, relationship, 148–149
   problems, 148–149
Meriwether, John, 300
Merrill Lynch, 278
Merton, Robert C., 300
Meta-infringement, 221
*Miller's Ale House, Inc. v. Boynton Carolina Ale
      House, LLC*, 149
Mishawaka Mfg. Co. v. Kresge Co., 3
M&M Characters, 4
Mobile telephone market, expansion, 1
Model growth patterns, 160

Monetary assets, 31, 32–33, 67
   analysis, 66–76
   considerations, 79–80, 166
   impact, 240
   return, 282
   value, 186
      calculation, 67e
      estimation, 71
Monetary recovery, 217–227
   accounting issues, 219–220
   attorneys, fees, 229–230
   awards, principles, 220–224
   corrective advertising campaign, 227
   counterfeiting/cybersquatting cases, statutory
      damages, 228–229
   defendant profits, 218–224
   enhancement, 227–232
   establishment, procedure, 230–232
   expense allocations, 219
   future lost profits, 225
   gross profit, 219
   head-start advantage, 226
   income streams, isolation, 219
   net income, 218
   net operating income, 218
   one-time events, 219
   out-of-period events, 219
   plaintiff damages, 224–227
   prejudgment interest, 229–230
   present lost profits, 225
   pretax net income, 218
   product liability claims, 227
   trial court, gatekeeper, 230–231
   unlicensed product sales, royalties, 226
Monetization, accomplishment, 238
Money, value (risk-free rate), 273–274
Monte Carlo analysis, usage, 292–293
Monte Carlo techniques, 184, 309–317
   variables, 309e
Moore, Frank S., 38
Morgenstern, Oskar, 303
Mortgages, 143
Mortgage servicing rights, 35
Mullins, David, 300
Multinational corporation, weighted average cost
      of capital, 281
Multinational enterprises (MNEs), 77, 80
Multiperiod excess earnings method, 255
Multiproduct business, 74
Murphy, William J., 47, 170

N
National Airlines, purchase, 98
Negative cash flow, 195
Neptune, example, 76–77
Nestle Holdings, decision, 134
Net book value, 56

Net cash flow (free cash flow), 124
  calculation, 126e
  usage, 179–180
Net economic benefit, present worth, 59
Net income, 218
Net operating income, 218
Net present value (NPV) calculations, 323
Net working capital, 32
New products
  adopters, impact, 291
  sales forecasting models (product diffusion),
    286–288
New York Stock Exchange (NYSE) stocks, 278
Nodes, 303
Noncontractual relationships, 37
Null hypothesis, 211

O

Objective probabilities, 301
  subjective probabilities, differences,
    300–301
Obsolescence
  cultural obsolescence, 152
  effects, 141
  functional obsolescence (FO), 85–86
  occurrence, 47
  product obsolescence, 150
  technological obsolescence, 150
Ocutt, John L., 47
Offer rejection, value (calculation), 306e
One-time events, 219
Operating income, differences, 179
Operating profit
  advantage, usage, 175
    example, 177e
  comparison, 125e
Operational software, 45
Option contract, information, 323
Option models, application, 324
Option pricing models, 323–325
Orderly liquidation, 53–54
Organization of Economic Cooperation and
    Development (OECD) Guidelines,
    international arm-s-length standards
    definition, 78
Organizations, marks (usage), 6
Original cost (fair value), 56
Original know-how, 251
Ostrofsky, Marc, 98
Outcomes, 310e
Out-of-period costs, 224
Out-of-period events, 219
Ownership
  future economic benefits, present
    value, 263
  issue, 80
  purpose, differences, 51

P

Package designs, 91
Packaging, trade dress category, 10
Pan American World Airways, bankruptcy,
    244, 246
Parameter estimates, 292
Paris Convention, 18
Parr, Russell, 136
Passbook loan, 241–242
Patent or padlock question, 41
Patents, 31, 43–44
  exceptions, 54
  licenses, rejection, 195
  trade secrets, integration, 41
  wars, 199
Patronage, undefined intangible, 39
p coefficients
  parameter estimates, 292
  values, 163
Peak sales, time/size (calculation), 293
Pearl-Reed model, 163
  example, 163e
Perception, effects, 331–332
Perpetual hypothesis, 164
Perpetuity, 102–103
  hypothesis, 144
Pfizer, Inc., Lipitor patent (loss), 93, 150
Physical depreciation (PD), 85, 86
  usage, 92
Piracy, economic consequences, 257
Pitt, William (the Younger), 322
Plaintiff
  damages, 224–227
  term, usage, 214
Pledging process, 235
Poison pill, 244
Political risk, 260
Portfolio audits
  chart, example, 330e
  relative value techniques, usage, 327
  steps, 327–328
Portfolios, 165
  management, knowledge (combination),
    326–331
  valuation audit, performing,
    326–327
Post-Its, brand (usage), 94
Potential value, 235
Prediction markets, 318
Preferred riskless, risk, 275
Preferred stock, valuation, 275
Prejudgment interest, 229–230
Preliminary consumer testing, 91
*Premier Pool Management Corp. v.
    Lusk,* 254
Premium price advantage, 174e
  impact, 174

Premium pricing, 118–119
  permission, 116
  technique, 118e
    alternative, 119e
Present lost profits, 225
Present value
  calculation, 175
  combination, 191
  formulas, 268
  formulations, 102
Presold business, representation, 35
Pretax income (increase), premium price
      advantage (impact), 174
Pretax net income, 218
Price advantage, 174
Price/earnings multiples, usage, 187
Price index, 88e
  obtaining, 88
Price premium method, ISO 10668 discussion,
      255–256
Primary exploitation, 110–112
Principle, interest (calculation), 267
Private label manufacturers, 121
Probability estimate, sensitivity analysis
      (performing), 307e
Process
  information, direct sources (absence), 49
  term, usage, 44
Product diffusion models
  combination models, 288
  pure imitative models, 288
  pure innovative models, 388
  types, 288–290
Production cost saving, 122, 124
  gross profit measurement, 123e
Production measures unit, 87, 90
  usage, 92
Production volumes, synergies, 122
Product liability claims, 227
Products
  appearance, 6
  cost reductions, 161
  curves, 289
  design, 129
    trade dress category, 10
  diffusion, 286–289
  disaster, 245
  engineering, 129
  extension, 116
    dissimilarity, 186
  fabrication, 129
  life cycle theory, stages, 160
  lines, sale, 222
  obsolescence, 150–151
  quality, 148
  sales, forecast, 285, 287–288
    diffusion models, 289e
  trademark/brand representation, 20–28

Product software, 45
Profitability
  absence, 243
  market share, association, 95
  reduction, 107–108
Profit measuring complexities, 218–220
Profits. *See* Defendant profits
  calculation, 220
  long-run expected growth rate, 278
Promotion costs, reduction, 116
Property
  adjustments, 97
  appraisal, 58
  arm's length transaction, 58
  classifications, 33
  comparable property, 95–96
  design/construction, 52
  exchange amount, 53
  importance levels, 50
  return on investment (ROI), 86–87
  rights, 50
  service capability, replacement, 84
  units, retirement data, 155
Proprietary technology, 41–42
Pry, Robert, 162
Public documents, royalty information, 198
Public market, 96
Published work, protection, 45
Purchase price allocations (PPAs), 142
  useful lives, assignation (example), 143e
Purchasing power
  provision, 116
  risk, 272
Pure imitative models, 288
Pure innovative models, 288
Purpose, ownership (differences), 51
Put, 323

Q
q coefficients
  parameter estimates, 292
  values, 163
Qiodan Sports Co., Jordan lawsuit, 152
Quaker Mill Company
  exploitation, 109
  trademark registration, 108–109
Quality control provisions, 191
Quantification techniques, 197–201

R
Racebrook Marketing Concepts, LLC, 99
Random Walk Down Wall Street,
      A (Malkiel), 314
Rate of return
  calculation, 126e
  components, 273–274
  determination, theoretical foundations, 269
  generation, 269

models, 274–278
Rate of return on book assets employed, 126–127
Rating techniques, 201–205
Ratio analysis, 319
Real rate of return, 274
Reasonable knowledge, substitution, 53
Recall expense, 246
Receivables, 240
Red Cross symbol, 23
Registrations, administration, 42
Reject offer branch, probability weighted value
    (comparison), 306–307
Relationships, 34, 37–38
    assembled workforce, 37
    company-distributor relationship,
        importance, 38
    customer relationships, 37–38
    distributor relationships, 38
    inertia, 37
Relative value technique, 326–331
Relief-from-royalty income stream, representation,
    133–134
Relief-from-royalty technique, 133–134
Remus, Paul C., 47
Renewal fees
    payment, 237–238
    responsibility, 238
Replacement cost, 56, 246
    calculation, 89
    depreciation, impact, 56
    estimation, 87–90
Replacement cost less depreciation (RCLD)
    (CRN), 86
Replacement cost new (RCN), premise, 85–86
Reproduction cost, 56
    depreciation, impact, 56
    estimation, 87–90
Required rate of return, 282e
    formula, 275
Residual market risk, 278
Residual, undefined intangible, 40
Residual valuation method, 321
Retail efficiencies, 122
Retailers trademarks, 26
    categories, 21
    importance, 23–24
Retailing, trademarks (importance), 26
Return on assets technique, comparison, 127e
Return on book assets, 127
Return on investment (ROI), 86–87
    principles, commerce (impact), 2
Revenue
    enhancers, 116
    forecast, work effort, 104–105
Reverse passing off, 217
Reverse product placement, 7
Rights, 34, 35–36
    business enterprise acquisition, 35

value, 135
Right to sublicense, 190
Risk
    anticipation, 186
    conceptualization, 300
    double counting, 170
    elements, 164–170, 272–273
    premium, 165, 273, 274
    qualitative terms, 165
    quantification, 284
    term, usage, 299
    uncertainty, differences, 299–301
Risk-free investments, 274
Risk-free rate, 273
R.J. Reynolds Tobacco Company, 221
Rolling back the tree, 306
Rolls-Royce trademark rights, purchase, 98
Royalties
    average rates, 200e
    award, 227–228
    base, 192
    benchmarks, 198
    calculation, 210e
    income stream, relief, 137e
    indications, 136
    information, 198
    payments, 190
    quantification, 195–197
    rate
        estimation, 211
    relief
        example, 178e
        method, 256
    revenue, future economic benefit, 120
    trademarks, association, 271
    usage, 133
Royalty rates
    formula, 192
    information, usefulness, 136
    knowledge, 201–202
R-squared statistic measures, 291
Rule 702 (Federal Rules of Evidence), 231–232

S
Sale-and-leaseback, 235
Sales curves (S-curves), 161–164
    Bass model, 163–164
    example, 286e
    Fisher-Pry model, 162
    Gompertz model, 161–162
    Pearl-Reed model, 163
    S-shaped curve, 290
    usage, 161
Sales revenue
    forecast, 119, 157
    increase, 205
Sales volume levels, 200
Salvation Army symbol, 23

Satisficing strategies, 326
Scandia Down Corp. v. Euroquilt, Inc., 3
Schiller, Philip, 1
Scholes, Myron, 300, 323–324
Scoring techniques, 201–205
Seafarer's aphorism
   Markov chain, 317e
   matrix, 316e
Search engine optimization (SEO), 254
Secondary exploitation, 112–115
   mark, 113
Secondary internal exploitation, 189
Secondary meaning, acquisition, 9
Secondary turnover, 146
Second stage companies, 280
Secured financing, 235–236
Securities and Exchange Commission (SEC),
   impact, 142
Securitization, 100, 236–237
   process, 235
Selling expenses, control, 122
Selling prices, reduction, 107
Semicommodity trademarks, 24–25
   categories, 21
Sensitivity analysis
   p, solutions, 308e
Sensitivity analysis, performing, 307e
Service mark, 5
Services
   extension, 116
   trademark/brand representation, 20–28
Shadow pricing, 320–321
Shareholder's equity, valuation (complication), 71
Shopping products, 28
Simple interest, 264, 266–267
Single-purchase model, 287
Snapple, economic problems, 148
Sonny Bono Copyright Term Extension Act, 44
Special purpose vehicle (SPV), 236
   sale, 237
Special risk premium, 260–261
Specialty products, 28
Specter, Arlen, 232, 257
Speedo swimwear trademark, sale, 98
Spokescandies, creation, 4
Spokespersons/spokescharacters, impact, 4
Sportscreme brand, sale, 98
Square Enix, 7
Standard & Poor's, 278
Staples (products), 28
Start-from-scratch aggregation, 92
Start-ups, 280
Stated preference data, extraction, 318–319
Stated preference methods, 317
Statement of Financial Accounting Standards (SFAS)
   No. 141 (Business Combinations), 55
   No. 142 (Goodwill and Other Intangible
     Assets), 55

State registration, USPTO control, 17
State trademark enforcement schemes, punitive
   damages, 228
*Statistical Analysis of Industrial Property
   Retirements* (Iowa State University Bulletin
   125), 154–155
Status goods, counterfeiting, 232
Statutory damages, 228–229
   quantification, 217
   rationale, 228–229
Steady growth, 103
Steinway, Inc., domain name, 216
Stock, preferred share (value), 275
Stoller, Leo, 254
Stradivarius, value, 43
Strategic score sheet, example, 328e
Strong franchises, 36
Student enrollments, 35
Subjective inputs, indirect techniques,
   133–137
Subjective probabilities, 301
   objective probabilities, differences, 300–301
Subjective scoring systems, 101
Subject property, arm's length sale, 97
Sublicense, rights, 190
Subscriptions, 143
   economic life, 144
Substitute trademark, 246
Substitution
   model, 162
   principle, 246
Subtraction logic, permutation, 121
Sue-or-settle example, 305
Suggestive marks, 9
Supply contracts, 143
Surrogate data, 160
Surrogate measures, 321–322
Surrogate models, usage, 133–137
Surrogate valuation measures, 322
Survivor curves, 154–157
   brands, relationship, 157
   example, 156e
   representation, 156
   shape, 155
Symbolic identifier, absence, 5
Symbols, motivators, 23

T
Tangible assets, 31, 33
   breakdown, 69e
   focus, 156–157
   high-technology tangible assets, 241
   impact, 241
   monetary assets, 67–69
   return, 282–283
   value, 186
     example, 69e
     estimation, 71

Tax basis, 57
Tax issues, 77–80
Tax regulations, compliance, 142
Technical obsolescence, 150–151
Technological change, substitution model, 162
Technology
  licenses, average royalty rates, 200e
  life extension, 151e
  royalty rates, trademark royalty rates
    (comparison), 201e
  technology-related intellectual property, 41
  trademarks, symbiosis, 151
Termination provisions, 190
ThinkPad laptop
  brand, 150
  trademark, 12
Third stage financings, 280
3dfx Interactive, Inc., bankruptcy proceedings,
  243
Three-brand market
  brand loyalty, 315e
  future, prediction, 316
Time, adjustments, 97
Time-to-market acceleration, 116
Time to peak sales, 293
Trade creditors, impact, 242
Trade dress, 6
  categories, 10
  non-functionality, 10–11
Trademark
  values (information), stock prices (impact), 321
Trademark assets
  risk, 169
  valuation, uncertainty/immeasurables, 297
  x/y coordinates, plotting, 329e
Trademark licensing economics
  rules, 211
Trademarks, 4–5, 31
  adoption, 216
  ad valorem taxes, relationship, 248–249
  amortization, 140–141
  application, 18–19
  arithmetical foundation, 266–268
  auctions, 99
  brands, relationship, 11–15
  business, attachment, 16
  buyer perspective, 12–14
  capture, 175
  collateral usage, 236
  complete valuation, 326
  cost method, usage, 90–94
  cost savings, 121–124
  counterfeiting, 257
  creation
    equity investment, impact, 243
    total cost, 197
  crossovers, 24
  decision making, 325

defining, 2–17
description, 15–16
descriptor, absence, 10
development, 91
dilution action, 221
direct techniques, 118–133
economic benefit, 107
  recognition, 107–108
economic life, 140–141, 144–154
economic terms, 15
enforcement
  actions. *See* Civil trademark enforcement
    actions.
  cases, harm (quantification), 213
  schemes, punitive damages, 228
establishment, cost, 92
examples, 4, 109–110
extension, 113
familiarity, 5
forms, 11
function, 3
goodwill, relationship, 15–17
  U.S. Supreme Court description, 16
guideposts, 23
harmonization attempts, 17
holding companies, 252–253
images, meaning, 2
implied guarantee attribute, 26
importance, 24–25
inclusion, 79
  OECD Guidelines, 79
income method, usage, 106
indefinite lives, 70
industrial/business setting, 26
internationality, 152
legal property rights, association, 92–93
legal strength, 309
legal underpinnings, 17–19
license
  creation, 79
  negotiation process, 247
licensing, 115
  rarity, 120
  transaction value, 191
licensing economics, 189, 193–195
  analytical technique, 203–205, 210–211
  scoring/rating techniques, 201–205
licensor exercise quality, 247
life extension, 151e
market method, usage, 98–101
market transactions, 96
monetization, accomplishment, 238
noun-descriptor usage, 10
noun, usage, 9
owner perspective, 12
patterns, 144–154
pluralizing, 10
portfolios, management, 327

Trademarks (*continued*)
  possessive usage, 10
  potential value, 235
  problems, example, 14
  products, market size, 309
  products/services, 20–28
  protection, 4, 19
  purchase, 95–96
  reanalysis, 169
  registration, 18, 91
  rights
    maintenance, 144
    securing, 17
  riskiness, 242
  role, 25
  royalties, association, 271
  royalty rates
    calculation, 206e–207e, 209e
    facts, 202
    technology royalty rates, comparison, 201e
  searches, 91
  significance, 9–11
  symbols, motivators, 23
  technology, symbiosis, 151
  third party, impact, 3
  timelessness, 139
  transactions, 95
  trolling, 253
  trolls, impact, 253–255
  types, 3–8
  umbrella sense, 3–4
  usage, 25
  U.S. treatment, 140–141
  value
    increase, 31
    residual value, representation, 173
    subtraction, usage, 184e
  verb, usage, 9
  versatility, 242
Trademark valuation, 1–2, 31, 83
  attempt, 120
  discounted cash flow, example, 182e–183e
  elements, 214
  exploitation scenarios, example, 185e
  goal, 271
  gross profit advantage, example, 176e
  importance, 36
  income allocation, example, 186e
  operating profit advantage, usage, 177e
  premium price advantage, 174e
  process, 20
  royalty, relief, 178e
  situations, 235
Trade name, 5
  foreign language meaning, linguistic search, 91
  identification, problem, 5
  inclusion (OECD Guidelines), 79

Trade secrets, 31
  definitions, 42
  patents, integration, 41
  protection, 42
Transactions, comparison, 319
Transfer pricing, 252–253
  taxation, 78
  transactions, illustration, 80e
Translator, calculation, 88e
Trended original costs, 87–89, 91
  calculation, 89e
Trial court, gatekeeper, 230–231
Triarc, 100
  trademarks, 237
True value, 52
25 percent rule, 211

U
Unanticipated events, 272
Uncertainty
  node, 303
    addition, 305e
    value, calculation, 306e
  risk, differences, 299–300
Undefined intangibles, 34, 38–41
  excess earnings, 39–40
  going concern value, 40–41
  goodwill, 38–39
  patronage, 39
  residual, 40
Underwood meat spread brand, sale, 98
Unexpected inflation, impact, 279
Unfair competition, 217
Uniform Trade Secrets Act, 42
United Nations symbol, 23
United States Patent and Trademark Office
      (USPTO), registration
  application rejection, 5
  refusal, 19
Unit of production measures, 87, 90
  usage, 92
Unlicensed product sales, royalties, 226
Unpublished work, registration, 44
Unrelated parties, 96
Unsought products, 28
U.S. Bankruptcy Code, Section 365(a), 194–195
U.S. bankruptcy law, impact, 247–248
Useful life, 141
  assignation, example, 143e
  limitation, 141–142
U.S. Second Circuit Court of Appeals, Nestle
      Holdings decision, 134
U.S. Trademark Act of 1946 (Lanham Act), 2, 214
  amendment, 17
  registration, proof, 18
  remedy, 233
Utility patent, defining, 44

V

Valuation, 31
  analysis, 48
    elements, 298–301
    strategies, 325–326
  arithmetic, ease, 48–50
  cash flow, importance, 124
  complete valuations, 326
  cost approach, 246
  cost method, 58
  directions, 244–248
  discounted cash flow (DCF) model, usage,
    178–184
  elements, 49e
  exercise, aspects, 298–299
  gross profit advantage, usage, 174
  income allocation basis, 186–187
  income approach, 246
  income method, 59
  inputs, difficulty, 48–50
  market approach, 247–248
  market method, 58
  methods, 57–59, 84e
  misconceptions, 47–48
  premium price advantage, 174e
  principles, 46–50
  process, 20
  ratios, 319
  standards, 83. *See also* International valuation
    standards.
  task, 111
  techniques, 298
  transaction, description, 47
Value
  balance, government regulation
    (impact), 320
  calculation, 127
  conclusion, 48
  cost, difference, 65–66
    understanding, 66
  fair value, 54–57
  financial statements, 65–76
  growth prospects, relationship, 96
  indicators, correlation, 84e
  market value, 52–54
  measurement, 56
  monetary terms, 61
  premise, 51–57
  results, interpretation, 298
  term, usage, 46–47

Value-added reseller, 28
Value Line, 278
Value, price/cost, differences, 51
Variables, 309e, 310e
Venture capital, 279–280
  companies, impact, 280
  rate of return, usage, 284
Venture sales/revenues (prediction), diffusion
    models (usage), 285
Victoria's Secret, license value, 226
Virtual marks, 7
Vivendi Universal, 100
  trademarks, 237
Volume premium method, 255
von Neumann, John, 303

W

Wal-Mart Corporation, 117
Warranty, 129
Washburn Crosby Company, 114
Washington Mutual, Inc. (WaMu), bankruptcy,
    243
Weak franchises, 36
Wear and tear, 85
Webner, W. Mack, 6
Weighted average cost of capital (WACC), 167,
    281–284
  allocation, 168e
    alternative, 168e
    business enterprise WACC, example, 281e
What-if questions, 133
Willfulness, definition, 223–224
Windows Vista brand, 117
Window tax, usage, 322
Wine.com domain name, purchase, 98
Wise Foods, Inc., trademarks (usage), 237
Word marks, U.S. court categorization, 9
Working capital, consideration, 282
World Intellectual Property Organization (WIPO),
    economic/social concerns, 257

X

Xerox trademark, adoption, 216

Y

Yield differential, 274

Z

Zack's Investment Service, 278
Zebco, 225